_HUMAN VARIATION

Races, Types, and Ethnic Groups

third edition

Stephen Molnar

Washington University

PRENTICE HALL, Englewood Cliffs, New Jersey 07632

Library of Congress Cataloging-in-Publication Date

Molnar, Stephen (date)
    Human variation : races, types, and ethnic groups / Stephen
Molnar.—3rd ed.
        p.   cm.
    Includes bibliographical references and index.
    ISBN 0-13-446162-2
    1. Physical anthropology. 2. Race. I. Title.
GN62.8.M63 1992
573—dc20   91-19227
                                                         CIP

Acquisitions Editor: Nancy Roberts
Editorial/production supervision and
    interior design: Helen Brennan
Cover design: Barbara Singer
Prepress buyer: Kelly Behr
Manufacturing buyer: Mary Ann Gloriande
Editorial Assistant: Pat Naturale

TO IVA
who worked so hard to make this book possible

© 1992, 1983, 1975 by Prentice-Hall, Inc.
A Division of Simon & Schuster
Englewood Cliffs, New Jersey 07632

Printed in the United States of America
10 9 8 7 6 5 4 3 2 1

ISBN 0-13-446162-2

Prentice-Hall International (UK) Limited, *London*
Prentice-Hall of Australia Pty. Limited, *Sydney*
Prentice-Hall Canada Inc., *Toronto*
Prentice-Hall Hispanoamericana, S.A., *Mexico*
Prentice-Hall of India Private Limited, *New Delhi*
Prentice-Hall of Japan, Inc., *Tokyo*
Simon & Schuster Asia Pte. Ltd., *Singapore*
Editora Prentice-Hall do Brasil, Ltda., *Rio de Janeiro*

_Contents

SEVEN
Human Variability and Behavior   257

EIGHT
The Future of the Human Species   294

——— **TABLES** ————————————————————————

FIGURES

Preface

Writing a new edition of a text on human biological diversity today has become a real challenge. The first edition, written sixteen years ago presented a problem of scarcity of material on human variation, today the opposite is true. There have been many advancements in biological methods that have been applied to questions of our species' composition; questions that are now considered important. The new investigations have resulted in a flood of data and now the problem is one of selectivity, what to include as examples of the ranges of variability of _Homo sapiens_ and how to explain the persistence of certain traits through time and space. In addition, there is a revival of racism, and ethnic awareness throughout the world that often causes authors to fall into the seductive traps of simple explanations. Issues thought settled by the time of the second edition (the arguments over racial inequality) have been resurrected at this time. We more and more frequently see and hear statements from many sources supporting the nineteenth century contention that race or ethnic membership is somehow important in evaluating individuals. It is not repeating history so much as it is a continuing, and at times, an intentional misunderstanding of the origins and meanings of human variation. To compound the problem, there are now one and one half billion more of us on the planet. The growth in numbers has been uneven, especially compared to the last century, and is now divided into a developed and lesser developed world. The result is vastly differing regional population densities. Further, human survival is threatened by a rise of new diseases as well as a return of some old ones. All of the factors contribute to the question of how to discuss human variation in 1991.

The major additions that were required have been in chapter two; the new genetics has been included in this expanded chapter to explain the finite structure of DNA and the locations of specific genetic regions. Restriction fragment polymorphisms have also been included with the globin genes as examples to differentiate between populations. This is followed by Chapter Three, Traits of Simple Inheritance, that includes updated discussions on DNA markers of human variation and revision and expansion of blood types of the red and white cells. Population variation of the HLA (histocompatibility) system is also included.

Chapters Four, Five and Six have been revised and expanded as required by newer data on complex traits, growth and adaptation. Though the basics have remained essentially the same, some new examples of population distribution have been added.

Chapter Seven still provides the background to biological determinism and the misuse of racial taxons. At this point near the end of the twentieth century it is disappointing to have to restate again and again the problems inherent in simple applications of classifications to a complex, polytypic species, but it is even more necessary when even national leaders attribute their countries successes to a "genetic homeogeniety." Both Chapters One and Seven provide current discussions.

Chapter Eight follows the same format as in the second edition but the arguments are based on current data (ca. 1991) on population size, growth rates, infant mortality rates and the changing disease environments. The question, "are we entering a period of ecological crisis" is as current now as it was in 1983, but the evidence is even more compelling. With increased population, major famines, new disease threats, and technological failures, the affects on human biological diversity must be considered. The chapter considers these issues as much as possible in the space available.

All chapters have current bibliographies, new figures, and tables. The Glossary has been expanded to include the newer technical terms.

I wish to acknowledge the responses from friends and colleagues that have helped to ease the burden of selecting topics for this edition. I am especially appreciative of the reviewers of the manuscript. Their comments were invaluable. A large debt is owed to the many students I have had the privilege to teach over the years. Keep asking your questions! I wish also to thank Sonia Wolf for the help with the new drawings. My appreciation also goes to the capable staff at Prentice Hall whose editorial assistance has guided me away from the many mistakes I otherwise would have made. Any errors that have managed to escape their watchful eyes are mine alone.

Last, but not least, I wish to express my profound appreciation to my partner in this project, my wife, Iva who encouraged me when I most needed it and who patiently typed and retyped the many manuscript drafts. Even with the aid of modern technology, a personal computer, the task was not easy.

Stephen Molnar

1

Racial Variation and Perception of Human Differences

DO HUMANS VARY?: AN INTRODUCTION

> No argument has ever been advanced by any reasonable man against the fact of differences among men. The whole argument is about what differences exist and how they are to be gauged. (Barzun, 1965:201)

There is no doubt about the fact of human variability. The usual division of our species into races, however, often depends on a faulty perception of human differences: We rely on a simple visual appraisal of appearances of size, form, and color to determine the distinctions between various groups. But even this simple appraisal suggests that _Homo sapiens_ consists of a large number of diverse populations whose range of variability is enormous (Figures 1-1 to 1-6). Such variety causes one to ponder the composition of our species and its origin, and casts doubt on any scheme that attempts to divide humanity into a few definite races or ethnic groups.

Some of the biggest differences exist in the color of the skin, because people range in pigmentation from a very pale color—for example, northern Europeans—to an extremely dark brown—for example, the peoples of the African Congo or New Guinea. Human stature also ranges widely—from the 4.5-foot pygmies in Africa and Oceania to the 6.5-foot

FIGURE 1-1
Australian Aboriginal Mother and Child. (Courtesy of Tasman Brown.)

Nilotic peoples of East Africa. Europeans themselves vary from short (in southern Europe) to tall (in northwestern Europe). Hair form, another trait that attracts a great deal of attention, varies from straight and long to short and spiral shaped.

Other differences are not so readily identifiable but, with some care, can be measured. For example, the size and form of the human face

FIGURE 1-2
An Ainu from Hokkaido, Japan. (Courtesy of John W. Bennett.)

FIGURE 1-3 A Creole Mother and Child from the Mauritius Islands. (Courtesy of Linda Sussman.)

differs considerably throughout the world, and the proportions of the lower limbs and the trunk vary over a broad range. Many more subtle differences between human populations, such as types and quantities of blood enzymes, blood groups, and other biochemical factors, can be determined only with the aid of laboratory instruments, but they exist nonetheless.

Just why is *Homo sapiens* such an extremely polymorphic, polytypic species? That is, how can we explain the individual variability within a population (polymorphic) or the distinctions between the human groups we frequently call races (polytypic)? Why are these several characteristics of skin, hair, blood, and body size distributed among the world's peoples in the way they are?

Human biological variability today appears to result from the influences of several natural forces that have been at work throughout human prehistory. The size of the populations, their isolation, and their adaptation to environmental stresses contribute to or distract from the survival of individuals or the group. Each population grouping also reflects, to some degree, the experiences of their ancestors and gives evidence of those elements in the environment that have been shaping the population through time. This modification throughout the generations is still pro-

FIGURE 1-4   **A Maori Male from New Zealand** (Courtesy of Auckland Institute and Museum.)

FIGURE 1-5
A Maori Mother and Child of New Zealand. (Courtesy of Auckland Institute and Museum.)

FIGURE 1-6
A Bushman of the Kalahari Desert, South Africa.
(Photo by A. A. Abbie. Courtesy of Australian Institute
of Aboriginal Studies.)

ceeding and may contribute to future population diversity. No matter
how we define racial groups today, their composition will undoubtedly
change over the generations to come because of the major alterations of
evolutionary forces through human adaptation, and because of continuing
migrations and interbreeding. These and other factors cause the extensive
changes in ethnic and racial boundaries as we shall discuss.

How have we become conscious of the varieties of *Homo sapiens* and
their places among living organisms in the world? This awareness developed gradually as a result of extensive explorations of the world by
Europeans during recent centuries. Explorers brought back specimens of
plants and animals unknown in Europe, and these, together with the
encounters with strange peoples, demonstrated the diversity in the living
world—and challenged many of the Europeans' long-established beliefs.
The idea that humans descended from an original pair was especially
difficult to accept after the discovery of such different kinds of people as
the Hottentots, Pygmies, and American Indians. A revival of Aristotle's
world view of idealized living forms scaled to fit within eleven grades of
development became most useful. However, as expressed by Lamarck
(1744–1829), the famous French naturalist whose ideas on the evolution
of life forms predated Darwin's, "man represents the type of highest
perfection of nature and the more an animal organization approaches

that of man the more perfect it is" (quoted in Mayr, 1982:353). With such graded categories, natural scientists were able to compromise the discoveries of these new peoples with current religious dogma by the arrangement of all living creatures into a scale from lower to higher categories from inanimate to animate with humans at the top in a graded series. This "great chain of being" arrangement greatly simplified the study of human variability and the idea of arranging human groups into an ascending order with Europeans at the top remained popular throughout the nineteenth century.

The "chain" concept fostered the belief that no two varieties of humans could occupy the same developmental level. So when the Hottentots and Bushmen were discovered, their appearance and language—which the European explorers considered to be like the chatter of monkeys—caused them to be placed in a lower category, nearly subhuman. Later, in the last half of the nineteenth century, when Darwin's evolutionary theory was gaining acceptance, the varieties of people were thought to represent past stages of development. Even before Darwin, there was a firmly held belief that many ancestral human pairs were created, each differing externally and internally in a way that suited them for a particular environment. These arrangements of our species into varieties were frequently complicated by the scientists' personal biases. They often thought that certain groups had been retarded in their progress toward civilization by environmental conditions. Naturally, because these schemes were proposed by Europeans, the Caucasians were considered to be thousand of years ahead of the other races and far superior.[1] Later, as studies of human diversity intensified in the nineteenth century, even European populations were divided into ethnic groups or races; the classic divisions were *Nordic, Alpine,* and *Mediterranean.*[2]

During the nineteenth century, several attempts were made to introduce scientific method into the study of human diversity in the form of mathematical analysis. For example, statistical methods were applied to the study of human variation in size, and the concept "average man" was introduced. But the notion that there existed an ideal, normal, or natural world has, for many hundreds of years, motivated us to seek patterns and to establish categories. These categories were organized and identified in terms of an ideal type of individual, supposedly representative of the group.

---

[1] This idea has persisted, as the following quotations illustrate. "As far as we know now, the Congoid line started on the same evolutionary level as the Eurasiatic ones in the Early Middle Pleistocene and then stood still for a half million years, after which Negroes and Pygmies appears as if out of nowhere" (Coon, 1962:659); "Great Scott! How many times must I point out that you do not need to use either that word or that concept! The Negro is a younger race. The public has been deceived as to this fact" (Putnam, 1967:165).

[2] See Ripley (1899) for the discussion of the races of Europe.

These "ideal types" work well for sorting out widely differing groups such as birds or butterflies or fish, though dealing with units or groups of similar organisms becomes more difficult. This difficulty increases when we search for forms that match notions of the ideal specimen, a factor that has caused many problems in studies of human evolution. Often the investigator had in mind an image of what the type specimen should look like and then searched until it was found, neglecting the deviations from this image. Such a simplified view of the natural world was applied to studies of human races well into this century. Kretschmer (1888–1964), who studied human body form (constitutional types), for example, emphasized in 1930 that this typological system was based on the most beautiful specimen, the rare and happy finds.

Such subjectivity impedes the understanding of the scope of human diversity and contributes to several simple stereotypes. Rather than acknowledge the variation of traits in populations, many natural scientists were content to view the human species as consisting of few "types" despite the accumulation of data on human diversity by the end of the nineteenth century. These types could, in turn, be applied to a division of our species into a few races that actually masked the individual diversities.

To add to the problem, physical traits were often confused with cultural habits of dress or language, and, though clothing and language may be, at times, useful devices to identify human populations, they should never be applied as if they had biological meaning. A classic example was the term *Aryan,* which originally was applied to a group of languages (Indo-European) related to Sanskrit, the language of ancient populations of northern India. Many writers have persisted in using this term as if it described a biological unit, even though Aryan, the linguistic term as used by Mueller, included groups as diverse as Iranians, Europeans, and Singhalese of Ceylon (Sri Lanka). Terms like *Celtic, Teutonic,* or *Slavic* are also frequently used to describe a biological unit, though these terms more accurately distinguish between language groupings.

In addition to language, groupings of human populations or races are often socially or culturally determined. For example, in much of Latin America the differences between "Indio" and "Mestizo" is but a simple matter of language and clothing. Mexican society identifies a person as Mestizo if he or she speaks Spanish and wears shoes, ignoring the degree of Indian or European ancestry. Even though these groupings are just as real to the observer as any biological fact, explanations of biological(eds.) variability should not be offered on this basis. Regardless, racial divisions are often described by such popularized terms as *European, Negro, Indian, Hispanic,* or *Jewish;* each includes many populations of numerous diverse characteristics. This mixing of units—the confusion between biological and social traits—posed a major problem for anthropologists and still adds confusion today. A major reason being that, race studies are, at least, partially founded in the assumption that certain basic units of humanity are of great antiquity. This results in the many schemes that have been offered for sorting our species into different numbers of races.

HUMAN VARIATION AND ITS CLASSIFICATION

The problem is not whether humans vary in biological makeup—of course we do. In fact, our species is very polymorphic, and few arguments have even been advanced against this fact. This variation is not always in the ways that have been described, however, because of the impressionistic means by which we usually have perceived human differences. The problem lies in the degree of differences that exist and how they are to be evaluated. Though human variation seems almost limitless and at times random, there are limits, often within well-defined boundaries. What are these boundaries, and how do they relate to humans' past and to human survival?

The modern systematic study of human diversity begins with an attempt to place populations in a classification system. Most classifications depend on the system established by the Swedish botanist Linneaus (Karl von Linnné, 1707–1778). Linneaus classified approximately 4235 species of animals into a series of categories in ascending order. First published in 1735, this system underwent modification throughout several editions and provides the basis for the classification in use today. An abbreviated example of the modern version that applies to us places *Homo sapiens* in the Order Primates with the several other closely related species (Figure 1-7).

Linneaus based his classification system on the assumption, current for his day, that species were of fixed type and number since creation. Species were seen as a unit of organisms that could interbreed only among themselves; an earlier description noted that "a species could not spring from the seed of another, different species" (Mayr, 1982:257). This sharp distinction between species would assist the process of classification. Further, Linneaus and other natural scientists accepted that the number of species were fixed and unchanging. All one had to do was to collect and classify samples of the life forms. But, as it turned out, Linneaus was confronted with growing evidence of the variety of organisms, and the categories had to be expanded and modified with each new edition of his *Systema Naturae*. This was especially true when human populations from the other continents were discovered by European explorers. A few of these exotic people were brought back to display before astounded audiences beginning with Columbus after his first voyage. Also the discovery of monkeys and apes in Africa and Southeast Asia presented challenges; where should these new humanlike animals be placed?

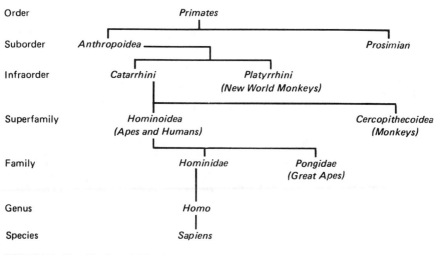

FIGURE 1-7   Classification of Primates.

Linneaus ignored the evolutionary implications of his classifications throughout several editions of his work, and he continued to maintain that species were fixed in number. Overwhelmed by the increasing evidence of nature's diversity, however, he gradually altered his position and allowed that certain varieties were unstable, a stand that suggested evolutionary change. Today, of course, biologists no longer consider special creation or the fixity of species but consider, rather, the fossil record and look to the natural diversity of biological organisms as evidence of evolutionary change caused by several factors discussed in the next chapter—change that contributes to the formation of new species or to extinction. Not only do we view species as a dynamic unit of the natural world, but we consider species in its environmental context as shown in this definition by Mayr (1982:273): "A species is a reproductive community of populations (reproductively isolated from others) that occupies a specific niche in nature."

The variety of humans was dealt with by Linneaus by expanding the species into subcategories called human varieties, listed in Table 1-1, together with classifications offered by eighteenth-century naturalists. These earliest classifications, later called *races,* were determined by several easily perceived biological differences. The criteria were mainly a comparison of skin color, but often the shape of the face and skull were used. Judging the form and size of the skull was an especially popular method for racial studies because ancient populations could be studied and supposed racial affinities could be determined from their skeletal remains. Often stature, hair form, and shape of the nose were used. Frequently, these traits were applied in combination in an effort to distinguish precisely

TABLE 1-1   Early Racial Classifications

LINNEAUS (1735)	BUFFON (1749)	BLUMENBACH[a] (1781)	CUVIER (1790)
American (Reddish)	Laplander	Caucasoid	Caucasoid
European (White)	Tartar	Mongoloid	Mongoloid
Asiatic (Yellow)	South Asiatic	American Indian	Negroid
Negro (Black)	European	Ethiopian	
	Ethiopian	Malay	
	American		

[a] This scheme for racial division was an expansion of Blumenbach's earlier one (1770). As he described the problem: "Formerly in the first edition of this work I divided all mankind into four varieties but after I had more accurately investigated the different nations of Eastern Asia and America; and, so to speak, looked at them more closely, I was compelled to give up that division, and to place in its stead the following five varieties as more consonant to nature."

Source: From Blumenbach, J. F., *Readings in Early Anthropology*, ed. J. S. Slotkin, 1965. Copyright © by Viking Fund Publications. Reprinted by permission of the publisher.

between populations. A large subjective component present in each of these classifications, however, led certain earlier workers to suggest that racial classification was unimportant. Also, the fact that all races could freely interbreed made it clear that no group could be very far removed from the original form of the species, and all shared close common ancestors.

Though the boundaries for these racial divisions were established as much on geographical distribution as they were on biological differences, behavioral attributes were also associated with biological criteria. Linneaus attributed behavioral as well as biological characteristics to each group. He defined *Homo European* as fickle, sanguine, blue-eyed, gentle, and governed by laws; he described *Homo afer* as choleric, obstinate, contented, and regulated by customs; and he characterized *Homo asiatic* as grave, dignified, avaricious, and ruled by opinion. These personality profiles that Linneaus offered of the racial groups he described provided a ready means of grouping behavior together with biological features. Although this practice may have been excusable in the eighteenth century, such confusion of cultural features with biological traits has often persisted in our society to this day. Though there has been little or no evidence to support correlations between behavior, character, and skin color since that offered by earlier writers on human diversity, we still read descriptions that claim to demonstrate correlations between race and a whole range of "native" abilities.

Following Linneaus, other natural scientists turned their attention to human classifications. A German physician, Johann Friedrich Blumenbach (1752–1840), the reputed "Father of Physical Anthropology," gave us several of the racial terms in wide use today. He classified humanity into five races: *Caucasoid, Mongoloid, American, Ethiopian,* and *Malayan.* To the usual criterion of skin color Blumenbach added hair form and facial characteristics with special attention to the shape of the skull. The shape of the skull was supposed to be a significant racial trait and was regarded as highly resistant to environmental influences. Blumenbach amassed many human skulls from all over the world for study and, in keeping with the eighteenth-century belief in ideal types, he searched to find the most perfect specimen. The skull that came closest to fitting this image of perfection was one that had been recovered from the Caucasus Mountains, in an area near Mount Ararat. The *Caucasoid* eventually became a term applied to a major category that encompassed the European, North African, and Middle Eastern populations.

During this period of studies of human variety, our affinity to the lower primates did not go unnoticed. Peter Simon Pallas (1741–1811), a German naturalist and student of Linneaus, provided the first family-tree diagram used in biology. In a communication to Blumenbach, Pallas described a diagram depicting degrees of morphological affinity between several animal groups. This tree, or "biological pedigree," depicted what may have been Pallas's belief in organic evolution (McCown and Kennedy, 1972). It definitely described a close affinity between *Homo sapiens* and the lower primates—a relationship, based on anatomical similarities, that was considered as a possibility by other naturalists; Buffon, a French naturalist (1707–1788), noted a greater resemblance between humans and orangutans than between humans and baboons. His conservatism, however, prevented him from accepting human and primate affinities. Despite the similarity in anatomy between our species and other primates, *Homo sapiens* was set apart by Buffon on the grounds that only *Homo sapiens* had a soul.

Blumenbach, Buffon, Linneaus, and others in the eighteenth century were handicapped in their attempts to work out a classification more reflective of the actual nature of human variability. They lacked the insights possessed by later generations of scientists who had additional evidence and a clearer understanding of evolution. In addition, Blumenbach and his contemporaries assumed that the taxonomic groups of humanity were fixed and unchanging, as they believed species to be, and that there was a distinct boundary between each race established at creation. The biological diversity that was apparent within each group was presumed to be a variation around the ideal racial type. The characteristics of a European, whose features and skull shape differed from the ideal Caucasoid type, would be explained as the result of climate, diet, or even social class. Such concepts and beliefs in racial diversity set the stage for modern studies of the human race throughout the nineteenth and most of this century.

As descriptions of additional human populations were offered, explanations of the origins of their diversity were sought. Climate was most often described as a significant influence (the Ethiopian, blackened by the sun, was the usual example offered), but this oversimplification ignored the influence of heredity. As a critic of the environmental-influences theory, Leonardo da Vinci observed that the black races of Ethiopia were not the product of the sun's effects, because black parents produce offspring who are black (Slotkin, 1965:91). "Domestication of mankind," a process that supposedly accompanied the development of civilization, was presumed to be another influence on race formation and was described by James Cowles Prichard (1786–1848) in *Researches into the Physical History of Man* (1813). In the second edition, published in 1826, Prichard rejected this domestication theory, however, and described the environmental influences and the close correlations between climate and physical type.

In addition to the question of origins or causes of racial variation, the classification of races itself was called into question. Prichard recognized early the problems imposed by dividing humanity into only a few fixed species, and he rejected attempts to divide the human species into "principal families," which was a common practice followed when divisions were made on the basis of skull shape. "It is by no means evidence that all those nations who resemble each other in shape of their skulls, or in any other peculiarity, are of one race, or more nearly allied by kindred to each other than to tribes who differ from them in the same particulars" (Prichard, 1826:28). Though he did reject such divisions Prichard described major types of *Homo sapiens* based on head form and coloration. He argued that this was done only to facilitate comparisons independently of any design to ascribe common origins. He suggested that there was no such thing as a Negro race in the customary sense: "Among those swarthy nations of Africa which we ideally represent under the term negro, there was perhaps not one single nation in which all the characters ascribed to the negro are found in the highest degree" (Stocking, 1973:48). This insight, though strikingly modern, is seldom recalled today.

The lack of correlation, when more than a single trait is used as a criterion, has been recognized again and again and renders any search for racial purity a futile, and often silly, exercise. Nevertheless, the attempt has been made repeatedly to work with idealized forms when classification of our species is attempted. The notion of ideal type has persisted into modern times as illustrated by the fact that Otto Ammon (1842–1911), a German anthropologist who had measured thousands of human heads and had frequently discussed Nordic and Alpine types of Europeans, could not produce a "perfect" specimen of either type. He confessed that he was not able to find a specimen perfect in all details (Montagu, 1974:454).

ANTHROPOMETRY: MEASURES OF HUMAN VARIATION

With the interest in head form and the many attempts at numerical description of its several features, there was a development of anthropometry, the physical measurements of human body form. Racial classifications in the eighteenth and nineteenth centuries relied heavily on these metric descriptions of both the whole body and of the skeleton. Affinities between human populations were determined, and associations between certain human groups and the apes were assumed. Perhaps it was inevitable that races would be arranged in an ascending scale with those placed lower presumed to be a link to apes. Though such a scheme was popular and accepted as a proven "fact" until even modern times, it was criticized and questioned by some. Prichard, in 1813, rejected any suggestion that the Negro was a connecting link to the ape; in fact, Prichard was inclined to look on racial categories as being merely arbitrary groupings established for convenience of the study of human variation, as we discussed previously.

The major reason that the size and shape of the skull had been given the most attention in anthropometric studies was the assumption that the skull form was a feature of the anatomy least resistant to change and, hence, cranial form was considered a good measure of one's ancestry. In addition, because the skull housed the brain, the head's shape and contours were supposed to be indicative of the brain's characteristics and even a measure of its quality. The belief that a person's character and intelligence were indicated by the morphology of his or her head has a long history. The study of these supposed interrelationships expanded and developed into a "science" at the beginning of the last century through the efforts of two German physicians, Franz Joseph Gall (1758–1828) and Johann Kaspar Spurzheim (1776–1832). Their work provided the basis for phrenology, a widely popular pseudoscience of the nineteenth century that examined and recorded the skull's contours, thought to provide a map or diagram of an individual's latent abilities and talents.

Later, in 1842, Anders Retzius (1769–1860) added a new index to cranial studies that described the general shape of the cranial vault. Retzius divided the maximum breadth of the skull by its maximum length, which gave a ratio known as the *cephalic index* (Figure 1-8). This index became an important element in cranial studies and was widely used after Retzius reported that European populations could be divided into three types based on their head shapes: *dolichocephalic* (long, narrow head); *mesocephalic* (intermediate shape); and *brachycephalic* (round headed, or short and broad shaped). The cephalic index, together with the two types of face form, orthognathic (straight faced) and prognathic (lower face projecting), provided another set of criteria for racial studies. As has frequently happened, these physical traits became regarded as indicators of abilities,

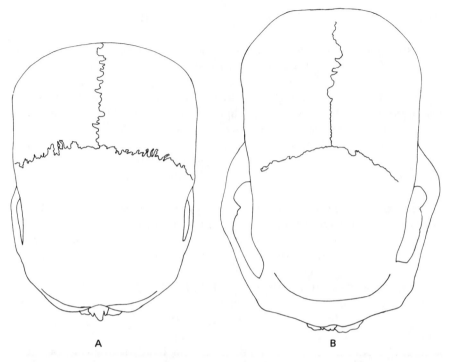

A   B

FIGURE 1-8   Representative Skull Shapes Viewed from Above. The broader skull (A) is classed as *brachycephalic* in contrast to the long and narrow shape of the *dolichocephalic* skull (B).

skills, and behavioral attributes. Face form together with the cephalic index provided Retzius with a means to divide European populations into four possible groups. Comparing cephalic indexes between populations, Retzius reported differences between the skulls of Finnish and Swedish populations. The round-headed Finns were considered an indigenous race, whereas the long, narrow-headed Swedes had supposedly descended from Indo-European Aryans who invaded Europe thousands of years ago from western Asia. Overall, the cephalic index has been popular for a long time, and it has been widely applied in studies of human variation even up to the midtwentieth century.

One of the leading scientists of the day who took an important interest in Retzius's work was Pierre Paul Broca (1824–1880), a famous French neurosurgeon. Broca applied his training and experience in comparative studies of craniology to provide further support to those who endeavored to relate human behavior to a particular head form. He was convinced that the measured shape of the skull was the best indicator of the quality of the brain. The concern with brain contents, and hence craniology as Broca developed it, was based on an interest in racial differences that he believed to be primordial. Broca assumed that because racial differences also find their expression in behavior, the brain had something to do with race (an assumption very much with us today, as we shall discuss). Broca worked with great care and treated his measurements with a fine precision. He did not stop with a mere numerical descriptive system but deduced from his measurements the racial history or even the social status of the group under study. He translated skull dimensions into a series of mathematical indexes and then deduced the personality and social attitudes of the long-dead individuals, together with their supposed biological affinities. However, after years of such efforts Broca admitted that no single criterion was sufficient to separate the races of humanity.

Though he contributed much to neuroanatomy and anthropology in the midnineteenth century and introduced several new techniques of analysis, his achievements have been overshadowed by the erroneous generalizations he made about social class and intelligence that were very similar to the imaginative speculations of the phrenologists. His attempt to associate lumps on the skull with various activity centers of the brain may be understood within the intellectual perspectives of nineteenth-century neuroscience. The attribution of character, race, and social class to skull form is more difficult to understand, especially because Broca admitted that several organic diseases contracted during childhood could cause deformation of the skull. Despite the work of Broca and many others, phrenology passed from scientific acceptability by the end of the nineteenth century. As one author writes, "Phrenology died a pauper's death in the late 19th century, victimized by the vicious ostracism of the period's most reputable anthropologists" (Haller, 1971:17). Though this pseudoscience disappeared quietly the racial classifications begun or supported by phrenologists, which relegated Mongolian, Malayan, Indian, and Ethiopian to inferior positions beneath the Caucasian, were seldom criticized or attacked.

While Retzius, Gall, and Broca were developing theories of craniology, several scientists in America were occupied with similar studies. Samuel Morton (1799–1851), a famous physician of his day, is best remembered for the thousands of skulls he collected; many were from American Indian remains but a sizable number came from other parts of the world. Morton believed, as did his European colleagues, that skull shape and size indicated race and character. They equated size of skull with intelligence and often reported smaller average cranial volumes for non-Europeans. Morton showed by his measurements that American Indians had a much smaller cranial volume than did the Caucasoid skulls in his collection.[3]

---

[3] Recent reexamination of Morton's measurements and his use of arithmetic means by Gould (1978, 1983) shows that there were, in fact, insignificant differences between the racial groups. The large differences reported by Morton could be demonstrated only if there had been selective bias in the selection of the measurements.

Because the European skulls in his collection had the largest cranial capacity, Morton concluded that Caucasoids were the most intelligent of the races—a contention brought up repeatedly in the century following Morton's studies. Therefore, the discovery of skulls of reputedly Caucasoid type in several of the large earth mounds located in the Ohio and Mississippi valleys of the midwestern United States were taken as proof that a vanished race of ancient Caucasian people was responsible for the construction of the vast and impressive earth works rather than the native Americans who were seen by the earliest European colonists in the eighteenth century.

Morton's work influenced many others, notably George Gliddon (1809–1857), a famous Egyptologist of his day. Gliddon eagerly and uncritically applied Morton's methods to cranial studies of the skeletal remains he recovered from Egypt to prove that the pharaoh and pyramid builders were, in fact, members of the Caucasoid race. This conclusion added support to the conviction held by scholars of the day that only the Caucasoids were capable of building higher civilizations. These kinds of studies and the conclusions they reached continued for many years through the early part of this century. Though now thoroughly discredited, this misuse of craniology was accepted as "scientific proof" of the racial composition of ancient populations.

Throughout the development of anthropometry there has been the belief that if only enough measurements are taken, then facts would emerge that would clear up the mysteries surrounding human origins and variations. Many populations were measured throughout Europe, and school children and military personnel were favorite subjects in the study of variability of the human form. Also, demographic data were now considered important and were assembled in large quantity. Given the vast number of measurements made in the course of anthropometric studies, a means of analysis had to be devised, and several mathematicians developed statistical methods. Foremost among the statisticians of his day was Lambert Quetelet (1796–1874), an astronomer and mathematician interested in social statistics. He gathered anthropometric measurements from many military conscripts, university students, and prison convicts. These data were compared with the measurements of a general sample from several populations in Europe. Comparisons of height, weight, and several body proportions showed significant differences between population samples. Because of these and other works, Quetelet was responsible for the concept of the "average man" (Stigler, 1986:170).

His statistical work and his descriptions of the "average man" lent support to the search for the ideal of beauty and perfection in humans. Quetelet was deeply influenced by the works of Camper and Blumenbach, and he accepted facial angle as a marker or indicator of intelligence (Figure 1-9). The series of studies he performed on army conscripts and

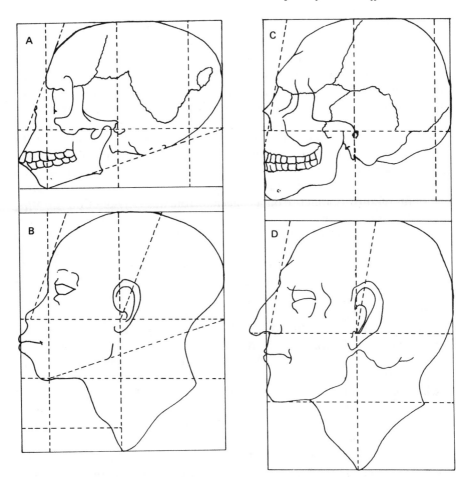

FIGURE 1-9 **Comparisons of Idealized Face Forms of the European and the African.** These are from descriptions by Peter Camper, a student of Linneaus. Camper emphasized the distinctions of the lower face that were described by an acute angle in the African (shown in diagrams A and B).

convicts in Belgium provided the raw data for many of the correlations of behavior with body form. These materials contributed to the application of probability statistics to predictions of behavior, a method that became widely accepted in both Europe and North America and provided a foundation for those works that attempted to identify criminal types from a few physical characteristics.

One of the major effects of Quetelet's work on population averages and "types" was to influence the establishment of a commission in the United States designed to examine army personnel during the Civil War. This "Sanitary Commission" examined and measured thousands of persons including many recently freed slaves and American Indians inducted into the army during the Civil War. The results provided an unparalleled opportunity for investigating race differences. Though the stated purpose of the commission was directed toward the practical goals of determining fitness of individuals for army duty, the commission's efforts provided a major study of human variability and was perhaps one of the earliest applications of anthropological theory to practical problems relating physique and endurance to job performance. Generally, the thrust of the study was to determine which races were most suitable for military service and for which job. As with most military, however, qualifications and aptitudes meant little in practice. The commission did generate large amounts of anthropometric data collected from a variety of ethnic groups.

Though the work of the Sanitary Commission is scarcely remembered today, it convinced scientists of the day of the usefulness of such racial variation studies. Joseph Le Conte (1823–1901) wrote in *Man's Place in Nature* (1878) that the scientists held the keys to proper race relations in America: "The scientist's methods and his understanding of evolution provided the basis for sorting mankind into a hierarchy of abilities" (Haller, 1971:35). These and many other similar statements were merely a reaffirmation of the prejudices that had been accumulating for generations. From such works, there developed a belief in "racial purity" and a conviction that strength of a nation depended on the maintenance of its pure stock (read "Caucasian"). Though supposedly based on a firm "scientific" foundation, such beliefs were seriously challenged by the end of the nineteenth century as new data were accumulated, and a clearer understanding was gained of the mechanisms of inheritance and evolutionary processes.

Race differences were not the only focuses of anthropometry. With the expansion of measurement techniques to include many features of the living human form, anthropometry was used for standard identification techniques in criminology. Studies of the physiques of convicted criminals were made, the assumption being that crimes were committed by biologically inferior persons. This school of thought was based mostly on the works of an Italian physician, Cesare Lombroso (1836–1909), who expounded the theory of the "born criminal." He was convinced that the presence of certain physical traits that deviated significantly from the average were atavistic remnants of our "ape" past and that these traits were indicators of a "savage" form of behavior. Through his extensive publications Lombroso cited a large list of "abnormalities"—such conditions as receding forehead, large ears, square and projecting chin, broad cheekbones, left-handedness, deficient olfactory and taste organs, and exhibitionism evidenced by addiction to decorating the body with tattoos. A person displaying five or more of these conditions, according to Lombroso, was a criminal type. For a time criminal anthropometry as well as the more generally applied somatology were widely used, and many people were studied to establish a relationship between behavior and physique. Though this idea tends to linger on, no evidence supports Lombroso's basic assumptions today, given our knowledge of environment and behavior. Lombroso eventually allowed that only 40 percent of the crimes were committed by persons with these atavistic traits.

One of the most famous and influential scientists to follow Quetelet's lead was Francis Galton (1822–1911), a cousin of Charles Darwin. As a mathematician, Galton was keenly impressed with the ideas of Quetelet and applied them to found the field of biometrics. Galton studied the inheritance of certain traits in twins and their families and, through this work, established testing procedures and means of comparing individuals or samples from entire populations. He was the first to carry out systematic intelligence testing and, together with his equally famous student and later colleague, Karl Pearson (1857–1936), offered as a plan for improvement of the human species by the regulation of marriage and family size, which he called *eugenics.*

Galton and his colleagues attempted to demonstrate through measurements and testing procedures the degree to which inheritance or environment influenced a person's behavior and abilities. He spelled out this position in detail in his book *Hereditary Genius* (1869) in which he traced the genealogies of many of Britian's leading families and noted the frequencies of the appearances of individuals who had distinguished themselves as scientists, lawyers, members of parliament, literary figures, and so forth. In any consideration of the relative influences of the environment (nurture) or heredity (nature) on the determination of mental ability, Galton would be placed more on the nature side of the nature-nurture argument. Though claims that behavior is influenced more by heredity than by environment have not stood the test of time very well and evidence remains speculative, the idea is still a popular one (see chapter 7). A major difficulty has been a lack of understanding of genetic mechanisms; another problem is that the idea of what constitutes a race is rather vague. These weaknesses were pointed out early in this century by Franz Boas (1858–1942), one of the founders of American anthropology who stated:

> If the defenders of race theories prove that a certain kind of behavior is hereditary and wish to explain in this way that it belongs to a racial type they would have to prove that the particular kind of behavior is characteristic of all the genetic lines composing the race. (Boas, 1911:253)

An additional problem was that many physical traits were treated as if they were permanent and unchanging throughout generations. Boas, in a series of studies of immigrant populations, showed the plasticity or changeable nature of supposed permanent characters, such as head or body form. He observed that the many constitutional types of which a race is composed cannot be considered as absolutely permanent. His *Report on Changes of the Bodily Form of Descendants of Immigrants* (1911) stands as a landmark study of interactions between environments and inheritance. This report described the different head forms found among children of immigrants. Children who were born in America significantly differed from their foreign-born parents in body size and form. They were larger and heavier than their parents, changes that were attributed to improved living conditions, especially nutritional (Boas, 1940).

In addition to ignoring environmental influences on body form, the greatest errors in classificatory schemes are: (1) to expect all characteristics to be shared by all members of the same group; and (2) to mix unrelated characteristics, as did Lombroso in describing his criminal types. Such "types" are no more real than the "average man." The simple visual appraisals often involve this sort of error, however. These distinctions, based on limited information, lead us to make faulty groupings of humans and faulty assumptions about the "worth" of these groups. The criteria we may use are not as interrelated as we imagine. Nose form and head shape or stature, for example, have small correlations with one another, and the skin color of the world's peoples has its own special relationship to the environment.

An outstanding development of the twentieth century has been the replacement of typological thinking with a populationist approach that considers the range of variability of our species and avoids a simple reliance on averages or means (Mayr, 1988). A consideration of variability and intermediates (the populationist approach) avoids the confusion that was faced by somatology in the early part of the century. At that point, after more than a hundred years of study, there were at least sixty systems for typing human body build, each probably equally valid. The variety plus the limited explanatory power of such typologies suggests more art than science. Each of the typing systems is successful only in emphasizing differences. In the long run, however, the most striking feature of our species is the similarities between peoples—a condition that, because these similar peoples live in such diverse environments, required careful study and explanation.

RACIAL BOUNDARIES: FACT OR FICTION?

Human history records many contacts among peoples from all areas of the world. The frequent and free interbreeding of these populations, whether Hottentot with European, African with American Indian, or Polynesian with Chinese, to mention a few examples, is a matter of record.

Such evidence has destroyed many of the myths of the last two centuries and has long established that we all belong to the same species. This situation has probably existed for hundreds of thousands of years, ever since ancestral human's mobility overcame geographical barriers. Despite this evidence confusion still occasionally arises over what are races and how racial boundaries can be identified.

The term *race* was applied to varieties of *Homo sapiens* in the middle of the eighteenth century by Buffon, the French naturalist mentioned earlier. Before this time, *race* described breeds of domestic animals, their group membership, or their descent from a common ancestor. Since then the term has been used in a variety of social and biological contexts and has become encumbered with contradictory and imprecise meanings. Many people take for granted that they know what race means and assume that scientific investigation has long ago proved the existence of significant human racial differences. Each time the term is applied, however, a definition must be provided so that the reader will know what concept it represented. There is even a considerable confusion over the number of divisions of humanity; as few as three and as many as thirty-seven races have been described. Two carefully written studies published in 1950 listed six and thirty races, respectively.[4]

The number of races and their boundaries remains a subject of dispute partially because of the lack of agreement on which traits identify a person's racial identity. Just what constitutes a race is a difficult question to answer, because one's classification usually depends on the purpose of classification; various approaches to taxonomy often have a built-in bias, especially when applied to humans. It is usually assumed that there is an actual structure or collection of organisms in the natural world awaiting classification. The sample definitions that follow give some idea of the confusion surrounding the race concept during the past forty-five years in biology as well as anthropology.

Definitions of Race

DOBZHANSKY: Races are defined as populations differing in the incidence of certain genes, but actually exchanging or potentially able to exchange genes across whatever boundaries (usually geographic) separate them. (1944:252)

Race differences are objectively ascertainable facts, the number of races we chose to recognize is a matter of convenience. (1962:266)

HULSE: . . . races are populations which can be readily distinguished from one another on genetic grounds alone. (1963:262)

[4] Boyd, 1950; Coon, Garn, and Birdsell, 1950.

BOYD: We may define a human race as a population which differs significantly from other human populations in regard to the frequency of one or more of the genes it possesses. It is an arbitrary matter which, and how many, gene loci we choose to consider as a significant "constellation." (1950:207)

GARN: At the present time there is general agreement that a race is a breeding population, largely if not entirely isolated reproductively from other breeding populations. The measure of race is thus reproductive isolation, arising commonly but not exclusively from geographical isolation. (1960:7)

MAYR: A subspecies is an aggregate of local populations of a species, inhabiting a geographic subdivision of the range of the species, and differing taxonomically from other populations of the species. (1963:348) It is a unit of convenience for the taxonomist, but not a unit of evolution. (1982:289)

BAKER: It is concluded that race may be defined as a rough measure of genetic distance in human populations and as such may function as an informational construct in the multidisciplinary area of research in human biology. (1967:21)

VOGEL AND
MOTULSKY: A race is a large population of individuals who have a significant fraction of their genes in common and can be distinguished from other races by their common gene pool. (1986:534)

Because of the prejudice surrounding the concept of human races and the misunderstanding of human biological diversity, the following definition, which substitutes *ethnic groups* for the term *race*, was offered.

MONTAGU: An ethnic group represents one of a number of populations, comprising the single species *Homo sapiens*, which individually maintain their differences, physical and cultural, by means of isolating mechanisms such as geographic and social barriers. These differences will vary as the power of the geographic and social barriers acting upon the original genetic differences varies. (1964:317)

The following broader, more descriptive attempt to define human groupings on an objective basis without regard to the biases of the day is a reminder of an earlier effort to treat human diversity and its allied social problems from the scientific basis of degree of genetic differences.

HUXLEY AND
HADDON: Populations differed from one another, Huxley and Haddon stressed, only in the relative proportions of genes for given characters that they possessed. "For existing populations," they maintained, "the word race should be banished, and the descriptive and non-committal term *ethnic groups* should be substituted." (quoted in Kevles, 1985:133)

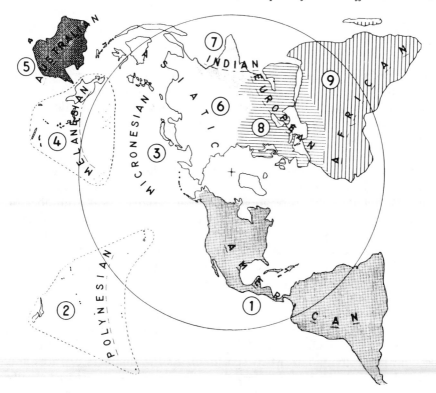

FIGURE 1-10   Polar-Projection Map of the World Showing the Limits of Nine Geographical Races Described by Garn (1961). Geographical barriers set off the race collections. (From Garn, S. M., *Human Races*, 1961. Copyright © 1961 by Charles C Thomas, Publisher, Springfield, Illinois. Reprinted by permission of the publisher.)

These definitions, though they appear quite diverse, have in common certain factors that they emphasize. The first is an assumption about the role of geographical distribution in race formation. Primarily, the divisions are based on the sharing of a common territory or space and that geography played some role in establishing boundaries until recent times (Figure 1-10). The second factor is that all agree on the importance of breeding populations in the possession of a collection of traits which sets the group apart. Beyond this there seems to be little agreement in terms or boundaries or groupings. There are some opinions that dividing humanity into racial groups distorts the facts and forces the investigator into erroneous channels of thinking.[5] The purpose for the classifications of human populations

[5] "To deny existence of racial differences within the human species is futile. The futility has been neatly demonstrated at our symposium. I find it amusing that those who questioned the validity of racial classifications have themselves used the word 'race,' or the term 'so-called race,' many times. Indeed, how else could they speak about human variation at all? The reliability and the usefulness of racial classifications have often been exaggerated" (Dobzhansky, 1968:166).

has continually plagued anthropologists for generations.[6] But regardless of the numerous ways of looking at human diversity or the evaluation of the utility of race groupings, the fact remains that many biological differences are real and cannot be described or explained away by simple statements. The concept of race is not merely a taxonomic problem of which group of populations fits together within a certain classification. It is a problem of the ways in which one views *Homo sapiens* in the perspective of time and space.

Even by the end of the nineteenth century scientists began to appreciate that there was no single physical criterion for distinguishing between groups of humans. However, it was believed that racial grouping could be delimited by association of several variables, and a number of writers proceeded to publish racial groupings that they believed reflect the actual variability of our species. A casual survey shows that at least fourteen different race typologies have been described in this century. Most of them started with the major racial stocks defined by Linneaus and Blumenbach, but they went further and subdivided each into several subgroups or local types.

This increase in subdivision illustrates the problem we often encounter in dealing with subspecies, either *Homo sapiens* or other mammals: The more we learn about the variability of the group, the more difficult it becomes to fix boundaries between them. As the numbers of races and local types of *Homo sapiens* grew, the number of groupings was simply increased. This is illustrated by the expanded studies of European populations that showed numerous contrasts. From southern to northern Europe and from eastern to western Europe, body form and size differed significantly as did hair and even skin coloration. To encompass this newly recognized diversity several authors simply added new racial subdivisions. For example, in *The Races of Europe* (1899), Ripley determined that European populations consisted of three races: Nordic, Alpine, and Mediterranean. The Nordics were tall, fair-skinned people with large doliocephalic heads who were the majority of the northwestern European population. The southern European Mediterranean race were short, brachycephalic people with dark complexions in stark contrast to the Nordics. The Alpines, most occupants of central and eastern Europe, possessed average head size and shapes intermediate between the two. Unfortunately for the study of race, individuals as well as whole population groups possessed mixtures of these traits and could easily be classified into one or the other of the races of Europe. This concern with the identification of significant groups continued into the middle of the present century when interest shifted toward the question of what race

---

[6] The difficulty encountered by authors of several recent anthropology texts when they attempt to deal with the race concept is described by Littlefield (1982).

actually is and what was the purpose of the classification. The following classifications show this changing concern.

Earnest Hooton in *Up from the Ape* (1946) defined race as a group whose members present individually identical combinations of specific physical characters that they owe to their common descent. He divided *Homo sapiens* into three main physical groups or main races, and subdivided these into an array of subcategories. His sorting criteria were primarily skin color, hair color, eye color, and hair form.

Coon, Garn, and Birdsell in *Races* (1950) described race as a population that differs phenotypically from all others. They distinguish six groups or "stocks" that grouped together thirty races. These races were determined on the basis of evolutionary status as reflected in certain features of the skull and body and special surface features, such as black skin and face form, that appear as special adaptations to the environments. In 1960 Garn offered a classification differing somewhat from that constructed in his work with Birdsell and Coon. He described nine races, which were geographically delimited collections of local races. The local races defined as breeding populations, the numbers of which in any geographical race were very large. A sample of thirty-two local races was listed as representative (Tables 1-2a, 1-2b).

Boyd, in *Genetics and the Races of Man* (1950), defined six races on the basis of certain blood-type frequencies. By 1963 the distribution of the different blood types throughout the world became better known, causing Boyd to increase his original six races to thirteen. The major increase was in the European group, from two to five. This expansion of the number of categories is clearly a result of the increased knowledge about blood types of the world's peoples (Table 1-3).

Carleton Coon described five groups of humans in *The Origin of Races* (1962), all of which he attempted to trace to mid-Pleistocene origins. These groups were referred to as subspecies, several of which were further divided—for example, Australoids, the aboriginal inhabitants of Australia and most of New Guinea, with a few remnant populations throughout Southeast Asia and the Philippines, were composed of full-sized people and hereditary dwarfs (Table 1-4). By a mixed criterion combining morphological traits (including skin color, blood type, and fossilized skeletal remains), Coon was able to divide-up *Homo sapiens* into major racial stocks—mostly geographical races including a diversity of local races.

RACES, POPULATIONS, AND SOME CAUSES OF VARIABILITY

Races or subspecies are collections of populations, and each is constantly changing as individuals are added through birth or lost through death. This creates a dynamic situation: Because of the nature of human

TABLE 1-2a   A Racial Classification[a]

1. Murraylan	16. Hindu
2. Ainu	17. Mediterranean
3. Alpine	18. Nordic
4. N. W. European	19. N. American Colored
4a. N. W. European Prototype	20. S. African Colored
5. N. E. European	21. Classic Mongoloid
6. Lapp	22. N. Chinese
7. Forest Negro	23. S. E. Asiatic
8. Melanesian	24. Tibeto-Indonesian Mongoloid
9. Negrito	25. Turkic
10. Bushman	26. Am. Indian Marginal
11. Bantu	27. Am. Indian Central
12. Sundanese	28. Landino
13. Carpentarian	29. Polynesian
14. Dravidian	30. Neo-Hawaiian
15. Hamite	

[a] The authors described this classification as a tentative list. They stated: "The foregoing list of 30 'races' might have been ten or 50; the line of discrimination in many cases is arbitrary. In some cases we have nearly adequate data on which to base descriptions, in others almost none at all. . . . If this list does nothing else, we hope that it will bring home to the student the realization that race is not a static thing at all, but that new races are constantly being formed through the mechanisms described earlier in this Lecture, and that a new race such as the 'Neo-Hawaiian' (#30) is just as real as an old one such as the Mediterranean (#17) or the Negrito (#9). History, in the biological as well as the cultural sense, is always in motion."

Source: After Coon, Garn, and Birdsell, 1950: 140. Copyright © 1950 by Charles C Thomas, Publisher. Reprinted by permission of the publisher.

TABLE 1-2b   Major Racial Stocks

1. *Negroid:* All peoples showing special adaptation to bright light and intense heat, wherever found.
2. *Mongoloid:* The same for adaptation to intense cold.
3. *White:* Peoples of the Old World, excluding Australia and the southeastern fringe of Asia, who possess neither of these two kinds of adaptation. Overseas settlers of the same origin, and similar phenotypical form.
4. *Australoid:* The native inhabitants of Australia, whom one of us (Birdsell) has shown to belong to two distinct races and to include one other type. Veddas of Ceylon, and possibly some other remnant populations in Malaysia.
5. *American Indian:* The descendants of the pre-Columbian inhabitants of North, Central, and South America.
6. *Polynesian:* The inhabitants of the outer islands of the Pacific, from New Zealand to Hawaii to Easter Island. While moderately variable, they show resemblances to Mongoloids, white Australoids, and possibly Negroids.

Source: After Coon, Garn, and Birdsell, 1950. Copyright © 1950 by Charles C Thomas, Publisher. Reprinted by permission of the publisher.

TABLE 1-3   Racial Taxonomy of *Homo sapiens*

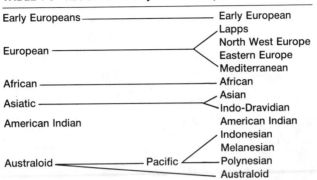

Source: Based on the frequencies of blood types in major groups of *Homo sapiens;* from Boyd, 1950, 1963.

reproduction, each individual inherits a unique combination of traits but in every population, the individuals share numerous characteristics. Because the breeding population (the basic group within the species) is regionally defined, these characteristics appear as clusters in space; these clusters are often identified as the basis for racial typologies. Because the "typical" or "average" individual is an abstraction, most of a population covers a wide range of variation that overlaps with other groups, causing a gradient or cline of variation to be distributed over a wide area (Figure 1-11). Identifying "types" on the basis of trait clusters (in populations) or their geographical distribution is not useful in the studying of human biological diversity as we shall see in the later chapters. The concept of racial types has no significance in itself, and only under certain specified conditions are racial taxonomies useful to the zoologist, as we describe in chapter 5.

The collections or concentrations of characteristics that we see today in certain regionally defined populations are probably the result of an ordering of genetic variability in response to the selective forces present

TABLE 1-4   Classification of Modern Races

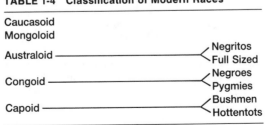

Source: After Coon, 1962, 1965.

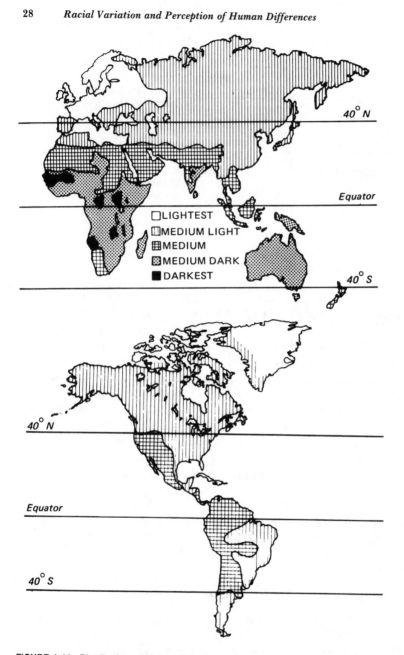

FIGURE 1-11   Distribution of Human Skin Color. (From Frisancho, A. R., *Human Adaptation*, 1979, St. Louis: The C. V. Mosby Co.; modified from Brace, C. L. and A. Montagu, *Man's Evolution*, 1965, New York: Macmillan.)

in each environment. The history of populations is, of course, important as it describes migrations and merging or separating of groups during the last few thousands of years.

For evolution of human diversity we might turn to the fossil evidence of our species' past; but it is not nearly complete enough to fill out an adequate record, nor are the total fossil remains capable of establishing a record of unilineal evolution leading to any of the modern races. Some workers have attempted to establish modern racial groupings in the fossil evidence, but all they have achieved is a demonstration of some similarities. From this presumed evidence of racial origins, they have drawn conclusions about the evolutionary position of modern groups. Regardless of what their race, subspecies, or stock is supposed to be, the fact is that all humans can freely interbreed, as colonization, wars, and armies of occupation have clearly demonstrated during the last several thousands of years.

Biological and cultural diversity are often confused; group membership (race or ethnic) is frequently determined by a mix of behavioral, linguistic, and biological traits. For example, the population of Mexico is derived from European, African, and Native American ancestors. Recent migrants to the United States as well as U.S. citizens who descend from colonists in the Southwest and California are classified as Hispanic. This is without regard to their complex heritage. Likewise persons from several of the other Latin American countries are lumped together in the Hispanic category much to the objection of Brazilians. The term *Hispanic* is based on a sharing of the Spanish language, which does not apply to Brazilians who speak Portuguese. What this example shows is the difficulty of classification of groups of people and how such classification obscures the diversity while not revealing much about population ancestry.

We so commonly and carelessly use such labels in our daily lives that we have come to assume that they are meaningful in the biological sense. To some degree the classifications have a biological component. For example, Jamaicans are dark skinned, unless, of course, the individual is of European rather than African descent. Likewise a migrant from Mexico is expected to have certain facial features and smaller body size, unless the person has several Spanish ancestors among his or her ancestry. These illustrations could be extended to include contrasts among Europeans as well—for example, the distinctions between northern and southern Europeans. For social or political purposes, the race-ethnic classification may serve a purpose, but they most often confuse the question of biological differences. The difficulty encountered by the U.S. government in collecting vital statistics, especially data on disease incidence, illustrates the confusion over race. To record race for the purpose of collecting infant mortality statistics, the race of infants of "mixed" parents is determined by these rules: (1) if one parent is white, the fetus or infant is assigned to the other parents race; and (2) when neither parent is white, the fetus or

Race
Fill ONE circle for the race that the person considers himself/herself to be.
   If **Indian (Amer.)**, print the name of the enrolled or principal tribe. ——▶

If **Other Asian or Pacific Islander (API)**, print one group, for example: Hmong, Fijian, Laotian, Thai, Tongan, Pakistani, Cambodian, and so on. ——▶

If **Other race**, print race. ——▶

○ White
○ Black or Negro
○ Indian (Amer.) (Print the name of the enrolled or principal tribe.)⌐

Asian or Pacific Islander (API)

○ Eskimo
○ Aleut

○ Chinese   ○ Japanese
○ Filipino ■   ○ Asian Indian
○ Hawaiian   ○ Samoan
○ Korean   ○ Guamanian
○ Vietnamese   ○ Other API⌐

○ Other race (Print race)⌐

FIGURE 1-12   Racial Classifications According to US Census of 1990

Item four on the census form requests a self identification of each member of the household and attempts to include all groups commonly thought of as "race, tribe, or ethnic group." There is some problem with even these broad categories since they do not allow for residents of several islands or regions (such as Hawaii, Samoa, Guam, Vietnam, or Korea). Blank spaces are available for "other race" and other "Asian or Pacific Islander." Source: Extracted from Census Bureau form; US Department of Commerce.

infant is assigned to the father's race. The exception is if the mother is Hawaiian, the infant is classified Hawaiian (U.S. Department of Commerce, 1989). This follows a long tradition that has treated children of ethnically mixed marriages as if they possess traits, especially behavioral traits, of the parent who is from the socially disadvantaged ethnic group.

Such confusion of traits, the mixing of inherited with socially derived traits, has continued to cause great difficulty for all those who deal with human diversity, from the census taker to human biologist. Terms must be carefully chosen whether talking of population, ethnic groups, or race so there is a clear, precise meaning. If population genetic variability is discussed, then the term *breeding population* is most useful because it implies a clear delineation of genetic boundaries. Ethnic group, conversely, is applied to a wide variety of poorly defined groups, from a group sharing a common language (for example, Hispanic) and little else to minorities who retain their identity through sharing of certain origins and traditions (for example, Native Americans). *Race* is a term originally applied to populations who shared close common ancestry and certain unique traits, but it has been so overworked and its applications are so broad and general that race is nearly useless and is often replaced by *ethnic group*. Classifications of race or ethnic group still appear and, in fact, were used in the 1990 census (Figure 1-12). Each respondent to the census is asked to choose a category from among those that are the traditional race types, and several national or ethnic groups. The results of this self-classification will be useful for several political and economic purposes, but the identification itself will reveal little about the actual range of human biological variation.

These examples and contrasts between terms show that we should not take for granted the categories into which we put people. We should not think of these categories as a reality of nature but should recognize them for what they are—a construct, a means of organizing the diversity of data describing our species.

I shall remind the reader of these problems throughout the book and I shall use, when necessary, the term *race* to mean a group or *complex* of breeding populations sharing a number of traits. When it is necessary to refer to a broader range of peoples like inhabitants of continents, then race will be used in a geographical sense—that is, "African" or "European." Whatever the application, the intent will be clear—to identify a major segment of *Homo sapiens* that differs in many ways from other such groups.

What, then, is the origin of human diversity? If race or subspecies is an artificial construct—a device of convenience to enable the human mind to organize information from the natural world—then origins cease to be an important consideration. Rather our concern should be with the possible responses to the environment that our species is capable of biologically. With this in mind, we attempt to sort out the different influences on *Homo sapiens*. The terms *race, group,* or *population* are used to refer to that geographically and culturally determined collection of individuals who share a common gene pool.

RECOMMENDED READINGS AND LITERATURE CITED

BAKER, P. T. 1967. "The biological race concept as a research tool," *Am. J. Phys. Anthrop.,* 27:21–25.

BARZUN, J. 1965. *Race: A Study in Superstition.* New York: Harper and Row.

BOAS, F. 1911. *The Mind of Primitive Man.* New York: Macmillan.

BOAS, F. 1940. "The relations between physical and social anthropology," in *Race, Language and Culture.* New York: Free Press.

BOYD, W. C. 1950. *Genetics and the Races of Man.* Boston: Little, Brown.

BOYD, W. C. 1963. "Genetics and the human race," *Science,* 140:1057–1065.

BRUES, A. M. 1977. *People and Races.* New York: Macmillan.

COON, C. S. 1962. *The Origin of Races.* New York: Alfred A. Knopf.

COON, C. S., S. M. GARN, AND J. B. BIRDSELL. 1950. *Races: A Study of the Problems of Race Formation in Man.* Springfield, Ill.: Charles C Thomas.

COON, C. S. 1965. *The Living Races of Man.* New York: Alfred A. Knopf.

DOBZHANSKY, T. 1944. "On species and races of living and fossil man," *Am. J. Phys. Anthrop.,* 2:251–265.

DOBZHANSKY, T. 1962. *Mankind Evolving: The Evolution of the Human Species.* New Haven: Yale University Press.

DOBZHANSKY, T. 1968. *Science and the Concept of Race.* New York: Columbia University Press.

FRISANCHO, A. R. 1979. *Human Adaptation.* St. Louis: C. V. Mosby.
GARN, S. M., ed. 1960a. *Readings on Race.* Springfield, Ill.: Charles C. Thomas.
GARN, S. M. 1960b. *Human Races.* Springfield, Ill.: Charles C Thomas.
GOULD, S. J. 1978. Morton's ranking of races by cranial capacity. *Science,* 200:503–509.
GOULD, S. J. 1983. *The Mismeasure of Man.* New York: W. W. Norton.
HALLER, J. S., JR. 1971. *Outcasts from Evolution.* Chicago: University of Chicago Press.
HOOTON, E. A. 1946. *Up from the Ape.* New York: Macmillan.
HULSE, F. S. 1963. *The Human Species.* New York: Random House.
KEVLES, D. J. 1985. *In the Name of Eugenics: Genetics and the Uses of Human Heredity.* New York: Alfred A. Knopf.
LITTLEFIELD, A., L. LIEBERMAN, AND L. T. REYNOLDS. 1982. Redefining race: the potential demise of a concept in physical anthropology. *Current Anthropology,* 23:641–655.
MAYR, E. 1982. *The Growth of Biological Thought: Diversity, Evolution, and Inheritance.* Cambridge, Mass.: The Belknap Press of Harvard University Press.
MAYR, E. 1988. *Toward a New Philosophy of Biology.* Cambridge, Mass.: Belknap Press of Harvard University Press.
McCOWN, T. D., AND K. A. R. KENNEDY, eds. 1972. *Climbing Man's Family Tree: A Collection of Major Writings on Human Phylogeny 1699 to 1971.* Englewood Cliffs, N.J.: Prentice-Hall.
MONTAGU, M. F. A. 1964. "Discussion and criticism on the race concept," *Current Anthrop.,* 5:37.
MONTAGU, M. F. A. 1974. *Frontiers of Anthropology.* New York: Putnam.
MORTON, S. G. 1839. *Crania Americana.* Philadelphia: J. Dodson.
PRICHARD, J. C. 1826. *Researches into the Physical History of Mankind,* 2nd ed., 2 vols. London: John and Arthur Arch.
PRICHARD, J. C. 1973. *Researches into the Physical History of Man,* ed. G. W. Stocking, Jr. Chicago: University of Chicago Press.
PUTNAM, C. 1967. *Race and Reality.* Washington, D.C.: Public Affairs Press.
RIPLEY, W. Z. 1899. *The Races of Europe.* New York: Appleton.
SLOTKIN, J. S., ed. 1965. *Readings in Early Anthropology.* New York: Viking Fund Publications.
STANTON, W. R. 1960. *The Leopard's Spots: Scientific Attitudes Toward Race in America, 1815–59.* Chicago: University of Chicago Press.
STIGLER, S. M. 1986. *The History of Statistics: The Measurement of Uncertainty before 1900.* Cambridge, Mass.: Belknap Press of Harvard University Press.
STOCKING, G. W., JR., ed. 1973. *Researches into the Physical History of Man.* Chicago: University of Chicago Press.
U.S. Department of Commerce. 1989. Monthly Vital Statistics Reports (Suppl.).
VOGEL, F., AND A. G. MOTULSKY 1986. *Human Genetics. Problems and Approaches,* 2nd ed. Berlin: Springer-Verlag.
WASHBURN, S. L. 1963. "The study of race," *American Anthrop.,* 65:521–531.

2

Biological Basis for Human Variation

Humans share similar modes of reproduction with most of the other mammals, and inheritance mechanisms are the same—the combination of certain material in the germ cells of male and female parent to produce a fertilized egg. These mechanisms of inheritance are the source of much of the vast diversity seen in the biological world. Though the variety may seem to be extremely random and unlimited, there are, in fact, limits to the extent and degree of variation in each species. *Homo sapiens,* the species with which we are most concerned, contains as much or perhaps more variation than any other mammalian group, but its diversity is also limited by certain processes. For many centuries, natural scientists had sought to comprehend and explain the processes of reproduction and the transmission of traits between generations. The explanations varied from a description of a "blending" of parental bloodlines, favored by animal husbandry, to a theory of "preformism"—the idea that the individual, in miniature form, existed in either the ova or sperm awaiting stimulation by fertilization to begin its development. None of these explanations could account for the ranges of individual similarities or differences among offspring and their parents. A thorough understanding of the mechanisms of inheritance was slowly gained through the accumulated work of many investigators from the nineteenth century into the middle of this century.

A significant, and perhaps initial, advancement was made in the middle of the last century by a botanist experimenting with plant hybridization. The discovery of the laws of biological inheritance by Mendel eventually led to the understanding of these mechanisms and provided the answer to a crucial question—the source of individual variation—a question that had plagued Charles Darwin.

PRINCIPLES OF INHERITANCE

Johann Gregor Mendel (1822–1884), often described as the founder of the science of genetics, spent most of his life as a member of the Augustinian order in a monastery in Brunn, Czechoslovakia. He had been an excellent student but was forced to discontinue his studies because of ill health and poverty. Upon entering the priesthood he was able to continue his education, in part, as preparation for teaching in the local secondary schools. Mendel studied in Vienna under leading natural scientists of the period and far from being an isolated, obscure, ill-trained monk as had been described, he was well educated for the period. Most importantly for the future of genetics, Mendel came under the influence of Franz Unger, a botanist whose theory on the importance of varieties in natural populations probably was the stimulus that caused Mendel to work on the problem of inheritance (Mayr, 1982).

Whatever the influence, Mendel spent years studying plant hybridization, and he is best known for his extensive experiments on cross-pollination of common varieties of sweet pea (Lathyrus). He cross-pollinated these plants for color, shape, size, and form of seed pod. Mendel was fortunate in his choice of these characteristics because they happened to be traits of simple inheritance: The plants bred true without intermediate traits—that is, each succeeding generation possessed traits like the parental generation. Analysis of these multiple crosses led Mendel to derive a hypothesis that an organism's characteristics were inherited as discrete units or elements and not through a blending of parental traits, as was assumed in Mendel's day.

In some of his earliest experiments Mendel crossed plants that had violet-red blossoms with white (colorless) ones and produced hybrids that all had violet-red blossoms. When these hybrids were crossed, however, they produced a mixture of white and violet-red (Figure 2-1). Also, plants of different stem length were crossed (tall with dwarf) and the F_1 (first filial) generation were all of the tall variety. Cross-breeding of plants of this hybrid generation (the F_2) produced a mixture of tall and short plants. Mendel sought to explain these results by hypothesizing that these traits were determined by a pair of elements. One of the elements, or heredity particles, was dominant to the other; they segregated independently each

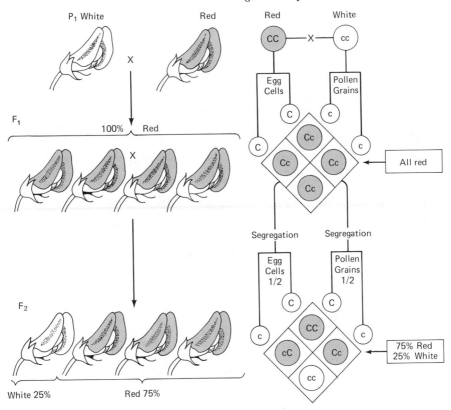

FIGURE 2-1 Diagram of Mendel's Experiments and the Results.

generation, a phenomenon called the *Law of Independent Segregation.* Mendel continued these kinds of experiments many times, and his results were close to a certain ratio of traits in the F₂ generation as diagrammed in Figure 2-1. The relative frequency of these traits is known as the *Mendelian ratio.*

Experiments crossing plants selected for a difference of two traits produced dihybrids with a certain ratio of these traits among the F₂ generation, as was the case with crosses of single traits. These results demonstrated that traits such as seed shape and color were determined by paired elements that independently assorted in ovule and pollen (Figure 2-2). The repetition of such experiments produced results that could be predicted because they always fell within close range of the expected, establishing the *Law of Independent Assortment.* Thousands of experimental crosses of plants, selecting for single or paired traits, proved the correctness of Mendel's hypothesis and demonstrated the mechanisms of inheritance.

Mendel's work remained unappreciated during his lifetime, partly

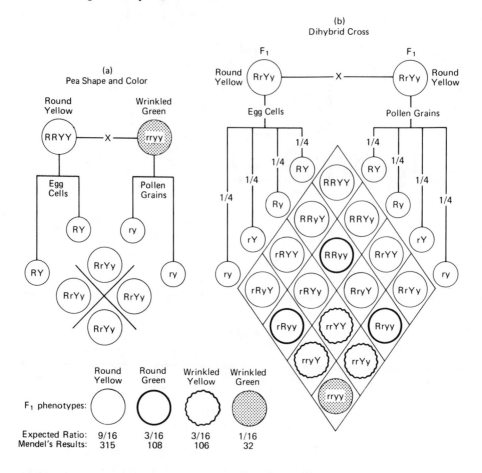

FIGURE 2-2 Independent Assortment: Mendel's Second Law.
When Mendel crossed plants, selecting for two characteristics at a time, he found that the paired factors for each character assorted independently. Diagram A shows the cross of plants to produce a "dihybrid" generation that, when crossed, produces four different characteristics, shown in diagram B.

because cellular structures and their functions were just being discovered and partly because of a choice of traits that just happened to have a simple mode of inheritance. It was not until 1900 that particulate inheritance was recognized as the mode of transmission of characteristics between generations. Three botanical researchers (de Vries, Correns, and Tschermak), working independently on plant hybridization, provided experimental support. Within less than a decade other scientists showed that inheritance of traits in animals also followed Mendel's laws. These studies and the thousands of experiments to follow during the early decades of this century established the foundations of modern genetics.

The Gene

In 1909, the element described by Mendel became known as the gene, a unit of inheritance, a term derived from the Greek root *gen* (to become or to grow out of). Each species has a specific quantity of genes numbering in the thousands or tens of thousands. It is estimated that our species, for example, has between fifty thousand to one hundred thousand genes. Geneticists recognized early that genes segregated as did the chromosomes, the darkly staining, threadlike bodies in a cell's nucleus. Groups of these genes are arranged lineally along the chromosomes. The locus, or position, of each gene in this linear sequence has a special significance for determination of a trait. For example, the reproduction of dihybrids for color and seed shape, as in Mendel's experiments, suggested that the locus for seed color is on a different chromosome than the locus that carries the gene for seed shape. In addition, there may be more than one form of gene for each locus—for example, one that determines that the seed is green or one that determines that the seed is yellow. These alternative forms of the gene for a particular characteristic were called *allelomorphs* from which the term *allele* is derived as used today to describe the variety of gene forms of a trait. Again, in reference to Mendel's study, we see that some alleles are dominant to others, as was the case with plant color shown in Figure 2-1. The paired combination of alleles, one carried at a locus on each of the chromosomes of the pair, is called the *genotype*. Hence, the genotype, or heredity type, for color may be CC, Cc, or cc. The trait that is the result of the genotype combination is the *phenotype* (the visible type or trait).

CHROMOSOMES AND CELL DIVISION

Each cell of an organism contains several pairs of chromosomes within its nucleus. When the cell grows and eventually divides as in cell reproduction, these chromosomes undergo several changes that alter their shapes before division. They reorganize from the irregular threadlike bodies of darkly staining material to form shorter, thicker structures. The chromosomes are recognized as independent bodies at this stage, and each appears as two joined strands. These strands are called chromatids and are held together at a point along its length called the centromere. During cell division, or *mitosis,* the chromatids of each chromosome are pulled apart; each is attracted to opposite poles of the cell, which become the center for the formation of the daughter cells (Figure 2-3). The end result of mitosis is to double the number of cells with an even distribution of chromosome materials between the daughter cells. During the interphase, or resting stage, the missing halves of chromosomes (the chromatids) are

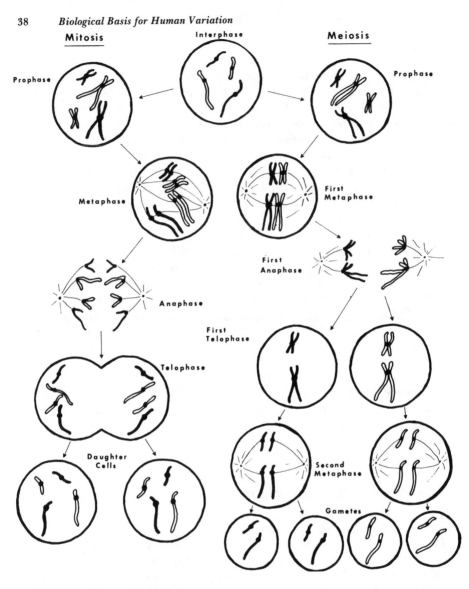

FIGURE 2-3   Stages of Cell Division.

These diagrams show the major steps that occur in cell division. A comparison between *mitosis* and *meiosis* illustrates the organization of the chromosomes at each stage.

Mitosis: This simple cell division starts with chromosomes as pairs of chromatids joined at some point along their length by a centromere. Through metaphase and anaphase stages the chromosomes are arranged in the equatorial plane of the dividing cell and, finally, the chromatids are pulled apart by the end of the anaphase. Telophase is the stage during which the cell membrane grows and eventually separates into two daughter cells.

Meiosis: The major distinction of meiosis is that through a process of reduction and division, daughter cells are produced that have one-half of the chromosomes of the parent cell. The chromosomes are aligned side by side along the equatorial plane in the first metaphase rather than end to end as in mitosis. By the end of the first anaphase the pairs have been separated into cells at a telophase stage, but these cells continue to divide. The second metaphase separates the chromatids into the germ cells called *gametes*.

duplicated from materials in the cells' cytoplasm, and the chromosomes are then completed and will be ready for the next cell division. The splitting of each chromosome in half and the movement of the chromatids into the daughter cell ensures that each cell has a full and identical complement of genes. Such a process allows tissues to grow and still maintain their identity and special functions.

The number of chromosomes of the body's cells, or diploid number, is a fixed number for each species. For example, *Homo sapiens* has forty-six, whereas the chimp and gorilla have forty-eight and the gibbon forty-four. The forty-six chromosomes in our species are arranged as twenty-three pairs, of which twenty-two are known as *autosomes* and one pair, the sex chromosomes, are responsible for sex determination. The sizes of the chromosomes of the same pair are identical, and, though there is some similarity between certain pairs, structural uniqueness of each pair of autosomes sets them apart and prevents the combining of chromosomes from different pairs, though rarely a fragment from one chromosome will attach to a chromosome of another pair (nonhomologous). This *translocation* causes severe disruption of the cellular functions, which almost always leads to destruction of the cell. If abnormal chromosome form or number occurs, the *zygote* (fertilized ova) seldom grows beyond a few divisions, and only rarely would it reach the embryo stage. There are, however, occasional abnormal combinations of chromosomes. The best-known example is *Down's syndrome,* formerly called Mongolism.[1] An individual with this affliction has forty-seven chromosomes instead of forty-six because of an extra chromosome at the twenty-first pair, or "trisomy." Down's syndrome includes a group of abnormal physical traits in addition to a varying degree of mental retardation. Several other syndromes, described subsequently, are due to abnormal numbers of sex chromosomes.

Because the number of chromosomes is critical and must remain constant from one generation to the next, a basic problem of sexual reproduction is how to ensure that an equal number of chromosomes is passed on to the next generation. Because sexual reproduction involves a combination of materials from two individuals to produce the offspring, this problem of the maintenance of the species chromosome number is solved by a process of cellular reduction and division known as *meiosis.* Meiosis is, to a certain extent, comparable with mitosis of somatic cell division with several important exceptions (see Figure 2-3). A major distinction is one of chromosome number: The dividing cell separates the homologous chromosomes shortly before division. The cells, now with only twenty-three chromosomes or one from each pair, continue to divide;

[1] Langdon Down, a nineteenth-century London physician, described patients with a particular type of congenital mental deficiency as "typical mongols." These individuals, because of their general appearance of a broad flattened face, epicanthic eye folds, and other features, were likened to the Mongoloid race.

during the second metaphase, the chromatids are pulled apart. The final stage produces cells, the gametes, with one-half the number of chromosomes, the haploid number.

The germ cells, whose major function is production of the gametes (eggs in the case of a female or sperm in the case of a male), are formed in specialized tissues found in the gonads. These cells undergo meiosis, which divides the chromosome pairs to form a gamete able to combine with a gamete of the opposite sex to form the fertilized egg or *zygote*. This fertilized egg pairs up chromosomes from each parent to duplicate the proper number of chromosomes for the species. This process of sexual reproduction is one of the most fundamental and important factors for the introduction of new varieties because it combines materials from two individuals. During meiosis each chromosome segregates independently from all of the others. Therefore, chromosomes that were provided to the individual at conception by the gamete from the male or female parent are often separated, so it is highly improbable that a person's gametes will contain an even distribution of the chromosomes that were inherited from each of the parents. Of the twenty-three individual chromosomes contained in a particular gamete, for example, fifteen may have been derived from those inherited from one parent and the remaining eight from the other parent. This independent assortment of chromosomes during meiosis is one kind of *recombination* that occurs during meiosis and contributes to diverse combinations of genes in each gamete. The mixing of proportions of one's maternal and paternal chromosomes during meiosis generates a variety of gametes; the total number of gamete types that can be produced by humans is 2^{23}, or more than eight million.

Another type of recombination, and one that is of primary importance in its influence on gamete diversity, is *crossover* during an early stage of meiosis. Crossover refers to an exchange of parts of nonsister chromatids of homologous chromosomes. The homologous chromosomes align in pairs, or *synapsis*. The chromatids of the pair of chromosomes are closely bound into a tetrad bundle, and when they begin to separate to opposite poles of the dividing cells there is a swapping of parts of the nonsister chromatids as illustrated in Figure 2-4. This breakage and rejoining after an exchange of corresponding parts is called *chiasma*, which causes a realignment of the linear arrangement of genes along each chromosome; the frequency of this occurrence or the chance that it will happen depends on the distance between gene loci (see Figure 2-4).

Neither type of recombination adds new genetic information into the population. It merely reassorts the genes so that individuals in each generation will have different gene arrangements and combinations, causing each person to be a unique creation. Because these gene arrangements or genotypes, discussed earlier, influence the characteristics, *recombination* is an important source of individual variability.

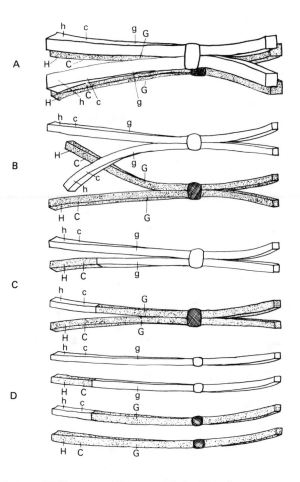

FIGURE 2-4 Crossover of X-Chromosome Fragments during Meiosis.

Occasionally, there is an exchange of fragments between homologous chromosomes (members of a pair). This exchange may take place due to breakage of chromatids during the prophase stage (shown in Figure 2–3). The parts are then rejoined to the other chromosome. The model of the X-chromosome illustrates the swapping of the section with the h allele (hemophilia) and c allele (color blindness) with the fragment carrying H (normal allele) and C (normal visual). This event occurs during prophase, steps A and B. Step C shows a separation of the chromosomes—each is broken apart into its chromatids, step D. The final result is a realignment of genes.

SEX CHROMOSOMES

The sex of an individual is determined by a combination of the X and Y chromosomes: If, at fertilization, two X chromosomes are combined, the individual will be a female; if an X is combined with a Y chromosome, the individual will be a male. Any deviation from these two combinations yields an individual with many abnormal characteristics. Occasionally (about once in every four hundred male births), an extra X chromosome is combined with the XY pair; the offspring is a male with poorly developed sexual characteristics and with some female ones as well (*Klinefelter syndrome*). If a female lacks an X chromosome (once in every 3500 female births), she will have a series of anatomical defects known as *Turner's syndrome,* and the diploid number will be forty-five instead of the normal forty-six. Males with the XYY condition have also been discovered. They are normal males, with the exception of their greater than average height. Early studies of this condition described a possible association with certain behavioral pathologies, and pointed to a supposed high frequency of the XYY condition among mental patients and prison inmates. Subsequent studies, however, found that only a few individuals with this syndrome are institutionalized (about 4 percent), whereas the remaining 96 percent of XYY males have normal behavioral patterns indistinguishable from the rest of the male population. The extra Y chromosome does not predispose a male to social pathology.

The major significance of the X and Y chromosomes in addition to sex determination is their influence on secondary sexual characteristics of form, size, and growth patterns. Males mature later (about two years) than females but are greater in body size. They also differ in body hair distribution and density, especially facial hair. In addition, males differ in bodily proportions; the pectoral girdle (shoulders) is broader than the pelvic girdle, whereas the reverse is true in females. The structural differences of X and Y chromosomes also contribute to male-female differences in the frequencies of certain traits.

The Y differs considerably in structure from the X. It is shorter, so that a region of the X is not represented by a corresponding region of the Y (Figure 2-5). Any genes appearing on the *nonhomologous* region of the X chromosome will not be paired up in male cells. Therefore, a certain number of genes on the nonhomologous region of the X chromosome will express their product without any influence from other alleles. This leads to the existence of certain recessive traits in our species that occur more frequently in the hemizygous male than in the female.

Usually, these X-linked traits are caused by recessive alleles. Because they are frequently paired with normal dominant alleles in the female, owing to the two X chromosomes, these traits rarely occur in women. Some of the better-known traits are hemophilia, red-green color blindness, and a deficiency of an enzyme, G6PD, which are due to recessive genes inherited, as shown in Figure 2-6.

There is little known about Y-linked genes. A peculiar hairy growth over the outer edges of the ears, hairy pinna, and hairy growth over the elbows are two traits that have been frequently mentioned following their discovery among males within several lineages in India. More recently,

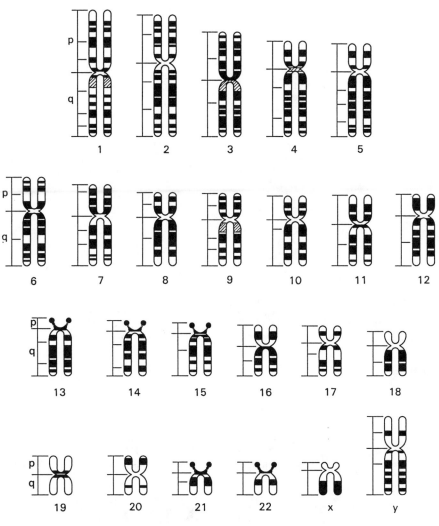

FIGURE 2-5   Human Chromosomes in Mitosis

This illustration is drawn from a photomicrograph of human chromosomes in mitosis. The twenty-two autosome pairs are grouped according to size (karyotype) and the sex chromosomes are placed separately after pair twenty-two. The dark bands illustrate the locations stained by specific chemicals. The short and long arms of each chromosome are designated by P and Q to assist in locating particular sites.

studies of regions of the Y chromosome (in some sexually dysfunctional males) with the aid of restriction enzymes (deoxyribonucleic acid [DNA] probes) have identified certain regions with particular influences on growth, testes development, and spermatogenesis (Vogel and Motulsky, 1986). These and other studies are beginning to define the role of the

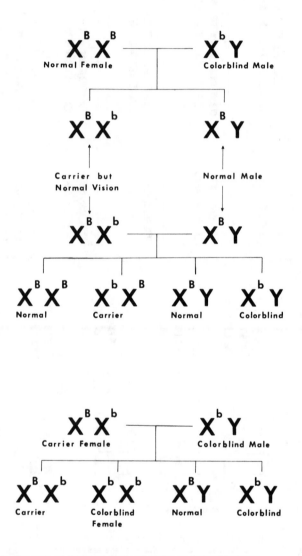

FIGURE 2-6   An Example of X-Linked Traits: Red-Green Color Blindness.

This diagram shows the various combinations that can produce a color-blind person. A normal female and color-blind male will produce all normal offspring. But a female carrying the recessive allele (b) has a 50-50 chance of producing a color-blind son, though all daughters will have normal vision. The more rare condition of a color-blind female is the result of a mating between a color-blind male and a carrier female.

Y-linked genetic loci in the development of male secondary sexual characteristics.

THE GENE, DNA, AND THE "CODE OF LIFE"

Knowledge of the gene as a unit of inheritance had undergone a slow but steady advancement over the first half of the century since the rediscovery of Mendel's experiments. The earliest and perhaps the most important of these advances was an understanding of the intergenerational transmission of traits; parents do not pass on characteristics but transmit the "information base" needed for their development. The association of such information with the darkly staining material in a cell's nucleus was made early in the century, about the time the term *gene* was used to designate the hereditary unit of information. This was followed by a recognition of chromosome pair, where the genes were thought to occupy a position or *locus* on each. The further advancements made in studies of cell structures and how they divide clearly demonstrated the basic mechanisms of particulate inheritance.

Understanding of the actual nature of gene structure and its varying functions, and how genetic mutations occur had to wait until a model was offered to define the structure of the nucleic acid components within the cell's nucleus. Though nucleic acid had been long suspected to be the hereditary material within the nucleus, the connection could not be made to the proteins that directed cellular processes and growth. These processes were thought to be dependent on the chromosome's involvement in the synthesis of products necessary for the cell's metabolism. The composition and structure of the nucleic acids seemed to be the key to understanding not only the nature of heredity but the functioning of the entire organism as well.

This led to a search for these products. For many years, investigators worked, with some success, to describe the structures of complex molecules, like proteins that were believed to control cellular metabolism or, in some cases, formed the basic components of body tissues. The structure of the nucleic acids and their relationship to protein molecules escaped definition until midcentury. In 1953, James Watson and Francis Crick offered a model to explain the molecular structure of deoxyribonucleic acid (DNA) a compound whose existence in the nucleus had been known for years. The model proved to be an accurate description of this complex structure, and their discovery had a momentous impact on biology and was just the type of breakthrough that the field needed to start a new phase of genetics research. The discovery was so important and basic to the understanding

Triplet Code

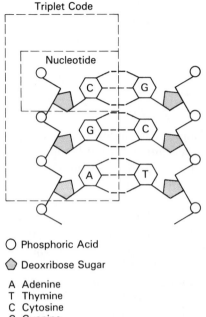

○ Phosphoric Acid

◇ Deoxribose Sugar

A Adenine
T Thymine
C Cytosine
G Guanine

(a)

FIGURE 2-7a
Nucleotide Structure, the Basic Unit of the DNA Molecule

A nucleotide is composed of a molecule of phosphate and a deoxyribose sugar to which is attached any one of four types of organic bases: adenine (A), thymine (T), cytosine (C), or guanine (G). This basic unit is attached to an adjacent nucleotide by bonding between phosphate and sugar molecules as shown. Three nucleotides, taken together, provide a particular *triplet code* because of the combination of the three organic bases they contain, and this code specifies a particular amino acid as discussed in the text.

of the genetic code of life that Watson and Crick were awarded a Nobel Prize in 1962.[2]

DNA is a long, repetitive structure made up of alternating phosphate and sugar (deoxyribose) molecules to which are attached one of four kinds of organic bases: thymine, adenine, cytosine, or guanine. The sugar-phosphate molecules form a basic backbone structure of DNA. The unit composed of sugar, phosphate, and base molecules is ·called a nucleotide (Figure 2-7a), which is joined with the next nucleotide; this process is repeated over and over until a long chain has been formed. The bases of the nucleotides are attracted to other bases on a complementary DNA strand, and the two are held together by a weak hydrogen bond. Each base only attracts one other type; thymine (T) is bonded to adenine (A) and cytosine (C) to guanine (G). The length of the two chains can be

[2] Many researchers in several fields laid the groundwork for molecular genetics, and Watson relates a very interesting and personal account of the events leading to the discovery of the DNA structure. He also describes the fierce competition among scientists to be the first to identify the functioning of this key molecule (Watson, 1980).

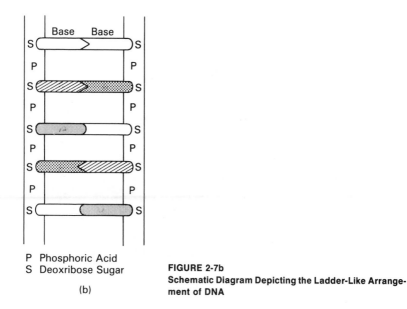

P Phosphoric Acid
S Deoxribose Sugar

(b)

FIGURE 2-7b
**Schematic Diagram Depicting the Ladder-Like Arrange-
ment of DNA**

The organic bases of opposite DNA strands are attracted and bound together by a weak hydrogen bond which causes DNA to be a double stranded molecule. Because of their chemical structures, adenine will bind only with thymine and guanine with cytosine. These base to base bonds form the "rungs" of the "ladder" while the series of sugars and phosphates are long side pieces to which the rungs are attached.

diagramed as a ladderlike structure; the long parallel structures are formed by the sugar and phosphate backbones, whereas the connecting rungs are the complementary base pairs (Figure 2-7b). The DNA strands are actually rotated about each other to form the double helix described by Watson and Crick.

The importance of the base-to-base attractions is well illustrated when a cell divides. The DNA strands pull apart, and the unbonded bases attract new nucleotides and bond with complementary bases. These nucleotides attach over the length of the original strands, forming two new double helical molecules (Figure 2-7c). This DNA replication on cell division is described as semiconservative; one of the old strands is joined with a newly formed strand so each of the daughter cells will end up with its proper DNA complement. This process occurs repeatedly during cell divisions to produce new tissue and, provided that all replication is correct (no mutations), the daughter cells will be identical to parental cells.

THE GENE: STRUCTURE AND FUNCTION

Once the nature of the nucleic acids in the nucleus was described the search was on for an explanation of how they related to cellular functions and division, and what relation these acids had to the transmission of

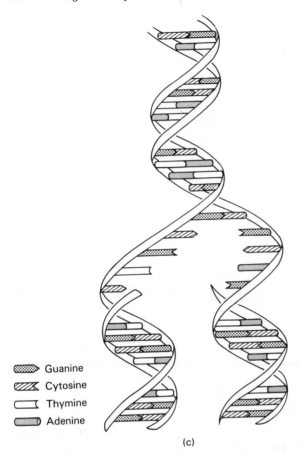

Guanine
Cytosine
Thymine
Adenine

(c)

FIGURE 2-7c Helical Shape of DNA Molecule and Semi-Conservative Replication

DNA molecules are rotated so they form a double helical structure; the sides formed by the sugar and phosphates and weakly bound bases are connected as shown in Figures 2-7a and b. When a cell divides the DNA molecules be must duplicated in such a way that the new cells will have the exact quantity and sequence nucleotides. This is achieved by a process of separation of part of the molecule at a time and bonding the complementary nucleotides to the exposed unpaired bases. When completed this process has created two daughter helixes, each composed of one of the original DNA strands bound to a newly synthesized one; a process called semi-conservative replication.

traits throughout generations of cells. The search was directed to protein molecules because of their functions. They provide support (structural proteins) as in the example of collagen, an important protein of skin, bone, and many other tissues in the body; regulate metabolic processes (enzymes), as in digestion, body temperature control, or production of skin pigment (tyrosinase); and influence gene expression through the action of thousands of enzymes in a cell or by hormones.

Proteins[3] constitute a class of chemical compounds made up of chains of smaller molecules (amino acids) linked together by peptide bonds. The total of these linkages are described as a polypeptide chain. The proteins are composed of 20 kinds of amino acids arranged in a linear chain in some combination. The chain may be a few dozen amino acids long as in human insulin, which has 51 arranged in two tightly bond chains, or a protein may contain 100 or more amino acids as in globin of human hemoglobin with 574 organized into four polypeptide chains, two alpha and two beta. The sequence or linear arrangement of the amino acids is critical and provides the protein molecule with a specific identity and hence its function. In Figure 2-8 the normal sequence is shown for the first 6 positions and position 26 of the 146 in the beta chain of human hemoglobin. A substitution of amino acid, valine, for glutamic acid changes the identity from hemoglobin A to hemoglobin S (sickle cell type), and under certain conditions its function (oxygen transport) is radically altered. Other substitutions also change hemoglobin type as shown. This importance of amino acid sequence raises the question of how cells and structures that synthesize proteins direct the correct organization of the polypeptide chains.

Because of a pattern of inheritance of different forms of proteins observed in family lineages over the years, protein synthesis was thought to be under genetic control. The genetic material, though considered to be in the nucleus, was not identified until after midcentury, however. The major compounds within the nucleus, the nucleic acids were, at first, ignored as the genetic code because analysis of their chemical composition showed a presence of only four kinds of organic bases. Any hypothesis that these bases existed in a regular structural sequence made it difficult to understand how only four units could determine the linear arrangement of twenty types of amino acids into a string of dozens or more. Also, the proportions of the bases varied between DNA and ribonucleic acid (RNA) compounds. The major works after 1953 provided many of the answers and opened up the era of molecular genetics, which has enormously expanded the understanding of cellular function and its inherited basis.

Genetic Code

Considering DNA as the genetic code, the problem of amino acid identification is solved when the nucleotides are "read" three at a time as a group instead of individually. Because each nucleotide is identical (phosphate and sugar) except for one of the four types of organic base attached, a group of three nucleotides give the probability of 4^3 or 64 different coded combinations (three positions at which one of four kinds

---

[3] The major organic molecules of living organisms are classified into four categories: carbohydrates (sugars and starches), lipids (fats), proteins, and nucleic acids.

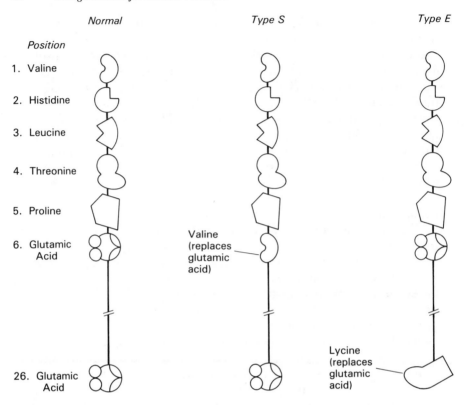

FIGURE 2-8   Amino Acid Sequences of Three Types of beta Globin

These diagrams depict the amino acids at the first six and at the 26th position. Normal, type S, and type E hemoglobin have the same sequence of amino acids at all 146 positions of the beta globin chains with two very important and specific exceptions. Type S has a substitution of valine for glutamic acid at position 6 while type E is the same as the normal for that position but has a replacement of lycine for glutamic acid at position 26.

of organic bases may occur). This code then could account for more than twenty amino acids with a number of "codes" left over. After much research, different DNA triplets were shown to code for particular amino acids, and some amino acids could be coded for by any one of several triplets; the DNA code was said to be redundant (Table 2-1). The problem that remained to be solved was how the DNA code in the nucleus could control synthesis in the cell's cytoplasm where the structures (ribosomes) and raw materials needed for the protein synthesis were located.

RNA.   This second nucleic acid compound proved to be the transporting agent or *messenger* that copied the code and relayed it to the sites of protein synthesis, the *ribosomes*. Figure 2-9 diagrams the basics of this

TABLE 2-1   Genetic Code[a]

AMINO ACID	DNA (TRIPLET)	mRNA (CODON)
Alanine (ala)	CGA, CGG, CGT, CGC	GCU, GCC, GCA, GCG
Arginine (arg)[b]	GCA, GCG, GCT, GCC, TCT, TCC	CGU, CGC, CGA, CGG, AGA, AGG
Asparagine (asn)	TTA, TTG	AAU, AAC
Aspartic acid (asp)	CTA, CTG	GAU, GAC
Cysteine (cys)	ACA, ACG	UGU, UGC
Glutamic acid (glu)	CTT, CTC	GAA, GAG
Glutamine (gln)	GTT, GTC	CAA, CAG
Glycine (gly)	CCA, CCG, CCT, CCC	GGU, GGC, GGA, GGG
Histidine (his)[b]	GTA, GTG	CAU, CAC
Isoleucine (ile)[c]	TAA, TAG, TAT	AUU, AUC, AUA
Leucine (leu)[c]	AAC, GAA, GAG, GAT, GAC, AAT	UUG, CUU, CUC, CUA, CUG, UUA
Lysine (lys)[c]	TTT, TTC	AAA, AAG
Methionine (met)[c]	TAC	AUG
Phenylalanine (phe)[c]	AAA, AAG	UUU, UUC
Proline (pro)	GGA, GGG, GGT, GGC	CCU, CCC, CCA, CCG
Serine (ser)	AGA, AGG, AGT, AGC, TCA, TCG	UCU, UCC, UCA, UCG, AGU, AGC
Threonine (thr)[c]	TGA, TGG, TGT, TGC	ACU, ACC, ACA, ACG
Tryptophan (trp)[c]	ACC	UGG
Tyrosine (tyr)	ATA, ATG	UAU, UAC
Valine (val)[c]	CAA, CAG, CAT, CAC	GUU, GUC, GUA, GUG
Terminating triplets	ATT, ATC, ACT	UAA, UAG, UGA

[a] Symbols for bases in nucleic acids: A (adenine); C (cytosine); G (guanine); T (thymine); and U (uracil), used as a substitute for T.
[b] Essential in diet of young child.
[c] One of the eight amino acids that humans cannot synthesize and therefore must be obtained from the diet.

process. It starts in the nucleus when an enzyme, *RNA polymerase,* causes the double strand of DNA to separate along a few triplets. The unbonded bases of one of the strands are temporarily bonded to complementary bases of RNA triplets (codons), which are formed into a chain as the enzyme moves along the DNA. Once a transcription has been made, the mRNA chain segment separates from the DNA. This process is repeated until a terminating triplet is reached (ATT, ATC, or ACT in Table 2-1). At this point a single-stranded messenger RNA (mRNA) has been produced, and the DNA strands are rejoined into the double helix as before.

The mRNA is only a primary messenger, however, because it includes a number of noncoding sequences of the gene, the *introns.* The primary mRNA undergoes a process of maturation that causes a looping of the strand over the intron area, which is then cut and discarded. The remaining ends are joined, linking together those segments of DNA that code for proteins, the *exons.* The finished mature product of mRNA then moves out to the ribosomes in the cytoplasm, the site of protein synthesis. This single chain of triplets (codons) provide an attraction for the bases of short strands of transfer RNA (tRNA) to attach temporarily. Each tRNA,

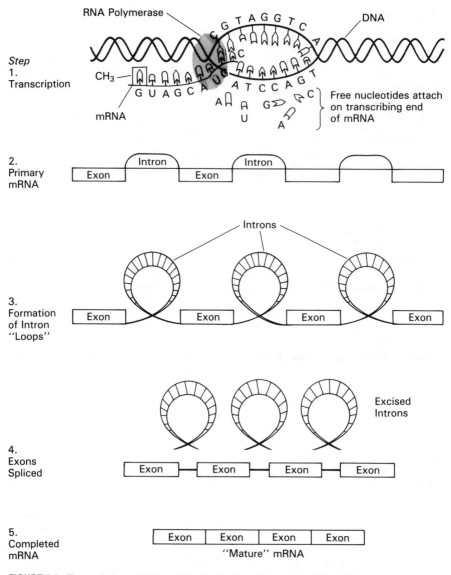

FIGURE 2-9 Transcription of DNA and the Synthesis of Messenger RNA (mRNA)

The five basic steps in the process of synthesizing mRNA to transcribe the DNA code are illustrated in this diagram. *Step One* begins by the separation of a segment of the double helix by the enzyme, RNA polymerase. The exposed bases of one of the DNA strands attract free nucleotides which become bound to one another, forming the single stranded mRNA which is a process similar to the formation of complementary daughter strands of DNA during replication. However, the major exception is that the mRNA soon separates, remains single stranded, and uses the base uracil to bind with adenine instead of thymine. The enzymes move along the DNA and the process is repeated, and when a length of DNA has been "read" the strands rebind to one another.

or anticodon because its bases are complementary to mRNA, carry a particular amino acid. When the codon-anticodon bonds are established, the amino acids, carried by the tRNA, form peptide bonds, and the process is repeated until the stop signal is reached. The completed protein molecule is thus produced (Figure 2-10). The tRNA are free to pick up more amino acids, and the process begins all over. The triplets (codons) of mRNA are listed with the corresponding DNA triplets and the amino acids in Table 2-1. This code is universal—that is, the amino acids have the same codons throughout all living organisms, whether amoeba or human, and the universality of the code provides strong supporting evidence for the unity of life.

To summarize, a single stranded nucleic acid (RNA) is made from one strand of the DNA molecule, the sense or template strand. This mRNA is complementary to all those triplet regions between a start-and-stop triplet sequence and includes the coding (exon) and noncoding (intron) regions of a gene complex. The introns are excised from the primary mRNA, and the exons are joined before it is released to the site of protein synthesis, the ribosomes. The mRNA begins to attract a tRNA that carries one amino acid specified by the codon-anticodon sequence. A series of these are attached along the strand, and the adjacent amino acids react to form peptide bonds resulting in a long chain that is the protein. From the diagrams and descriptions it is apparent that the mRNA faithfully replicates from the DNA, a complementary chain of triplets that must be modified by removal of those noncoding portions, the introns, because the DNA carries many more triplet units than are used in the protein synthesis process. The discovery of this excess of nucleotide material leads to a reexamination of chromosome structure and the basic nature of the human genome.

Chromosomes at Molecular Level

Since the description of chromosomes, their structure, and their change during cell division early in this century, information has reached a point where the finer, molecular components can be defined. We now have a sharper focus of not only what is transpiring at the genetic level, but we also have a fairly good idea of how all the genes fit together to form these large structures in the nucleus, the chromosomes.

Step Two is reached when the transcription is completed and the primary mRNA is separated. At this step the mRNA contains a copy of all of the DNA, both exons and introns.

Step Three is a maturing process which causes the introns, non-coding portion, to contract and form loops which result in shortening the mRNA bringing the exons closer together.

Step Four excises the intron loops and splices the exons together.

Step Five produces the now shortened and completed strand of mature mRNA which contains the code to direct the production of polypeptide chains of amino acids.

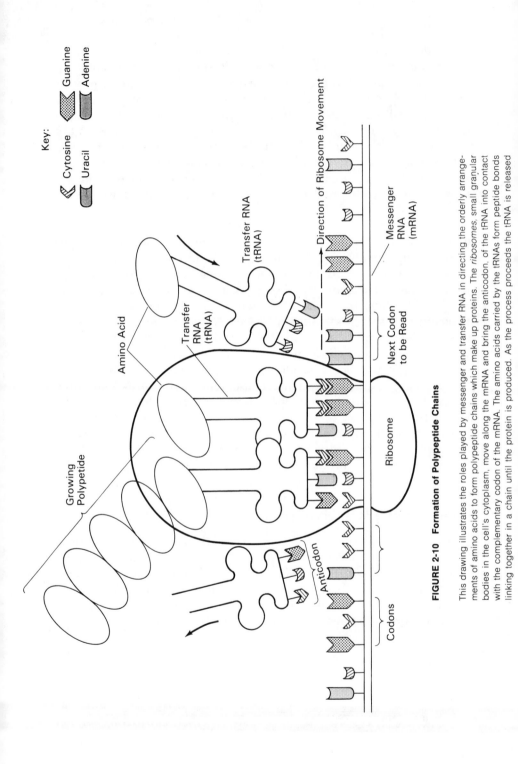

Key:

- Cytosine
- Uracil
- Guanine
- Adenine

Growing Polypeptide

Amino Acid

Transfer RNA (tRNA)

Transfer RNA (tRNA)

Direction of Ribosome Movement

Messenger RNA (mRNA)

Next Codon to be Read

Ribosome

Anticodon

Codons

FIGURE 2-10 Formation of Polypeptide Chains

This drawing illustrates the roles played by messenger and transfer RNA in directing the orderly arrangements of amino acids to form polypeptide chains which make up proteins. The *ribosomes*, small granular bodies in the cell's cytoplasm, move along the mRNA and bring the anticodon, of the tRNA into contact with the complementary codon of the mRNA. The amino acids carried by the tRNAs form peptide bonds linking together in a chain until the protein is produced. As the process proceeds the tRNA is released

The human genome contains enough DNA for more than one million genes, but the real number is closer to one hundred thousand or even less. This means that a large excess of DNA is replicated and transmitted between generations of cells but is not used in the coding of protein synthesis. This excess, actually most of the DNA, has other than genetic functions because DNA fragments may be regulatory, provide start or stop signals, or function simply as spacing devices as in the case of the introns. The scope of this excess may be appreciated by some comparisons. If stretched out to full length, the DNA equivalent in the total haploid genome of a gamete is a molecule of one meter long, which contains about one billion triplets. All of the DNA must be contained in a cell nucleus with the dimensions of 10 nm by less than 1 nm, however. This placement of such a large mass in a restricted space is made possible by compaction because of "super coiling" of the helical structures.

The total DNA of the human genome is divided into chromosomes, and each is a long continuous chain of DNA coiled and compacted; the longest chain is 82 mm and the shortest, the Y chromosome, is 2.15 mm. At the beginning stages of mitosis or meiosis (discussed earlier) a chromosome is composed of two chromatids held together by a centromere somewhere along its length. A visualization of this arrangement is provided by the drawing in Figure 2-11, which compares components of a chromosome at the structural, microstructural, and submicroscopic levels. This knowledge of the fine structure of the chromosome, together with knowledge of the nucleotides and triplets of the gene, has contributed to a clearer understanding of genetic loci and has enabled the mapping of portions of the genome. In fact, a major project is now underway to map the entire human genome, the identification and labeling of the position of each gene site.

Regions along the DNA strand of a chromosome have certain noncoding functions or contain codes for particular gene products. The region or locus for certain genetic traits, identified earlier by linkage studies in family lineages described before, has been confirmed and are now clearly established by investigations of chromosome structure at the molecular level. This advancement in our knowledge of inheritance has been made possible by the discovery of a class of bacterial enzymes that can cut the giant DNA molecule into shorter strands at specific base pair locations. These enzymes, *endonucleases*, have opened up a whole new frontier for genetic studies.

Endonucleases. These restriction enzymes, so called because they cut the DNA molecule at specific points along the chain, have enabled investigators to separate out the entire one meter length of the human genome DNA into many shorter fragments. These fragments are of varying lengths (number of base pairs [BP]), and each has a specific triplet

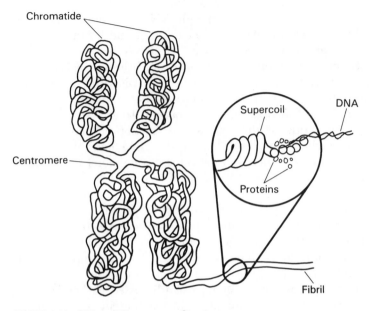

Chromatide

Centromere

DNA

Supercoil

Proteins

Fibril

FIGURE 2-11   DNA and Chromosome Structure

This diagram illustrates, at several microstructural levels, the relationship of DNA strands to its chromosome. The *chromatids* are shown as densely compacted DNA linked together at a point near their centers, the *centromere*. The lower right chromatid shows a section of a fibril which is further magnified to illustrate the supercoiled DNA structures it contains. Further expansion of this segment reveals the particles of proteins and an individual DNA molecule. **Source: Modified and redrawn from Vogel and Motulsky, 1986**

sequence at the point of cleavage; the triplet sequence plus one or two other nucleotides provide a point of attraction for one of these enzymes. Cleaving the entire human genome can produce about five hundred thousand fragments of from one hundred to ten thousand BP in length. These fragments can be separated by the *Southern blotting* method, a technique that separates the different fragments in an electric field and preserves them on a nitrocellulose filter (Southern, 1975). Basically, the technique takes advantage of the fact that fragments differ not only in size but in electric charge as well, a characteristic that will cause the fragments to move at different rates of speed through an agarose gel plate when an electric current is applied (electrophoresis). Once the fragments are separated, the fluid medium, a buffer solution, is blotted out by squeezing the gel between a weight, blotting paper, and the filter (Figure 2-12). This removes the fluid and leaves the fragments trapped and dispersed on the nitrocellulose filter as they were in the gel.

The hydrogen bonds of these DNA fragments are broken by treatment with an alkali solution separating the double strands. The now

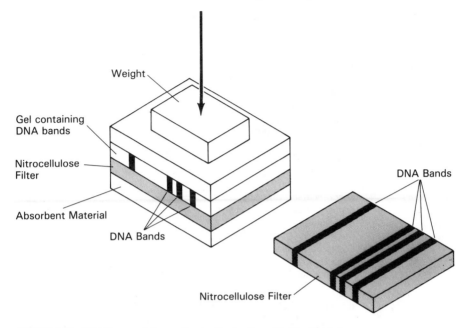

FIGURE 2-12   DNA Fragment Separation by the Southern Blotting Technique

The weight in the drawing compresses the gel layer and squeezes the buffer fluid on to a nitrocellulose filter. The porous filter allows the fluid to pass through to the absorbent material while retaining the DNA fragments. These fragments are positioned as bands relative to one another as they were on the gel.

single-stranded fragments with specific base sequences can be examined individually by special chemical staining or by use of a radioactive probe. This probe is a short strand of DNA of known base sequence labeled with a radioactive isotope of phosphorus. The DNA probe combines with the complementary DNA strands and forms a double-helical structure on the filter. A piece of photographic film is exposed to the radioactive labels over a period of several days. The result is a series of dark bands on the film that identifies the positions of those fragments that had combined with the probes. Because five hundred thousand fragments are an impossible number to deal with at one time, the chromosomes are first separated and then examined individually. The chromosome DNA may be cut by one or more restriction enzymes[4] and the resulting fragments are then treated by the Southern blotting method.

DNA probes.   A large and ever-growing "library" of genes has made it possible to pinpoint the location of a gene on a particular chromosome. The probes are radioactively labeled single-stranded DNA, which attach

---

[4] There are more than 150 restriction enzymes (endonucleases) known at this time.

**TABLE 2-2   Examples of Genetic Diseases
Detected by Gene Probes**

Disease

Achondroplasia
alpha1-antitrypsin deficiency
Diabetes mellitus (type I)
Globin gene cluster (alpha)
Globin gene cluster (beta)
Growth Hormone deficiency
hemophilia A
hemophilia B
HLA genes
Immunoglobulin genes
Lesch-Nyhan syndrome
Osteogenesis imperfecta (type II)
Phenylketonuria
Prealbumin (amyloidosis)
Sickle cell anemia
Thalassemias
Thrombosis III deficiency

* Selected from various sources. For a complete
listing see, Cooper and Schmidtke (1986).

to the complementary fragments forming a hybrid double helix on the filter as described earlier. This allows for identification of specific genes or gene clusters because of the way in which the DNA probes are produced, by a method called *reverse transcription*. Where mRNA is available for proteins of known amino acid sequence, as in the case of the hemoglobins, insulin, and so forth (Table 2-2), an enzyme, reverse transcriptase, assembles DNA nucleotides complementary to the mRNA chain. This process is, as the name signifies, the reverse of the transcription process that occurs in the cell nucleus to produce the mRNA. The difference is, of course, that the molecular geneticist assembles complementary DNA (cDNA) in the laboratory using mRNA material as a template. The cDNA, when treated, becomes a "probe" to hybridize with the DNA fragments produced on cleavage of the chromosome DNA by restriction enzymes.

Briefly, a gene product of interest is identified (enzyme, structural protein, and so forth), and the mRNA is obtained from a cell or assembled in a test tube, which is possible when the amino acid sequence of the gene product is known. The mRNA provides a template for the synthesis of cDNA. The cDNA is used as a probe to locate the gene sequence on a chromosome fragment. A similar method, in situ hybridization, also uses a radioactive DNA strand but adds the probe to chromosomes in the metaphase of cell division. The probe hybridizes with the intact chromosome DNA at a specific segment. These methods have enabled many highly imaginative genetic studies and, as investigation of human chro-

TABLE 2-3   Sampling of Human Genes Identified by In Situ Hybridization

GENE AND BASE PAIR [BP] LENGTH	LOCALIZATION CHROMOSOME AND REGION
beta-Globin (4400 BP)	11 p
alpha-Globin (800 BP)	16 p
Insulin (900 BP)	11 p 15
LGH (550 BP)	17 q 22–24
Interferon	9 p 2.1-pter
IFN alpha + beta	12 q 24.1
Ig (6600 BP)	14 q 32
Ig Kappa (10500 BP)	2 p 12
alpha-Fetoprotein (380 BP)	4 q 11–22
serum albumin (1600 BP)	4 q 11–22
Ig C lambda (203 BP) (gene family)	22 q 11
Myosin MHC (2200 BP)	17 p 1.2 pter
Collagen-gene	7 q 22

IFN   Interferon, gamma or immune type
Ig   Immunoglobins
LGH   Growth hormone (Lactogenic gene cluster)
Selected from: Vogel and Motulsky, 1986.

mosomes expand at an accelerating rate, the number of useful probes and their applications increase rapidly (Table 2-3). Development of these processes have taken place over years of intensive biochemical work, and many are highly sophisticated—so much so that no brief description can do them justice. For more details and elaboration of additional investigation to identify or "map" the human genome, the reader is directed to texts like Hartl (1988), Nichols (1988), or Vogel and Motulsky (1986).

GENE CLUSTERS AND RESTRICTION FRAGMENT LENGTH POLYMORPHISMS (RFLP)

The various means of identifying gene location and the gene's finer structure have revealed some complications. The studies documented many more polymorphisms of DNA than were expected, but, at the same time, there has been some clarification of the excessive amounts of DNA present in the human genome as noted earlier. Because of the intensive study of human hemoglobin for the last forty years, the genes, gene clusters, and RFLP of this protein may be used to illustrate some recent discoveries.

The genes that regulate synthesis of the alpha- and beta-globin genes have been located on two different chromosomes; the alpha-globin gene of 800 BP units on the eleventh and the beta-globin gene of 4400 BP units, on the sixteenth. The identification of the beta-globin gene offered

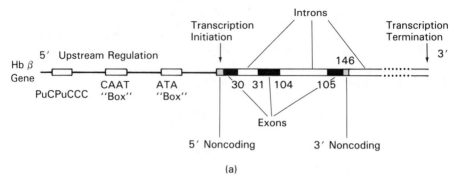

(a)

FIGURE 2-13a   Diagram of the beta Globin Gene of Human Hemoglobin

The *introns* (non-coding) and *exons* (coding) regions of the gene are shown as well as the transcription initiation and termination "boxes." The numbers indicate the location of the codon for a corresponding amino acid position of the beta globin.

some unexpected results. In the process of hybridization of beta-globin DNA with complementary DNA (cDNA), some loops of unpaired nucleotides were produced on the beta-globin strand that were visible under an electron microscope. These were segments of DNA not present as complementary regions on the cDNA. The explanation of the results was straightforward. Because the cDNA was a true copy of the mRNA made by reverse transcription, and because the mRNA represented the amino acid sequences of beta globin, then the unpaired DNA sequences were regions that were not transcribed into the completed mRNA. The unpaired regions were introns, as described earlier, and three are shown in the beta-hemoglobin (Hb) gene diagramed in Figure 2-13a. The Hb gene actually is a cluster of three groups of nucleotide triplets (the black boxes) separated by noncoding units, the introns (white boxes). The gene is transcribed, and in step one all groups are represented. Then the introns are excised, the three exons are joined, and the mRNA is complete. These interesting findings opened up a new realm of investigation. First, the search is on for the function, if any, of the introns. The second area of interest is the evidence that the gene exists "in pieces" as a cluster of nucleotides along a portion of the chromosome 11 DNA. There are, in addition to the Hb gene, several other genes (embryonic globin, for example) in this cluster and a "pseudogene," a DNA sequence similar to the functional gene[5] but not transcribed (Figure 2-13b). Additionally, the wide use of several restriction enzymes revealed a great diversity in the

---

[5] After consideration of units of nucleotides called exons, introns, and even pseudogenes, it is necessary to redefine the term *gene*. It may be best defined as that region of the DNA that contains the nucleotide sequence code for the production of a polypeptide chain through the vehicle of a mRNA chain.

TABLE 2-4   Frequency of DNA Polymorphic Sites in Beta-Globin Gene Cluster in Selected Ethnic Groups

POLYMORPHISMS	GREEKS	AMERICAN BLACKS	SOUTHEASTERN ASIANS
Taq I (1)[a]	1.00	0.88	1.00
Hine II (2)	0.46	0.10	0.72
Hind III (3)	0.52	0.41	0.27
Hind III (4)	0.30	0.16	0.04
Pvu II (5)	0.27		
Hinc II (6)	0.17	0.15	0.19
Hinc II (7)	0.48	0.76	0.27
Rsa I (8)	0.37	0.50	
Taq I (9)	0.68	0.53	
Hinf I (10)	0.97	0.70	0.98
Rsa I (11)			
HgiA (12)	0.80	0.96	0.44
Ava II (13)	0.80	0.96	0.44
Hpa I (14)	1.00	0.93	
Hind III (15)	0.72	0.63	
Bam HI (16)	0.70	0.90	
Rsa I (17)	0.37	0.10	

[a] Numbers in parentheses refer to the sites illustrated in Figure 2-13b, which are cut by the restriction enzymes.

Source: Modified from Vogel and Motulsky, 1986.

size, and triplet sequences in the noncoding regions near the beta-globin gene.

RFLP. Because of the attention directed to the study of abnormal Hbs, considerable information has been derived about the RFLP polymorphism. Table 2-4 lists some of the major restriction enzymes used to cut the beta-globin gene cluster at different points. These sites, or points of cleavage in the DNA molecule, are illustrated in Figure 2-13b. The

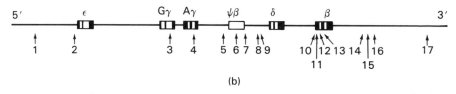

(b)

FIGURE 2-13b   Diagram of the beta Globin Gene Cluster

The coding parts of DNA are frequently linked to other DNA clusters which play no role in the production of the protein; in this case, globin. However, the thousands of base pairs of this cluster may be cut at specific sites by selected enzymes. The resulting fragments can be used to distinguish between populations and sometimes even individuals. The numbers in this diagram represent sites that are cut by the endonucleases corresponding to those listed in table 2-4.

considerable variation between individuals is due to single substitutions of nucleotides. Because much of the DNA between gene clusters is noncoding, these substitutions causing sequence variation have no known functional consequences—at least not at this stage of our knowledge. Some of these variations in cleavage sites, producing fragments of different base sequences called haplotypes, occur in greater frequency in one population compared with another. As shown in Table 2-4 the RFLP produced by PVUII (Figure 2-13b, number 5) occurred only in the DNA sample obtained from the Greek population. The Hine II restriction site is recorded at high frequency in Greeks and Asians, but is low in American blacks. This work with RFLP sampled in populations from around the world has opened up a whole new frontier in the study of human genetic diversity as explored in the next chapter. Because much of this polymorphism has no apparent functional significance, the RFLP serve well as population markers suggestive of a common history and of interpopulation relationships. Finally, the RFLP are the result of changes in the base sequences or *mutations*, but these are mutations in the noncoding regions and likely do not influence survival. There are mutations, however, in the coding region that affect gene products that do influence survival.

MUTATION

The change in the genetic code or *mutation* is a rare and random event. The several examples of alterations in amino acid sequences of hemoglobin are the results of point mutations, or changes in a BP within the exon. Fortunately, mutations occur at very low rates in humans, between about one to around forty per one hundred thousand gametes (Table 2-5). The rates for point mutations that change the globin genes have not been

TABLE 2-5 Estimated Human Mutation Rates for Selected Traits

AUTOSOMAL DOMINANTS	MUTATION PER MILLION
Gametes	
Achondroplastic (dwarfism)	10–14
Retinoblastoma (eye tumor)	6–18
Huntington's disease (progressive, degeneration of central nervous system)	1
Neurofibromatosis (tumors of nervous system)	13–25
Marfan's syndrome (disorder of connective tissue)	4–5
X-Linked Recessives	
Hemophilia A (bleeder's disease)	20–30
Duchenne's muscular dystrophy	30–100

calculated, however. Mutations occur randomly and they cannot be predicted, although experiments have increased rates of mutations under the influence of ionizing radiation. The intervening sequences of chromosomal DNA, the introns, appear to undergo more rapid mutation as the results from the studies of the RFLP show. These changes introduce a great deal of measurable variety in the human gene pool, but they apparently do not affect survival.

Mutations, although usually detrimental, are an important source of new genes introduced into a population—thereby increasing the frequency of alleles at the different loci. Mutations are, therefore, the ultimate source of variability of a species, and, as such, are the foundation for the wide diversity we see in the biological world. The definition now must be expanded to include the RFLP and consideration must be given to the particular region of the DNA where the BP change occurs and the effect that it may have on the organism.

FORMAL HUMAN GENETICS

At this point, following a discussion of the finer structure of the gene, the reader might be tempted to conclude that genetic knowledge started with the discovery of DNA and insight into the effects of mutations began with the availability of restriction enzymes. No such conclusion is warranted, however, because the study of *formal genetics*—that is, the crossing of generations of experimental animals, insects, and bacteria to produce a particular series of traits in the offspring—has laid the foundation for much of our knowledge of genetics. Human subjects have played an equally important role in development of formal genetics. Even though *Homo sapiens* is a complicated organism with between fifty and one hundred thousand genes, a great deal has been learned about trait inheritance from studies of our own species. Through analysis of traits over several generations, certain human characteristics have been related to simple gene combinations. Studies of human pedigrees and the identification of easily perceived phenotypes, even centuries ago, have added to our understanding of *dominant* and *recessive* inheritance. For example, Maupertius, a French astronomer of the eighteenth century, traced the appearance of extra digits (fingers or toes) through four generations of a family lineage and described the condition as a dominant trait, likewise, other writers of the period described the "bleeder's" disease suffered by some males of the royal families of Europe (Glass, 1955).

Dominant Inheritance

Some traits are inherited as dominants—that is, the presence of a single dominant gene will cause the traits to be expressed. *Achondroplasia,* a type of human dwarfism caused by arrested growth of the long bones owing to a defect in cartilage development, is an example of a phenotype determined by a single dominant gene. This gene appears in a population by a mutation that has been reported at a high rate in certain northwestern European populations (see Table 2-5). A person who possesses the mutant gene for this condition will be much shorter than normal because of a failure of growth of the arms and legs; the body trunk is usually of the normal size. Another well-known affliction, the *Hapsburg lip*, made famous by numerous individuals of this royal family of central Europe, is also determined by a dominant gene. Individuals with this condition have a protruding lower jaw and enlarged lower lip, and chances are that half of their children will show the same abnormality. A white streak or forelock in the hair is also the result of the action of a dominant gene. These simple, easily perceived dominant traits fully express their characteristics each generation, and a simple ratio or proportion exists: If one parent has the trait, there is a 50 percent chance that each child conceived will also possess it. If both parents have the trait, then the probability that their children will have it increases to 75 percent (Figures 2-14a, 2-14b).

FIGURE 2-14 Dominant Inheritance: Examples of Abnormal Traits

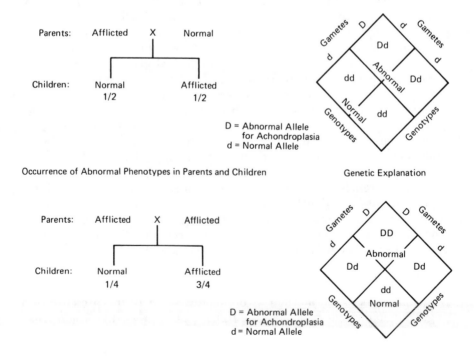

Recessive Inheritance

Unlike simple dominant genes, the presence of recessive genes cannot always be detected and sometimes cause characteristics to appear in children of unafflicted parents, often to their dismay. Rather than blame one's grandparents or argue that devilish forces are at work, it is best to recognize that humans possess many genes whose actions or potential actions are masked by the expression of the more dominant allelic form. Such genes, called *recessives*, can cause a characteristic to appear in an individual only when they combine as a pair (homozygous combination). Many human traits are determined in this way.

An example is a well-known condition that interrupts the synthesis of melanin pigment and causes the individual to be without color in the hair and skin; such an individual is known as an *albino*. This condition occurs in European populations only about once in twenty thousand births, but once in three thousand births in several Nigerian populations. In most of these cases the parents were normal but each was a carrier of the recessive gene for albinism; these genes may combine on conception to produce an offspring who had the recessive pair. Another example is provided by the ABO blood-group system. The gene that determines type O blood is recessive to both the A and B alleles. Hence, it often happens that parents, neither of whom is type O, have an offspring with type O blood. This indicates that the parents were carrying the type O gene, a recessive whose presence is masked by the action of either the A or the B allele (Figure 2-15).

The ratio of recessive trait occurrence in each generation depends on the gene combinations of the parents and is somewhat more difficult to determine than the simple dominant ratio. If neither parent has the

FIGURE 2-15   Inheritance of ABO Blood Types

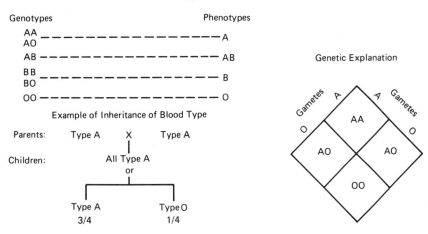

Occurrence of Abnormal Phenotypes in Parents and Children   Genetic Explanation

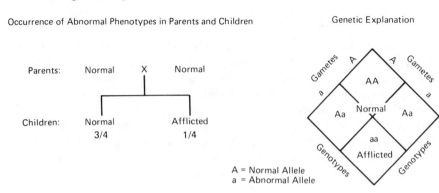

Occurrence of Abnormal Phenotypes in Parents and Children   Genetic Explanation

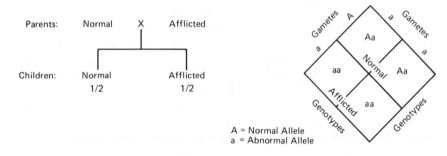

FIGURE 2-16   Recessive Inheritance: Examples of Abnormal Traits

trait but both are carriers of the recessive gene, there is a 25 percent chance that a child they produce will have the trait. If one parent is the carrier and the other parent has the trait, however, then there is a 50 percent chance that their child will have the combination (Figures 2-16a, 2-16b).

Gene Combinations and Interactions

The preceding examples shown in Figures 2-15 and 2-16a, 2-16b illustrate the relationship between genotype and phenotype; a certain allele or pair of alleles will determine a particular trait. Many human traits, however, are of complex inheritance, and several genes may determine the phenotype through their combined action. Such traits are called *polygenic*. Human skin color, for example, varies over a wide range throughout our species because the synthesis of the pigment is under the control of several genes. Studies that have measured the light-reflectance characteristics of untanned skin surfaces showed that offspring of one black and one white parent measured between the ranges of their parents (Figure 2-17). This position of skin reflectance matches closely that

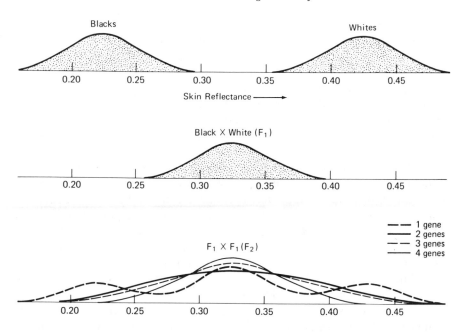

FIGURE 2-17   Skin-Color Distributions in Blacks and Whites. (From Bodmer, W. F., and L. L. Cavalli-Sforza, *Genetics, Evolution, and Man.* Copyright © 1976. San Francisco: W. H. Freeman and Company.)

Skin color is measured by the skin reflectance for light of 685 mμ wave length. For the F_2 generation, distributions shown are those expected under various hypotheses about the number of genes involved. Observations on F_2 and backcrosses tend to resemble those expected if the trait is determined by three of four genes.

suggested by the hypothesis that three or four genes are responsible for the inheritance of skin color.

These measurements of skin reflectance are made on skin from an unexposed area of the body to avoid the tanning influence of the ultraviolet rays of the sun. If exposed, then skin pigment in most people will increase; even those with naturally dark skin will increase pigmentation. This illustrates environmental influence (sunlight) on a genetically complex phenotype (skin color), and the outcome of this interaction is a highly variable reflectance property. This property is measurable as a quantitative trait, or described as a multifactorial trait because of the genetic and environmental interactions.

Numerous other multifactorial traits studied in humans demonstrate a range of environmental and genetic influence. Several *congenital* diseases (present at birth) and diseases of mature adults tend to "run" in families; there is a history of appearing in one spouse's pedigree because some genetic factor(s) are passed on to the offspring. Birth defects like neural tube defects, cleft palate, club foot, and heart defects are examples. The midlife diseases such as hypertension, adult diabetes (type II), and coronary heart disease are other multifactorial conditions frequently studied in reference to combinations of familial and environmental influence. The blood pressure of close relatives of a hypertensive person is higher, on average, than for that age group in the general population. Likewise, the relatives of diabetics often show a lessened ability to regulate blood sugar levels and are at risk for developing the disease in later life if excess carbohydrates are consumed.

Body size and proportion are other multifactorial traits with a strong genetic component. When intergenerational comparisons can be made there are significant resemblances between parents and offspring. In many countries, however, children grow faster to become larger adults than in previous generations. This long-term trend, extending over much of this century, reflects reduction in disease, improved living conditions, and better diets as we shall discuss later in chapter 4.

Further, complexity of the genetic system may cause a trait to vary in frequency or expression. There are genes that are known to influence more than one trait, and these genes are said to be *pleiotropic*. Because the primary products of gene action are polypeptides (chains of amino acids) shown in Figure 2-10, they may be part of a biochemical pathway leading to the production of several other products. For example, a recessive allele that prevents the production of an enzyme needed in the metabolism of an essential amino acid, phenylalanine, can indirectly cause severe damage to the central nervous system through the accumulation of toxic levels of this amino acid. This condition, resulting from the inheritance of the pair of recessive genes controlling phenylalanine metabolism, is known as *phenylketonuria* (PKU). In addition, persons homozygous for this gene will have paler skin and a reduced thyroid activity because phenylalanine is not converted into a necessary ingredient for the synthesis of another amino acid, tyrosine. This amino acid is the precursor from which melanin, the skin pigment, is made. It also is the basic compound from which thyroxine (the active iodine compound of the thyroid gland) is formed.

Another contributor to phenotypic diversity is that genes do not always cause a character to be expressed in the same way, and sometimes the phenotype does not appear at all, even though the genotype for it is known to be present. For example, the pedigree of the family that possessed a muscle defect of the small finger, which causes the digit to be permanently bent, showed a distribution of the autosomal dominant gene through four generations. One of the males in the third generation lacked this inherited defect though he passed along the gene to both of his daughters in the fourth generation. This skipping of generations is an event that occurs when a gene is partly or incompletely penetrant. In some individuals autosomal dominant traits may be severer than in other persons. This condition, known as variable *expressivity*, is illustrated by the presence of extra fingers or toes, known as *polydactyly*. A dominant gene causes the presence of extra fingers or toes, but the gene is not always expressed in the same way. Sometimes an extra digit will appear on the hands or feet, or sometimes only a single digit will be present on one or the other appendages. These and other recorded family pedigrees illustrate some of the variety of expressions of complex traits. To understand them and their intergenerational transmission, it is necessary to consider the organization and clustering of human populations as they influence future generations.

BIOLOGICAL UNITS

The discussion of the mechanisms of inheritance and the effects of genes on individuals now must be considered in the context of the groups or units within which individuals interact. These are the groups that alter their total genetic composition through time in response to the forces of the environment. The group contains a certain range of individual variability for many characteristics, but the most favorable traits are present in the highest frequency with some exceptions. The major concern is the variation and distribution of traits between generations. Equally important is the geographical distribution or spatial clustering of traits into groups.

Species

The venerable idea of species is based on an observation of the striking discontinuity of life forms in nature. The study of this discontinuity among groups of living organisms developed into a discipline that recognized a species as something "different," and used these differences to classify plants and animals in the natural world. The earlier classifications, based on simple morphological traits, did not consider the range of variability; there was often misunderstanding, as illustrated by descriptions of polytypic species that emphasized an idealized form. This old typological approach has been replaced in biology by the recognition of the biological diversity in many species and the difficulty encountered when attempts are made to differentiate between groups of organisms solely on the basis of a few select morphological features.

The species concept has undergone a long history of development and change, especially in this century. As more has been learned about variation and its genetic basis, the definition of species has focused more on genetic variability, isolating mechanisms, and ecology. For example, many authors today stress reproductive isolation, natural habitat, and ecological niche in their attempts to define species. This follows Mayr's observations described in his extensive and important review of animal species (Mayr, 1963). Mayr referred to *species* as the largest and most inclusive reproductive community and noted that a species is also an ecological unit. But even this perspective underwent further development as illustrated by the definition that he offered years later, "a species is a reproductive community of populations (reproductively isolated from others) that occupies a specific niche in nature" (Mayr, 1982:273).

Population

The nature of species, especially those of wide-ranging complex organisms, encompass a concept of gene pool today. The species' gene pool is composed of divisions or groups of interbreeding organisms called populations. Within each of these populations are collections of individuals who bear a part or a small sample of the total species gene pool for the term of their life-span. These individuals form what is described as a breeding population or *deme* and collectively represent a portion of the species. Within each population the gene combinations are reassorted each generation through the mechanisms involved in the reproduction process. The total number of combinations of all genes creates a *gene pool* whose composition will depend on the degree of interbreeding between populations; also, natural forces may alter the gene pool each generation. The distribution of characteristics among the individuals of a population may be described by a normal curve, as in the case of stature or skin color discussed earlier. This concept of gene pool contrasts to the idea of type or average, which emphasizes the central tendency (arithmetic mean). Typological comparisons between groupings of individuals or populations throughout the species rely on arithmetic means, stressing differences between one type and another, whereas, in reality there is often a great deal of similarity between widely dispersed populations within our species. The *populationist* view considers the distribution of traits throughout the gene pool and attempts to show the similarity or dissimilarity between adjacent populations, which could be illustrated by the wide range of overlap of these normal curves of a population. Geographical distributions of many gene frequencies form a continuum over a wide area, and the gene frequencies of each population overlap those of its neighbors. The effect can be a smooth *clinal* distribution of gene frequencies.

FACTORS OF VARIATION AND EVOLUTION

Evolution has been described as "descent with modification," a definition that refers to a gradual change of populations of organisms throughout tens of thousands of generations, changes that accumulate and lead to the formation of new species.[6] Such a definition is applicable to studies of paleontological species in comparisons with their modern living descendants who may be diverse in form, as in the examples of the variety of primate species living today. Many of these primate species can be traced through the fossil record to a few common ancestors tens of millions of years ago. This is an abbreviated way of describing an aspect of Darwin's theories of evolution. He emphasized that the world is not constant and that the diversity of living forms were joined by descent from common ancestors. The similarities of certain characteristics among groups of species has been demonstrated through comparisons of morphology; hence, humans are grouped with the great apes, especially African, rather than with baboons because there is greater anatomical similarity (see Figure 1-7). The development of techniques that compare blood proteins and DNA have validated these earlier observations.

Since Darwin, the knowledge of genetics, and now the clearer understanding of the nature of the gene, has contributed to a new form of the definition of evolution. Geneticists and many anthropologists describe evolution as change in gene frequencies in a population from one generation to the next. This cannot be considered evolution unless these changes persist as a new pattern over time. The accumulation of these changes, often under the influence of natural selection, are described as *microevolution*. There are an abundance of examples found in simpler organisms, but it is more difficult to demonstrate microevolution among living humans as we shall describe in the following chapters. Considering the new knowledge of genetics and the recognition of the significance of a species' environment, about midcentury, *evolution* was understood as a change in the adaptation and in the diversity of population of organisms. According to Mayr (1982), such a definition emphasized the dual nature of evolution that was a vertical phenomenon of adaptive change, and a horizontal phenomenon of diversity among populations. The degree of change and its rate over time were subject to a variety of forces that affected population composition throughout the generations.

Stability or change within a biological unit (the breeding population or gene pool) depend on a great many factors. If these factors balance out so that a net change occurs and persists over generations, the result is evolution. If the elements that cause change are counteracted by those that tend to maintain stability, then there will be no net change in gene-pool composition. Such stability is, of course, an ideal situation. The actual condition of a population may be small gene-frequency variation among several generations, partly because each generation varies somewhat in number of individuals and in age distribution and sex ratio—more so in

---

[6] Evolution is a change in the pattern of adaptation and in the diversity of populations of organisms that persist over time (Mayr, 1988:163).

former times with high mortality rates than today with a longer life expectancy at birth. Treating population equilibrium or disequilibrium has always presented a problem because demographic as well as genetic factors must be considered. An important step was taken with the recognition of Mendelian genetics followed by the development of the foundation of population genetics.

Hardy-Weinberg Equilibrium

Early in this century, even after particulate inheritance was recognized, there still was considerable confusion about the relationship between dominant and recessive alleles. The question frequently raised was: If one allele was dominant to another, would not the dominant one eventually, after a period of time, come to be the most frequent allele in the population? The answer is no, of course not. In 1908, an English mathematician, G. H. Hardy, and a German physician, W. Weinberg, independently of each other, offered a mathematical formula $(p + q)^2$, which described in simple terms the proportion of a pair of alleles in a randomly mating population living under stable conditions. This formula explained why the dominant allele would not increase.

If the symbols of A and a are used to indicate the alleles, then the gametes (sperm and ova) will carry one or the other allele, and recombination through reproduction will occur at a constant frequency. The following combinations are expected:

		SPERM	
		A	**a**
OVA	**A**	AA	Aa
	a	Aa	aa

This simple table shows that one AA genotype is reproduced for every two Aa combinations and every one aa genotype—the *Mendelian ratio*. In the hypothetical situation in which the allele A and a are present in equal numbers in a population, one-half of the gametes carry the **A** allele and one-half carry the **a**. Let **p** equal the frequency of **A** and **q** equal the frequency of **a**. Then the allele frequencies of all combinations can be derived from the following table:

		FREQUENCY OF *SPERM* CARRYING ALLELES A and a	
		p (.5)	q (.5)
FREQUENCY OF *OVA* CARRYING ALLELES A AND a	p (.5)	p^2 (2.5)	pq (.25)
	q (.5)	pq (.25)	q^2 (.25)

Adding up the frequencies of all combinations to derive a total for the population we get

$$p^2 + 2pq + q^2$$
$$(0.25) + 2\,(0.25) + (0.25)$$
$$p^2 + 2pq + q^2 = 1$$

and then $(p + q)^2 = 1$ because it is the binomial expression of the quadratic equation. Taking the square root of the equation we get

$$\mathbf{p + q = 1}$$

which is a mathematical way of saying that, in a sexually reproducing population, the total number of alleles at any locus is equal to unity. Therefore, if we know the frequency of one, then the other can be determined (expressed as $p = 1 - q$, or $q = 1 - p$). This should be easy to comprehend if one recalls that only a single allele is present at a locus on a chromosome (though the other chromosome of the pair may carry another allelic form of the gene). In our example of two allelic forms, it is an either-or situation; the A or a is present. Given the random mating conditions, each type of sperm has equal opportunity to fertilize each type of egg, so the 1:2:1 Mendelian ratio of the genotypes AA, Aa, and aa will be maintained throughout the generations, and there will be no change in gene frequency. The *Hardy-Weinberg Law* states that the frequencies of p and q will remain the same throughout any number of generations given a stable, random-breeding population isolated from other populations.

An example can be made of the number of individuals who are taste sensitive to the chemical *phenylthiocarbamide* (PTC), a substance that is bitter tasting to most persons but tasteless to about 25 percent of the Europeans tested. It was found some years ago that this tasting ability was due to a dominant allele (T). So a person either TT or Tt was a taster, whereas the homozygous recessive tt was a nontaster. If a random sample of a population shows that there are 250 nontasters out of 1000, then 25 percent of the populations have the genotype tt. The gene frequency of the recessive allele (q) in this example can be calculated: $q^2 = 0.25$ and $q = \sqrt{0.25}$, which is equal to 0.5 or one-half of the alleles for the PTC locus are the recessive form. The frequency of the dominant allele (T) would then be 0.5 or $(1 - q)$. Nevertheless, even though the alleles are of equal frequency in the population, three quarters or 75 percent of the individuals have the taster phenotype. This is simply explained by reference to the ratio of the genotypes previously shown. One-half of the recessive alleles (t) are combined with the dominant alleles to form the heterozygote who is a taster (Tt). Throughout future generations, assuming random mating

TABLE 2-6   Frequencies of Offspring from All Types of Matings

GENOTYPES OF PARENTS	FREQUENCY OF MATINGS	FREQUENCY OF OFFSPRING			NUMBER OF INDIVIDUALS		
		TT	Tt	tt	TT	Tt	tt
TT × TT	p^4	p^4	—	—	625	0	0
TT × 2 Tt⎫ 2 Tt × TT⎭	$4p^3q$	$2p^3q$	$2p^3q$	—	1250	1250	0
TT × tt⎫ tt × TT⎭	$2p^2q^2$	0	$2p^2q^2$	—	0	1250	0
2 Tt × 2 Tt	$4p^2q^2$	p^2q^2	$2p^2q^2$	p^2q^2	625	1250	625
2 Tt × tt⎫ tt × 2 Tt⎭	$4pq^3$	—	$2pq^3$	$2pq^3$	0	1250	1250
tt × tt	q^4	—	—	q^4	0	0	625
All Types	1	p^2	$2pq$	q^2	2500	5000	2500

Adding up each column gives a total of $p^2 + 2pq + q^2$ = (all types of matings) and the numerical example adds up to a total of 10,000. This table shows, in a randomly mating population of this size with p of .5, that the numbers of individuals with the three genotypes will be distributed ¼ TT (2500), ½ Tt (5000), and ¼ tt (2500) each generation. Under conditions of stability, as described earlier, this distribution will remain unchanged throughout any number of generations.

with respect to taste sensitivity, the gene frequencies of these alleles will remain the same, and there will be the same number of individuals who are tasters (Table 2-6).

The Hardy-Weinberg formula in addition to random mating assumes that certain conditions exist that contribute to population stability; if these conditions are maintained gene frequencies will remain invariable throughout any number of generations. Few natural populations fit this model situation exactly, but the basic formula established a reference against which change can be measured, and it provides a useful tool in studies of variation and evolution. The forces for change in a population's gene frequencies are *mutation, natural selection, genetic drift* (a sampling error), and *migration*.

Mutation

As noted earlier, the change in a gene results in an alteration in its action and introduces a new variety of allele. This adds differing genotypes within a population. Mutation is the ultimate source of all genetic variation in a population and may provide a species with an ability to respond to a variety of environmental conditions. Some mutations, however, cause such a radical metabolic change that an organism cannot survive; many more are detrimental but are not lethal. Still other mutations may affect changes in the way organisms metabolize certain substances, resist parasites, or produce antibodies against infectious disease. A question frequently raised in the past was whether or not mutations are "bad." All are seen now as an error in genetic coding. The influence on survival of such an error, or change in code, will be taken up in the following chapters. At this point we only consider mutations as a source of disturbance of genetic equilibrium in a population.

In *Homo sapiens,* mutations apparently occur at a low rate, though this rate is influenced by certain forces (for instance, ionizing radiation) from natural or human-caused sources. The results from exposure to radiation cannot be predicted—that is, which genes will mutate is not known. Some human mutation rates that occur because of unknown causes have been measured in family lineages and are listed in Table 2-5. As shown, the rates are very low and population gene frequencies will be disturbed only slightly, but a mutant gene may convey an advantage and contribute to increased fitness in certain environments where selective forces favor the carrier of the mutant. This will cause the frequency of the mutant allele to increase rapidly in just a few generations.

Natural Selection

Though chance plays a role in the production of variation within a population of sexually reproducing organisms, the range of variability and composition of a breeding population is limited. All possible genotypes are not represented in each generation with equal frequency. There are factors that limit the extent of population diversity and determine the gene frequencies from generation to generation. A major factor that acts to limit and stabilize genetic diversity is called *natural selection.*

Some individuals, because of their genome (total genetic complement), reproduce at a higher rate than others and, thus, contribute more offspring to the next generation. Such persons, because of their reproductive success, are the fittest, in the sense of *Darwinian fitness* (those who produce the most offspring). Conversely, those who reproduce fewer offspring are less fit and have a lesser influence on future gene pools. The genotypes that confer a reproductive advantage of some degree to the organism will expand within a population throughout generations, and the gene frequencies will increase.

There are several mechanisms that determine reproductive success; the sum total of all those processes that determine survival and reproduction are lumped under the term *natural selection.* The word *natural* indicates that there are certain conditions that exist in the environment within which the organism lives that are relatively advantageous to some individuals. These natural conditions are in contrast to those created by the animal breeder who selects chickens or cattle and breeds only those animals who possess the economically desirable traits—for example, rapid weight gain. Selective breeding is a good example of artificial selection for desirable characteristics. Darwin, offering an explanation of how evolution occurred, noted that what humans have done in a limited way in an effort to domesticate plants and animals, nature has achieved on a grand scale through natural selection.

The effect of natural selection is the maintenance of certain desirable characteristics throughout the generations. Mutations, which occur spontaneously, may convey an advantage under certain environmental conditions; the number of individuals possessing the mutant allele will increase each generation, perhaps slowly or rapidly, depending on the life-span of the organisms and the intensity of selection. The rise in the number of insect species that have been found to be resistant, or even immune, to the effects of certain insecticides are examples.

Resistant strains of the common housefly began to appear throughout the world within two years after the insecticide DDT was used in an effort to control this pest. It appears that larvae of the resistant strains develop faster and survive better in a crowded environment than the DDT-susceptible strains. Studies of the resistant insect strains showed the presence of a certain enzyme (dehydrocholorinase) aided in the metabolism of the insecticide. This enzyme was also present, but in lower quantities, among those flies most susceptible to DDT. It is not difficult, then, to reconstruct an evolutionary history for the flies that depicts a population heterogeneous for this trait (a mix of flies with high and low quantities of the enzyme). When their environment shifted drastically with the introduction of DDT, the resistant strain of flies survived longer and reproduced in greater numbers until a majority in future generations were of the resistant type. The varieties were already present, probably because of past mutations; if the rapid reproduction of flies is considered, then a slight advantage of one genotype over another would cause major changes in the populations response to their environment.

Other examples of environmental change and natural selection is the rise of bacteria strains resistant to certain antibiotics, a resistance that has made them more difficult to control. Each of these examples shows environmental changes caused by human intervention and is an excellent demonstration of the operation of natural selection on simpler organisms. Many populations of complex organisms also provide evidence for the action of natural selection, as in the case of the spread of rabbits in Australia and the attempts to control their population boom.

The European wild rabbit was introduced into Australia in 1859 when a colony of twenty-four were turned loose on an estate in Victoria in the southeastern part of Australia. By 1928 the fast-breeding rabbits, without any natural predators in their new homeland, had multiplied to an estimated five hundred million, spread over much of Australia. The rabbits became a major pest, destroying grazing land and crops, and causing millions of dollars worth of damage each year. All attempts to control the rabbits with traps and poisons proved futile until 1950 when a virus (myxoma), lethal to rabbits, was introduced into the population. From the first infection induced among rabbits in South Australia, the virus spread into most areas, killing 95 percent of the rabbits by 1953. After this drastic decline, however, the population recovered and began to increase because of the survival and reproduction of a few individuals whose genetic complement provided them with some degree of immunity. In addition, the virus itself underwent a transformation, and new strains appeared that were less lethal. Selection favored the disease-resistant rabbit, and there was a coadaptation of the virus and host (rabbit). For a virus to survive long enough to multiply and to be transmitted to another host, it must not be too lethal. If the rabbit dies before the virus can be transmitted to a new host (usually by mosquito), then the virus strain also dies. Selection therefore favored a less deadly virus and a rabbit with a degree of resistance to the infection. These results have been verified many times in laboratory tests and thus provide an illustration of the action of selection.

Reproductive success is the mark of fitness and ensures the survival of the species and the successful adaptation to environmental fluctuations. The mere success of a population's reproductive capacity may contribute to rapid increases followed by sharp declines. A case in point is the rapid breeding field mouse (*Microtus awalis*). The female is fertile at thirteen days old and if bred will produce a litter (four to six) twenty days later. Fertilization can occur again immediately after the female gives birth, and a second litter can follow within twenty days. These mice have been bred in captivity and can produce twenty-four litters within twenty months. Such frequent reproduction increases the population to a point where it far exceeds the carrying capacity of the environment (usually measured in terms of available food), and widespread destruction of the resources occurs followed by a rapid population decline or "crash." Within months, the cycle can be repeated. Selection exerted by disease and the limitation of food resources tend to check population size, but in the case of rapid breeders, insects, and even some mammals, the extremes in maximum and minimum population sizes can be enormous.

Slow-breeding animals have a different sort of problem. The elephant, the slowest of the mammals with a gestation period of twenty-two months, may, under favorable conditions, reproduce six offspring during its reproductive span. Even slight environmental variations can have profound effects. Droughts and diseases work a heavy toll and may have been responsible (probably aided by human predators—the Paleolithic hunters of the New World) for the extinction of the mammoths (prehistoric elephants) in the Western Hemisphere eight thousand years ago. In the case of the human species, with a shorter gestation period of nine months, as is discussed later, we, too, have a limited reproductive potential because of a lengthened dependency period of the young and a relatively short reproductive period of the female (compared with life-span). Human reproductive potential is further restricted by numerous regulations imposed by society that forbids sexual intercourse between many classes of relatives. The net result is a reduction in the absolute numbers of offspring produced, which often is below the biological potential. In sum, natural selection refers to all those features of a population's environment that influence reproduction and survival contributing to a steady production of individuals over the generations who, as Darwin described, have a reproductive advantage.

In the case of human populations, natural selection is much more complicated as will be explained in the following chapters. Throughout our history some populations have increased, whereas others have declined. Diseases once a deadly menace have now declined to be replaced by others; in this decade, mortality from a previously unknown disease—the acquired immune deficiency syndrome (AIDS)—has risen dramatically. Until the last few centuries human existence had always been precarious; periods interspaced with high mortality and high fertility were the rule until human adaptation underwent a dramatic improvement. First, the Neolithic revolution, when plant and animal domestication began about ten thousand years ago, was a very successful adaptation that contributed to major population increases. Then, again, during the Industrial Revolution of two hundred years ago, western Europe underwent a population "explosion;" fertility rates went up, and death rates declined dramatically. A short time later, the rest of Europe and certain other parts of the world followed in this new pattern. Today, many national groups are undergoing a similar experience of population increase but at much higher rates. Those countries with the major growth throughout the period of the Industrial Revolution are now experiencing a lowering of birth rates together with a reduction of mortality rates, which has brought the annual increase of population down to a low level. There has been, throughout human history, disproportionate growth among human populations. No one regional group has predominated for very long, and the tendency for fluctuations in population growth are described in the last chapter.

Gene Flow

In addition to growth, there has been a considerable population movement throughout human history, and much of this migration has occurred in the last few centuries. The migration and mixing of peoples increase genetic exchange, and populations who were previously isolated in past centuries have undergone a considerable change in gene frequencies. Interpopulation contact through migration, trade, or warfare have had a major influence on genetic variability of many parts of *Homo sapiens*.

This gene flow, as it is often called, is a factor that reduces the influences of isolation and prevents the development of unique gene combinations within a breeding population. It has the potential for introducing new gene combinations, causing the population to be more heterogeneous. The relative influence of gene exchange between breeding populations depends, of course, on the size and length of time in contact. Invading armies, colonists, travelers, and traders have all had an effect on genetic distribution among the populations of our species. The distribution of gene frequencies today and in the recent past is quite different from the way it was before the major colonial expansion of western Europe beginning in the fifteenth century.

Genetic Drift

A critical factor influencing gene frequencies from generation to generation is the total number of individuals who make up the effective breeding population (males and females in their reproductive years). When this number is very small, there is the possibility that all gene combinations will not be represented in the next generation. This may be described as a *sampling error* or *genetic drift*. The chance distribution of the genotypes of offspring from the mating of heterozygotes can serve to illustrate the influences of population size on sampling error. When there is a mating of heterozygotes (**Aa** × **Aa**), there is a probability of 25 percent that the offspring will be **AA**. If the couple produces five children, then the probability is less than 0.1 percent that they all will be genotype **AA,** whereas there is 1.5 percent chance that three children will have this genotype (Table 2-7). Should either of these unlikely events occur and more **AA** genotypes are produced than either **Aa** or **aa,** the frequency of the recessive allele, **a,** would decrease through chance alone in a population with only a few matings each generation. The larger the number of

TABLE 2-7   Distribution of Offspring of Two Heterozygous Parents (Aa × Aa)

GENOTYPE OF FIRST OFFSPRING	PROBABILITY OF FIRST OFFSPRING	GENOTYPE OF SECOND OFFSPRING	PROBABILITY OF SECOND OFFSPRING	TOTAL PROBABILITY
AA	1/4	AA	1/4	Both offspring AA, 1/16
AA	1/4	Aa	2/4	AA followed by Aa, 2/16
AA	1/4	aa	1/4	AA followed by aa, 1/16
Aa	2/4	AA	1/4	Aa followed by AA, 2/16
Aa	2/4	Aa	2/4	Both offspring Aa, 4/16
Aa	2/4	aa	1/4	Aa followed by aa, 2/16
aa	1/4	AA	1/4	aa followed by AA, 1/16
aa	1/4	Aa	2/4	aa followed by Aa, 2/16
aa	1/4	aa	1/4	Both offspring aa, 1/16

matings, the greater the probability that all genetic combinations will be reproduced, so the gene frequencies will remain stable from one generation to the next. By contrast, the fewer the matings each generation, the smaller the sample of the total gene pool. Under this condition there will be a greater chance that certain genes will not be passed on because of the small size of the sample.

There are several examples where genes have become fixed at high frequencies in human populations within just a few generations. Island populations throughout the Pacific and other regions, as well as religious colonists whose beliefs have resulted in self-imposed isolation, document the influence of population size on gene frequencies. The smaller the size of the effective breeding population (ratio of males and females of reproductive age to total population), the greater the chance of gene frequency change between the generations. A case in point is a religious isolate in western Pennsylvania, the "Old Order Dunkers."

This religious group can trace their origins to 1708 in the Rhineland area of Germany with the establishment of a sect of the German Baptist Brethren. The American colony began in 1719 when twenty-eight persons arrived in Pennsylvania. These initial colonists were joined by others from the same Rhineland region. The New World colony flourished and grew in number until religious dissent caused the sect to split into three divisions in 1881. The smaller division retained the original beliefs and practices of the earlier settlers and became known as the "Old German Baptist Brethren" (Dunkers). About 1950, there were fifty-five communities spread over the Midwest, with a few in California and Florida. Three of these communities remained in the area of Pennsylvania where the colony began and where the communities were examined by a team of medical and genetic experts.

This extensive study by Glass and his coworkers (Glass et al., 1952) focused on several genetic characters, the blood groups of the ABO, Rh, and MN systems, as well as certain complex traits. Their findings showed that the Dunkers differed significantly from the average trait frequencies of the U.S. population. The Dunker isolate of three hundred persons also differed significantly from populations living in those regions of Germany from which the group's ancestors had migrated. Blood type A and blood type M were much more frequent in the Dunker sample, for example. Other phenotype distinctions were observed in the population, which were believed due to the small size of the effective breeding population (there were only 90 parents) and because of its isolation over the generations. Though it is difficult to document sampling error (genetic drift) in humans, this case study provided some interesting data to support population size as a factor in gene frequency change. In addition, there is the genetic composition of the colony's original founders to consider.

The influence of the founders' gene combinations is another form of sampling error and is referred to as *founders' effect* (Mayr, 1963). Because of the improbability of a small group of colonists representing all of the variety of the parent population, this initial error in sampling will have a major influence on future generations of descendants from the founding population. This restricted sampling, or "bottleneck" effect may be repeated in future generations if, through natural catastrophe or disease, the population loses large numbers of their people over a short period. Consider the example of the small South Atlantic island of Tristan da Cunha, midway between South America and Africa. The 270 persons occupying the island in 1961 could trace their ancestry back to the original 15 colonists consisting of soldiers, shipwrecked sailors, and a few women who arrived in 1816.

The lonely, isolated island has no natural harbor to shelter ships from the rough seas, and its environment is harsh so that except for an occasional individual, there has been no immigration. Despite these restrictions the population grew to 103 in 1855, when it suffered a set back with the departure of all but 33 persons. A second bottleneck occurred when a small boat with 15 males aboard capsized, leaving no survivors. Following this disaster many of the widows and their offspring emigrated, reducing the island from 106 to 54. The population again recovered to reach 270 by 1961. These events have caused some rare genetic recessive traits and unique gene frequencies to exist among the modern-day descendants.

Even larger populations, descendants of a few founders, will often contain a high frequency of rare genetic defects. An example of such detrimental genes reaching high frequencies is the inherited defect *porphyria*. This metabolic disorder prevents chemical conversion of the porphyrin compound, the iron-bearing pigment of hemoglobin, and results in the excretion of excessive amounts in the urine. Persons with the South African type of porphyria, inherited as an autosomal dominant gene, are ultrasensitive to sunlight, which produces severe skin lesions. The accumulation of porphyrin in the blood leads to several symptoms of the digestive tract and nervous system disorders; persons with the affliction are sensitive, as well, to certain types of drugs like barbiturates. This metabolic defect is rare throughout the world with most cases reported in the Afrikaans population. The gene responsible for this affliction has been traced through genealogies back to 1688, which identified a young girl from Rotterdam and her spouse, another immigrant from the Netherlands. The eight-thousand carriers of the porphyria gene today are descendants from this marriage. These findings are not surprising considering that an estimated one million of three million Afrikaans are descendants of forty original couples settling in the Cape area (Dean, 1963).

Random Mating

The Hardy-Weinberg Equilibrium assumes that matings occur without regard to genotype—that is, they are random. Persons marry without considering blood-group genotypes; for example, persons do not select a mate of type A blood and reject type B. Therefore, calculations for many of the human gene frequencies will not be disturbed by a nonrandomness of breeding. Random breeding in another sense does not usually apply in the choice of mates, however, because a number of social as well as biological criteria are considered. In human populations all males and females do not have an equal chance of mating, and there are several barriers that reduce random mating. One is *positive* assortative mating, which describes a tendency for "like" to marry "like." Tall people tend to marry tall people, and short people tend to marry short people. Also there is a high positive correlation between the intelligence quotients (IQs) of husband and wife. Persons frequently marry those within their social circle and, until just a few generations ago, geographical distance played a major role in mate selection; marriages occurred most often between individuals who lived nearby. Though the distances between prenuptial households is steadily increasing, marriage to "the boy or girl next door" was more fact than fiction until quite recently (see chapter 5).

Another factor that has reduced random matings is society's rules that prohibit matings between close relatives. All societies enforce some form of an incest taboo that forbids marriages between persons of some degree of biological relationship, which always includes the nuclear family—parents and offspring within this restricted category. An exception is brother-sister unions that were favored in several ancient civilizations like the Egyptian, Hawaiian, and Incan to maintain the royal blood line. Beyond the nuclear family, relationships are defined in many different ways. Modern societies frequently forbid marriages between first and second cousins. In many states it is illegal to marry one's cousin of any degree, whereas only first cousins are prohibited in other states; in at least one state (Wyoming), first-cousin marriages are permitted if the woman is older than fifty years of age. In the past, however, many primitive cultures preferred certain types of cousin marriages. Also, several royal families of Europe have, for centuries, tried to maintain political alliances by intermarriages, frequently between cousins. The Hapsburg empire of Central Europe was founded on such alliances, for example. For most of humanity, however, the tendency has been to outbreed depending on distance, economy, religion, and availability of potential mates owing to population size.

The degree of outbreeding depends largely on the size of a community; just how many persons are there in a population who might be suitable mates? In the smaller villages there are few eligible marriage partners of the right age who are not relatives, and a young man who is seeking a bride, for example, will have few choices. He may persuade a young woman from another village to become his spouse and to migrate to his village, he himself may migrate, or, as often happens, he may marry a cousin if his society and family permits. Thus, one expects to see a greater number of consanguinal marriages (those between genetic relatives who are usually first or second cousins) in a smaller community. Examinations of several breeding isolates show a high negative correlation between size and frequency of cousin marriages—that is, the smaller the size of the population, the greater is the number of first-cousin marriages.

The outbreeding, or population *exogamy*, has had the effect of reducing homozygosity and increasing heterozygosity. The effects of increased heterozygosity in a population is expressed through individuals of greater size, improved general health, and increased fertility. Population *endogamy*, inbreeding, causes the reverse. The few studies of the effects of human inbreeding suggest the existence of a "hybrid vigor" or heterosis for humans similar to what has been described for other species. By contrast, children of *consanguineous* matings (marriages of relatives of some degree) are smaller in size, have a higher frequency of congenital abnormalities, and exhibit greater mortality during the first six years of life (Morton, 1958, 1961; Schull and Neel, 1965). Inbreeding increases the chance of pairing deleterious recessives in the offspring because of the probability that related parents may be carriers of the same recessive because of their sharing of a close common ancestor. The consequences of this increased homozygosity of recessive alleles is shown by an increase in genetic disease measured in certain populations. There is a greater frequency of consanguinity among parents of affected offspring than among general population (Table 2-8).

GENES AND POPULATIONS: A SUMMARY

Mendel's experiments laid the foundation for modern genetics. The significance of these experiments was that they clearly demonstrated, for the first time, particulate inheritance, and the concept of inheritance by a blending of traits was at last put to rest. There are several points that should be emphasized. The first is that genes are transmitted in groups because they are a part of the chromosomes that exist as paired structures except when separated at meiosis to form the gamete. At this point in cell division, each chromosome goes its own way; there is an independent assortment that occurs, as Mendel showed with his experiments with dihybrid plants. Another way of describing this chromosome assortment is to consider that in humans, who have forty-six, one-half of the chromosomes are provided by each of the parents. This is not necessarily,

TABLE 2-8   Percentages of Affected Offspring
of Cousin Marriages

TRAIT	% CONSANGUINITY[a]
Albinism	19–24
Alkaptonuria	30–42
PKU	5–15
Tay Sachs	27–53
Xeroderma pigmentosum	20–36
Ichthyosis congenita	30–40
Congenital total blindness	11–21

[a] This indicates the frequency of consanguinity of those parents who produced affected offspring. This should be weighed against the average for the general population, which is less than 1 percent.

Source: From Curt Stern, *Principles of Human Genetics*, 3rd ed., W. H. Freeman & Company. Copyright © 1973.

however, the same order in which they will be passed to the children, each of whom will not get a fixed portion of their grandparents' genes. The gametes that humans produce all contain a mixture of chromosomes from each of the parents so it is highly improbable that any person will possess one-fourth of his or her genome from each grandparent.

A second point to consider is that a crossing of heterozygotes produces results that will usually differ somewhat by chance alone from the Mendelian ratio (1:2:1). This is to be anticipated, though, and simple statistical tests can show whether this deviation significantly differs from the expected or if it differs simply because of a chance variation. If the difference is significant, then one of the forces known to influence gene frequencies may be involved.

In considering a Mendelian population (breeding population), those sources of variation and the forces for stability will have to be identified and compared to understand any change in gene frequency throughout the generations. Sources of new genetic material (mutations) cause small, minor changes in gene frequency in contrast to migration, which can disturb equilibrium in a single generation. If the mutation is one that conveys an advantage, then natural selection can cause a rapid rise in the frequency of the new allele. Mutations, as discussed, play the role of supplying new genetic material and, considering the complexity in the copying of the genes at meiosis, it is surprising that mutation rates are so low. It is likely that many more mutations occur than have been measured and that these mutations are responsible for the wide range of biochemical variability that we are beginning to recognize in the human species. Most of these deleterious mutations are, fortunately, masked by the normal allele except in those rare cases in which they are combined in the homozygote. We now know of the many variations in DNA fragment lengths, recently described, that frequently occur from either crossovers or from base pair changes.

Population size is a critical consideration in any study of human variation because of the possibility of loss of alleles through chance alone. The *effective breeding population* consists of those in their reproductive years (generally considered between fifteen and forty-four years of age) and is, on the average, roughly one-third of the total population. Add to this the restrictions imposed by society's rules dictating the matings allowed, and chance can be seen as a major factor in gene frequency change. Also, chance plays a role in reproduction (the variety of gametes is an example), but human behavior channels a good bit of genetic variability along a certain course, as we describe later.

This chapter has provided an overview of the biological basis of human inheritance and variability. These basic concepts are developed throughout the balance of this book and appropriate examples given. The examples offer evidence that *Homo sapiens* is subject to basic biological laws. Though human behavior may alter the direct effect of the forces acting on a species, our total gene combinations are still related to certain environmental variables that exert selective forces. The appreciation of the importance of these forces enables us to understand the development of biological diversity.

RECOMMENDED READINGS AND LITERATURE CITED

BODMER, W. F., and L. L. CAVALLI-SFORZA. 1976. *Genetics, Evolution and Man*. New York: W. H. Freeman.

DEAN, G. 1963. *The Porphyrias: A Story of Inheritance and Environment*. Philadelphia: J. B. Lippincott.

GLASS, B., M. S. SACKS, E. F. JAHN, AND C. HESS. 1952. "Genetic drift in a religious isolate: An analysis of the causes of variations in blood group and other gene frequencies in a small population," *Am. Naturalist*, 86:145–159.

GLASS, B. 1955. "On the unlikelihood of significant admixture of genes from the North American Indians in the present composition of the Negroes of the United States," *Am. J. Hum. Genet.*, 7:368–385.

HARTL, D. L., D. FREIFELDER, AND L. A. SNYDER. 1988. *Basic Genetics*. Boston: Jones and Bartlett.

MAYR, E. 1963. *Animal Species and Evolution*. Cambridge, Mass.: Belknap Press of Harvard University Press.

MAYR, E. 1982. *The Growth of Biological Thought: Diversity, Evolution, and Inheritance*. Cambridge, Mass.: Belknap Press of Harvard University Press.

MAYR, E. 1988. *Toward a New Philosophy of Biology*. Cambridge, Mass.: Belknap Press of Harvard University Press.

MORTON, N. E. 1958. "Empirical risks in consanguineous marriages: Birth weight, gestation time, and measurements of infants," *Am. J. Hum. Genet.*, 10:344–349.

NICHOLS, E. K. 1988. *Human Gene Therapy*. Cambridge, Mass.: Belknap Press of Harvard University Press.

SCHULL, W. J., AND J. V. NEEL. 1965. *The Effects of Inbreeding on Japanese Children*. New York: Harper and Row.

SOUTHERN, E. M. 1975. "Detection of specific sequences among DNA fragments separated by gel electrophoresis," *J. Mol. Biol.*, 98:503–517.

STERN, C. 1973. *Principles of Human Genetics*, 3rd ed. New York: W. H. Freeman.

VOGEL, F. AND A. G. MOTULSKY. 1986. *Human Genetics: Problems and Approaches*, 2nd ed. Berlin: Springer-Verlag.

WATSON, J. D. 1980. *The Double Helix: A Personal Account of the Discovery of the Structure of DNA*. New York: W. W. Norton.

3

Human Biology I: Traits of Simple Inheritance

Humans have a complex genome of great diversity as we shall begin to discuss in this and succeeding chapters. With the rise of molecular biology and analysis of DNA structure, more and more is learned about the many human phenotypes of simple inheritance determined by a dominant or recessive allele. The expression of these monogenic phenotypes is little influenced by the environment, in contrast to the polygenic traits. Some of the better-known monogenic traits include the various blood-group systems, abnormal hemoglobins, and numerous serum proteins. Recently, the use of restriction enzymes to "cut" the DNA molecule at precise locations has added considerable knowledge of the restriction fragment length polymorphisms (RFLP) in many population groups. The list of genetic markers is continuously growing as improved techniques enable the identification of additional polymorphisms, many of them enzyme systems or proteins of the blood serum. These monogenic traits are described as discontinuous; each trait is either present or absent, in contrast to the broad ranges of the polygenic traits discussed in the next chapter. In the study of population genetics and of those factors that cause changes in gene frequencies, monogenic traits are most useful. Some of these simply inherited traits have also been used as markers to estimate the degree of genetic distance between populations and their probable ancestral relationships.

BLOOD COMPONENTS AND INHERITED TRAITS

Blood serves the vital functions of transporting oxygen and nutrients throughout the body and of removing the waste products of metabolism. Blood consists of specialized cells, *erythrocytes* (red blood cells), whose function is to transport oxygen to the tissues, and a yellowish fluid, the plasma. This fluid part of the blood contains a variety of components vital to the metabolism. Major plasma constituents are *albumin,* a group of large protein molecules that combine with and transport several substances; *fibrinogen,* blood-clotting agents; and *globulin fractions,* small granular bodies (Figure 3-1). Another type of cell—the *leukocyte,* or white blood cell (mainly granulocytes and lymphocytes)—is also found in the blood. Normally there are few of these cells in circulation, but during infection their number rises dramatically as the body's defense against invading organisms.

In our discussion of inherited polymorphisms of the blood we are especially interested in the gamma-globulin fraction that includes immunoglobulins, antibodies that attack the foreign substances entering the body (usually bacteria or proteins). These *antibodies,* our main line of defense, are protein molecules that have the ability to attach to certain other chemical molecules on the surfaces of micro-organisms. This attachment causes a group of these organisms to cling together (agglutinate). Many foreign substances such as pollen, mold, virus, or bacteria may stimulate the synthesis of antibodies in the host's body; substances with this property are called *antigens.*

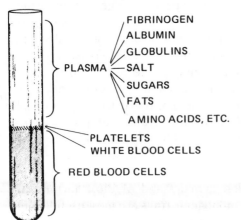

FIBRINOGEN
ALBUMIN
GLOBULINS
PLASMA — SALT
SUGARS
FATS
AMINO ACIDS, ETC.
PLATELETS
WHITE BLOOD CELLS
RED BLOOD CELLS

FIGURE 3-1
Blood Components. When a sample of blood is placed in a test tube and spun in a centrifuge the heavier components settle to the bottom with the lighter products and fluids at the top. The diagram lists these major components, the types of cells, and the products in the plasma.

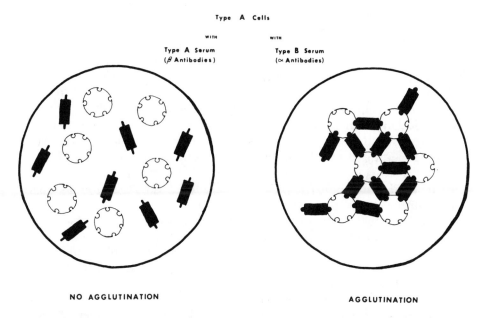

Type A Cells

WITH | WITH
Type A Serum (β Antibodies) | Type B Serum (α Antibodies)

NO AGGLUTINATION   AGGLUTINATION

These diagrams show the relationships between red blood-cell antigens (type A) and the two types of serum. No agglutination will occur when type-A cells are mixed with serum from a type-A person. The antibodies are anti-B type (β antibodies) and are not attracted by the combining sites of the type A (left diagram). When type-A cells are mixed with serum from a type-B person, the anti-A antibodies (α antibodies) combine with the cells and agglutination occurs, causing the cells to cling together in a group (right diagram).

FIGURE 3-2 Diagram of Antibodies-Antigen Reactions.

The antigen is often a complex molecule with multiple combining sites or locations where antibodies may connect and may be viewed as a simple model shown in Figure 3-2. The antibody, however, is a simpler structure and has fewer combining sites. When the antibody connects with an antigen, there are still sites available to connect with other antibodies and antigens until all combining sites are full. The result is a linkage together of all the foreign antigens. This interaction ultimately makes it possible for the body's defense to destroy foreign substances or to render them harmless by preventing their multiplication. The efficiency of this system depends on the ability to produce antibodies of the right kind and in sufficient quantities.

Blood Groups

There are antibodies in each person's system that are, of necessity, compatible with the individual's own circulatory system. If blood from one person is mixed with blood from another, however, then a reaction may occur between the antigens and antibodies of the two individuals. Experiments that mixed red blood cells of one species with samples of serum from another resulted in an attraction between the red blood cells causing them to cling together or agglutinate. This attraction suggested that there was some substance that attached to a sticky part of the red blood cell surfaces. Likewise, when samples were taken from different humans, the agglutination would occur frequently but not always. These serological experiments during the last quarter of the nineteenth century indicated that there were some distinct differences in the surface components of the red blood cells and those within the blood serum. There was further demonstration of the variety of human blood components when blood transfusions were attempted on a large scale, for the first time, during the Franco-Prussian War (1870–1871).

Before 1900, transfusions were used only as a last resort in an attempt to save the patient's life. Often the transfused blood would cause shock and even death because of agglutination of the incompatible antibodies and red cells as we now know. At times, though, transfusions were successful because some mixtures of blood were compatible. In 1900 Karl Landsteiner, an Austrian immunologist, began to analyze systematically the pattern of agglutination between the blood donor and recipients. Tests were made by mixing the blood serum from one person with red blood cells from another. Only certain combinations caused an agglutination of the red cells. If a reaction occurred between serum from person A and red cells from person B, Landsteiner found the reverse was also true; serum from B would agglutinate cells from A. Throughout thousands of tests Landsteiner found these results to be consistent, but there were some individuals whose cells could not be agglutinated by either anti-A or anti-B serum. Transfusions could now be made safely if the donor and recipient bloods were matched.

Since this original discovery, many other major blood groups have been identified by cross-reaction between red blood cells and serum from different individuals, and also by reaction of blood cells to specially prepared antiserum. Such antiserum is prepared by injecting human cells into laboratory animals (for instance, rabbits), and samples of antiserum made by the animal are extracted. This antihuman antiserum is then tested against a variety of human blood samples and the reactions tabulated. By testing blood cells taken from numerous individuals, agglutination reactions are noted with some and not with others. Extracts of plant compounds have also been applied in this way. Table 3-1 lists several of the more clinically important blood groups including those useful today in the study of human genetics.

The *ABO blood group* is the best known of a growing list of the red-cell antigens because of its medical importance; since its discovery, millions of people throughout the world have had their blood types recorded.

TABLE 3-1   Major Blood Group Systems

SYSTEM	ANTIGENS	GENOTYPES	PHENOTYPES	DATE OF DISCOVERY
ABO	A_1, A_2, B	OO, AA, BB, AB	O, A_1, A_2, B, AB	1900
Lewis	Le^a, Le^b	Le^aLe^a, Le^bLe^b, LeLe	Le(a+b−), Le(a−b+), Le(a−b−)	1946
Rh	(see Table 3-3b)			
MNSs	N, N, S, s	MS/MS, MS/Ms, Ms/Ms, MS/NS,MS/Ns,Ms/NS, Ms/Ns,NS/NS,NS/Ns, Ns/Ns	M, N, MN, S, s, Ss	1927
P	P_1, P_2	P_1P_1, P_1P_2, P_2P_2, P_1p, P_2p, pp	P_1, P_2, p	1927
Lutheran	Lu^a, Lu^b	Lu^aLu^a, Lu^aLu^b, Lu^bLu^b	Lu (a+b−), Lu (a−b+)	1945
Kell	K (Kell) k (Cellano)	KK, Kk, kk	K+k−, k+k+, K−k+, (K−k−)	1946
Duffy	Fy^a, Fy^b	Fy^aFy^a, Fy^aFy^b, Fy^bFy^b, FyFy	Fy (a+b−), Fy (a+b+), Fy (a−b+), Fy (a−b−)	1950
Kidd	Jk^a, Jk^b	Jk^aJk^a, Jk^aJk^b, Jk^bJk^b	Jk (a+b−), Jk (a+b+), Jk (a−b+), Jk (a−b−)	1951
Diego	Di^a	Di^aDi^a, Di^aDi, DiDi	Di (a+), Di (a−)	1955
Sutter	Js^a	Js^aJs^a, Js^aJs, JsJs	Js (a+), Js (a−)	
Auberger	Au^a	Au^aAu^a, Au^aAu, AuAu	Au (a+), Au (a−)	1961
Xg	Xg^a	Xg^aY, XgY, Xg^aXg^a, Xg^aXg, XgXg	Xg (a+), Xg (a−)	1962

Sources: Based on Buettner-Janusch, 1966; Giblett, 1969; and Race and Sanger, 1975.

of people throughout the world have had their blood types recorded. Analysis of these data and comparison of ABO types in families has shown that the type was passed on by Mendelian inheritance.[1] The antigens are under the control of at least three alleles at a locus on chromosome 9; the alleles A and B are codominants, whereas the type O allele is recessive. The genetics of the ABO system become more complex as additional alleles are detected. For example, there are actually two types of A, A_1, and A_2, which increase the number of alleles at the ABO locus to four.

Within the blood plasma of each person there are antibodies related

[1] The inheritance of blood types as Mendelian characters was demonstrated by Hirszfeld and von Dungern in 1910, but they identified only two alleles, A and B. Their work stimulated many others; Bernstein, in 1924, established that there were, in fact, three alleles that determined the ABO blood types (Mourant, 1983).

to the "type" of red-cell antigen. The antibody type as well as the antigen type are under genetic control, and the pattern of inheritance is listed as follows:

GENOTYPE	PHENOTYPE	ANTIBODIES
	(BLOOD TYPE)	
AA	A	anti-B
AO		
BB	B	anti-A
BO		
AB	AB	none
OO	O	anti-A,B

This diagram illustrates that the genotypes AA and AO determine the same blood type (the type of antigen carried by the red blood cell). Persons of this type will have anti-B antibodies in their plasma, so blood from a type-A person cannot be donated to a type-B person. These antibodies are "naturally" occurring—that is, they appear to have been determined by the ABO alleles. They are normally present in a person's serum, and their production need not be stimulated by an antigen from external sources. The antibodies (A and B) in a type-O person are somewhat different; they are smaller in size, and their reactions are weaker.

Soluble ABO Antigens and Modifying Genes

When the ABO group was first studied it was assumed that type O was simply the absence of antigens A and B, and a type-O person's blood would not react to either antisera. Further study showed that certain antisera could be found that would react with type-O blood cells. The reaction indicated the probability of an antigen on type-O cells and was designated *type H*. The antigen is a molecular fragment on the surface of the blood cell that is common to both the A and B antigens, because type-A and type-O blood cells will also react with the anti-H serum. The reaction is weaker than that of the cells from a type-O person and the order of strength of reactions is $O > A_1 > B > A_2$. This H substance may be identifiable in the saliva and other bodily fluids just as the antigens of type A and B of most persons may be present in soluble form (around 75 percent in the British Isles and higher in other regions).

The presence of soluble ABH antigens in bodily fluids such as saliva, tears, semen, milk, gastric juice, and other watery secretions is determined by a dominant allele at another locus, and the person who is homozygous or heterozygous is described as a secretor. The inheritance of the ability to secrete the ABH antigens in soluble form is shown by the following genotypes:

GENOTYPE	PHENOTYPE
Se Se ──────────→	secretor
Se se ──────────→	secretor
se se ──────────→	nonsecretor

The existence of these water-soluble forms has made it possible to study the structure of the ABH antigens because it can be manipulated chemically, whereas the red-cell antigen form cannot be extracted from the cell's surface without altering the antigen's structure and identity.[2]

Bombay Blood Type

The discovery of persons in India whose red blood cells did not agglutinate when mixed with anti-A, anti-B, or anti-H serum added evidence that other genetic loci influenced the expression of the ABO blood types. These persons should have had an ABO type given the evidence from the studies of their family pedigrees, but they did not. Further surveys showed that this rare condition is seldom found in any population except among Mohorati speakers in and around Bombay, India, where the frequency is about one in thirteen thousand, and on Reunion Island in the Indian Ocean (Gerard et al., 1982). Such persons are said to have the *Bombay* blood type and lack ABH antigens on red blood cells or the soluble form in the serum.

This condition, the Bombay type, is inherited as a simple recessive and may be understood as the lack of a substance that is essential as a precursor for the structure of the A or B antigen. A simple diagram illustrates the requirement of a sugar-protein chain, determined by a dominant allele (H), so the AB or H type may be present.

GENOTYPE(H)	GENOTYPE(ABO)	BLOOD TYPE
HH	Precursor AA	A + H
	AO	
Hh	Precursor BB	B + H
	BO	
	OO	H
hh	None (any ABO)	Bombay

In other words, the antigen characteristic of A or B on the red cell or in

---

[2] The blood group substances on the surface of the red blood cells are composed of a chain of sugars and proteins (glycoproteins) that are alcohol soluble and cannot easily be analyzed. The soluble forms of the ABH substances have been extensively studied, however. The relative positions of the sugars, fructose and galactose, along the chain determines the identity of the antigen (Race and Sanger, 1975).

soluble form requires the presence of the H substance. Those who lack the H allele are described as Bombay blood types.

Lewis Blood Group

The alleles for the secretor phenotype are independent of the ABO locus though they determine the presence or absence of ABH substances in their soluble form as described. There is a close relationship, however, between the secretor gene locus and the *Lewis* blood-group system, and both function as modifiers of the ABO system. There are three types of individuals known in the Lewis system: Le $(a+b-)$, Le $(a-b+)$, and Le $(a-b-)$. No Le $(a+b+)$ individuals have been identified. A person who types Le $(a-b+)$ is also a secretor, but a person who is Le $(a+b-)$ is not. A person who does not react to the Lewis antiserum and who is not a secretor is designated Le$(a-b-)$. The Lewis system is under the control of a pair of alleles, designated Le and le, but the expression of the product of these alleles as antigens Le^a and Le^b depends on the combined interactions of the Lewis and secretor system (Table 3-2).

Rhesus (Rh) Blood Group

The *Rh system* is second to the ABO in clinical importance and is the one most often involved in a blood disease of the newborn, *erythroblastosis fetalis*. In this disease, the red cells of the developing fetus are destroyed by antibodies made in the mother's blood in a response to stimulus from

TABLE 3-2 Relations Between Red Cell and Soluble Antigens: The H, Secretor, and Lewis Loci

GENOTYPES			ANTIGENS ON CELLS			ANTIGENS IN MUCOUS SECRETIONS		
H	SECRETOR	LEWIS	ABH	Le^a	Le^b	ABH	Le^a	Le^b
HH	Sese			LeLe	+	−	+	+
	+ +							
Hh	Sese			Lele				
HH	sese	LeLe	+	+	−	−	+	−
Hh		Lele						
hh	SeSe	LeLe	−	+	−	−	+	−
	SeSe	Lele		Bombay				
hh	sese	lele types	−	−	−	−	−	−
HH	sese	lele	+	−	−	−	−	−
Hh								
HH	SeSe	lele	+	−	−	+	−	−
Hh	Sese							

Source: Modified from Harrison et al., 1988.

certain antigens on the fetus red cells, antigens that the mother does not possess. Though the disease was known for many years, no explanation was possible until 1940 when Landsteiner and Weiner showed that anti-Rh serum[3] agglutinated red cells of about 85 percent of white New York patients tested. The remaining 15 percent did not react to the serum and were identified as Rh negative. The research continued and, about a year later, the investigators discovered that mothers who had given birth to infants suffering from a hemolytic disease (erythroblastosis) were Rh negative; their blood cells did not react to the anti-Rh factor, but their infants did (Figure 3-3).

Since the 1940s numerous studies of the Rh system have revealed many Rh antigen types that are inherited through Mendelian mechanisms. Because of the number and complexity of the reactions to antisera tests, two different explanations have been offered to describe the kinds of

FIGURE 3-3
Reaction of an Rh Negative Mother to Her Rh Positive Fetus

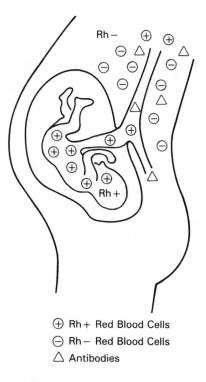

⊕ Rh+ Red Blood Cells
⊖ Rh− Red Blood Cells
△ Antibodies

If the fetus of an Rh negative mother and Rh positive father is Rh positive there is the risk of the mother becoming sensitized by the fetal red blood cells. A few of these cells may enter the mother's blood stream and, because they are Rh+, they will stimulate the production of antibodies. These antibodies can freely cross the placenta and destroy the fetal red blood cells.

[3] Anti-Rh serum was produced by rabbits when they were injected with red cells from Rhesus monkeys.

reactions and modes of inheritance. The hypothesis by Fisher and Race, postulates that the reactions or potentials for reactions are inherited as if they were determined by three closely linked loci, each with two alleles (each allele determines one antigenic response to an antiserum). They used the notations Cc, Dd, and Ee to represent the pair of alleles at each locus; the lowercase letters do not indicate recessitivity or dominance, because each allele determines the presence of an antigen, though an antibody for d has not been discovered yet. Because the three loci are so closely linked and crossover rarely occurs, the loci are written together as a combination (haplotype) to represent the genotype. A typical genotype might appear as

$$\frac{\text{CDE}}{\text{cde}}$$

which shows that all antigens in the systems are represented and would interact with the antiserum especially prepared for these tests. By contrast, Weiner, the codiscoverer of Rh, postulates that there is only a single locus with eight allelic genes, each responsible for determining an antigen that can combine with three or more kinds of antibodies. Both hypotheses are equally valid, though some immunologists prefer one over the other, and both notation systems are used to indicate blood type in the Rh system.

Each parent in this example (Table 3-3a) would test positive for C, but, because they are heterozygous for the alleles, the probability is that one out of four offspring would be negative for this antigen. The female, according to her genotype, is homozygous for gene d. She would not react to the anti-D serum test (this individual would be considered Rh negative). Because her husband has both d and D, however, there is a 50 percent chance that a child produced by this mating would have the D allele and

TABLE 3-3a   Mode of Inheritance of Rh System (Fisher-Race Notation)

MALE GENOTYPE	FEMALE GENOTYPE
CDE	Cde
cde	cdE

Genotypes of offspring		
gametes	Cde	cdE
CDE	CDE / Cde	CDE / cdE
cde	cde / Cde	cde / cdE

TABLE 3-3b   Genetic Notation and Rh Antigens

ALLELIC GENES (WEINER SYSTEM)	ANTIGENS (SPECIFIC ANTISERA REACTIONS)	THREE GENE LOCI (FISHER-RACE SYSTEM)
R^0	Rh_0, hr^1, hr^{11}	cDe
r'	rh', hr''	Cde
r''	rh'', hr'	cdE
R^1	$Rh_1{}^1$, (Rh_0, rh^1, hr^{11})	CDe
R^2	Rh_2 (Rh_0, rh^{11}, hr^1)	cDE
R^z	Rh_z (Rh_0, rh^1, rh^{11})	CDE
r^y	rh_y (rh^1, rh^{11})	CdE
r	rh (hr^1, hr^{11})	cde

would be Rh positive. There is also a possibility, in this case, of the fetus's stimulating anti-D antibody production in the maternal system.[4] The anti-D antibodies from the mother's bloodstream easily cross through the placenta into the fetal circulation, where they agglutinate and then destroy the blood cells (see Figure 3-3). When such an event occurs, there is the risk of the fetus's developing the erythroblastosis disease. The risk increases with each pregnancy because the mother's system is sensitized by carrying previous Rh negative fetuses and the anti-Rh antibodies are at a high level. Naturally, if the genotype of the fetus is negative for D, there would be no danger.

The genes for the Rh antigen system do not determine antibodies, as in the case of the ABO system, which has naturally occurring antibodies. Theoretically any of the six antigens has a potential to stimulate antibody production, but only D and C seem to cause trouble in the incompatible pregnancies just described. Incompatibility may also occur in the ABO blood-group system, and some hemolytic disease has been reported in type A or B infants born of type O mothers.

MN System

The *MN system* was first discovered in 1927 when Landsteiner and Levine were able to prepare two types of antiserum against human red cells that would identify three types of individuals.[5] The symbols M and

---

[4] Except in unusual circumstances, blood cells do not cross the placenta to exchange between maternal and fetal circulation. At birth, however, when the placenta is separating from the uterine wall, a few fetal cells can enter the maternal circulation. If the mother's blood type is different from the fetus, then her system will make antibodies. The level will rise with each pregnancy, and so will the risk of a fetus or newborn suffering from a hemolytic disease caused by maternal antibodies against the fetal red cells.

[5] Many of the blood-group systems have been discovered by mixing blood cells with antiserum made from plant extracts or with antihuman serum made by injecting human red cells into certain animals, usually rabbits. This results in antibodies against a variety of the proteins attached to the human red cell. This procedure provides a way of detecting a range of individual variation.

N were used to describe the genotypes of this new system. Inheritance of MN type appeared to be of this kind:

MN	X	MN	Genotypes (parents)
MM	MN	NN	Genotypes (children)
M	MN	N	Phenotypes

These alleles are codominants, and each determines a characteristic response to antiserum. The heterozygote (MN) individual would react with both antisera and would distinguish this individual from the persons who react only with anti-M or anti-N. Unlike the ABO or the Rh systems, the MN system does not appear to have any medical importance—probably because no antibodies are known to occur in humans. Antibodies neither occur naturally (the genetically determined ones as in the case of the ABO blood group) nor are induced (as in the Rh system).

An antigen closely linked to the MN locus is referred to by the term S. There appear to be only two alleles at this locus, Ss, with S dominant, so there are three genotypes: SS, Ss, ss. Both SS and Ss would be positive to the anti-S test, whereas s would not react to the antiserum. The S and the MN loci are linked so closely that there are no known cases of crossover. This means, as in the Rh system, that the genes are transmitted as a unit, a haplotype: MS, NS, and so on.

The MNS system is evenly distributed among most of the world's peoples with some major exceptions. The American Indians have a high frequency of haplotypes MS and Ms, in contrast to Australian Aboriginals, who have extremely high frequencies of N, especially Ns. The significance of these distributions, while interesting to the anthropologist, has yet to be determined, though they have been used as one more bit of evidence to compare ancestral relationship.

Duffy Blood Group

In addition to the systems already considered there are several less well-known blood groups. These groups are discovered, often by accident, when a patient has an unexpected reaction to a blood transfusion or gives birth to an erythroblastic infant even though the mother was Rh +. Careful immunological studies eventually identify the particular antigen involved. Family and population tests with the new antisera often show a variety of responses among the people, and a new antigen system is established. Often these systems are under the control of a single pair of alleles, and some of these new antigens prove useful in population genetic studies because of their distribution among our species. Such a system, which has

TABLE 3-4   Duffy Blood Group

GENOTYPE	PHENOTYPE
Fy^aFy^a	Fy (a + b −)
Fy^aFy^b	Fy (a + b +)
Fy^aFy^o	Fy (a + b −)
Fy^bFy^b	Fy (a − b +)
Fy^bFy^a	Fy (a + b +)
Fy^bFy^o	Fy (a − b +)
Fy^oFy^o	Fy (a − b −)

relatively little clinical importance but is valuable as a genetic marker, is the *Duffy blood group.*

There are two Duffy antisera, designated anti-Fy^a and anti-Fy^b. Most people around the world react to either one or the other antiserum, and many react to both. Ninety percent of central and West Africans and many African-Americans, however, are negative for Fy^a and Fy^b. Given these data, together with family studies, it appears that three alleles are involved: Fy^a, Fy^b, and Fy^o (Table 3-4).

Because Fy^a is virtually lacking in African populations, this blood type has proved useful for determining European admixture in African-Americans. In persons of European descent the frequency of Fy^a reaches a high of 90 percent, though it has not been widely studied in other groups except Africans (Table 3-5). Lack of the alleles in central Africa may be related to the incidence of malaria. There have been studies that reported that the Duffy antigens acted as red-cell surface receptors for the vivax malarial parasite causing it to cling to the red blood cell, thereby facilitating its entrance into the cell. Because of this attraction, persons lacking the Fy^a and Fy^b antigens would possibly be more resistant to the parasites. Should subsequent work support this initial observation, then natural selection could be demonstrated to favor Fy^o individuals in an environment with vivax type malaria (see chapter 6 for discussion of malaria and natural selection).

Diego Blood Group

Originally, this antigen was identified among certain Venezuelan Indians who had up to 30 percent positive response to the antibody (anti-Di^a). Its subsequent discovery among other Native American populations has caused it to be called an "American Indian" gene. It also occurs in some east Asian populations and among a few Papuan populations in New Guinea. The Diego type is absent in Europeans, Africans, and Eskimos. Too few population surveys, however, have been made to establish a more complete distribution. The Diego antigen causes no

TABLE 3-5   Frequency of Duffy Allele Fy^a in Various Populations

POPULATION	FREQUENCY OF Fy^a ALLELE (PERCENT)
Africa	
Upper Volta	0
Dahomey	0
Ghana	0
Nigeria	0
Kenya	
Kamba	0
Giryama	9.5
Bechuanaland	
Bushman (Central)	27.9
Bushman (Pooled sample)	31.2
South West Africa	
Bushman	15.7
Hottentot	27.9
Republic of South Africa	
Bantu	11.8
Congo	
Bantu	7.8
North America	
Black	21–26
White	43

Sources: Based on Hiernaux, 1966; and Reed, 1969.

medical problems but does add to a growing array of genetic markers that may distinguish between major population groupings.

Lutheran Blood Group

This system has not yet proved useful for population studies, as most of the world's peoples are Lu^b (0.96 in Europeans, 0.97 in Africans, and 1.0 in Asians). Tests thus far have identified only two alleles—Lu^a and Lu^b—though one example of Lu (a−b−) has been discovered in a single family lineage. The allele Lu^a is very rare and totally absent in many populations (Australian Aboriginals, Asians, and American Indians). The main interest of this system is its possible autosomal linkage to the secretor locus discussed earlier.

Xg Blood Group

The Xg system is X-linked and has been frequently studied because it provides an additional locus to assist in the "mapping" of the human X chromosome. A single antibody is known, anti-Xg^a, which identifies two types, Xg (a+) and Xg (a−). Family pedigrees suggest that the antigen is inherited as a codominant trait; Xg^aY males and Xg^aXg^a females react strongly to the antisera. The erythrocytes of Xg^aXg females have a weaker, more variable reaction. There has been no significant variation of frequency in the populations tested so far.

Blood Groups: An Overview

Studies of the red-cell antigen systems provide a way of distinguishing between individuals on the basis of their reactions to several antisera. These responses, as we have discussed, are determined by substances (antigens) on the surface of the blood cell that have a certain specific identity; they appear to be inherited, as shown here. In certain blood groups, the ABO and MN, for example, most of us respond in predictable ways. For the rarer, lesser-known systems, reactions to the antisera tests have been recorded less frequently (as an example, the Diego system). There are many more systems (the "private" antigens) that describe cross-reactions with antisera that are rare and have been identified only in a single family.

The great diversity of human blood types was illustrated by Stern (1973) when he described a study of 132 individuals who were tested for nine blood groups. Different combinations of the types of the nine systems were seen in 129 persons. If additional tests were added, it would be hypothetically possible to identify a person from blood type alone, just as can be done from fingerprints and is now accomplished by comparisons of DNA fragments.

This complexity need not concern us, however, nor should the student become dismayed at the large variety of human blood types. The variety merely demonstrates some of the broad polymorphisms of our species, which can be useful. The systems listed here provide a vital tool for the study of human genetics, identifying paternity and determining monozygous twins. Population studies also show that the red-cell antigens offer a means for analysis of population migration, admixture, and, perhaps, for study of the forces of natural selection because many distributions may be more different than would be expected from chance alone as we shall describe in chapter 6.

WHITE BLOOD CELL (WBC) (LEUKOCYTE) ANTIGENS

Another major cellular component of the blood, the *leukocytes*, has become an increasingly important focus for the study of inherited antigens. The leukocytes, or WBC are a group of cells whose function is to protect the body against infectious organisms and, normally, they are present in small numbers; about nine thousand compared to five million red blood cells in a microliter of blood. When the body is challenged by a micro-organism, the number of WBC increase dramatically; a large portion of these, about 40 percent, are lymphocytes found mostly in the lymph nodes, thymus, and spleen. The two different forms, T lymphocytes and B lymphocytes participate in the immune response by the production of antibodies. The effectiveness of these responses, including the activities of the other WBC (the *granulocytes* that engulf some of the foreign microbes and waste products) depends on the antigenicity of the invading organisms and the degree of similarity or dissimilarity to the host's tissues. In other words, the functioning of the WBC in their protective role depends on their antigen types and the antigen identity of the foreign substances, a process similar to the reaction of an Rh− pregnant woman to her Rh+ fetus described earlier. After years of research on the immune system, skin grafts, and organ transplants, the WBC are recognized as having a highly variable antigen system, even more complex than that described for the red blood cell (RBC) antigens.

There are many differences between the WBC and RBC. The WBC are found not only in the blood serum within the blood vessels but are also distributed throughout most tissues of the body in virtually every fluid surrounding the somatic cells. This wide distribution and their antibody functions explain, in part, the rejection of skin grafts and organ transplants. Attempts, over the years, to graft skin from one person to another failed because the recipient's system rejected the graft as material foreign to its own immune system. Grafts between identical twins proved to be successful, however. This success of twin grafts suggested that the immune-rejection process was genetically determined. Further evidence was provided by studies of the blood serum from patients who had been given multiple transfusions; their serum contained a variety of agglutinins (antibodies). Tests of these antibodies against blood samples taken from the general population resulted in the agglutination of WBC in 60 percent of the cases (Dausset et al., 1972). That is, some of the WBC "types" introduced into the patient through transfusion-stimulated antibody production and some did not. The individual's WBC were not affected by the antibodies in his or her own serum, however. Following this evidence of individual differences in the ability to produce a variety of antibodies of specific identity, family and twin studies were conducted. The results obtained by cross-typing and matching blood cells of close relatives established the mode of inheritance of WBC antigens. These earlier studies were followed by many others during the next three decades and have identified a large complex system of WBC antigen types.

Histocompatibility System (HLA)

The HLA, or antigen types of the WBC, is the most polymorphic system known, thus far, for humans. The antigens are, like the RBC antigens, molecules of sugars linked to a protein as part of the cell's surface membrane. They also come in a variety of forms, and their presence is detected by a reaction with an antibody. In addition to its location on the WBC, these antigens are also found widely dispersed throughout and are attached to all other cells except RBC, sperm, and certain placental cells.

The antigen types are determined by five loci on chromosome 6 and designated: HLA-A, HLA-B, HLA-C, HLA-D, and HLA-DR. Because there are from eight to forty alleles at each locus, the resulting multiplicity of allelic combinations of the five loci make any simple designation impossible. Normally, a person's HLA system is expressed as a *haplotype,* the listing of the allele present at each of the loci. For example, in a study of 334 people in England, the haplotype HLA *A1-B8-DR3* was found among 10.4 percent, which was a world high for this particular haplotype, whereas it was only half as frequent in most other western Europeans. By contrast, the most frequent haplotype found among Japanese populations was HLA *A24-BW52-DR2*, which occurred in 7.8 percent of the sample. Table 3-6 summarizes a variety of HLA haplotypes distributed among several population groups (Bodmer et al., 1987). With a clearer understanding of the antigenicity of the HLA system, tissue matches may be obtained by identifying the haplotypes of close relatives, a procedure that is a vital step in the preparation for organ transplants. Another important aspect is the protective function of the WBC in the immune system, outlined earlier. During the past 15 years, frequent associations have been reported between HLA types and certain diseases.

In addition to its clinical significance and because of its diversity throughout the species, the polymorphisms of the HLA system provide another set of genetic markers of human variability. Several geneticists and anthropologists have used such data to trace population migrations and to reconstruct ancestral relationships on the basis of HLA haplotype similarity or dissimilarity. The number of loci and the variety of alleles provide a means of gaining a closer perspective of interpopulation relationships.

HEMOGLOBINS AND RED BLOOD CELL (RBC) VARIANTS

Approximately 85 to 90 percent of the protein of the human RBC consists of the complex protein molecules *hemoglobin.* Hemoglobin is composed of four polypeptide chains, two *alpha chains* of 141 amino acids each and two *beta chains* of 146 amino acids each. Each of the four contains a *heme* group, a large molecule (porphyrin ring) containing an atom of iron that gives blood its red color. These iron atoms, within the center of the heme groups, will combine with two atoms of oxygen in the lungs and then transport it throughout the circulatory system to tissue where the oxygen

TABLE 3-6   Major HLA Haplotypes of Selected Populations

HLA HAPLOTYPES			POPULATIONS[a]												
			1	2	3	4	5	6	7	8	9	10	11	12	13
			percent of total sample												
A1	B8	DR3	10.4	5.1	5.1	7.1	8.9	9.1	12.1	5.3	—	1.5	3.7	3.6	2.2
A2	B35	DR4	0.1	—	0.4	0.1	—	—	—	—	1.9	—	14.8	3.6	—
A2	B35	DR5	—	0.4	0.7	0.4	—	—	—	5.3	0.6	—	—	—	—
A2	B35	DRW8	0.3	0.4	0.4	—	—	—	0.8	2.6	0.9	—	7.4	—	—
A2	B44	DR4	4.0	1.8	1.1	1.2	3.6	1.5	2.7	—	—	—	—	—	—
A24	B35	DR4	—	0.2	—	0.1	—	—	—	2.6	0.9	0.8	14.8	—	—
A24	B7	DR1	—	0.4	—	0.2	—	—	—	—	4.5	—	—	—	—
A24	BW52	DR2	—	—	—	—	—	—	—	—	7.8	—	—	—	—
A24	BW54	DR4	—	—	—	—	—	—	—	—	6.2	—	—	—	—
A26	B38	DR4	0.1	0.1	—	0.1	0.6	—	—	7.9	—	—	—	—	—
A28	BW58	DRW6	—	—	—	—	—	—	—	—	—	—	—	—	6.7
A3	B7	DR2	4.5	2.9	1.1	3.7	5.3	3.0	6.6	—	—	—	—	—	—
A30	B13	DR7	0.8	0.9	0.4	0.6	2.4	3.0	1.2	5.3	—	11.3	—	3.6	—
AW33	BW65	DR1	0.1	0.5	0.4	0.5	—	1.5	—	7.9	—	—	—	—	—

[a] Populations: 1. English, Celtic, Dutch, Scandinavian; 2. German, French, Italian, Spanish, Swiss; 3. Austrian, Yugoslavian Czech, Hungarian; 4. American, Canadian; 5. Australian; 6. South African Caucasoids; 7. other Caucasoids; 8. Jewish Ashk; 9. Japanese; 10. Chinese (including Chinese subsets); 11. American Indians; 12. Mexican; and 13. black Africans.

Source: Modified and selected from Bodmer et al., 1987.

is needed. The transport of oxygen and its release and the uptake of carbon dioxide as part of tissue respiration is a complex process dependent on several factors, and one of the major factors is the amino acid composition of hemoglobin.

The structure of hemoglobin is among the most thoroughly studied of any of the proteins. Its large size and number of amino acids lends itself well to a technique of analysis called *electrophoresis*. This is a method of separating proteins by applying an electric charge to proteins in solution or gel medium (Figure 3-4). Proteins with different amino acid composition move at various rates of speed in an electric field and, after a time lapse, those molecules with a higher charge move further from the origin than those of a lesser charge. This method has been used many times and numerous protein polymorphisms have been identified through separation of the polypeptide chains of different amino acid compositions. For

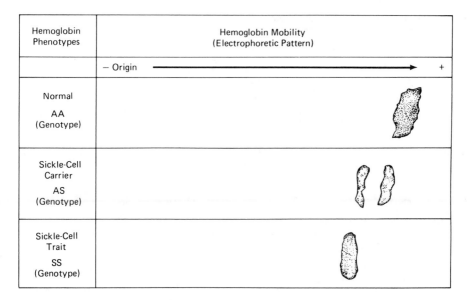

Hemoglobin Phenotypes	Hemoglobin Mobility (Electrophoretic Pattern)		
	− Origin ⟶		+
Normal AA (Genotype)			
Sickle-Cell Carrier AS (Genotype)			
Sickle-Cell Trait SS (Genotype)			

FIGURE 3-4 Separation of Hemoglobins by Electrophoresis.

example, these methods have identified several forms of human hemoglobin; thirty-six alpha-chain and fifty-seven beta-chain variants are known. Many of these variants differ by only a single amino acid in the entire polypeptide sequence of 141 (alpha chain) or 146 (beta chain). A sample of these changes in amino acid sequences are listed in Table 3-7. Certain amino acid substitutions reduce or radically alter hemoglobin function and may cause metabolic diseases such as *sickle-cell anemia* or *thalassemia*. There are other hemoglobin forms, however, that apparently do not interrupt the normal RBC function of oxygen transport.

The sequence of amino acids in hemoglobin is under genetic control as noted earlier. If the symbol of normal hemoglobin is Hb^A and Hb^S signifies the abnormal sickling type, then the mode of inheritance can be written:

$$Hb^A Hb^S \quad \times \quad Hb^A Hb^S \quad \text{parents}$$
$$Hb^A Hb^A \quad Hb^A Hb^S \quad Hb^S Hb^S \quad \text{children}$$

The Hb^S gene causes a single amino acid substitution, valine for glutamic acid at position 6 in the beta chain (see Table 3-7). The alleles Hb^A and Hb^S are codominant, and a heterozygote produces a combination of both normal and abnormal hemoglobin. RBC of the heterozygote will then contain molecules of both types, but with a larger proportion of the hemoglobin A. The homozygous recessive ($Hb^s Hb^s$) produces only hemoglobin molecules with the valine substitution.

TABLE 3-7   Major Alternation in Amino Acid Sequences

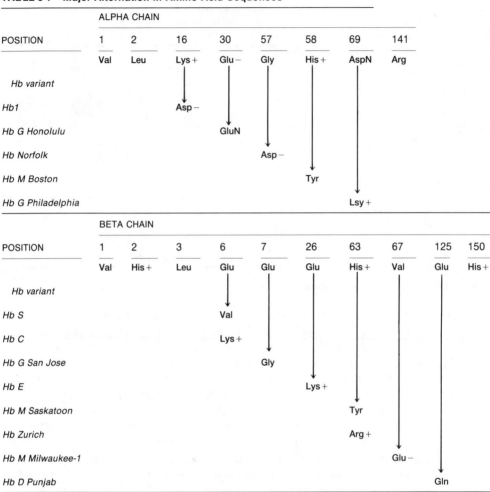

ALPHA CHAIN								
POSITION	1	2	16	30	57	58	69	141
	Val	Leu	Lys +	Glu −	Gly	His +	AspN	Arg
Hb variant								
Hb1			Asp −					
Hb G Honolulu				GluN				
Hb Norfolk					Asp −			
Hb M Boston						Tyr		
Hb G Philadelphia							Lsy +	

BETA CHAIN									
POSITION	1	2	3	6	7	26	63	67	125	150
	Val	His +	Leu	Glu	Glu	Glu	His +	Val	Glu	His +
Hb variant									
Hb S				Val					
Hb C				Lys +					
Hb G San Jose					Gly				
Hb E						Lys +			
Hb M Saskatoon							Tyr		
Hb Zurich							Arg +		
Hb M Milwaukee-1								Glu −	
Hb D Punjab									Gln

Source: Reprinted by permission from Watson, James D., *Molecular Biology of the Gene*, 4th ed. Menlo Park, Calif.: The Benjamin/Cummings Publishing Company, Inc., 1987, figure 8–8, p. 193.

This simple alteration in hemoglobin structure causes the cell to undergo a deformation in shape when oxygen is taken up by the surrounding tissues. As oxygen is given up by the hemoglobin molecules, the chains begin to alter their spatial orientation and will change to a series of helical-shaped fibers. The more oxygen removed the more hemoglobin molecules will alter until enough of these long fiber bundles have formed that, in turn, deform the blood cell. The shape of the deformed cell is crescent or sickle-like in appearance instead of its normal shape; hence the term *sickle cell* (Figure 3-5a, 3-5b, 3-5c). Persons with the

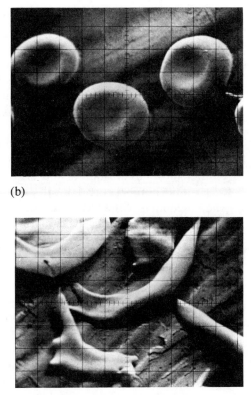

(b)

(c)

FIGURE 3-5   **(a) and (b) Normal Human Red Blood Cells, as Photographed in a Scanning Electron Microscope.** The magnification in (b) is about five times that in (a). (c) Some sickled human red blood cells, also photographed in a scanning electron microscope. (From Buettner-Janusch, J., *Physical Anthropology: A Perspective,* 1973. Copyright © 1973 by John Wiley & Sons, Inc. Reprinted by permission of the publisher.)

sickle-cell trait may survive for long periods with few cells sickling, depending on the rate of oxygen consumption. When, however, there is a greater demand for oxygen, which would occur during vigorous exercise, the tissues take up more oxygen from the RBC, causing more of the molecules to become deoxygenated; shape change follows, which brings on a sickling crisis. The cells distort and clog smaller blood vessels, especially in the peripheral circulatory system, and then they are destroyed by the body's own immune response.[6] The hemoglobin is released from

---

[6] The lifetime of a human red blood cell is between ninety and one hundred days; after this period, the cell is broken apart (hemolysed). Many of the constituent parts are preserved and "recycled" to be used again in the manufacture of new red blood cells. If this rate of synthesis of new red cells is exceeded by the rate of hemolysis, then anemia results.

the red blood cell when it bursts apart. Anemia and a whole host of associated afflictions will result (Figure 3-6). Depending on age, work habits, diet, and geography, a homozygote Hb^SHb^S may be at greater or lesser risk. A laborer is at greater risk than a person who has a sedentary occupation, for example. Exercise in the thinner atmosphere in the mountains or flying in planes with unpressurized cabins could bring on a crisis. By contrast the heterozygote carrier of the trait enjoys a degree of protection from the risk of a sickling crisis. The presence of Hb^A molecules mixed with the Hb^S prevents or reduces the probability of the abnormal hemoglobin forming fibers. The heterozygote's RBC function normally under most circumstances and only rarely do the cells sickle.

The homozygote Hb^SHb^S is a near-lethal combination because all hemoglobin is of the S type, and sickling crises may be frequent. Individuals with this combination have a high mortality rate. Though there are reports of some adult homozygotes leading normal productive lives in Ghana, West Africa, the odds are against individuals with the trait (Konotey-Ahulu, 1982). Only a few live to adulthood; average life expectancy is only twenty years in the United States and lower in Africa. Despite the high risk caused by possession of the Hb^S allele, it occurs at high frequency (10 to 20 percent) in many populations. These populations are distributed throughout central Africa, around the Mediterranean, among a few groups in eastern Turkey, and in parts of India (see chapter 6). Type E hemoglobin has a much more limited distribution; its highest frequencies occur among populations in India, Southeast Asia, and New Guinea. The distribution of these abnormal hemoglobins closely corresponds to the incidence of malaria and may reflect a resistance to the malarial parasite in the circulation. No hemoglobin abnormality is known to exist among native peoples of the New World. Abnormal hemoglobins in the New World occur in persons who are descendants of African slaves and a few others who have migrated from areas where these hemoglobin types are found.

Thalassemia, or Cooley's anemia, originally described an inherited condition of anemia found among many of the populations in several countries bordering the Mediterranean Sea. This condition is inherited as an autosomal dominant allele that depresses the synthesis in the beta-Hb chain (beta thalassemia), resulting in an imbalance of the quantity of alpha and beta chains. Such cells are unstable and are lost at a rapid rate in the homozygous person who will have a severe form of anemia (thalassemia major), and few survive childhood without medical care. The heterozygotes (thalassemia minor) may have a milder form and are usually free of symptoms. The reduction of beta-Hb production in the heterozygote is somewhat compensated for by a continued synthesis of the fetal hemoglobin form well into adult life. Despite this severe selection against the heterozygote, thalassemia is widespread throughout much of the Old World. In certain regions of Italy, for example, 35 percent of the people

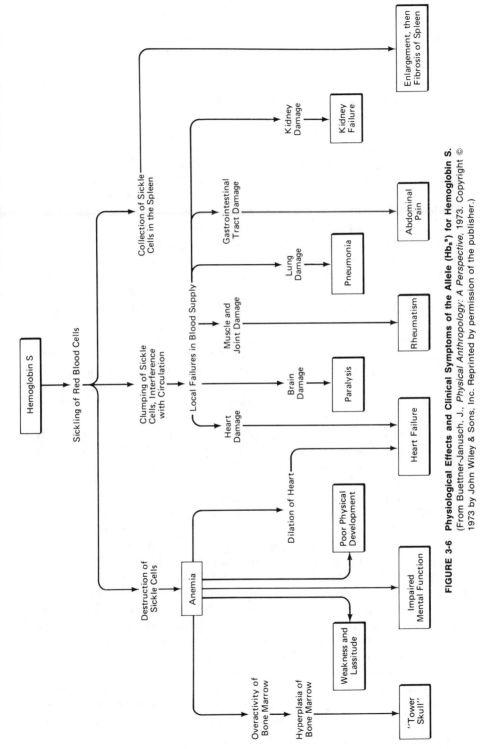

FIGURE 3-6 Physiological Effects and Clinical Symptoms of the Allele (Hb$_s$^{s}) for Hemoglobin S. (From Buettner-Janusch, J., *Physical Anthropology: A Perspective*, 1973. Copyright © 1973 by John Wiley & Sons, Inc. Reprinted by permission of the publisher.)

have some form of thalassemia. Similar high frequencies are seen in many North African populations, and in some Southeast Asian groups a different thalassemic gene frequency exceeds 15 percent.

Since the early days of the investigation of Cooley's anemia there has been an ever-expanding research effort in the studies of abnormalities of hemoglobin production. A remarkable number of mutations have been reported at the hemoglobin locus that reduce or prevent synthesis of the polypeptides resulting in shortened life-spans of the blood cells and anemias of varying degrees of severity. The discovery of this diversity of genes controlling synthesis of both chains has led to a clearer understanding of the synthesis of this vital protein. These variant forms of hemoglobin synthesis are classified as the *thalassemias*.

Here, rather than there being a single substitution of an amino acid as in the examples of the other abnormal hemoglobins, the synthesis of one or the other polypeptide chains is impaired. The type of thalassemia that retards beta-chain synthesis results in Hb with a surplus of alpha-chain peptides. The reverse is true when alpha-chain synthesis is blocked; an excess of beta polypeptides occurs. Each form of thalassemia is under the control of genes at different loci on chromosome 16 (alpha globin) and chromosome 11 (beta globin).

G6PD deficiency, a defect in the metabolism of the RBC that causes anemia under certain conditions, is an inherited condition in which there is less than normal activity of an enzyme, glucose-6-phosphate dehydrogenase (G6PD). Energy for cellular metabolism is provided by the conversion of glucose to lactate, and G6PD catalyzes the initial step in this conversion. The altered form of the G6PD enzyme is less efficient in its function and results in a reduced energy level in RBC. Also, the RBC's fragility is increased in persons with a G6PD deficiency who are prone to hemolytic anemia because the cells have a tendency to lyse (burst) when exposed to certain drugs, infective agents, or parasites.

The drug sensitivity of the RBC of certain people has been recognized since the 1920s when synthetic antimalarial drugs were first introduced as substitutes for quinine. Adverse responses were noted among many Asian soldiers serving in the British army. Later, in World War II and the Korean War, sensitivity was noted in about 10 percent of black American soldiers who suffered from anemia following administration of drugs such as primaquine. At the time, though a G6PD deficiency was not identified as the reason, it was recognized that some conditions existed in the RBC of these patients that caused cell destruction when exposed to these drugs. The anemia diminished when the source of irritant was removed and cell count returned to normal.

This transient form of anemia, which also appears as an allergic reaction of some persons on exposure to plant components of the fava bean, has been known throughout the Mediterranean for many years.

Fava beans have been a dietary staple of many populations of the region for centuries; hence the condition of sensitivity to the bean and plant pollen has been called *favism*. The similarity between the two types of anemic responses, one to antimalarial drugs and the other to the plant substances, is now established. The exact nature of the deficiency was determined in the late 1950s through laboratory tests devised to identify the susceptible individuals. It was found that the susceptible individuals had lower G6PD activity in their RBC than those persons whose cells did not hemolyze (burst apart) under the test procedures.

Once these test procedures were refined and proved effective in identifying afflicted individuals, many thousands of blood samples were examined. Deficiencies were found to occur more frequently in males than in females, suggesting that G6PD synthesis is under the control of an X-linked locus, which is now mapped to the same region as the color blindness and hemophilia loci. Males, with normal G6PD have quantities of type A or type B, the most common type, whereas the deficient males have either A − or B − type. Females who are G6PD deficient would be homozygotes for the defect A − or B − alleles. Heterozygote females tend to have a mixture of normal and abnormal RBC because only one of the X chromosomes are active in each of the cells of the blood-forming tissues.

Since these original studies, two hundred other variants of G6PD have been reported (Table 3-8). Fortunately, most of these are quite rare and only about one-half of the variants appear to be sensitive to hemolytic agents. These variants exist in numerous populations from New Guinea to India, Italy to Africa, and throughout the Middle East. The highest frequency of G6PD deficiency is found in countries around the Mediterranean, particularly among Egyptians and populations on the island of Sardinia. The variant Gd(A−) is frequent—about 20 percent among

TABLE 3-8   Classes of Some Common G6PD Variants

CLASS	POPULATION	ENZYME ACTIVITY
Gd B	Majority	Normal level
Gd A+	African	Near normal
Gd A−[b]	African	10–60% of normal
Gd B−[a,b]	Mediterranean	0–5% of normal
Gd Canton[a,b]	Chinese	4–25% of normal
Gd Anant[b]	Thailand	Near normal
Gd Mahidol[b]	Thailand	5–16% of normal
Gd Mahidol[b]	Thailand	5–16% of normal
Gd Hektoen	Thailand	Above normal

[a] Sensitive to fava bean.
[b] Sensitive to certain oxidizing drugs.
Sources: Data selected from McKusick, 1986; Vogel and Motulsky, 1986.

Africans. The more severe variant form, Gd(B −), is found in frequencies of 15 to 20 percent in Greece, Sardinia, and the Middle East (Beutler, 1983:1635).

Finally, these red-cell variants, the abnormal hemoglobins, G6PD deficiency, and thalassemia, are not confined to a single geographical area nor are they unique to a particular "racial" group. The genes for these variants are widespread throughout many of the world's peoples and closely follow the distribution of malaria. No explanation of migration and admixture has been able to account completely for these distributions. Major migrations of the world's peoples have undoubtedly been involved in the dispersal of these mutant genes, but other factors are also important, as is shown in chapter 6.

POLYMORPHISMS OF SERUM PROTEINS[7]

In addition to hemoglobins and red-cell enzymes, many serum proteins are polymorphic. Their synthesis is under genetic control, and when mutations occur there are slight structural changes similar to those described for the hemoglobins. Blood serum, the fluid part of the blood with fibrin removed, provides a variety of easily studied proteins. Electrophoresis techniques readily separate many protein fractions into different groups (Figure 3-7). The several globulin fractions show an enormous range of variability and the albumins once thought to be a protein of little variation, now are also known to be highly polymorphic. Many polymorphisms of the globulin and albumin system have been detected, and significant differences between racial groups have been recorded. The meaning of this diversity is not always apparent, but some clues are provided by the following examples.

Immunoglobulins (Gamma Globulins)

These are a group of antibodies specific for certain foreign antigens introduced as mold, pollen grains, or the proteins of an infectious organism. Each person has the capacity to synthesize an enormous number of different antibodies, and this synthesis occurs within the B-lymphocyte cells in circulation. Only a small part of this antibody production capacity is realized, however, because it depends on the stimulation of the B cells. Once stimulated, the cells begin to divide producing identical cells that secrete the antibody specific to the antigen. This is one of the means by which the body defends against infections and other harmful agents. The other major defense mechanisms are the macrophages, a type of white

[7] A locus with two or more alleles is considered polymorphic if the least-frequent alleles have a frequency of greater than 1 percent.

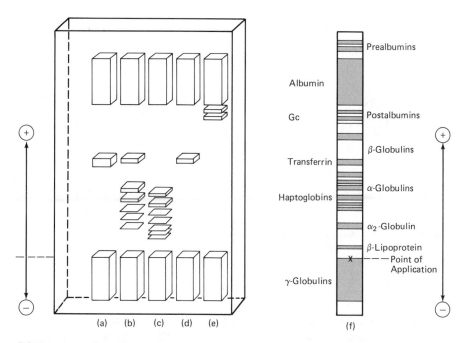

FIGURE 3-7   Relative Electrophoretic Mobilities of Protein Constituents of Human Serum. (a), (b), (c) Haptoglobins, phenotypes Hp 1-1, Hp 2-1, Hp 2-2, respectively; (d) transferrin, TfC; (e) group-specific component,-phenotype Gc 2-1; and (f) composite showing relative electrophoretic mobilities of important constituents of serum. (These diagrams show the relative positions of the various components after electrophoresis in alkaline starch gels; variations in conditions of electrophoresis lead to changes in resolution of some of the proteins.) (From Buettner-Janusch, J., *Physical Anthropology: A Perspective*, 1973. Copyright © 1973 by John Wiley & Sons, Inc. Reprinted by permission of the publisher.)

blood cell that engulfs and destroys foreign substances, and the T lymphocytes in the thymus gland that regulates the immune responses of the other cells.

This group of slow-moving globulins consists of highly variable and complex protein molecules composed of four polypeptides, a pair of "heavy chains," each linked to a smaller or "light chain" (Figure 3-8). Most of the heavy chain is a constant region, a stable amino acid sequence, whereas the part that is linked to the light chain is highly variable. The amino acid arrangement of the light chain varies to conform to the identity of the antibody that attaches to this region. Comparisons of the constant heavy chain regions among the immunoglobulins reveal five classes whose functions vary (Table 3-9).

The IgG group of immunoglobulins is the most plentiful and have been extensively studied. The constant part of the heavy chains shows a great deal of polymorphism and are described as the GM system, which has at least twenty specific antisera reactions. Though some of these

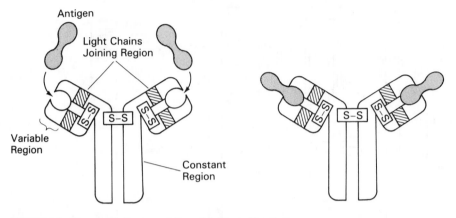

FIGURE 3-8   Diagramatic Representation of Antibody Structure

The antibody is a complex of light and heavy chains of polypeptides linked together by two sulfur atoms (S-S). They consist of a basic constant chain linked to a variable region which has a structure specific for a particular antigen. This recognition site binds and inactivates the antigen as illustrated.

reactions are inherited as simple codominant alleles and the amino acid sequence of each region of the chain is under control of a separate locus, it is not clear how many genetic loci are involved. The loci do appear to be closely linked, each with several codominant alleles.

There is a variation in the frequency of occurrence of several of the *GM types* among the world's populations that have been tested. Table 3-10 illustrates this variation of the major GM groups. The haplotypes are the clusters of specific GM types that occur together in an individual. They apparently are transmitted genetically as a unit, and distinct differences are found between several populations. This distribution of the antibody system's polymorphisms suggests varying levels of ability to react to certain classes of disease-causing organisms. Combinations found in some populations but not in others suggest that natural selection is operating, but direct correlations between GM types and a particular disease have not been made.

TABLE 3-9   Types of Immunoglobulins

TYPE	PLASMA CONCENTRATION (μ/ml)	FUNCTIONS
IgG	12,100	Inactivates bacteria & virus
IgA	2600	Neutralizes toxins
IgM	930	Inactivates bacteria & virus
IgD	23	Unknown
IgE	0.5	Activates allergic responses

TABLE 3-10   Common GM Haplotypes in Various Populations Tested for Nine Factors

	A	B	C	D	E	F	G	H	I	J	K	HAPLOTYPES	
European	+	+	+									A	(1, 17, 21)
(Caucasoids)												B	(1, 2, 17, 21)
Mongoloids	+	+						+	+			C	(3, 5, 13, 14)
												D	(1, 5, 13, 14, 17)
Ainu	+	+						+		+		E	(1, 5, 14, 17)
New Guinea	+	+	+						+			F	(1, 5, 6, 17)
Australian	+	+										G	(1, 5, 6, 14, 17)
												H	(1, 13, 17)
African (Negroids)				+	+	+	+					I	(1, 3, 5, 13, 14)
												J	(2, 7, 21)
Bushmen	+		+				+			+	K	(1, 5, 17)	

Source: From Harrison et al., 1977. Copyright © 1977 Oxford University Press. Reprinted by permission of the publisher.

Haptoglobins

The haptoglobins are another group of serum proteins that are of particular interest. They are part of the alpha$_2$ globulins and have the capacity to combine with the free hemoglobin released into the plasma when a red blood cell lyses. This attachment to the haptoglobin prevents the hemoglobin from being lost through excretion in the kidneys. The haptoglobin-hemoglobin complex is carried by the circulatory system to the site where new red blood cells are formed, and the hemoglobin is "recycled." Alternatively, the hemoglobin complex is transported to the liver where the heme is converted to bilirubin. Three types of haptoglobin have been identified, each apparently under genetic control through the action of a pair of nondominant alleles. The genotypes and phenotypes would appear as follows:

GENOTYPES	PHENOTYPES
Hp^1Hp^1	Haptoglobin 1-1
Hp^1Hp^2	Haptoglobin 1-2
Hp^2Hp^2	Haptoglobin 2-2

The occurrence of different haptoglobins varies widely (Table 3-11). The

TABLE 3-11   Geographic Distribution of Hp[1] Gene

POPULATION	NUMBER TESTED	Hp[1] FREQUENCY
Europe		
Norway	1000	0.36
France	406	0.40
England	218	0.41
Italy (South)	752	0.32
Poland	151	0.36
Africa (North)		
Nigeria: Yoruba[a]	99	0.87
Senegal	398	0.63
Africa (East)		
Uganda[a]	165	0.63
Africa (Central)		
Congo: Metropolitan	151	0.77
Tutsi	86	0.52
Pygmies[a]	125	0.40
Africa (South)		
Zulu	113	0.53
Hottentot	59	0.51
Bushmen	113	0.29
Asia		
China: Hong Kong	122	0.29
Japan	822	0.28
Thailand	682	0.24
South India: Tamils	291	0.09
Todas	89	0.35
Pakistan	392	0.21
North America		
Alaska: Eskimos	418	0.30
Arizona: Navajo	263	0.45
New Mexico: Apache	98	0.59
Mexico: Lacandon	89	0.92
Central America		
Panama: Cuna	174	0.38
South America		
Ecuador: Quechua	192	0.78
Bolivia: Aymara	71	0.70
Brazil: Xavante	78	0.46
Pacific Islands		
Australian Aborigines		
North Queensland	493	0.17
New Guinea	82	0.66
Philippines	293	0.38
Samoa	80	0.59
Tonga	200	0.60

[a] Hp[0] phenotype greater than 10 percent.

Source: From Giblett, E. R., *Genetic Markers in Human Blood*, 1969. Copyright © 1969 by F. A. Davis, Co. Reprinted by permission of the publisher.

highest frequency of Hp^1 appears in tropical populations. Though the adaptive significance is not yet clear, it may be related to a type of environmental selection, because Hp^1 has a greater affinity for Hb and hence a higher binding capacity. This may be an advantage in certain populations where hemolytic anemia is very high. Persons with Hb^SHb^A or Hb^SHb^S genotypes would appear to benefit from Hp^1.

Transferrins

Another serum protein variant is a beta-globulin (transferrins) that binds atoms of iron and transports them to the tissues as needed, especially to the bone marrow where hemoglobin is formed. Also, transferrins assist in the absorption of iron through tissue membranes, especially dietary iron through the gut wall. These functions are graphically illustrated in persons with a rare recessive gene that results in a total lack of transferrin (McKusick, 1975). These persons suffered from severe iron deficiency anemia despite an excess of the mineral.

Transferrins exist in at least seventeen forms as identified by electrophoresis methods, and each seems to be under genetic control of an autosomal nondominant allele. The several variants fit into one of the three groups: most are in group TfC and a slower group (TfD), whereas only a few types occur in a rare group, TfB. These polmorphisms are distributed unevenly throughout the species, and several populations have only a single type (Table 3-12). The significance of this polymorphism of the iron-binding protein is not known, but there may be some relationship to its binding capacity. Such a difference would make certain forms more efficient in some populations, as was suggested for haptoglobins. An increase in combining capacity would be advantageous to populations in which a large percentage of the people were subject to chronic anemia. Any advantage, no matter how slight, in the absorption and transport of this vital element would contribute to survival.

INBORN ERRORS OF METABOLISM

Some of the most useful of the genetic markers in the study of human populations are defects in the metabolism. Many of these defects are due to a lack of enzymes that regulate important steps in our intermediate metabolism. Because of these deficiencies, proteins are not synthesized, carbohydrates are not converted to energy, lipids (fats) are not properly utilized, or essential substances are not transported or stored. Examples of all of these problems have been identified in the human genome, many of which are due to a recessive allele. Fortunately, most of these inherited conditions are extremely rare with only a few cases identified in the

TABLE 3-12   Frequencies of Three Transferrin Groups

POPULATION	NUMBER TESTED	FREQUENCY		
		Tf C	Tf B's (Fast)	Tf D's (Slow)
Asia				
India				
Tamil	291	1.000		
Toda	89	1.000		
Ceylon				
Singhalese	159	0.988	0.006 B_2C	0.006 CD_1
Tamil	140	1.000		
Veddah	64	0.890		0.094 CD_1 0.016 D_1
Japan	822	0.984	0.001 BC	0.015 CD
Africa				
Nigeria				
Habe	120	0.850		0.150 CD_1
Fulani	111	0.937		0.063 CD_1
Fulani	68	0.838		0.147 CD_1 0.015 D_1
Ibo	70	0.871		0.129 CD_1
Congo				
Nonmetropolitan	446	0.933		0.067 CD_1
Pygmy	121	0.934		0.066 CD_1
South Africa				
Hottentot	59	0.932		0.068 CD_1
Zulu	116	0.974		0.026 CD_1
Bushmen	113	0.876		0.115 CD_1 0.009 D_1

Source: After Buettner-Janusch, 1966. Copyright © 1966 by John Wiley & Sons, Inc. Reprinted by permission of the publisher.

medical literature. A catalogue of Mendelian traits in humans has been prepared that lists these genetic defects together with all known traits of the human genome and is updated periodically (McKusick, 1986).

The few examples described subsequently illustrate how a slight change in a single step in a biochemical pathway can have major, sometimes fatal, consequences. Since Garrod's classic paper in 1902 describing an inherited biochemical defect, *alkaptonuria,* there has been a continuous search for other such disorders, and many inherited enzyme defects have been reported. Most of these traits are diseases, a pathology of the metabolism. Some manifest themselves as a block in a biochemical pathway and are easily identified, such as PKU, or they may appear as a complex phenotype, like *emphysema,* the destruction of membranes of the lungs. A partial list of the more common recessive diseases in *Homo sapiens* is provided in Table 3-13. These examples all suggest the extent of the possibilities of error in a complex metabolic system like our own. All ethnic groups, have their share of inherited diseases, though some occur

TABLE 3-13   Incidence of Common Recessive Diseases

DISEASE	INCIDENCE PER MILLION BIRTHS
Severe mental defects (excluding aminoacidurias)[a]	800
Deafness (severe)[a]	500
Cystic fibrosis	400
Blindness[a]	200
Adrenogenital syndromes[a]	100
Albinism	100
Phenylketonuria (PKU)	100
Treatable aminoacidurias (excluding PKU)[a,b]	50
Untreatable aminoacidurias (excluding PKU)[a,b]	50
Mucopolysaccharidoses (all forms)[c]	50
Tay-Sachs disease	10
Galactosemia	5
Total	2365

[a] These diseases exist in multiple forms.
[b] Aminoacidurias are diseases, like PKU, that are caused by accumulation of an amino acid because of an enzyme block owing to an inborn error of metabolism. Some thirteen diseases are included under these two headings.
[c] Mucopolysaccharidoses are diseases, like Hurler's syndrome, that are caused by a defect in the metabolism of certain types of complex sugars (the mucopolysaccharides), whose accumulation in various tissues causes a variety of gross developmental abnormalities.

Source: From Jones, A., and W. F. Bodmer, *Our Future Inheritance: Choice or Chance*, 1974. Copyright © 1974 by Oxford University Press. Reprinted by permission of the publisher.

more frequently in certain populations than in others because of a past history of natural selection, size, or migration.

Phenylketonuria

Phenylketonuria (PKU) is a disease caused by the inheritance of an autosomal recessive gene. Individuals homozygous for this allele are unable to metabolize an essential amino acid, phenylalanine, which occurs in nearly all proteins. In a normal person and in the heterozygote, the excess taken in through the diet that is not used for protein synthesis is oxidized into tyrosine. The homozygote recessives have a block in their metabolic pathway (Figure 3-9), and large quantities of phenylalanine—up to fifty times normal—accumulate in the blood. Some of this excess is oxidized, through another pathway, to phenylpyruvic acid. The PKU defect actually affects a series of biochemical steps. At certain of these steps other enzyme defects occur that are inherited as recessives. One of these is *alkaptonuria*, which causes alkaptones to be excreted in the urine. These cause an affected person's urine to turn black when exposed to the air. No severe effects result from this condition, at least none comparable with those of

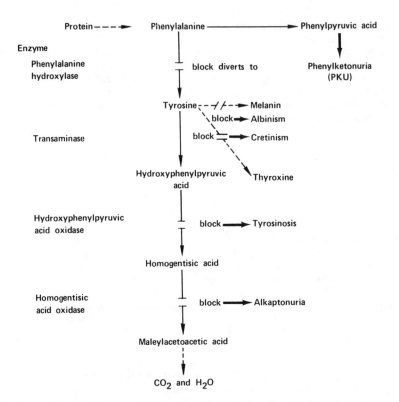

FIGURE 3-9   Metabolic Pathway for Phenylalanine and Tyrosine. The first step in the metabolic breakdown of the essential amino acid phenylalanine is mediated by a liver-produced enzyme, phenylalanine hydroxylase. This enzyme is responsible for the substitution of an OH group for an H atom in phenylalanine, converting it to the amino acid tyrosine. Tyrosine, in turn, through a series of intermediate steps is converted into melanin, the skin pigment, and other substances. It is also broken down further along the pathway illustrated, in which the existence of intermediary steps is indicated by dotted arrows. If phenylalanine hydroxylase is absent, phenylalanine is in part converted into phenylpyruvic acid, which accumulates, together with phenylalanine, in the bloodstream. These substances are toxic to the central nervous system and lead to phenylketonuria. Other genetic metabolic defects in the tyrosine pathway towards oxidation are also known. As indicated in the diagram, absence of enzymes operating between tyrosine and melanin is the cause of albinism. Two other blocks illustrated produce tyrosinosis, a rare defect that causes hydroxyphenylpyruvic acid to accumulate in the urine, but requires no treatment, and alkaptonuria, which makes urine turn black on exposure to air, causes pigmentation to appear in the cartilage, and produces symptoms of arthritis. Another block in a different pathway, somewhat more complex, produces thyroid deficiency leading to goiterous cretinism. (From Lerner, M. I., and W. J. Libby, *Heredity, Evolution and Society*, 2nd ed., 1976. W. H. Freeman and Company. Copyright © 1976.)

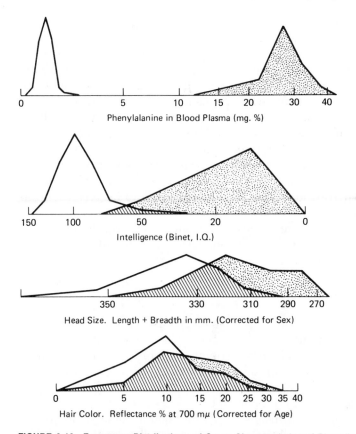

Phenylalanine in Blood Plasma (mg. %)

Intelligence (Binet, I.Q.)

Head Size. Length + Breadth in mm. (Corrected for Sex)

Hair Color. Reflectance % at 700 mμ (Corrected for Age)

FIGURE 3-10   Frequency Distributions of Some Characteristics of Phenylketonuria in Phenylke-tonuric Patients (Shaded) and in Control Populations. Hair color and head size show pronounced overlap, and intelligence shows some overlap. The level of phenylalanine in the blood, however, is higher in all phenylketonurics than in controls. If intelligence were the only phenotype used in the analysis, the genotype would be said to be non-penetrant in a small proportion of cases. When plasma level of phenylalanine is the phenotype, the genotype is found to be fully penetrant. (From McKusick, Victor A., *Human Genetics*, 2nd ed., 1969. Copyright © 1969 by Prentice-Hall, Inc. Redrawn from Penrose, *Ann. Eugenics*, 16 (1951), 134.)

PKU. Darkly pigmented granules appear in the affected person's cartilage, however, and occasionally symptoms of arthritis result. This metabolic defect is rare, approximately one case in a million.

The excess levels of phenylalanine and phenylketones are substances toxic to the developing central nervous system of the infant and young child. If the two substances persist in the bloodstream, they do severe damage to the brain. Untreated, the PKU individual will suffer severe mental retardation and that person's IQ will be significantly lower than normal; a victim's usual IQ range is from 20 to 80 (Figure 3-10).

The Guthrie test for PKU in newborns was begun in the 1960s in Europe, North America, and Asia; since then, millions of infants have been examined. Europeans and Americans of European descent had the highest frequencies from one in six thousand to about one in twenty thousand births. It is extremely rare among Japanese, African-Americans, and Ashkenazi Jews. Even among Europeans the gene frequency for the PKU recessive is highly variable; eastern Ireland has about one PKU infant per seven thousand births (a calculated gene frequency of 0.014) in contrast to one in eighteen thousand births in London (a gene frequency of 0.007). Scandinavian populations have even lower frequencies (0.0038), whereas in several eastern European populations the PKU trait is nearly as high as eastern Ireland. These tests have proved to be very useful in the identification of those infants at risk and, if the PKU condition is identified at birth, treatment begins immediately. By carefully managing the dietary levels of the amino acid, phenylalanine, the infant can grow and will develop normally.

Albinism

Many of the inborn errors of human metabolism require sophisticated biochemical methods to identify, but a few traits result in obvious, easily recognized phenotypes. The most striking and highly visible of these phenotypes is *albinism,* total or near total lack of pigmentation in skin, hair, and the iris of the eyes. Albinism has been recognized in many populations for centuries, and the condition varies in frequency from one in 20,000 births among Europeans to one in 2,000 in some West African populations. In several small, isolated, inbred populations the frequency is reported to be as high as 1 in 146 live births; the Cuna, a Carib Indian group occupying islands off the Caribbean coast of Panama, and the Hopi of Arizona are populations with such an exceptionally high frequency of albinos.

There are several types of inherited defects in the synthesis of melanin, the pigment of the skin. The majority of albinism is due, however, to a recessive allele that causes a lack of the enzyme, tyrosinase, which is necessary for the conversion of the amino acid tyrosine to melanin. Other inherited defects in melanin synthesis have been identified and have raised doubts about a single locus explanation when an albino couple gave birth to two normally pigmented children. The phenomenon of *complementation* (the additive effect of gene products from different loci) was offered to explain how two individuals, apparently with the same defect, produce phenotypically normal individuals. Though both parents lacked pigmentation, mother and children tested positive for tyrosinase. The father tested negative for this enzyme, as expected for an albino (type I). The explanation is that at least two different genetic loci are involved in the production of melanin. The albino parents were homozygote recessive at different loci, which is illustrated in the following way:

Parents   *aaBB* × *AAbb*
(Albino)   (Albino)

Children   *aABb*
(normal)

There are several other types of albinism, and several additional cases of complete or partial depigmentation have been reported. These are recessive traits, but at least one example described is due to a dominant allele (McKusick 1986).

Some Variations in Sugar Metabolism

The major source of energy for the metabolic processes of the body is a simple sugar, glucose derived from several kinds of complex carbohydrates of the diet. These complexes of starch and sugars must first be broken down into simpler structures in the small intestine so they can be absorbed into the bloodstream. This hydrolysis or cleavage into smaller molecular structures is mediated by enzymes for that particular carbohydrate compound. For example, *amylase* is the enzyme that brings about the hydrolysis of starches, *sucrase* the enzyme for sucrose (cane sugar), and *lactase* the enzyme that causes hydrolysis of milk sugar, lactose. There are many more enzymes that play essential roles in the digestion, energy conversion, or storage of carbohydrates that are ingested by the human diet. A reduction or an absence of certain of these enzymes are known to be inherited as described subsequently.

Lactase Deficiency

As in the case of most mammals, the newborn human's source of food for the first few months or even years (in some cultures) is the milk secreted by the mother's mammary glands. In addition to protein and fat, the secretion contains an important carbohydrate, lactose, the principle source of energy for the growing infant. This milk sugar is a complex molecular structure that cannot be absorbed into the blood stream. It must be first split into its simpler components, glucose and galactose, which are then absorbed through the cells lining the upper intestinal tract and enter the bloodstream. The enzyme, *lactase,* catalyzes this breakdown of the lactose sugar, and the enzyme is secreted in large quantities by the cells lining the walls of the upper intestinal track in infants and young children. Following the weaning period as the individuals change their diet to solid food, the lactase enzyme reduces to 10 percent or less of the level present in the infant. The level and activity of the enzyme may be maintained into adult life in some individuals or disappear altogether depending on the continued use of fresh milk from dairy herds and on the presence of an autosomal dominant allele for lactase.

Most humans, in recent times and even today, rarely consume milk after weaning; even many pastoral peoples ferment the milk in some form before consumption and seldom use it fresh. In its fermented form, bacteria do the job of the lactase and split the milk sugar into products easily digested. Most humans are classified as lactose malabsorbers. Virtually all Asian and Africans are malabsorbers as well as many Europeans (Table 3-14). There are populations, however, in which a high frequency of adults maintain the ability to digest lactose, and these are found mainly in Europe and among a few pastoral tribes in East Africa. All have a long history of direct consumption of fresh milk from their cattle, goats, or reindeer. This experience over the centuries, plus a genetic factor, has contributed to a population with a high rate of lactose digestion. Careful analysis of family pedigrees in Finland, for example, showed that those adults who were unable to digest lactose had inherited the lactase deficiency as an autosomal recessive trait; adults who were absorbers were either homozygous dominants or heterozygotes, and the malabsorbers were homozygous recessives (Flatz et al., 1982; Sahi, 1978).

Avoidance of fresh milk is an indicator of malabsorption because of

TABLE 3-14   Frequency of Lactase Deficiency

GROUP	NO. OF SUBJECTS	PERCENT DEFICIENT
American Negro	97	74 (approximately)
Batutsi (Rwanda)	12	17
Bahina (Angola)	11	9
Australian Aborigines		
Papunya (all less than 15 years old)	25	90
Maningrida (age range 6 to 48 months; mean 22 months)	19	80
Greenland Eskimos	32	72
American Indian (Chami, Colombia)	24	100
American Indian	3	67
Chinese	20	85
Formosa	7	
United States	3	
Philippines	10	
Baganda (Africa)	17	94
Bantu (Africa)	35	89
Thai (Thailand)	140	97
Thai (Thailand)	75	100

Source: Based on McCracken, 1971.

the gastrointestinal distress caused by undigested lactase while the use of fresh milk is taken as evidence of effective digestion. Anecdotal evidence describes a high frequency of the lactase persistence allele among many of the cattle herders of East Africa. Among the Orma, a cattle herding people of Kenya, fresh milk is frequently consumed, especially during the dry period. All adults and children partake without the distressful symptoms of the malabsorption syndrome, except for one twelve-year-old male of mixed parentage; his mother was Bantu, an agricultural group living nearby (Ensminger, personal communication 1990). Similar observations have been offered for Europeans where the observed differences in use of milk by adults have been confirmed by laboratory tests for lactase phenotypes (Flatz et al., 1982). In sum, milk-using experience has contributed to a high frequency of the gene for adult lactase persistence in some peoples of the world.

Galactosemia

There are several other genetic abnormalities of carbohydrate metabolism, though, fortunately, most are rare. One of the better-known defects is *galactosemia*, which is the inability to convert galactose to glucose. This metabolic defect is inherited as an autosomal recessive trait. Persons homozygous for the allele lack the enzyme (galactose-1-phosphate uridyltransferase) necessary to convert galactose, one of the sugars produced when a molecule of lactose, milk sugar, is split during digestion. Heterozygotes have quantities of the enzyme that are intermediate between normals and the afflicted person.

Within a few days or weeks of birth, the afflicted infant begins to show signs of distress and an impairment in its ability to digest milk. If allowed to go untreated, the accumulation of galactose in the blood leads to several serious conditions: stunted growth, enlarged liver, mental retardation, and cataracts. Fortunately, galactosemia is rare (from 1 in 65,000 births in Europe to 1 in 118,000 reported in Massachusetts), but the several known cases may be due to a recessive at different loci. The galactosemia cases do provide, however, another example of inherited defects in metabolism that result in the lack of a single enzyme (Vogel and Motulsky, 1986).

OTHER METABOLIC DEFECTS

In addition to inherited disorders of carbohydrate metabolism, there are several examples of enzyme deficiencies that affect the organic bases of the DNA or the lipid (fat) coverings of nerve fibers. Some are quite rare, occurring only in a few inbred lineages, whereas others are present at distressingly high frequencies. McKusick (1986) lists several thousand for which the mode of inheritance is known. A few disorders are described below as examples of those genetic defects that are of anthropological interest.

Errors in Purine Metabolism

Whenever there is an excess of purines like the organic bases of the DNA and RNA nucleotides, adenine and guanine, for example, the compounds are converted through several steps to an ultimate end product, uric acid. A normal person excretes a soluble form of the excess uric acid through the urine. There are several metabolic abnormalities, however, that cause uric acid to accumulate in the tissue in crystalline form, causing much pain. *Gout* is a common term for this disease, which actually occurs in several forms and more often in males. Some individuals have a tendency for this disease because of an inherited enzyme defect, which appears to be an X-linked recessive trait. Overeating, especially a diet high in proteins, increases the uric acid produced and can bring on the symptoms of joint pain and swelling.

Another form of purine acid metabolism deficiency is accompanied by an elevated uric acid excretion and a peculiar form of self-destructive behavior. The afflicted child, always male, chews off his lips and if not restrained will bite off the ends of the fingers. This Lesch-Nyhan syndrome has attracted much attention since its description in the 1960s, and biochemists have identified an enzyme deficiency in the pathway of conversion of the purine nucleic acids. The deficiency is inherited as an X-linked recessive trait, and though the female carrier can be identified she does not show any of the symptoms.

Errors in Pyrimidine Metabolism

The end products of pyrimidine (organic bases like cytosine, thymine, and uracil) metabolism are highly soluble, unlike the products of purine metabolism. Thus, an overproduction of pyrimidines does not cause any pathological symptoms to appear, but there are certain enzyme deficiencies in pyrimidine metabolism that are inherited and that result in certain detectable compounds. One such compound is beta-aminoisobutyric acid (BAIB). This substance is formed by the breakdown of pyrimidines, and is further reduced to carbon dioxide and ammonia by the action of a transaminase enzyme. High rates of excretion have been measured in some people who are homozygous for this recessive allele. Their metabolism is otherwise normal except for the excretion rate of BAIB. In addition, persons undergoing radiation treatment for cancer excrete large amounts because of the high rate of destruction of DNA in the cancer cells.

There appears to be no pathology associated with high excretion of BAIB. Persons who are low excretors (less than 40 mg/day) appear to be no more or less fit than high excretors (300 mg/day). With the exception of a correlation with radiation treatment for cancer just noted, there appears to be no disease correlation for BAIB excretion. There is a significant geographical distribution of populations with high excretors, however (Table 3-15). Many excretors are seen among Asians; in contrast, Europeans and Americans of European descent tend to be low in number (only 10 percent are high excretors). Among African-Americans, excretors are more frequent, but they still number far below the percentage of high excretors in Asian populations. Though the meaning of this metabolic variation is not clear and fitness does not appear to be influenced, the phenotype provides another interesting marker for the study of human polymorphisms.

TABLE 3-15   Distribution of BAIB Excretors

POPULATION	NUMBER TESTED	FREQUENCY OF HIGH EXCRETORS
North America		
European descent		
Michigan	71	0.03
Texas	255	0.10
New York	218	0.10
New York	148	0.11
African descent		
Michigan	25	0.20
New York	38	0.15
Indians		
Apache	110	0.59
Apache	113	0.42
Eskimo	120	0.23
Chinese	33	0.45
Japanese	41	0.41
Central America		
African descent (Black Caribs)	285	0.32
Asia		
India	16	0
Thailand	13	0.46
Marshall Islands		
Rongelap	188	0.86
Utirik	18	0.83

Source: After Buettner-Janusch, 1966. Copyright © 1966 by John Wiley & Sons, Inc. Reprinted by permission of the publisher.

Tay-Sachs Disease

This disorder of the lipid metabolism allows the accumulation of a glycolycial compound in the cytoplasm of brain cells because of a lack of an enzyme hexosaminidase. The glycolycial at elevated levels eventually destroys the central nervous system, resulting in severe mental retardation and blindness. The afflicted infant or child usually dies before age five. There are several disorders of this type, but the best-known and most frequently reported is Tay-Sachs disease (infantile amaurotic familial idiocy) among Ashkenazi Jews (1 in 6000 births). This frequency contrasts to the 1 in 500,000 non-Ashkenazim births. The disease is due to an autosomal recessive allele, and an estimated one in forty persons of Ashkenazim origin are carriers of the defective allele. Persons who are carriers show no symptoms of the disease, but they have less than normal concentrations of the enzyme. The persistence of the high frequencies of this detrimental gene has perplexed scientists for years and thus far only two explanations have been offered, a high degree of inbreeding or a selection favoring the heterozygote in an environment with a high incidence of tuberculosis infection.

DNA MARKERS OF HUMAN VARIATION

The discovery and development of restriction enzymes during the past ten years has provided a means of studying human variability at the genetic level. Instead of examining the end products, or final result of gene action (blood groups, hemoglobins or other proteins and enzymes discussed earlier), the ability to cleave DNA or RNA molecules into smaller fragments enables scientists to study the fine structure of the gene itself. Because the bulk of DNA is apparently not involved in coding of structural or regulatory genes, most of these nucleotides may vary through mutation without affecting function. The studies of DNA gene clusters of several important proteins, for example, reveal the existence of a great deal more diversity among humans at the molecular level than had been previously supposed. The fragments of these nucleotide sequences provide some excellent population markers.

RFLP (Restriction Fragment Length Polymorphisms)

The action of the endonucleases (restriction enzymes) may produce one or more fragments of varying lengths as described in chapter 2. In practice, several restriction enzymes are used to cleave the DNA of a gene cluster at different sites. There are seventeen restriction sites known to exist along the sixty-eight kilobases of the beta-globin gene cluster, for example. These restriction sites are polymorphic in that cleavage may or may not occur because of a different base pair (BP) at that point in the nucleotide chain (indicated by + or −). This polymorphism will result in several fragments of varying lengths. The listing of cleavage sites together denotes the haplotype.

The sickle-cell gene is found to be in a gene cluster whose DNA will produce different length fragments because of polymorphisms at several restriction sites. These differences distinguish between three African population groupings, the *Senegal, Benin,* and *Bantu* because of their haplotypes for eight restriction site polymorphisms (Table 3-16). The sickle-cell gene among Arabian and Indian populations was recently found to have a fourth haplotype. The existence of these differences in the base sequences in the beta-Hb cluster have been explained by independent mutations in each of four regions (Hill and Wainscoat, 1986). Another view is that, because the gene cluster region is subject to high rates of recombination and the Hb S gene is under intense selection favoring the heterozygote, it underwent only a single mutation in the Mideast and then spread rapidly by population diffusion (Livingstone, 1989). The question of sickle-cell origin is by no means settled, but the evidence to date does show an important application of RFLP haplotypes and does offer several new perspectives.

Ever since Kan and Dozy (1978) reported DNA polymorphisms of the beta-globin gene cluster, the studies with restriction enzymes have offered a new and valuable means of examining human variability at the gene level. The growing number of endonucleases (more than two thousand) at this time offer unlimited possibilities to compare haplotypes for the RFLP of the human genome, and several laboratories are accumulating a sampling of cells from a variety of populations. These cells,

TABLE 3-16 Restriction Site Haplotypes for the Beta Hemoglobin S Gene

HAPLOTYPES[a]	RESTRICTION SITES[b]	
Senegal	− + − + +	+ + +
Benin	− − − − +	+ − +
Bantu	− + − − −	+ + +
Arab-Indian	+ + − + +	+ + −

[a] Haplotypes found in populations in three African regions, Arabia and India.
[b] Combinations of DNA sites cut by restriction enzymes above and below the beta Hb gene S. The + indicates a fragment cut at this site and − no reaction to the enzyme.

Sources: Data selected from Livingstone, 1989 and Williams, 1985.

usually lymphoblasts, are grown and multiplied in cultures to provide quantities of DNA for analysis. This DNA provides a data bank of genetic markers of significantly different population clusters around the world (Cavalli-Sforza et al., 1986). The applications of these data to questions of population origins or admixtures are just beginning to be realized on a large scale as, for example, in a recent study of South American Indians (Kidd and Kidd, 1990). Their study is an extension of the ongoing work to describe RFLP frequencies among the world's populations, which to date have been mostly Asian, African, or European.

DNA Fingerprints

An even finer focus of our view of DNA polymorphisms has enabled the identification of a single individual because of the uniqueness of certain DNA regions. These regions, repeat sequences or "minisatellites" in the noncoding regions (introns), are hypervariable. That is, a chromosome may have many repeats of these minisatellites, and unequal crossovers during DNA replication contribute to the polymorphisms we have described in gene clusters like the beta globin. The frequency of variation in these repetitive sequences causes heterozygosity to be common and provides markers that enable individual identification.

Gill and Jeffreys took advantage of this marker diversity in the study of human *myoglobin*, the oxygen-transporting protein of muscle. They isolated a fragment of DNA near the myoglobin gene containing a thirty-three base sequence, which was repeated more than twenty times within the fragment. The repetitiveness of the minisatellite attracted their attention; after cloning, a probe specific for the region was produced. Applying the probe by methods described in chapter 2 to other DNA sequences they found that the minisatellite was repeated frequently throughout the entire genome. Comparison of samples taken from several people showed a pattern of hypervariable regions specific to the individual. That is, the alignment of the pattern of dark bands on the film, the regions of hybridization with the radioactive probe, differed between every person tested except monozygotic twins (Gill et al., 1985). There was nearly 100 percent heterozygosity in small populations, and a study of four generations of an inbred lineage demonstrated that the bands followed the laws of Mendelian inheritance, but new bands frequently appear in children because of crossover during replication (Vogel and Motulsky, 1986).

These hypervariable regions have proved useful in the resolution of questions of paternity or maternity; the child will have a closer resemblance to the parent than to a nonrelative. Also, the DNA fingerprinting has proved to be useful in criminal cases. Often tissue, blood, or semen has been used to establish the identity of a suspect, and this evidence has contributed to conviction.

OTHER POLYMORPHISMS OF ANTHROPOLOGICAL INTEREST

Taste Sensitivity

There is a wide range of taste sensitivities in humans. Some of us detect chemical compounds more easily than others. Hence, detection of levels of saltiness, bitterness, or sweetness in foods and beverages differ among us all. There is good evidence that some of this sensitivity is inherited. This has been thoroughly demonstrated by at least one substance. Perhaps no other polymorphism is so easily detected by a simple test as is taste sensitivity to a substance called phenylthiocarbamide (PTC). In high concentrations this substance tastes bitter to some people but not to others. Since the accidental discovery of this condition more than fifty years ago, millions of people have been tested, and the frequency of tasters and nontasters has been calculated.

This ability to detect the substance PTC is determined by a dominant allele (T): Persons who are TT or Tt can detect the bitter taste. In almost all populations tested there are tasters and nontasters, but as more careful tests have shown lately, there are various degrees of sensitivity. The homozygote dominant individual (TT) is more sensitive than the heterozygote (Tt) or the homozygote recessive (tt), and can detect the bitterness in more dilute solutions. The frequency of the nontaster is shown in Table 3-17. We can see high frequencies of nontasters in several major racial divisions, so the frequency of the T gene may be useful comparing groups of *Homo sapiens*. Variations in taste sensitivity also exist in several subhuman primates; studies have reported taster variation in chimpanzees and rhesus (Eaton and Gavan, 1965).

The significance of this polymorphism is not certain, but there is some suggestion of a relationship between thyroid-gland activity and ability to taste PTC. The nontasters seem to be more susceptible to thyroid deficiency, and a higher frequency of nodular goiter is found among them than in tasters. Several plants of the Cruciferae family (cabbage, turnips, mustard greens, and so on) contain this thiocyanate group, which is responsible for the bitter taste in PTC. This substance is part of the thioglucosides, chemical compounds that can block iodine absorption of the thyroid gland under certain conditions. One hypothesis explaining the taster polymorphism is that tasters were able to reject plants containing substances that act as thyroid depressants and, thus, consciously avoided those substances that affect thyroid function.

Cerumen (Ear Wax)

The waxy substance that accumulates in our ears has two forms that are under control of a pair of alleles. The wet, sticky form of wax is determined by a dominant trait, whereas the dry, flaky form is determined

TABLE 3-17   Frequency of Nontasters

POPULATION	NUMBER TESTED	PERCENT NONTASTERS
Formosan (Natives)	1756	1.8
Cree and Beaver Indians (N. Alberta)	489	2.0
Ramah Navahoes	264	2.0
Chinese (in Malaya)	50	2.0
Africans, mostly West African	74	2.7
Bantu, Kenya	208	3.8
Aborigines (Senoi), Malaya	50	4
Lappish (Finland)	140	6.42
Japanese (Brazil)	295	7.11
Japanese (Japan)	656	8.23
Chinese (in London)	66	10.6
Negro (white admixture; Brazil)	534	12.83
Chilean	216	13.43
Jewish (north Africa)	340	15.00
Malays	50	15.6
Malayan	237	16.04
Northeastern Hindu (Riang)	401	16.21
"Cabocio" Brazil	258	16.28
Negritos, Malaya	50	18
Jewish (Ashkenazim; Europe)	440	20.68
Jewish (non-Ashkenazim; Balkan)	101	21.78
Northeastern Brazilians	296	23.31
Belgian	425	23.76
Portuguese	454	24.0
Spaniards, northeastern	306	24.8
White (Italian admixture; Brazil)	74	24.32
Basques, Spain	98	25.0
Eskimos, N. Alaska	68	25.8
Arab (Sudan)	1963	25.40
Tamils in Malaya	50	27.2
Finns	202	29.2
U.S. white	3643	29.8
Hindu	256	29.30
Norwegians	266	30.5
White (Rio de Janeiro, Brazil)	164	30.49
Danes	314	31.8
Swedish	200	32.00
English (London)	541	32.90
Indian (Guajiro, Venezuela)	100	40.00
Eskimos, Labrador	130	41
Bombay Indians	200	42.5

Sources: Based on Allison and Blumberg, 1959; and Saldanha and Nacrur, 1963.

by a recessive trait. In addition to the stickiness or dryness, the waxes differ in their lipid (fat) content and in the quantity of antibodies that they contain.

The wax types vary throughout the world's populations. A majority of Asians (80 to 90 percent) have the dry type, in contrast to Europeans and Africans, who usually have the wet ear wax. Among Asians and populations of Asian descent, though, there is a cline of variation that correlates with temperature. Dry ear wax is less frequent in the more southerly populations, and the wet type is found more often among tropical populations in both Asia and America. For example, 93 percent of Mayan Indians in the Yucatan of southern Mexico have the wet type of ear wax. Because of this clinal distribution and because of lipid and antibody differences, there is a possibility that wet ear wax may serve some protective function in hot, humid climates. There is no conclusive evidence, however. The distribution of cerumen alleles provides another example of the growing list of polymorphisms that require further study before their adaptive significance can be understood (Petrakis et al., 1967).

TRAITS OF SIMPLE INHERITANCE: SOME CONCLUSIONS

During the past fifteen years, the advances in human biology have been remarkable, and not only have many new genetic markers been reported but their chromosome location has been noted as well. Additional population data have also been obtained, and frequency distributions are readily available. The greatest single achievement, however, has been the studies of the finer structure of the gene, those numerous fragments that separate the functional pieces. The use of DNA fragments has aided in describing human diversity, and these DNA pieces of varying lengths have been added to a growing list of polymorphisms. The study of human biological diversity has moved from an examination of the end product of gene action to the recording of the actual gene itself, but these developments have not been an unmixed blessing. The studies have revealed an enormous range of variability right down to the level of individual identification by chromosomal DNA. The comparisons of populations now must consider this new information, and anthropological explanations become ever more important as we shall discuss in later chapters.

RECOMMENDED READINGS AND LITERATURE CITED

ALLISON, A. C., AND B. S. BLUMBERG. 1959. "Ability to taste phenylthiocarbamide among Alaskan Eskimos and other populations," *Human Biol.*, 31:352–359.
BEUTLER, E. 1983. "Glucose-6-phosphate dehydrogenase deficiency," in *The Metabolic Basis of*

Inherited Disease, 5th ed., eds. J. B. Stanbury, J. B. Wyngaarden, D. S. Fredrickson, J. Goldstein, and M. Brown. New York: McGraw-Hill, pp. 1629–1653.

BODMER, J. G., L. J. KENNEDY, J. LINDSAY, AND A. M. WASIK. 1987. "Applications of serology and the ethnic distribution of three locus HLA haplotypes," *Br. Med. Bull.,* 43:94–121.

BUETTNER-JANUSCH, J. 1966. *Origins of Man.* New York: John Wiley.

BUETTNER-JANUSCH, J. 1973. *Physical Anthropology: A Perspective.* New York: John Wiley.

CAVALLI-SFORZA, L. L., J. R. KIDD, K. K. KIDD, C. BUCCI, A. M. BOWCOCK, B. S. HEWLETT, AND J. S. FRIEDLAENDER. 1986. "DNA markers and genetic variation in the human species," *Cold Spring Harbor Symposia on Quantitative Biology,* 51:411–417.

DAUSSET, J. W., AND J. COLOMBANI. 1972. *Histocompatibility Testing 1972.* Copenhagen: Munksgaard.

EATON, J. W., AND J. A. GAVAN. 1965. "Sensitivity to P-T-C among primates," *Am. J. Phys. Anthrop.,* 23:381–388.

EDLIN, G. 1990. *Human Genetics.* Boston: Jones and Bartlett.

FLATZ, G., J. N. HOWELL, J. DOENCH, AND S. D. FLATZ. 1982. "Distribution of physiological adult lactase phenotypes, lactose absorber and malabsorber in Germany." *Hum. Genet.,* 62:152–157.

GANONG, W. F. 1977. *Review of Medical Physiology,* 8th ed. Los Altos, Calif.: Lange Medical Publications.

GERARD, G., D. VITRAC, J. LE PENDU, A. MULLER, AND R. ORIOL. 1982. "H-deficient blood groups (Bombay) of Reunion island," *Am. J. Hum. Genet.,* 34:937–947.

GIBLETT, E. R. 1969. *Genetic Markers in Human Blood.* Philadelphia: F. A. Davis.

GILL, P., A. J. JEFFREYS, AND D. J. WERRETT. 1985. "Forensic applications of DNA fingerprints," *Nature,* 318:577.

HARRISON, G. A., J. M. TANNER, D. R. PILBEAM, AND P. T. BAKER. 1988. *Human Biology: An Introduction to Human Evolution, Variation, Growth, and Adaptability,* 3rd ed. New York: Oxford University Press.

HARRISON, G. A., J. S. WEINER, J. M. TANNER, AND N. A. BARNICOT. 1977 *Human Biology. An Introduction to Human Evolution, Variation, Growth and Ecology.* 2nd ed. Oxford: Oxford University Press.

HIERNAUX, J. 1966. "Peoples of Africa from 22° N to the equator," in *The Biology of Human Adaptability,* ed. Paul T. Baker. Oxford: Clarendon Press.

HILL, A. V. S., AND J. S. WAINSCOAT. 1986. "The evolution of the alpha and beta-globin gene clusters in human populations," *Hum. Genet.,* 74:16–23.

JONES, A., AND W. F. BODMER. 1974. *Our Future Inheritance: Choice or Chance.* Oxford: Oxford University Press.

KAN, Y. W., AND A. M. DOZY. 1978. "Polymorphism of DNA sequence adjacent to the human beta-globin structural gene: Relationship to sickle mutation," *Proceedings of the National Academy of Science,* 75:5631–5635.

KIDD, J. R., AND K. K. KIDD. 1990. "Characterization of the R. Surui and Karitiana at 21 polymorphic DNA loci," [abstract], *American Journal of Physical Anthropology,* 81:249.

KONOTEY-AHULU, F. I. D. 1982. "Ethics of amniocentesis and selective abortion for sickle cell disease," *Lancet,* 1:38–39.

LERNER, M. I., AND W. J. LIBBY. 1976. *Heredity, Evolution and Society,* 2nd ed. New York: W. H. Freeman.

LIVINGSTONE, F. B. 1989. "Who gave whom hemoglobin S: The use of restriction site haplotype variation for the interpretation of the evolution of the beta^s-globin gene," *Am. J. Hum. Biol.,* 1:289–302.

MCCRACKEN, R. D. 1971. "Lactase deficiency: An example of dietary evolution," *Current Anthrop.,* 12:479–500.

MCKUSICK, V. A. 1969. *Human Genetics,* 2nd ed. Englewood Cliffs, N.J.: Prentice-Hall.

MCKUSICK, V. A. 1975. *Mendelian Inheritance in Man.* Baltimore: Johns Hopkins Press.

MCKUSICK, V. A. 1986. "The gene map of *Homo sapiens:* Status and prospectus," *Cold Spring Harbor Symposia on Quantitative Biology,* 51:15–27.

MOURANT, A. W. 1983. *Blood Relations: Blood Groups and Anthropology.* New York: Oxford University Press.

PETRAKIS, N. L., K. T., MOLOHON, AND D. J. TEPPER. 1967. "Cerumen in American Indians: Genetic implications of sticky and dry types," *Science,* 158:1192–1193.

RACE, R. R., AND R. SANGER. 1975. *Blood Groups in Man*, 6th ed. Philadelphia: F. A. Davis.

REED, T. E. 1969. "Caucasian genes in American Negroes," *Science*, 165:762–768.

SAHI, T. 1978. "Intestinal lactose polymorphisms and dairy foods," International Titisee Conference, Titisee, 13–15 October 1977. *Hum. Genet.*, 50:107–143.

SALDANHA, P. H., AND J. NACRUR. 1963. "Taste thresholds for phenylthiourea among Chileans," *Am. J. Phys. Anthrop.*, 21:113–120.

STERN, C. 1973. *Principles of Human Genetics*, 3rd ed. New York: W. H. Freeman.

VOGEL, F., AND A. G. MOTULSKY. 1986. *Human Genetics*, 2nd ed. Berlin: Springer-Verlag.

WATSON, J. D. 1987. *Molecular Biology of the Gene*, 4th ed. Menlo Park: W. A. Benjamin.

4

_Human Biology II: Traits of Complex Inheritance_____

Many human phenotypes are often used to identify individuals and label groups. Traits such as skin color, face form, body size, and head shape have all been applied to the classification of "races." Population similarities in their characteristics of color, size, and body form, however, do not necessarily denote common ancestry or membership in a particular "racial stock." Because of our expectations, appearances can be deceiving! Frequently it is difficult, or even impossible, to define clear-cut boundaries on the basis of one or a combination of these phenotypes.

These traits are the result of a complex of interacting environmental forces and the products of several genes. Such traits are described as _polygenic_ because a number of genes interact with the environment to form the phenotype, as in the example of skin color. Several genes influence the development of skin pigmentation, which in turn may be affected by the ultraviolet portion of the solar radiation spectrum. Numerous other environmental factors influence trait variation as is well illustrated by a diversity of human body form and size. Though a person may inherit genes for large size, poor nutrition or disease occurring at critical growth stages will limit size below maximum potential. Also, there can be variation in growth because of unique individual responses to these stresses, as in the case of children in the same family. These and other phenotypes of complex inheritance vary over a continuous broad range within a population, and there is a great deal of overlap between groups.

HUMAN FORM AND ITS VARIABILITY

The different sizes, shapes, and colors of the world's peoples are often described as representative of certain distinct groups, each possessing special typical features. Seldom do we appreciate that the range of human diversity extends in gradual degrees throughout the species. The human form varies over a wide range of sizes and shapes, and there is considerable difference among human populations living today. From pygmoid peoples to tall, slender Nilotics of East Africa, and from Eskimos to southern Europeans, we find that the ratio between stature and body weight differs in ways that may reflect environmental conditions of climate, diet, and disease as well as the genetic influence.

Body Size

The height of normal adults in our species ranges from around four feet to well over six feet. These limits are exceeded occasionally but seem to represent a norm for modern stature. This variation in human stature is distributed among the world's peoples in some very interesting ways. Though there appears to be a tendency toward taller people farther from the equator (as in northwestern Europe) and shorter people nearer the equator, numerous exceptions exist. There are many examples of tall people living close to very short or even pygmoid groups. For instance, the Mbuti pygmies of the Ituri Forest in the Congo are just a few hundred miles from a group who are considered the tallest people in the world, the Watusi. Another contrast in body size is seen among Native Americans of the Southwest; Hopi of northern Arizona average four to five inches less in stature than the Papago who live about two-hundred miles to the south. Every racial or ethnic group seems to have its tall and short peoples, and stature covers such a broad range that general statements are precluded. Figure 4-1 offers diagrams depicting mean statures for several populations of our species. Though the Pygmy is at the low end of the range, several other populations have comparably short stature.

In all populations there are a range of sizes—people who are taller or shorter than average just as there are differences of sizes among siblings. These differences reflect an influence of the genetic component as described later in the chapter under variations in growth. One of the most clearly defined differences in size owing to genetic influence is seen when comparisons are made between adult males and females. Males tend to be larger than females in any population, and though there often are

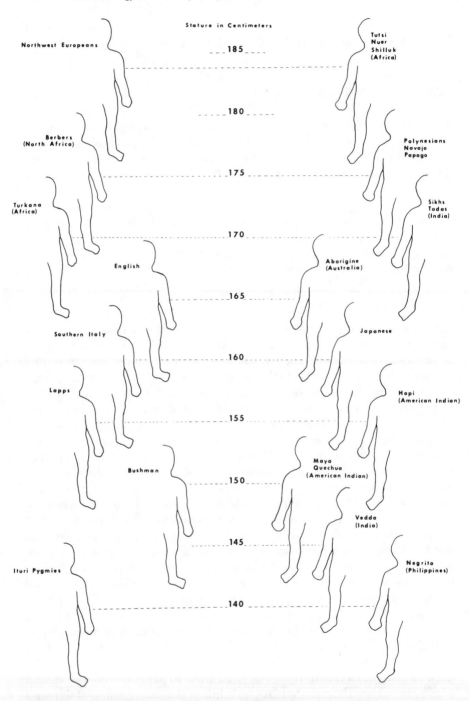

FIGURE 4-1   Diagram of Stature Variation between Populations.

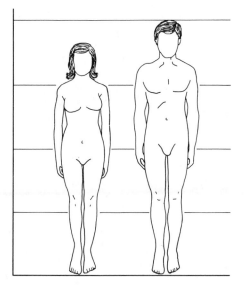

FIGURE 4-2
Sexual Dimorphism: Differences in Size, Shape and Proportion of Male and Female Body Form

This drawing depicts the average 5–7 percent difference between male and female. Some populations show a greater or lesser dimorphism. Shape and proportions also vary due to secondary sexual characteristics and differences in the relative widths of the pectoral and pelvic girdles.

taller females and shorter males, average male size exceeds female body size by 5 to 10 percent (see Figure 4-2). This difference between the sexes is referred to as *sexual dimorphism* and refers to the many other contrasts in body size and proportions as well as to stature.

Body Form

A relatively simple way of determining body proportion is to compare a person's standing height with his or her sitting height. The *cormic index*[1] or ratio between the two measurements indicates proportion of stature owing to the legs or the trunk. In populations with relatively short torsos and long legs, such as the Australian Aboriginals and many Africans, the cormic index is less than 50 (a ratio of 50 would indicate the legs and trunk plus head were approximately the same length). The tall stature of Nilotic groups in East Africa north of Lake Victoria (Dinka, Shilluk, Nuer) is due more to their very long legs than to trunk length, whereas most descriptions of the Pygmies note their elongated trunks, and short legs and long arms. Many Chinese populations, as well as groups of American Indians and Eskimos, have cormic indices as high as 54 percent, which indicates rather long trunks and short legs (Figure 4-3). Likewise, the ratio of arm to leg length (intermembral index) indicates another bodily

---

[1] Sitting height divided by standing height.

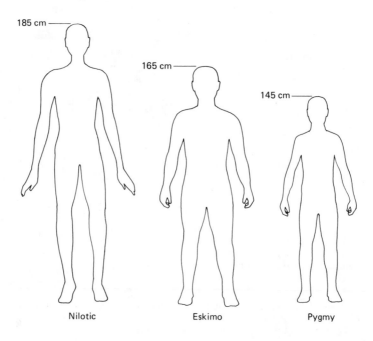

FIGURE 4-3   Drawings of Three Distinct Body Forms: Nilotic, Eskimo, and Pygmy.
Three distinct body forms are represented in this drawing. The Nilotic form illustrates a tall, slender shape found among many of the pastoralists of East Africa (Watusi, Masai, and Nuer). The Eskimo shape is in stark contrast with shorter stature and heavier body. By comparison, the Pygmy is not only the shortest and lightest human but has a relatively long torso with short legs.

proportion and shows some population differences. Though many populations show a tendency toward a particular body form, characteristics of shape are not reliable as a single racial criterion. A case in point is provided by the results of an extensive anthropometric survey of Australian Aborigines. Abbie (1975) reported extremes in stature of 146 to 190.6 cm for males and 137.6 to 174.3 cm for females; the cormic index ranged from 40.8 to 53.4 cm for male and 41.3 to 54.3 cm for females.

Body Weight

As with size and shape, weight also varies over a wide range, but it does not correlate closely with stature: Some tall people are light in weight compared with heavier shorter people. Adult weight ranges from about seventy to more than two hundred pounds depending on diet and, perhaps, to genetic factors as well. There seems to be little racial variation in body weight or in response to a surplus dietary intake, though many groups of American Indians, Pacific Islanders, and Australia Aboriginals become extremely obese when they change to the high-carbohydrate, high-fat diets

FIGURE 4-4   Steatopygia of a !Kung female.

Steatopygia is one of the characteristics for which the Bushmen of South Africa are famous. It is an enormous increase in the size of the buttocks by an accumulation of fatty tissue. The shape is maintained and the weight is supported by an addition of fibrous tissue. The condition is most accentuated in females.

typical of American populations today. Usually, the excess weight is stored as layers of fat just below the skin distributed over the body but more concentrated over the abdomen. There are some striking examples of differences, however, in the distribution of excessive subcutaneous fat, as in the case of *steatopygia* of Hottentot and San or !Kung women of South Africa, who, when well fed, develop especially large buttocks (Figure 4-4). In this condition, the buttocks are expanded by an enlargement of fat cells that are supported by bands of fibrous tissue. This may be an adaptation to high environmental temperatures because the concentration of fat cells in one region would lessen interference with the body's ability to dissipate metabolic heat through the skin's surface. Normally excess dietary calories are stored as a layer of fat just below the skin surface. The fat layer, if evenly distributed over most of the body, acts as insulation and would reduce the dissipation of body heat through radiation, a decided disadvantage in the hot climate of the homelands of these people.

Though dietary quantity and quality affect bodily proportions and weight, there is a close correlation with mean annual temperature. Generally speaking, in colder climates people are much heavier for their height than people in warmer regions, and the ratio between height and weight of the individual may be even more significant than limb ratios or

TABLE 4-1   Body Size and Stature-Weight Ratio

POPULATION (MALES)	STATURE (CENTIMETERS)	WEIGHT (KILOGRAMS)	RATIO
Kazakh (Turkestan)	163.1	69.7	2.34
Finland	171.0	70.0	2.44
Iceland	173.6	68.1	2.55
Eskimo	161.2	62.9	2.56
England	166.3	64.5	2.58
Sicily	169.1	65.0	2.60
Venezuela	164.2	62.4	2.61
Ecuador	157.7	57.5	2.73
North China	168.0	61.0	2.75
Scotland	170.4	61.8	2.76
Yambasa (Africa)	169.0	62.0	2.78
Berbers	169.8	59.5	2.85
Korea	161.1	55.5	2.90
Mahratta (India)	163.8	55.7	2.94
Central China	163.0	54.7	2.98
Thailand	161.0	53.2	3.03
Japan	160.9	53.0	3.04
Sundanese	159.8	51.9	3.08
Annamites	158.7	51.3	3.09
Batutsi (Africa)	176.0	57.0	3.09
Kikuyu	164.5	51.9	3.17
Hong Kong	166.2	52.2	3.18
Vietnam	157.6	49.1	3.21
Burma	161.5	49.9	3.24
India	163.0	48.2	3.38
Efe	143.8	39.8	3.61
Pygmies	142.2	39.9	3.56
Bushmen	155.8	40.4	3.86

Sources: Based on data from Dobzhansky, 1962; and Frisch and Revelle, 1969.

trunk limb proportions. Table 4-1 lists some representative populations selected for their variation in size and for the extreme temperature of the habitats. All racial groups consist of some populations who have high stature-weight ratios (indicating a tall, thin person) as well as groups with low ratios (short and heavy). Among groups in the warmer regions, particularly the wet tropics, there is a tendency to have a slender build, whereas in contrast, populations in the temperate or arctic regions are heavier for their stature. A further example of the relationship between climate and body size is illustrated in Figure 4-5, which plots average weights of several populations against mean annual temperatures of their environments. These examples of body form and size variability under differing environments demonstrate the great plasticity of human development. The responses to conditions of climate, diet, and disease are characteristically human and cross all ethnic and racial boundaries.

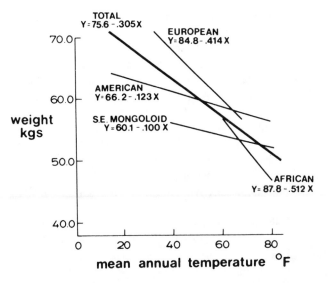

FIGURE 4-5   **Total Regression of Weight on Mean Temperature and Some of Its Component Intra-varietal Regressions.** Reprinted by permission from Roberts, D. F., *Climate and Human Variability*, 2nd ed. Menlo Park, CA: Cummings Publishing Company, 1978. Figure 2, page 18.)

Pygmies. These populations of small people are exceptional in their small size and bodily proportions, and are in stark contrast to all other *Homo sapiens.* The general relationships between body size, diet, climate, and growth seen in many of the world's peoples do not seem to apply to these dwarfed peoples. They are short in stature, well below the mean for the smallest in any population, but they have a long torso with short appendages; many Pygmies tend to be heavy in proportion to their height. There are several Pygmy and Pygmoid populations in some of the world's more remote tropical regions.

Today approximately 150,000 Pygmies live in small groups scattered throughout the tropical rain forests of central Africa, from near Lake Tanganyika in East Africa to Gabon and Cameroon in the West. These groups are believed to be remnants of prehistoric tropical forest dwellers who have been progressively reduced and thinly scattered over the area as agriculturalists began to occupy portions of the tropical rainforest approximately two-thousand years ago. The Pygmies have been pushed farther and farther into the more remote, agriculturally less desirable regions until, today, the largest numbers of Pygmies in Africa are concentrated in central Africa around the Congo basin and along the tributaries of the Congo River. In these areas the Pygmies have established a close trading relationship with the Bantu-speaking agricultural groups, trading the proceeds of the hunt for cultivated foods. The best known are the

Efe, Batwa, and Bakanga who live in the regions east of Kisangani (Stanleyville) in Zaire. A few groups, such as the Babinza, however, live in the western region of central Africa; these western groups are far less numerous and more widely dispersed. It is interesting to note that the shortest people in the world, the Mbuti of the Ituri rain forests in southeast Zaire, live within two to three hundred miles of the tallest people, the Tutsi of Ruwanda.

Pygmoid populations called Negritos, sometimes referred to as Oceanic Pygmies, are dispersed throughout many of the more remote areas of South Asia, the Philippines, and New Guinea. They are found in the jungles of the Malayan Peninsula and on the island of Sumatra; these are the Semang and the Senoi (Sakai), who are only slightly taller than the average African Pygmy, with a mean stature of 152 cm (five feet). Off the west coast of the Malayan Peninsula are the Andaman Islands, inhabited by three distinct groups of Negritos: the Minicopies, the Onge, and the Garawa. They all are similar in features and a bit shorter than the Semang, 149 cm (four feet, ten inches). The Onge are quite fat, and the women develop large fleshy buttocks, similar to the steatopygia on the San and Hottentot females. On the Philippine Islands of Mindanao, Palawan, and the northern part of Luzon are a few remnants of Pygmoid populations. Among the best known are the Aetas, whose mean stature has been given as 147 cm (four feet, nine inches). Other Negrito groups are found in the remotest parts of the mountains of western New Guinea; the Tapiro tribe, with a mean stature of 144 cm (four feet, seven inches), is an example.

The general characteristics of the Negritos, besides small stature, are very dark skin color, woolly hair, scant body and facial hairs, broad nose, and slight to moderately developed brow ridges. All groups do not share equally in these features, and there is a considerable variation between certain populations. In the case of skin color, some Negritos, as in the Philippine populations, have lighter brown or even yellowish skin, whereas the Andaman Islanders have very dark brown to black skin. Facial features also differ considerably, from smooth, rounded foreheads to heavy brows (usually in New Guinea groups) that match well the facial features of many Australian Aboriginals.

A major problem that has puzzled students of human variation has been the origins of these dwarfed peoples, which centers on the question of the relationship between the two divisions, the African Pygmies and the Southeast Asian Negritos. How are they related? Do they, as once supposed, share close common ancestry, or are they members of a unique Pygmoid race? Casual visual comparisons suggest that they are descendants from the same ancestors because of their comparable size, skin color, and hair form. In the past, Pygmies and Negritos had been classified as a single race, and certain anthropologists even suggested elaborate migration routes to get the ancestors of Southeast Asian Negritos from an African homeland to their present distribution. Other studies of Pygmoid peoples have pointed out, however, that the African Pygmy and Negrito are two independent types with only their short stature and certain other features in common (Boyd, 1963). Each Pygmoid population studied shared several traits of blood type and protein composition with their normal-sized neighbors. In fact, dwarfed peoples, in general, may be no more than local inbred populations (Abbie, 1967). The question of cause of the Pygmoid condition is still unresolved. Some clues may be provided by the studies of African Pygmies, which showed that the cartilage of their long bones do not respond normally to growth hormones, which stimulate the cartilage development in the growing bone. The Pygmies had sufficient quantities of this hormone, but their bones appear to be much less responsive. Such studies have yet to be performed on other dwarfed peoples.

HEAD SIZE AND SHAPE

The shape and size of the head have been under intense study by many generations of anthropologists, and numerous descriptive measurements have been devised. The human head has been of special interest because of the wealth of well-preserved skulls from prehistoric times. Representative skulls from extinct ancient populations often show a collection of characteristics that apparently sets them apart and have been used to suggest relationships between past and present populations.

Among the many skull features examined, the one most frequently used in the past for establishing racial groups has been the shape of the head defined by the cephalic index, as noted earlier. This index, the ratio of the breadth to the length of the skull, provides an approximation of shape. The skull of our species varies from long and narrow to short and broad—a variation of cephalic index from 70 (breadth = 70 percent of length) to about 90. Certain populations tend toward one or the other end of the range as indicated in Table 4-2, which lists Australian Aboriginals with the narrowest heads, whereas, at the other end of the range, Norwegian Lapps have the broadest head shapes.

Despite its frequent use in the past, the index has to be discounted as an important racial criterion because of its broad range and because there are similar indices found for such disparate groups as Quechua of the Andes and central Europeans, Norwegians and Otomis (American Indians), and Africans and Australian Aboriginals. If cranial and facial dimensions, describing face and head shape, are taken in combination and examined by modern statistical techniques, however, then distinctions are found among many populations. Degrees of relationships—that is,

TABLE 4-2   Cephalic Indices

GROUP	MEAN INDEX
Australians (Arnhem Land)	71.8
Central Bantu	74.1
South Africa (Bushmen, Hottentots)	75.1
Vedda	75.6
Ituri Pygmies	76.5
New Guinea and Melanesia	77.7
Eskimo	78.0
Madagascar and Indian Ocean	78.7
Sioux (central United States)	79.6
Iran, Armenia, Assyria	80.2
Japanese	80.8
Norwegians	81.0
Eastern Chinese	81.7
Germans	82.5
Negritos (Philippines)	82.7
Hawaiians	84.0
Norwegian Lapps	85.0

The index is obtained by taking the ratio of maximum skull breadth divided by maximum skull length times 100.

Sources: Data from Biasutti, 1959; and Harrison, Weiner, Tanner, and Barnicot, 1977.

the distances from a common ancestor—have been estimated in this way. The average cranial-facial morphology of Northern Europeans differs significantly from southeastern Europeans, for example. The cranial remains of ancient peoples who overran central Europe throughout recorded history have also been differentiated by this method (Schwidetzsky, 1982). The peopling of the Pacific and the Americas present a challenge to the prehistorian but are now being aided by extensive comparisons of cranial-facial shape (Brace, 1990; Pietrusewsky, 1990).

Such studies are possible if care is taken in selecting dimensions of various features because there is a strong component of inheritance regulating growth and the final form of the structure. The component of inheritance in head shape was demonstrated by Osborne and De George (1959), who compared monozygotic and dizygotic twins and showed a closer similarity between the monozygotic (identical twins) than between nonidentical or dizygotic twin pairs. The mode of inheritance is not known, however, because head shape is not a simple character depending on a single gene; rather, it is determined by a multiple gene complex subject to strong environmental influences. The overall rate of growth and body size also influences shape because there is a positive correlation between stature and skull length; taller individuals have longer heads. Because of these factors, plus the pattern of distribution of cranial shape, cephalic index remains an element of interest in the study of bodily proportions.

TABLE 4-3   **Range of Cranial Capacity in Some Fossils and Modern Humans, Including Two Pongids**

	RANGE OF CRANIAL CAPACITIES
Chimpanzee	275–500 cm^3
Gorilla	340–752
Australopithecine	450–700 (approximately)
Homo erectus (Pithecanthropus, Sinanthropus)	850–1250
Neanderthal	1100–1700
Homo sapiens	1000–2200

Sources: Based on Montagu, 1960; Schultz, 1926; and Tobias, 1971.

It should be considered as a part of the overall growth and development pattern influenced by environmental factors, however. For example, Beals (1984) made a broad-ranged comparative study of head shapes and found a close correlation between environmental temperature and head shape. Populations in colder climates had, on the average, rounder heads than peoples in the tropics, a characteristic that is likely to be of adaptive significance. The relationship of surface area and mass of parts of the mammalian body form influence the radiation of metabolic heat and affect temperature regulation.

Cranial Capacity and Brain Size

Perhaps more speculation and nonsense has been written about the size of the human brain and its relationship to intelligence than about any other aspect of our anatomical variability. This is probably because the size of the cranial vault differs so much among peoples today and has increased throughout the fossil record of human evolution (Table 4-3). The estimated volume of the cranial vault or cranial capacity increased from a low of 450 cubic centimeters (cc) in one of the earliest hominids, the Australopithecines, to the highest in modern *Homo sapiens*. The modern range for brain volume, estimated from cranial capacity,[2] was achieved relatively early in human evolution, approximately one hundred thousand years ago, among the Neanderthals of Europe. In fact, the estimated mean size of the Neanderthal fossils' cranial capacity (1450 cc) is actually higher than the mean for modern humans (1345 cc).

The increase of brain size during the last two or three million years of evolution is an extremely important event for studies of human paleontology, and comparisons of cranial capacities of the different fossils can be useful. There is a wide range in variation in modern populations, however, and the lower end of the range is well below the volumes

---

[2] The size of the human brain may be estimated from the total cranial vault volume because 80 percent of the total volume of the adult is occupied by brain mass.

estimated for certain early hominids—*Homo erectus,* for example (see Table 4-3).

Yet, there is no evidence that the individuals with small cranial capacities, and hence small brains, are any less intelligent than persons with larger cranial vaults. The differences in modern populations' brain size do not have any relevance to mental ability. As von Bonin (1963) a foremost neuroanatomist, once stated, the correlation between brain size and mental capacity is insignificant in modern *Homo sapiens.* The wide-ranging differences among the members of the same population show no correlation to behavior differences as an example. In fact, many famous statesmen and literary figures in recent history had cranial capacities at either end of the range; from Anatole France and Turgenev (1100 cc) to Oliver Cromwell and Lord Byron (2200 cc). Also, females average 10 percent smaller cranial capacities than males; a difference that is related to the smaller average female body size. In addition, the volume of the brain is difficult to measure, either by estimation from cranial capacity of the dry skull, the head of the living individual, or from the brain at autopsy. The methods used will influence the results. Also, the size of the brain is closely correlated with body size; most studies, especially the earlier ones, seldom considered the overall size of the individual or took note of the age at death, another variable.[3]

Nevertheless, there are authors, even today, who insist on recording and emphasizing racial differences in cranial capacity as if it were a meaningful indicator.[4] Because of this persistent use of estimated brain size, Figure 4-6 is included here and lists some select groups. Before the reader draws any conclusions, it should be pointed out that variation of ± 100 cc about the mean is evident within most European populations, and among these populations means may differ as much as 400 cc. In sum, individuals with larger or smaller cranial capacities are normally functioning and intellec-tually competent individuals, and large-headed and small-headed persons are found in all race and ethnic groups. The similarities or differences become even clearer when body size is considered.

The major changes during the evolution of the brain are more likely to have been qualitative rather than merely a gross alteration in size.[5] In addition, it is not so much a matter of gross size as it is a ratio of brain to body size. The human brain weighs approximately 2 percent of the total body weight, or a ratio of 1:45, whereas the gorilla brain-body ratio is 1:400. Even though humans stand near the top of the list of primates in

---

[3] For an evaluation of brain size variation see Tobias, 1970.

[4] For an example of misuse of fifty-year-old studies of brain size to support racist theories while ignoring recent results see Burnham, 1985.

[5] Holloway, 1966, discusses the quantitative and qualitative differences between human and chimp brains in relationship to gross body size.

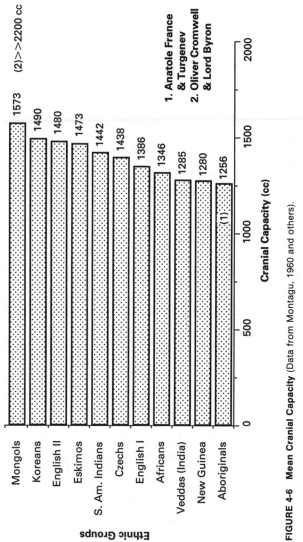

FIGURE 4-6 Mean Cranial Capacity (Data from Montagu, 1960 and others).

149

TABLE 4-4   Brain-Body Ratios

SPECIES	BODY WEIGHT	BRAIN-BODY
Homo sapiens	61.5 kg	1:47
Chimp	56.7	1:129
Gorilla	250	1:420
Night monkey	9	1:84
Capuchin	3.1	1:43
Galago	0.2	1:40
Deer	65	1:310
Rat	0.2	1:122

brain-body weight ratios, they are not the largest (Table 4-4). The marmoset (the smallest platyrrhine monkey of South America) has a ratio of 1:19, and the squirrel monkey of South American a ratio of 1:12. No one would argue that these primate brains are qualitatively comparable to *Homo sapiens*', however, for as Holloway (1966:309) states: "One c.c. of chimpanzee cortex is not equivalent to one c.c. of human cortex, nor is it likely that any equivalent measure can be found."

FACE FORM

The human face is highly variable in its shape and size, and distinctly individual forms occur. We can easily recognize our friends by their facial appearance, and we automatically and even subconsciously group people according to their expressions or dimensions and proportions of the face. One worker went so far as to divide faces into ten different categories or types, from the elliptical to oval, including such classifications as rectangular and pentagonal. Even with many gradations among these categories, it was still impossible to apply them to all members of a population. Any scheme devised to describe facial characteristics of certain populations is just a rough approximation that will include only a portion of the individuals in the group. The form of the mouth, prominence of the chin or nose, and the position of the eyes are visual clues that enable recognition. We all group people into broad categories and we see these groupings as related to the major racial divisions of our species; the terms Eskimo, Aboriginal, or Chinese project a mental image of what a person in that category looks like before we ever see the individual. Figure 4-7 offers an example of the human diversity of face form. Little is known about the causes of such diversity or about the genetic influences. The soft tissues of the face are arranged in any number of ways and change with age; family resemblances are strong and population affinities are usually clear. Also, there appears to be a geographical distribution of face form that

FIGURE 4-7 Faces of *Homo sapiens* This composite photograph illustrates the range of variability of our species. Source: Courtesy of United Nations.

suggests some adaptation to climate; the flat, broad face of northern Asian peoples have been described as an adaptation to cold ever since the earliest days of anthropology. There are few physiological studies to support such an explanation, however. A clearer understanding of facial structures is provided by studies of the facial skeleton.

Human face shape is complex and is the result of several large and small bones organized about three basic structures; the eyes, the nose, and the mouth. The development and placement of these structures must be coordinated to provide sufficient space and symmetry to enable the functions of sight, respiration, and alimentation, each with special requirements of shape, size, and position in the overall facial arrangement. The spacing of the orbits of the eyes, for example, influence the visual field and effect appearance to a large extent while the size of the nasal aperture allows for inhalation through the upper respiratory tract and is related to the bony structures of the roof of the mouth and the midface. The mouth, in turn, has a size and shape closely related to the size and spacing of the teeth in the dental arcade.

The shape of the human face has changed a great deal from the heavy prognathic structure, possessed by our fossil ancestors, to the reduced structure in modern *Homo sapiens* that is rather small in proportion to our large human head. This change has come about through evolutionary processes, as our ancestors relied less on their jaws and teeth for procuring and manipulating food, which, in turn, reduced the natural selection for large facial bones. The structures of the face, whose major function is to support the chewing apparatus, therefore diminished in size.[6] These structures are primarily the brow ridges (the ridge of bone over the eyes), the cheek bones (or zygomatic arches), and of course the upper and lower arches of bone that support the teeth.[7] With a reduction in these elements, the human face began to take on a new look, and the proportions were drastically altered. All of the world's populations did not undergo exactly the same pattern of change, however, nor were their faces altered at the same rate. Many of the facial features have maintained large sizes in some populations, such as the Eskimo and Australian Aboriginals.

One rather distinctive facial characteristic clearly involved in the evolutionary process is prognathism, the forward protrusion of dental arches. A comparison of modern humans with recent or ancient and fossil Neanderthals illustrates the reduction in the lower face of modern humans (Figure 4-8). Many modern populations today have prognathic profiles, yet this does not indicate a close affinity with fossil ancestors; rather, it is the result of the presence of large teeth in broad dental arches. Because the major purpose of the bony structures in this part of the face is the support of the dentition, the bone arches of the maxilla and mandible are correspondingly large.

Teeth have proved to be significant in the study of human variability because of their importance as evidence in evolution and adaptation to environmental conditions. Teeth served *Homo sapiens* well as cutting, grinding, and shearing implements in past times, as the heavily worn dental remains of prehistoric and earlier historic humans demonstrate (Brace, 1962; Molnar 1971). In fact, human survival up until recent times depended a great deal on a sturdy dentition and a heavy, well-formed skeleton (Figure 4-9). With the rise of technological efficiency in dealing

[6] For a discussion of these functions see Brace and Mahler, 1971; and Molnar and Ward, 1977.

[7] The amount of structural reinforcement provided by large brow ridges and cheek bones is by no means settled. There are close correlations, however, between tooth and palate size and the bones of the face.

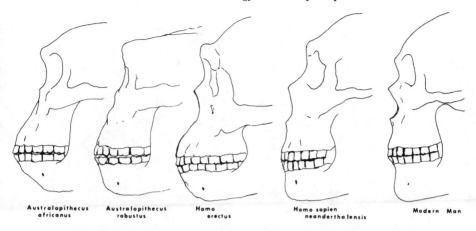

FIGURE 4-8   Alveolar prognathism. These sketches diagram the facial distinctions of several phases of human evolution. In contrast to the modern profiles, the lower face—mainly the anterior tooth row and chin—was much more robust and the teeth protruded further forward. The cheek bones (zygomatic arches) and brow ridges were also larger in earlier human ancestors.

with the raw materials necessary to sustain life, however, there was less reliance on the dental arches as implements: so in modern times our teeth often are looked on as annoying items of our anatomy that frequently require dental treatment.

Teeth have characteristics of shape and size that increased the dentition's utility as a chewing implement, extra molar cusps and reinforced enamel ridges are examples. Throughout evolution these characteristics varied from population to population so that, today, the racial groups of the world show considerable diversity in these dental features because of the differences in selective forces for sturdy teeth that have been operating on each group. Tooth size, especially the diameter of the molar crown, shows great variation. From the large crowns of the Australopithecine molars (approximately 15-mm diameter in the cheek-to-tongue direction) to the small sizes of many European populations (11.5-mm diameter of the first molar) the dentition of humans and their ancestors has steadily reduced in size over time. This reduction has not been equal nor has it been constant in all of the world's peoples; today some people, such as the Australian Aboriginals, still possess large teeth (Table 4-5).

Shovel-shaped incisors is another dental feature that occurs more frequently in certain populations than others. This term describes an incisor tooth that has thickened margins on the lingual surface (tongue side of the tooth). These raised surfaces provide structural reinforcement that prevents or reduces the possibility of breakage. In many Asian

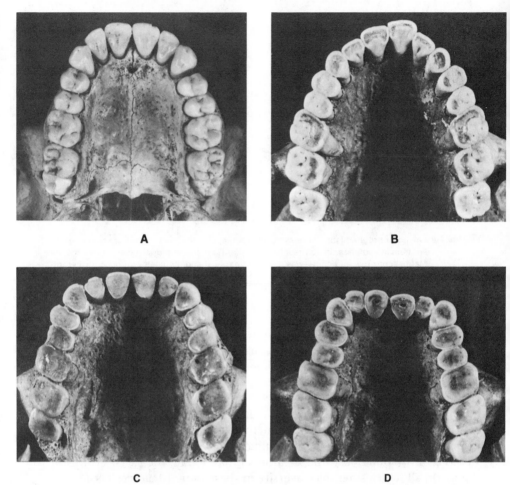

FIGURE 4-9 Examples of Worn Teeth in Prehistoric Populations. The upper dental arch is shown at several stages of wear. The unworn teeth of a sixteen year old (A) are compared to three adults who have suffered various degrees of tooth loss because of a tough abrasive diet requiring heavy chewing. A younger adult, about twenty-five (B), shows less wear than C, a thirty-five year old, and D, a forty-five year old.

peoples, Chinese, for instance, most individuals have these types of incisors, and children suffer far less from breakage of the upper central incisors in childhood accidents than do European children.

Several other features of the dentition also show a great deal of variability and, in some cases, have been grouped according to race. More often, though, there is only a variability in the frequency of the occurrence of the particular trait, and all the major groups of humanity possess it to some degree. The molar cusps are an example, because their number and

TABLE 4-5   Dimensions of Lower First Molar of Fossil and Modern Humans

	LENGTH (M-D)		BREADTH (B-L)	
	Mean	Range	Mean	Range
A. Africanus	13.87	11.60–16.50	13.04	11.30–15.00
A. Robustus	14.57	11.80–16.40	13.77	11.50–15.50
H. Erectus	12.74	9.90–14.70	12.02	10.10–13.70
H. Neanderthal	11.69	8.00–14.00	11.13	9.00–12.70
H. Sapiens	11.55	9.00–14.10	10.99	8.30–13.00
Australopithecines	14.34	11.60–16.50	13.53	11.30–15.50
Neanderthal	11.41	8.00–14.00	10.97	9.00–12.70
Mt. Carmel	11.56	10.50–13.00	11.18	10.50–11.50
Australian Aborigine	12.30	11.00–14.00	11.90	10.00–13.50
Pecos Pueblo	11.96	10.78–13.01	10.74	9.46–11.92
American Whites (2)	11.90	10.10–13.20	10.60	9.60–11.40
American Blacks	11.90	10.60–13.40	10.80	9.80–11.90
E. Greenland Eskimo	11.81	10.60–12.60	11.32	10.10–12.50
Sub Saharan (Africa)	11.77	9.50–14.10	11.16	8.80–13.00
New Britain	11.75	10.00–13.60	11.36	10.10–12.60
American Indian	11.68	10.00–13.30	11.28	10.00–12.45
Gillmanuk (Indon.)	11.60	10.00–13.40	11.00	9.60–12.20
Aleuts	11.45	10.10–12.80	10.50	9.20–11.30
Caucasoid	11.21	9.80–13.00	10.74	9.20–12.70
American Whites (1)	10.95	9.40–12.70		
Bushmen	10.90	10.00–12.00	10.20	9.00–11.30
Lapps	10.80	9.20–12.80	10.22	8.30–12.20

Source: After Wolfpoff, 1971. Copyright © 1971 *Studies in Anthropology*, Case Western Reserve University. Reprinted by permission of the publisher.

TABLE 4-6   Shovel Shaped in Upper Median Incisors

POPULATION	PERCENT MALE	PERCENT FEMALE
Chinese	66–89	82–94
Japanese	78	
Mongolian	62–91	91
Eskimo	84	84
Pima Indians	96	99
Pueblo Indians	86–89	86–89
Aleut	96	
American Black	12	11
American White	9	8

Sources: Based on Carbonell, 1963; and Comas, 1960.

arrangement on the molar crown has often been used to identify racial affinity. Some groups frequently do tend to have one or another pattern; for example, there are very seldom less than five cusps on the lower first molar of the Australian Aboriginal, whereas the first molars of many Europeans tend to be reduced in size with only four cusps. Many individual Aboriginals differ from this "typical" pattern, however, and often have a sixth cusp. So it is with other "racial" characteristics of the teeth; though members of a group may have a higher frequency of one or more dental traits, they are seldom unique possessors and other segments of humanity may have the same traits (as in the case of shovel-shaped incisors, Table 4-6). To sum up, the range of variability of the dentition of modern *Homo sapiens* is so great that several characteristic features must be considered together before racial or population affinity is described.

Morphology and Size

Tooth morphology and size are under close genetic control and have been shown to be very stable through time, a feature that enables comparisons of skeletal as well as living populations. These traits must be considered as a group, or cluster as Turner (1990) has done successfully to establish common ancestry and to trace origins. He compared the frequencies of twelve different dental traits, including shovel-shaped incisors as they occurred among Asians, Native Americans, and Pacific peoples and offered strong evidence for Northern Asia as the original homeland of Native Americans while establishing a distinctive difference among Asian and Pacific populations. The advantage of his method is that skeletal remains, thousands of years old, could be used to determine the presence of the traits in different world regions.[8]

---

[8] The trait frequencies were analyzed by multivariant computer methods, and clusters were derived that arranged representative samples in "trees" or dendrograms that placed populations according to similarity.

NOSE FORM

The nose dominates the midfacial region, and contributes a great deal to a person's distinctive identity. Form and size varies over a wide range; there are people with short, broad or long, narrow noses and all combinations in between. The linear measures are easily made on either the living or on the dry skull and many thousands of measurements have been recorded. *Nasal index* (width/length × 100), an approximation of shape like cephalic index, is also easily derived and has received a great deal of attention because nose shape has a pattern of geographical distribution and was once thought to be a distinctively racial trait. In some ethnic groups a certain shape does appear more frequently. An index of 104 describes a nose that is slightly wider at the nostrils than it is long; it is found among the Pygmies of the Ituri Forest area in Central Africa and Aboriginals in Central Australia. Narrower noses, represented by low indices (85 and below), are found among numerous groups throughout the world, in many American Indians, North Africans, Europeans, and Eskimos. A narrow or a broad nose form is not confined to any particular race. For example, the long, narrow noses found among the peoples occupying the highlands of east Africa are in contrast to the wide noses of the tropical dwellers in the Congo Basin.

Because the nose performs the vital functions in the upper respiratory tract of filtering, warming, and moistening the inspired air, its size and shape variation among populations has been frequently studied. The nose is lined with mucosal membranes covering a dense bed of fatty tissues through which a rich supply of blood flows. These membranes can secrete large amounts of water, up to 1 liter per day, which serves to moisten the inspired air. The moistening function serves to help maintain the inspired air at the relative humidity of 100 percent as required by the lungs. Other structures of the respiratory track contribute moisture, but the lining of the nose serves most effectively in this function. This means that the amount of total surface area of the internal nose and adjacent structures become more important in drier areas. Natives of arid regions of the world have a longer, narrower nose form; a geometric shape that provides the greatest surface area per unit size.[9] Among desert and mountain peoples the narrow nose is predominant and even in the colder and drier climates the Eskimos have a narrow nasal aperture, which provides an efficient mechanism for warming as well as moistening the inspired air. It is a simple matter of geometry that a high, narrow nasal opening can warm and moisten air more efficiently than a short, broad one, and in climates where the moisture content of the air is very low, selective forces act on this particular nose form, whether the dryness is due to intense

---

[9] For a discussion of shape, size, and surface area see Wolpoff, 1968.

TABLE 4-7   Mean Nasal Indexes of Select Populations

POPULATION	MEAN NASAL INDEX
South African Bushmen	103.9
Mbuti Pygmies	103.8
Aborigines (Australia)	99.6
Northern Bantu	95.5
Central Bantu	93.8
Vedda (India)	85.5
American Indian (Plains)	72.0
Eskimo	68.5
European	66.0
Iran	63.7

heat or intense cold. Table 4-7 shows examples of average nasal indices among populations living in a variety of climates.

Because face form is a result of a complex of the growth processes of several facial bones, any single feature is the result of interacting forces. This is especially true of nose form, whose width is related to the size and proportion of the upper dental arch. As the palate gets wider, the nasal aperture becomes broader and the Australian Aboriginals are a good example. Though most live in some of the driest areas of the world, their noses are extremely broad as noted earlier. This dimension is related to the large anterior teeth and to chewing processes exerted on the dental arches during childhood, which stimulates the palatal growth. Also, prognathism tends to be associated with a short, broad nose, and a significant correlation has been found between the length of the skull base and nasal width.

These factors of climatic influence and structural interrelationships suggest that human face form is extremely complex and that numerous variables are involved in growth and development to a certain adult form. Conclusions should not be drawn too quickly about relationships between any two populations solely on the basis of a similarity in structure because face form, like other bodily dimensions, develops according to local factors of natural selection acting on the genes that regulate growth. It is not necessary to postulate migrations and intermixtures to explain similarities between populations, as was once done for the Nilotic face form found in groups like the Nuer, Watusi, and other East African pastoralists. At one time their long, straight noses were believed to be due to contact and interbreeding with Caucasoid groups from western Asia. Subsequent genetic studies have not borne this theory out. No doubt, during a period of thousands of years, contact with western Asian populations may have occurred and some interbreeding may have resulted, but people with the Nilotic face are the result of local selective forces acting on the population; it is not merely a matter of interbreeding between races.

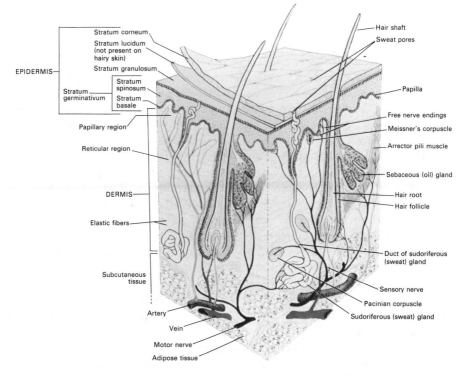

EPIDERMIS—
- Stratum corneum
- Stratum lucidum (not present on hairy skin)
- Stratum granulosum
- Stratum germinativum
  - Stratum spinosum
  - Stratum basale
- Papillary region
- Reticular region

DERMIS—
- Elastic fibers

Subcutaneous tissue
- Artery
- Vein
- Motor nerve
- Adipose tissue

- Hair shaft
- Sweat pores
- Papilla
- Free nerve endings
- Meissner's corpuscle
- Arrector pili muscle
- Sebaceous (oil) gland
- Hair root
- Hair follicle
- Duct of sudoriferous (sweat) gland
- Sensory nerve
- Pacinian corpuscle
- Sudoriferous (sweat) gland

FIGURE 4-10   Structure of Skin and Underlying Subcutaneous Layer. (From Tortora, Gerard J., *Principles of Human Anatomy*, 2nd ed., 1980. Copyright © 1980 by Gerard J. Tortora. Reprinted by permission of Harper & Row, Publishers, Inc.)

HUMAN SKIN

The human body is clothed in a protective covering of renewable, elastic skin consisting of a several structures organized in two major layers, the dermis and epidermis (Figure 4-10). The innermost or *dermal* layer consists of thick collagenous fibers and contains the blood vessels, nerves, hair follicles, and gland cells (sweat, sebaceous, and apocrine). This layer is covered by a thinner protective sheath of *epidermis*, which protects the dermis from the outside environment, especially solar radiation. Epidermis is a tissue of four cellular layers that act together to provide the basic protection of the body as well as a place to synthesize vitamin D_3.

The lowest epidermal layer, *stratum germinativum*, contains long columnar cells that make contact with the dermis; within this layer are also specialized cells, the *melanocytes*, which synthesize the brown-black pigment granules, melanin. These granules are found scattered throughout the upper layers of the epidermis. The next layer is the *stratum granulosum*, where the cells have changed their shape and are more densely packed together providing a concentration of keratin, a protein synthesized by these cells. *Keratin* is a dense, relatively inert substance that is the major constituent of nails, hair, and the outer flaky layers of skin. There are two other layers: a thin translucent one, *stratum lucidum*, and a dense *corneum*, composed of fused cells now consisting almost entirely of keratin, which is the outermost layer and provides a protective boundary. This surface varies considerably in thickness from one region of the body to the next; the more protected are thin, whereas areas like the palms of the hands and the soles of the feet are relatively thick.

The skin, in addition to its protective role, has many varied functions. It is an excretory organ that expels large quantities of waste products and chlorides in the water excreted by sweat glands. Skin is also important for regulation of body temperature through the evaporation of sweat or, conserving body heat by means of a network of muscle fibers that are able to contract the skin (the cause of goose bumps) and reduce heat loss when exposed to cooler air. In addition, most skin is a factory producing pigment granules (melanin) and vitamin D. Because of our concern with human racial differences, and because skin color has been a major taxonomic criterion used, the causes of color and the importance of melanin is now considered at length.

The color of *Homo sapiens'* skin, an easily perceived trait, has been used for many centuries as a criterion to divide humans into racial groups as discussed in chapter 1. Even the terms black, brown, white, and yellow are widely applied and accepted as a means to distinguish between groups of our species. The belief that humans come in a few primary shades is well ingrained in our culture, as is the belief that similarity of color indicates common ancestry. The facts are quite different, and perhaps in no other character are we so diverse as in our skin coloration. We come in all varieties, from the very pale Lapplanders to the dark brown inhabitants of the tropical rain forest of central Africa, such as the Pygmies or their neighbors, the Bantu. Even within the same population there is a significant difference in pigmentation between males and females, and between children and adults.[10]

Skin color is caused by several factors. In fair-skinned people the blood flowing through the innermost layer of the skin (dermis) contributes to the pinkish hue, and together with the several substances in the circulatory system (bilirubin and free hemoglobin, for example) largely determine the color of untanned skin. Keratin of the dead skin cells in the corneum has a yellowish tinge and also contributes to skin color as is demonstrated by the calluses on the palms of the hands and soles of the

---

[10] See Abbie, 1953, for a discussion of pigmentation of Aboriginals of central Australia or Hulse, 1967, for a description of variations of Japanese skin color.

feet. The lightness or darkness of the human skin, however, depends mainly on the amount of *melanin* made by the melanocytes.

The ability of humans to endure direct exposure to solar radiation for prolonged periods varies and largely depends on the concentration of melanin, which functions as a filter to prevent the sun's rays, in the ultraviolet portion, from penetrating through the epidermis to the dermal layer where blood vessels, nerves, and gland cells are located. Some studies showed that heavily pigmented skin filtered out about 95 percent of the ultraviolet, whereas fair skin blocked only about 50 percent.[11] Ultraviolet radiation can also be blocked by keratin, which is quite dense in thicker corneum layers. The skin of many Mongoloid peoples, for example, has a thickened corneum that scatters or filters the ultraviolet even though fewer melanin granules are present. In the dark skin of Africans, even the corneum is packed with melanin granules, which adds to its protection.

What is especially significant to our investigation of human variability is the considerable range of difference in melanin. The number of melanocytes is approximately the same in all races, and even albinos have a normal amount of these cells. Differences in melanin production must be due, then, to a difference in the activity of these cells. This activity is under the control of several genes; probably between four to six loci are involved. Offspring of a fair and a dark parent will produce melanin at an intermediate level. In dark-skinned peoples, the cells apparently function at a high level, synthesizing large quantities of melanin, whereas in the fair-skinned northern Europeans, the cells make very little melanin. The melanocytes are stimulated by ultraviolet radiation, however, and will synthesize greater quantities of melanin in the presence of sunlight. This photosensitivity explains the ability of the lighter-skinned people to tan during the summer months. Factors of sex and age also influence melanin density. Newborns of dark-skinned parents are light in color, sometimes even pink, and as they grow older their skin darkens like their parents'. In addition, females of any population are usually lighter than the males. These factors of age and sex may have relevance to survival.

Variations in quantities of melanin and its resulting filtering of the sun's rays have a very important consequence in altering the skin's ability to synthesize vitamin D_3 (cholecalciferol), which is formed in the skin by the action of ultraviolet radiation on a steriod (7-dehydrocholesterol) in the dermal layer. There is no variation in the quantities of steroid, but there are significant differences among people in the conversion to vitamin D. The development and maintenance of healthy bone depends on the presence of of the vitamin. Little, if any, ultraviolet energy penetrates to lower skin levels of darkly pigmented people during the winter months

---

[11] See Fitzpatrick and Jimbow, 1985; also see discussion on skin color and adaptation in chapter 6.

in the temperate zone, however, which explains why they are at risk for the vitamin D deficiency disease, rickets, when they move into the northern cities of Europe and America.

EYE COLOR AND HAIR COLOR

Melanin granules also determine the various shades of *eye color* by the distribution and density of the pigment in the iris. Blue eyes occur when there is little melanin present scattered throughout the iris structure. The light reflected from the relatively depigmented upper layer is in the blue range of the visible light spectrum. So blue eyes occur most often in fair-skinned persons. Variations in the density of the pigment and its distribution cause a graded color series from pale blue to brown. Though eye color tends to be related to the degree of skin melanin, darker eyes do occur in individuals with fair skin. This suggests that different gene loci control the production and distribution of eye pigment.

Hair color is also determined by the degree of melanin present and generally correlates with skin color. Most humans have dark hair, ranging from brown to black, and there appears to be an aging factor influencing hair color. Many children of European ancestry are fair haired until adolescence. The persistence of fair hair throughout adolescence is associated with fair skin. In central Australia, however, many Aboriginals have blond hair as children, which appears in stark contrast to their dark skin. As they reach adolescence, their hair usually darkens, but some maintain light hair color throughout their lives. The reason for the blondness among the Aboriginals is still open to speculation and is a lively topic for discussion. Blondness of the Australians is apparently due to a gene or genes for the trait and not because of some European admixture because those individuals with the blond trait have all Aboriginal characteristics, and the evidence for a lack of European genes is reinforced by carefully collected genealogies.[12] The peculiar example of the contrasts between hair and skin pigment raises the question of the complex inheritance of pigmentation of hair, skin, and eye color and suggests the possibility that the dark skin of Pacific peoples may be due to genes different from African populations.

Hair Form

When the skin of our species is compared with other mammals, the first distinction noticed is the near hairless, naked appearance. On closer inspection, however, the skin is not hairless; even apparently naked areas

---

[12] See Birdsell (1981:325) for a discussion of the cline for hair color in central Australia.

have about the same number of hair follicles as do our furrier primate relatives. Human hairs are finer, thinner in diameter, shorter, and most are relatively colorless. The distribution, density, and color of body hair, though, is subject to vast individual differences, and some racial groups have denser body hair than others. For example, there is a relative lack of facial hair among male Asians and Native Americans in contrast to the heavy beards of many European males, and the beards and dense body hair of the Japanese Ainu. Body hair distribution also shows significant sexual dimorphism with females of all races having less, and there is a near total lack of facial hair.

The hair on the head also varies considerably in length and form, from straight to wavy or curly, and the spiral "peppercorn" shape. Asians have straight hair that is thicker than the wavy or curly hair of many Europeans. Frizzy or woolly hair is the form of most Africans, and the San or !Kung are noted for their short, spiral hair. The adaptive significance of hair form is not understood, but it is likely that certain forms, woolly or spiral, allow for an air space between the scalp and outer edges that insulates the head from the intensity of the sun's heat in the tropics. Such an insulating mechanism would be an advantage to the !Kung hunters of South Africa or the Melanesians in New Guinea. As is the case with these other polygenic structures we have discussed, the distribution, form, and color of hair are inherited. The number of genes involved, though, are not known, but, some inherited defects of hair structure have been reported. One rare form of special interest, "woolly" hair, was discovered in a large family kindred living in an isolated region of Norway. Their hair grows to only a short length before the ends break off and gives the appearance of the frizzled or woolly hair form seen in some Africans. The "woolly" hair condition is different, however, and is inherited as an autosomal dominant trait.

FACTORS OF GROWTH AND DEVELOPMENT

The growth and development of the body's organs and structures are under control of a complex of genes that interact with the environment to produce the traits previously discussed. Nutrition, climate, and disease all act to regulate how we grow and at what rates. Also, there are individual and ethnic variations in body form and size. For example, though American-born Japanese are taller and heavier than their relatives in Japan, they retain the same body proportions. It is difficult, however, to sort out the genetic influences from the environment even though most growth differences appear to be environmental. Early childhood malnutrition, as an example, retards growth but there may be a catch-up period of accelerated growth if nutrition is improved later in childhood. Because

TABLE 4-8   Classification of Growth Periods

PERIOD	MALE	FEMALE
I. Infancy (neonate)	Birth–1 year (First 4 weeks)	Birth–1 year (First 4 weeks)
II. *Childhood*	*1–16 years*	*1–16 years*
early	1–6 years	1–6 years
mid	6–9 or 10 years	6–9 or 10 years
late	9 or 10–16 years	9 or 10–16 years
III. Puberty (in late childhood)	13–14 years	12–13 years
IV. Adolescence	14–18 or 20 years	13–18 or 20 years
V. Adult	20 years +	20 years +

Source: After Krogman, 1972. Copyright © The University of Michigan Press. Reprinted by permission of the publisher.

of a population's history of enduring marginal diets for many generations, it is possible that there has been natural selection for individuals who can best subsist under such conditions and may adapt by slower, prolonged growth. Such persons would suffer less from effects of malnutrition and have a capability to respond better during any catch-up period. An example is provided by the !Kung of South Africa whose small size may be due to a genetic adaptation to their desert environment (Howell, 1986). Some improvement in the environment and nutritional status of these people over the past decades is the likely cause of a small increase in mean stature since 1935 (Tobias, 1975). The genetic factors of populations with a history of nutritional deprivation have not yet been identified, however.

What has been clearly established is that there are several markers or "way-stations" that may be used to measure the relative quality of human growth. All humans pass through these well-defined periods during which growth may accelerate or slow down. The age or time of certain periods—the onset of puberty, for example—varies from group to group. The passage through these stages is relatively the same, however; all humans spend approximately one-third of their life preparing for the remaining two-thirds. These growth periods are listed in Table 4-8. Note that male and female timing is nearly the same except for an earlier onset of puberty in the female.

Comparisons with other mammals show that the time spent at each of these growth periods varies widely among species (Table 4-9). Humans are the most long lived and, though their gestation is not significantly different from the great apes, a greater amount of time is spent in childhood and adolescence. This lengthened development period is a major characteristic of our species and the increased time allows for a longer learning period, which is an important correlate to our increased brain size and development. Throughout human evolution the lengthened

TABLE 4-9 Developmental Periods of Select Mammal Species

SPECIES	GESTATION (IN DAYS)	AGE AT PUBERTY	LONGEVITY (IN YEARS)
Rat	22	6–9 (weeks)	4–5
Rabbit	31	6–9 (months)	10–15
Dog	63	6–8 (months)	15–20
Cat	63	12–15 (months)	20–30
Pig	112	7–8 (months)	12–20
Elephant	660	9–14 (years)	60–70
		PRIMATES	
Bush-baby	120–146	1½–2 years	14
Lemur	120–140	1½–2 years	27
Rhesus	150–180	2–4 years	29
Baboon	180–190	2½–3½ years	29
Gibbon	210	8–10 years	31
Orangutan	220–270	8–13 years	30
Chimpanzee	216–260	8–9 years	41
Gorilla	250–290	6–8 years	33
Human	260–280	13–15 years	[a]

[a] Though average longevity ranges from 45 years to 75 years in different societies, there have been frequent reports of persons living beyond the century mark.

learning period has been turned to an advantage in the development of culture.

The average birth weight of American whites is 3.3 kg (American blacks average 5 percent less); to achieve this size during the 270 days of gestation, the original weight of the fertilized ova must be increased several billions of times. From conception to birth the single cell is transformed into a complex organism consisting of billions of cells divided into numerous specialized tissues. Growth and development must occur at varying rates so each unit will have its correct functional proportion by birth. The embryo grows at a linear rate of 1.5 mm/day during the second month, which is an enormously rapid growth rate; for example, if this rate were continued after birth, a thirty-foot-tall adult would be produced. From about the eighth week, growth slows until the sixth and seventh months, when fetal growth begins to accelerate. After this peak during the fetal stage, infant and child growth slows but begins to accelerate again in late childhood to another peak in adolescence (the "growth spurt").

Different body regions grow at varying rates at different stages as in the example of the head, which accounts for a major proportion of growth during the fetal and infancy stages (Figure 4-11). This emphasis on cerebral development, one of the hallmarks of our species, is illustrated by the body-weight and brain-weight changes from the second month of gestation through the seventh year (Table 4-10). The brain weight accounts for 93 percent of the total weight, until the last four months of fetal

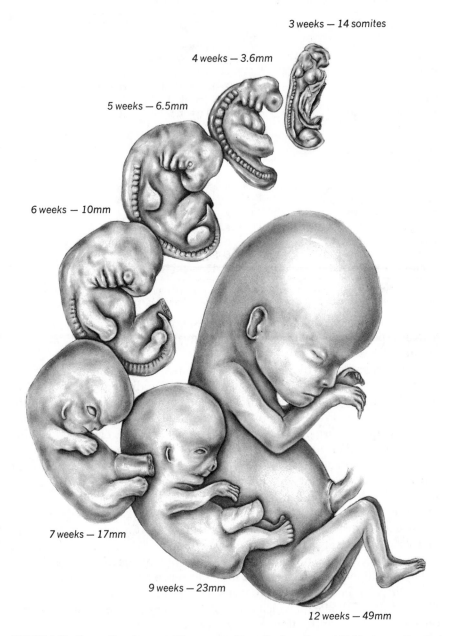

3 weeks — 14 somites

4 weeks — 3.6mm

5 weeks — 6.5mm

6 weeks — 10mm

7 weeks — 17mm

9 weeks — 23mm

12 weeks — 49mm

FIGURE 4-11   Human Developmental Sequences. (From Harrison, R., and W. Montagna, *Man*, 2nd ed., 1973. First edition copyright © 1969 Appleton-Century-Crofts. Reprinted by permission of Prentice-Hall, Inc., Englewood Cliffs, N.J.)

TABLE 4-10 Age Changes in Brain Size

AGE	BODY WEIGHT	BRAIN WEIGHT	% OF BODY SIZE	VOLUME OF BRAIN	CRANIAL CAPACITY	PERCENTAGE
Newborn	3100	380.0	12.3	330	350	94.3
3 months	—	—	—	500	600	83.3
6 months	—	—	—	575	775	74.2
9 months	—	—	—	675	925	73.0
1 year	9000	944.7	10.5	750	1000	75.0
2 years	11,000	1025.0	9.4	900	1100	81.8
3 years	12,500	1108.1	8.9	960	1225	78.4
4 years	14,000	1330.1	10	1000	1300	76.9
6 years	17,800	1359.1	7.6	1060	1350	78.5
9 years	25,200	1408.3	5.6	1100	1400	78.6
12 years	37,100	1428.0	3.8	1150	1450	79.3
18 years	59,500	1444.5	2.4	1200	1500	80.0

Sources: Based on Tobias, 1971; and Young, 1971.

development, when other parts of the body begin to enlarge rapidly; then the brain is only approximately 10 percent of total weight. This brain size is the maximum that the fetal metabolism can maintain because of the brain's higher energy requirement. From birth until the seventh year the brain increases much more rapidly than other tissues (except for the lymphoid tissues). At seven years of age a person has about 95 percent of his or her adult brain weight and brain development is nearly completed.

By comparison, after the first year of life, other tissues become slower in their growth until adolescence, when body size increases rapidly and the reproductive organs mature. The weights of several organs at various growth stages show a linear increase from birth to adult (Table 4-11). By the time puberty is reached, the brain is very close to its adult weight. The thymus gland, a lymphoid organ in the lower neck that functions as part of the immunological system, decreases in size by contrast. Body size and proportions of head, trunk, and legs also change.

Growth Rates

The several growth processes that occur at varying rates are under the influence of factors noted previously. The interplay of these factors may lead to retarded or advanced growth. At each point in time we are expected to be at a particular point in our life cycle, but many of us deviate from this established norm. We may be taller or shorter than our classmates, reach puberty earlier or later, or our skeletal system may develop at other than expected rates. In other words, our developmental age often will not coincide with our chronological age. One good measure of growth and development is the degree of skeletal development or "skeletal age."

TABLE 4-11   **Average Weights (in Grams) of Organs at Different Ages**

	NEWBORN	% OF ADULT WEIGHT	1 YEAR	6 YEARS	PUBERTY	ADULT
Brain	350	26%	910	1200	1300	1350
Heart	24	8	45	95	150	300
Thymus	12	80	20	24	30	0–15
Kidneys (both)	25	8	70	120	170	300
Liver	150	9	300	550	1500	1600
Lungs (both)	60	5	130	260	410	1200
Pancreas	3	3	9	—	40	90
Spleen	10	6	30	55	95	155
Stomach	8	5	30	—	80	135

Source: Reproduced with permission from Lowrey, G. H.: *Growth and Development of Children,* 7th ed. Copyright © 1978 by Year Book Medical Publishers, Inc., Chicago.

Skeletal maturation.   Most bone development begins during the embryonic period when the bones' characteristic shapes are formed in *cartilage*; the exceptions are cranial bones and the clavicle, which are developed from *membranous* tissues. During the latter part of the embryo state, mineralization of the cartilage starts from ossification centers and progressively increases until major portions of the bones have calcified. Bones continue to grow by this process of cartilage formation and then mineralize with calcium phosphate throughout childhood and adolescence, infusing the cartilage with this hard substance. Figure 4-12 shows the development and growth of the femur starting from a basic cartilage shape at two months prenatally (A). Primary ossification begins at four months from a center in the midshaft of the long bones, the *diaphysis* (B). At birth a major portion of the diaphysis is calcified and a secondary ossification has appeared (C); other centers will appear and begin to grow as indicated.

Throughout childhood the secondary centers of ossification become established and contribute to growth. The ends of the bones, or *epiphyses*, remain separated from the diaphysis by a cartilage plate until late in adolescence when they fuse with the diaphysis. It is through this process of cartilage formation, followed by mineralization, that growth occurs. The active formation at the epiphyses near the end of the long bones contributes to an increase in length. Each bone of the skeleton has a characteristic growth rate, and skeletal age or maturation is based on the degree of ossification of these centers and on their ultimate fusion with the main shaft (Figure 4-13).

In young children many bones of the skeleton remain unfused, and some bones (in the wrists, for example) have not yet begun to form. Radiographs of the hands of a child from the fourth to the seventh year

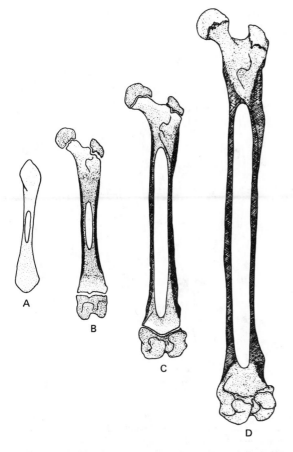

FIGURE 4-12   Diagram of Long Bone Development and Calcification Illustrated by a Human Femur.

show the development of the wrist bones (*carpals*), which begin to develop at different times during early childhood. Their relative sizes and degree of calcification show quite clearly (Figure 4-14). The fingers (*phalanges*) and the adjacent *metacarpals* (wrist bones), which grow in a pattern similar to the long bones of the arms and legs, show up clearly in this radiograph. The details of the diaphyses and associated epiphyses are shown at various stages. Thousands of individuals in many populations have had their hands radiographed during several years of growth, and standards of skeletal age have been established relative to chronological age. In this way, individuals with retarded growth may be identified early and, if owing to dietary or hormonal deficiencies, corrective measures can be taken.

There are many examples of deviation in skeletal development and epiphyseal fusion rates that are more due to general health and nutritional

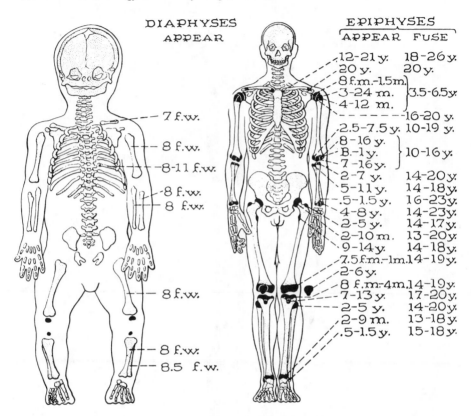

FIGURE 4-13 First appearance of the shafts (diaphyses) and joint ends (epiphyses) of the appendicular skeleton (f.w.: fetal weeks; f.m.: fetal months; m.: months; y.: years). (From Robertson, G. G., "Developmental Anatomy," in *Morris' Human Anatomy*, 12th ed., ed. B. J. Anson. New York: McGraw-Hill Book Company, 1966. Reproduced by permission.)

status than to racial differences. The timing of skeletal growth is much the same in all children, though Asian children are slightly more advanced. There is a clear sexual dimorphism; females are between one to two years earlier in their skeletal development.

Skull. At birth, the bones of the cranium are separated by unossified membranes, which allow great flexibility and permit the passage of the infant's head (averaging 35 cm in circumference) through the birth canal. Starting from birth, there is considerable activity at the ossification centers and the cranial bones increase in size until they meet and eventually fuse, later in adult life. Certain cranial bones, however, fuse soon after birth. For example, the halves of the mandible fuse at the mandibular symphysis (the chin region) during the first year, and also the left and right halves of the frontal bone of the skull fuse along a suture through the middle

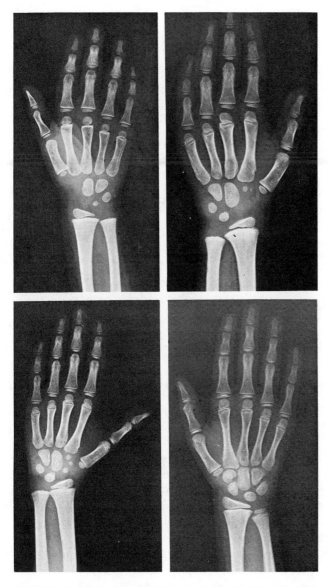

FIGURE 4-14 The development of the carpal bones (wrist bones) and the appearance of the epiphyses of the metacarpals and phalanges at ages four (top left), five (top right), six (bottom left), and seven (bottom right). (Reproduced with permission from Lowrey, G. H., *Growth and Development of Children*, 7th ed. Copyright © 1978 by Year Book Medical Publishers, Inc., Chicago.)

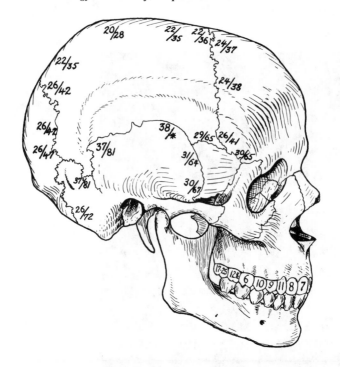

FIGURE 4-15   Suture Closure of the Skull. The superior figures indicate the age at which the portion of the suture commences to obliterate, the inferior figures, the age at which obliteration is completed. The * indicates that the suture never completely closes. The figures on the upper teeth give the usual ages in years of the eruption of each permanent tooth. Owing to the great variability involved, these figures must be used with caution. (From Montagu, M. F. Ashley, *An Introduction to Physical Anthropology*, 3rd ed., 1960. Courtesy of Charles C Thomas, Publisher, Springfield, Ill.)

of the forehead. Other cranial bones remain separated for many years and are joined at an irregular unmineralized junction (the sutures). These sutures gradually calcify with age, and the adjoining bones eventually become fused together. The older the individual, usually by middle age, the less distinct will be the cranial sutures. This process of cranial bone mineralization covers a broad time range because each suture fuses at a different rate (Figure 4-15).

Dental maturation.   At birth, the deciduous teeth are nearly complete and some are ready to erupt within the first few months. Below their roots, buried deep within the bones of the jaws, are the developing permanent teeth, which gradually replace the deciduous teeth as the individual grows (Figure 4-16). This process of dental development is long and complicated; starting at about the sixth week in the embryo and

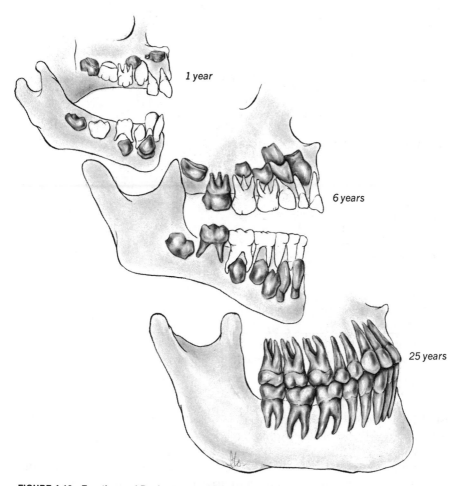

FIGURE 4-16   Eruption and Replacement of Primary and Secondary Dentition. Permanent (secondary) teeth are shaded. (From Harrison, R., and W. Montagna, *Man*, 2nd ed., 1973. Reprinted by permission of Prentice-Hall, Inc., Englewood Cliffs, N.J.)

continuing until the sixteenth year, there are some teeth in various stages of development while other teeth are fully formed.

The first teeth (deciduous incisors) erupt during the sixth to ninth month while the crowns of the permanent first molars, incisors, and canines are just beginning to form. This process of development and eruption continues until the twenty-first year (an average among North American whites) when the third molar (wisdom tooth) erupts, if the person is fortunate. Often, the third molar is impacted within the bone and must be removed surgically. The timing of dental development is

TABLE 4-12   Chronology of Human Tooth Development

TOOTH	ONSET OF CALCIFICATION	CROWN (COMPLETED)	ERUPTION	ROOT (COMPLETED)
Deciduous				
Central incisor	4–4.5 months (in utero)	1.5–2.5 months	6–8 months	1.5 years
Lateral incisor	4.5	2.5–3	8–10	1.5–2
Cuspid	5	9	10–20	3.5
First molar	5	5.5–6	12–16	2.5
Second molar	6	10–11	20–24	3
Permanent				
First molars	Birth	2.5–3 years	6 years	9–10 years
Central incisors	3–4 months	4–5	7	9–10
Lateral incisors	10–12	4–5	8	10–11
Canines (cuspid)	4–5	6–7	11	12–15
First premolars (bicuspid)	1.5–2 years	5–6	10	12–13
Second premolars (bicuspid)	2–2.5	6–7	11	12–14
Second molars	2.5–3	7–8	12	14–16
Third molars	7–10	12–16	[a]	18–23

[a] The eruption time of the third molars is highly variable, with a range of 16–22 years.
Sources: Modified from Logan and Kronfield, 1933; and Schour and Massler, 1944.

listed in Table 4-12. Note that the crowns are completed, and eruption occurs before the roots are fully formed.

Tooth-calcification sequences are fairly regular and provide a good indicator of age analogous to the skeletal ossification centers. Eruption times, however, are quite variable and are subject to several factors. There are strong environmental influences caused by diet and disease. Earlier eruption appears to be the rule among higher socioeconomic groups. Sex differences also exist; tooth eruption is, on the average, a few months earlier in females. No definite genetic pattern has been established, though there have been several reports of racial differences in tooth eruption. Tooth eruption among Europeans and American whites is later than among American Indians, Asians, and African Americans. Australian Aboriginals appear to have the earliest tooth eruptions, especially the third molars that have been known to erupt as early as 13 years.

Sexual maturation.   Toward the end of childhood (eight to nine years in females and ten to eleven in males), a series of biological changes begins that continues during a period of several years, transforming a child into a young adult. This is the period known as puberty or adolescence. After gradual deceleration of growth from its peak during the seventh fetal month, the body gradually begins to increase its growth rate with the approach of puberty. Changes occur in hair patterns and bodily proportions, and the sex organs begin to mature and increase in size. Approximately two years after entering this stage the individual begins the *adolescent growth spurt* (a time of rapid gain in size). The voice deepens (in males), breast development begins to be apparent (in females), and other secondary sexual characteristics appear—changes in fat distribution and development of hips (in females), for example, and increase in shoulder size in males. Pubic and axillary hair begins to appear in both sexes, and males start to show signs of facial hair.

There are wide individual variations in the time of the onset of the growth spurt, depending on sex, diet, general health, and, perhaps, genetic factors. In males, the growth spurt may occur anywhere between twelve and sixteen years, approximately two years later than in females (ten to fourteen years). After a year, growth decreases but continues slowly into the early twenties in males and the late teens in females. If measurements are taken throughout a person's growth years (longitudinal study), then a rapid gain can be easily seen, as shown in Figure 4-17, which plots average height increment gains for early- and late-maturing groups. Some individuals may gain 10 cm or more in height in a single year. Similar changes occur in weight, fat distribution, and bodily proportions. These changes, however, are more gradual and continue over longer periods.

There is no clear-cut indicator of sexual maturity in the male; the increases in the sizes of the sex organs and their hormonal secretions are gradual and continue over a long period. In the female, *menarche*, the onset of the first menses, which occurs within a year of the growth spurt, is an excellent marker dividing prepuberty- and postpuberty phases, however. There has been a trend over the past century toward a decrease in age at menarche, especially among children of the developed countries. For example, where records have been kept for one and a half centuries an average of seventeen years was registered in 1840 (Table 4-13). Today the average age at menarche is between twelve and fourteen, with 95 percent occurring between 11 and 15 years of age in the United States. No further decrease in age has been recorded, and there are several indications that the trend toward earlier menarche has ceased.

Neither race nor climate appears to be a factor in the timing of female maturity, though both have been examined extensively during the past few decades (Eveleth and Tanner, 1976). More likely menarche is related to those environmental factors that contribute to accelerated growth and changes in body composition. During and immediately after the growth spurt, female weight gain is greatest for the fat content of the body—a 120 percent increase compared with the lean body component

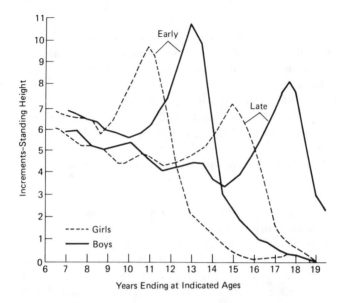

FIGURE 4-17   Amount of Increase in Height per Year of Early-Maturing and Late-Maturing Girls and Boys. Although late-maturing girls show the peak rate of growth almost two years later than early-maturing boys, they still reach this stage nearly two and a half years before late-maturing boys reach the same peak velocity of growth. The curves of growth for height and weight are related to the maturation of the skeleton. This, in turn, is related to maturation in general (including the hormonal changes associated with sexual maturation). (From Tanner, J. M., *Growth at Adolescence*, 1962. Copyright © 1962 by Blackwell Scientific Publications, Ltd. Reprinted by permission of the publisher.)

(muscle and bone) increase of 49 percent. This significantly shifts the lean body mass to fat ratio from 5:1 prepuberty to a 3:1 ratio at menarche. In contrast, the male body composition is around 5 or 6 to 1. Rose Frisch (1988) has argued convincingly that it is this surplus that provides a critical fat mass needed to support the energy requirements of the female reproductive physiology. A minimal amount of 17 percent is needed to initiate menses; in a girl of 165 cm (65 inches) tall, a total body weight of 49 kg (97 lb) is needed, or 38 kg (83.8 lb), for a person 155 cm (61 inches). The earlier attainment of these sizes, as in the case of children in well-off socioeconomic groups with optimum nutrition, contributes to earlier age at menarche. By contrast, in populations where children are relatively malnourished, girls grow more slowly, enter their growth spurts later, and weight gain is significantly lower than those in well-nourished populations—all contributing to a later menarche.

Children of the Bundi tribe in the highlands of New Guinea, for example, have the slowest growth, and girls reach menarche at about 18 years, the oldest recorded in the world today. Additional evidence is provided by European populations who lived through the hardships of

TABLE 4-13   Age at Menarche

POPULATIONS	AVERAGE AGE (YEARS)
European	
Various populations	12.5–13.5
Nineteenth century	15–17
New Zealand	
Maori	12.7
European	13.0
United States	
Afro-Americans	12.5
Euro-Americans	11–15
Chinese	
Hong Kong	12.5–13.3
Africa	
Nigeria	14.1
Uganda	13.4
Watusi	16.5
Hutu	17.0
New Guinea	
Bundi	18.0

Sources: Eveleth and Tanner, 1976; Frisch, 1988; Senderowitz and Paxman, 1985.

two World Wars. Many populations subsisted for long periods at or near starvation diets. The average age at menarche increased by two years to age 16, a point not too far from the late eighteenth-century levels.

The accumulation of these and other data from many studies of the health and welfare of children reveal some striking contrasts between generations and point to some significant trends. During the past century children are reaching maturity early, as described above, and are larger at all ages than previous generations.

Longitudinal Growth Trends

Growth data from several European countries and North America show an average gain of 1 cm in adult height per decade during the last century. To a large extent, this is part of a trend toward earlier maturation; individuals obtain their adult height at an earlier age. Males in the United States today reach their adult height at around eighteen years, whereas their great-grandfathers did not attain their full adult height until age twenty-six. Improved living standards in many societies have enabled children in many populations to grow to their maximum genetic potential; this increase in size during the past several generations is called *secular trend* (Figure 4-18). The graphs compare average heights of four groups from age four to twenty-three and show a 15-cm increase in adult height since 1833. The group of boys measured in 1833 were factory hands

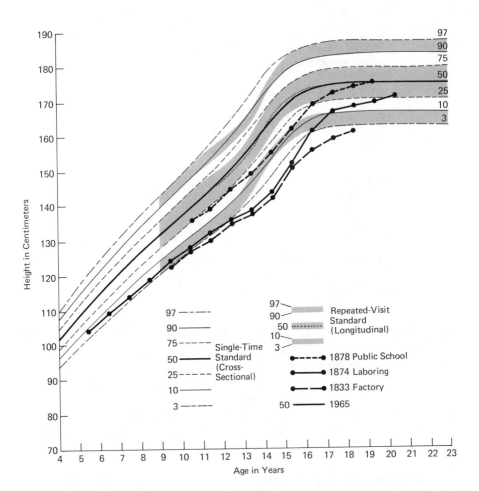

FIGURE 4-18 Secular Trend in Height. Secular trend in height is shown by surveys of the height of English boys in the years 1833, 1874, and 1965. Data are reproduced on a standard growth chart. "Single-time standard (cross-sectional)" refers to the average result from cross-sectional surveys. "Repeated-visit standard (longitudinal)" refers to average result from longitudinal surveys. The numbers 97, 90, 75, and so on indicate percent of the male population shorter than a given height. (From Tanner, J. M., "Growing Up," September 1973. Copyright © 1973 by Scientific American, Inc. All rights reserved.)

whose growth was retarded in late childhood and adolescence. Their height at age fourteen was a full 20 cm less than the standard of 1965, but slow growth over a prolonged period made up for some of this deficit. This catch-up period suggests that depressing environmental effects are more influential on growth rate than on final size.

Ethnic and Environmental Influences

Boys and girls in the developed countries are heavier and taller than their parents. The secular increase in size has caused the height and weight tables of a generation ago to be outdated. Reasons for this trend are often related to a general improvement in nutrition and health care, and to more adequate housing.

This phenomenon occurs in all groups whose socioeconomic circumstances allow the children to be raised at optimum levels of nutrition and health. The secular increases cut across ethnic boundaries. African-Americans, for example, also show an increase of body size over the past few generations despite the higher morbidity and mortality rates; however, this increase is significantly less than that of American whites. In addition, comparisons of Europeans, Africans, and Asians who are raised under similar economically well-off circumstances show few differences. The growth of Africans and Europeans is very much alike, but Chinese are shorter at all ages and complete their growth earlier. By contrast, groups of similar genetic composition raised under differing environmental circumstances differ in average body size at all ages. Children whose parents are members of professional or managerial classes mature earlier and are 2 cm taller than children whose father's occupation is unskilled labor. At adolescence, the difference between children of these classes increases to 5 cm. Comparisons of seven-year-old children, grouped according to socioeconomic class based on the father's occupation and number of children in the family, are shown in Figure 4-19.

Further evidence of these characteristic growth responses to varying environments have been documented by many records of immigrant populations and their children as in a study of stature increase among second-generation Italian-Americans in the Boston area (Damon, 1965). Stature increased from the oldest to the youngest age groups sampled, which were divided into decades from twenty to fifty-nine years of age. The greater stature of the youngest age group suggests that as economic standards and hence living conditions improve, the populations average stature and weight increase.

The many studies of human growth demonstrate that the effects of environment are quite similar for several ethnic groups. Variation in the tempo of ossification among several populations appears to be determined entirely by environment. Distinctions are seen, however, in body form and proportion, which appear to be under closer genetic control than body size. Malnourished Europeans will grow to become smaller adults, but they will maintain the same bodily proportions as the better nourished. Also, though identical twins raised in different homes may differ considerably in size, their bodily proportions remain the same. Consideration of these relative influences of genes and environment will make it easier to

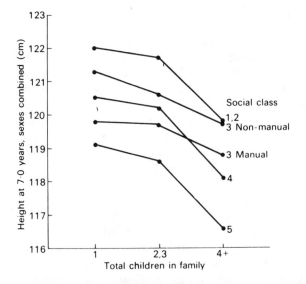

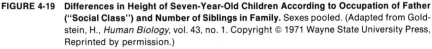

FIGURE 4-19   Differences in Height of Seven-Year-Old Children According to Occupation of Father ("Social Class") and Number of Siblings in Family. Sexes pooled. (Adapted from Goldstein, H., *Human Biology*, vol. 43, no. 1. Copyright © 1971 Wayne State University Press, Reprinted by permission.)

understand human variability of form and size, though there appear to be few racial distinctions.

RECOMMENDED READINGS AND LITERATURE CITED

ABBIE, A. A., AND W. R. ADEY. 1953. "Pigmentation in a central Australian tribe with special reference to fair-headedness," *Am. J. Phys. Anthrop.*, 11:339–359.

ABBIE, A. A. 1967. "Book review: *The Living Races of Man*," *Current Anthrop.*, 8:113–114.

ABBIE, A. A. 1975. *Studies in Physical Anthropology*, vols. 1 and 2. Australian Institute of Aboriginal Studies, RRS5, Canberra.

BEALS, K. L., C. L. SMITH, AND S. M. DODD. 1984. "Brain size, cranial morphology, climate, and time machines," *Current Anthrop.*, 25:301–330.

BIRDSELL, J. B. 1981. *Human Evolution*. New York: Houghton Mifflin.

BIASUTTI, R. 1959. *Razze e Popoli della Terra*, 2nd ed., 4 vols. Torino: VTET.

BOYD, W. C. 1963. "Four achievements of the genetical method in physical anthropology," *Am. J. Phys. Anthrop.*, 65:243–252.

BRACE, C. L. 1962. "Cultural factors in the evolution of the human dentition," in *Culture and the Evolution of Man*, ed. M. F. Ashley Montagu. New York: Oxford University Press.

BRACE, C. L., AND K. D. HUNT. 1990. "A nonracial craniofacial perspective on human variation: A(Australia) to Z(Zuni)," *Am. J. Phys. Anthrop.*, 82:341–360.

BRACE, C. L., AND P. E. MAHLER. 1971. "Post-pleistocene changes in the human dentition," *Am. J. Phys. Anthrop.*, 34:191–204.

BURNHAM, S. 1985. *Black Intelligence in White Society*. Athens, Ga.: Social Science Press.

CARBONELL, V. M. 1963. "Variations in the frequency of shovel-shape incisors in different populations," in *Dental Anthropology*, D. R. Brothwell, ed. Elmsford, N. Y.: Pergamon Press.

Comas, J. 1960. *Manual of Physical Anthropology.* Springfield, Ill.: Charles C Thomas.

Damon, A. 1965. "Stature increase among Italian-Americans: Environmental, genetic, or both?" *Am. J. Phys. Anthrop.*, 23:401–408.

Dobzhansky, T. 1962. *Mankind Evolving.* New Haven: Yale University Press.

Eveleth, P. B., and J. M. Tanner. 1976. *Worldwide Variation in Human Growth*, Biological Program 8. New York: Cambridge University Press.

Fitzpatrick, T. B., and K. Jimbow. 1985. "Human skin color: Origin, variation and significance," *J. Hum. Evol.*, 14:43–56.

Frisch, R. 1988. Fatness and fertility. *Sci. Am.* 258:88–95.

Frisch, R., and R. Revelle. 1969. "Variation in body weights and the age of the adolescent growth spurt among Latin American and Asian populations, in relation to calorie supplies," *Hum. Biol.* 41:185–212.

Goldstein, H. 1971. "Factors influencing the height of seven year old children—results from the National Child Development Study," *Hum. Biol.*, 43:92–101.

Harrison, G. A., J. Weiner, J. M. Tanner, and N. A. Barnicot. 1977. *Human Biology*, 2nd ed. Oxford: Oxford University Press.

Harrison, R., and W. Montagna. 1972. *Man.* Englewood Cliffs, N. J.: Prentice-Hall.

Holloway, R. L., Jr. 1966. "Cranial capacity and neuron number: A critique and proposal," *Am. J. Phys. Anthrop.*, 25:305–314.

Howell, N. 1986. "Feedbacks and buffers in relation to scarcity and abundance: Studies of Hunter-Gatherer populations," in *The State of Population Theory: Forward from Malthus*, (eds.) D. Coleman and R. Schofield, pp. 156–187. Oxford: Basil Blackwell.

Hulse, F. S. 1967. "Selection for skin color among the Japanese," *Am. J. Phys. Anthrop.*, 27:143–156.

Krogman, W. M. 1972. *Child Growth.* Ann Arbor: University of Michigan Press.

Lasker, G. W. 1973. *Physical Anthropology.* New York: Holt, Rinehart and Winston.

Logan, W. H. G., and R. Kronfeld. 1933. "Development of the human jaws and surrounding structures from birth to the age of 15 years," *Am. Dent. Assoc.* 20:379.

Lowrey, G. H. 1978. *Growth and Development of Children*, 7th ed. Chicago: Year Book Medical.

Molnar, S. 1971. "Human tooth wear, tooth function and cultural variability," *Am. J. Phys. Anthrop.*, 34:175–190.

Molnar, S., and S. C. Ward. 1977. "On the hominid masticatory complex: Biomechanical and evolutionary perspectives," *J. Hum. Evol.*, 6:557–568.

Montagu, M. F. A. 1960. *An Introduction to Physical Anthropology*, 3rd. ed. Springfield, Ill.: Charles C Thomas.

Montagu, M. F. A. 1965. *Introduction to Physical Anthropology.* Springfield, Ill.: Charles C Thomas.

Osborne, R. H. and F. V. Degeorge. 1959. *Genetic Basis of Morphological Variation.* Cambridge, Mass.: Harvard University Press.

Pietrusewsky, M. 1990. "Craniofacial variation in Australasian and Pacific populations," *Am. J. Phys.Anthrop.*, 82:319–340.

Roberts, D. F. 1978. *Climate and Human Variability.* Menlo Park: Cummings.

Robertson, G. G. 1966. "Developmental anatomy," in *Morris' Human Anatomy*, 12th ed., ed. B. J. Anson. New York: McGraw-Hill.

Schour, I., and M. Massler. 1944. "Development and growth of teeth," in *Oral Histology and Embryology*, ed. B. Orban. St. Louis: C. V. Mosby.

Schultz, A. H. 1926. "Fetal growth of man and other primates," *Quart. Rev. Biol.*, 1:493–495.

Schwidetzky, I., and F. W. Rösing. 1982. "European population of the high and late medieval period (1000–1500)—comparative statistical studies on historical physical anthropology," *Hum. Biol.* [Budapest] 10:39–47.

Senderowitz, J., and J. M. Paxman. 1985. "Adolescent fertility, worldwide concerns." *Population Ref. Bureau* Vol. 40, no. 2.

Tanner, J. M. 1962. *Growth at Adolescence.* Oxford: Blackwell Scientific.

Tanner, J. M. 1973. "Growing up," in *Readings from Scientific American, Biological Anthropology*. New York: W. H. Freeman.

Tobias, P. V. 1970. "Brain size, grey matter and race-fact or fiction," *Am. J. Phys. Anthrop.*, 32:3–26.

TOBIAS, P. V. 1971. *The Brain in Hominid Evolution*. New York: Columbia University Press.

TOBIAS, P. V. 1975. "Anthropometry among disadvantaged peoples: Studies in Southern Africa," in *Biosocial Interrelations in Population Adaptation*, (eds.) E. S. Watts, F. E. Johnston, and G. W. Lasker, pp. 287–305. The Hague: Mouton.

TORTORA, G. J. 1980. *Principles of Human Anatomy*, 2nd ed. New York: Harper and Row.

TURNER, C. G. II. 1990. "Major features of Sundadonty and Sinodonty, including suggestions about East Asian microevolution, population history, and late Pleistocene relationships with Australian Aboriginals," *Am. J. Phys. Anthrop.*, 82:295–317.

VON BONIN, G. 1963. *The Evolution of the Human Brain*. Chicago: University of Chicago Press.

WOLPOFF, M. H. 1968. "Climatic influence on the skeletal nasal aperture," *Am. J. Phys. Anthrop.*, 3:405–424.

WOLPOFF, M. H. 1971. *Metric Trends in Hominid Dental Evolution*. Cleveland: Press of Case Western Reserve University.

YOUNG, J. Z. 1971. *An Introduction to the Study of Man*. Oxford: Clarendon Press.

_5_

Distribution
_of_
Human Differences

The term *race* has been applied to units as small as local breeding populations (demes) or to large groups of populations occupying entire continents (geographical race). Race has also been used quite frequently to describe a cultural or political group (Jewish, Aryan, English, and so on). Another casual use of the term is shown by the phrase *the human race*, which has nothing to do with biological classification. Ethnic group is more and more frequently used today as a substitute for groups presumed to be of different genetic ancestry than the majority population—as in the case of Hispanic ethnic groups in the United States. The results of such varied and inappropriate usage have misled the reader and have obscured meaningful application. Further, the varied criteria used to delineate racial boundaries have added materially to the confusion over the need for race classification in human biology studies. Comparisons of traits of simple inheritance yield different results than do a comparison of complex traits; the geographical distribution of red cell antigens and histocompatibility (HLA) types differ markedly from each other and do not correspond well with quantitative traits like body form.

The question of how the human species should be divided for description and study has always been a difficult one, particularly because many racial differences are trivial in comparison to species differences and because most human alleles are shared by all populations. Often genetic polymorphisms per loci is smaller among the geographical races than it is among populations within the same race. These factors, together with the reality of population variability, have caused several biologists to avoid or even to abandon the use of the race concept as a viable tool for the study of human diversity. Hiernaux (1964:43), for example, observes: "In my opinion, to dismember mankind into races as a convenient approximation requires such a distortion of the facts that any usefulness disappears." The facts to which Hiernaux refers are the many sources of evidence of human diversity, which include the several traits we discussed in the preceding chapters. The distribution of these traits is broader than generally appreciated and some distributions cut across population and geographical boundaries.

There is general agreement, however, that an understanding of human biological diversity is basic to comprehending human adaptation. Some workers consider racial classification as a useful means of studying adaptation and epidemiology because they view races as "natural units" (Polednak, 1989). Others dismiss race as but an artifact of *Homo sapiens'* past. Many believe that traits should be considered individually and not as a group or cluster unless the resulting classification, based on one character, reflects the variability of others (Livingstone, 1964:47). More and more frequently, in the past decade, the breeding population has been the unit of study.

Regardless of one's definition or application of the concept, we should remember the point raised earlier: There is no reason to assume there is now, or ever has been, a *fixed number* of races. If we keep this in mind, we can avoid the trap that so many nineteenth-century naturalists fell into: "If races change, how do races come to be?" This logical impasse retarded the study of human biology for many generations. In fact, we are only now beginning to appreciate the complexity of our very polytypic species, whose variability is a result of a series of interactions between the social and biological systems.

Human variability as it is distributed through time and space depends on a multitude of factors. Several are the same factors that operate on any biological population and influence gene frequency throughout the generations, as described in chapter 2. Humans are highly mobile and are able to manipulate the environment at will to affect adaptation, however, and these abilities affect the elaboration of complex social systems that regulate behavior—particularly breeding behavior. The establishment of abstract boundaries or mating circles within populations and the custom of excluding outsiders to some degree are strong factors in directing gene flow and determining the shape of the new generation in an increasingly nonrandom way.

The history of a population—how long it has lived in a given area, what selective forces have been acting on it, and what contacts it has had with other populations—helps determine the distribution of human variability. The effects of the European colonization of the world dramatize the significance of mass movements of people. Smaller-scale, more gradual changes can also occur through interpopulation contact and through the establishment of sedentary populations, both of which occur as consequences of new technology or subsistence patterns such as agricultural activities.

If we consider these factors that influence the distribution of our species, then any grouping of human variability into units, populations, races, or subspecies become a much more viable means of studying human diversity. The way in which we choose to group human populations depends, of course, on our purpose, and we must keep this purpose in mind when working with these groups. For example, one should not establish races or ethnic units on the basis of sociopolitical or religious criteria and then explain or interpret their existence in biological terms. The same stricture applies to groups established on the basis of geographic boundaries. The so-called natural boundaries do not prevent interpopulation contact, though distance does, of course, reduce gene flow. Likewise sociopolitical or religious differences may influence the composition of the next generations but only to a degree. The significance of this influence is determined by the humans involved and by their society. The religious and violent political differences in Northern Ireland, for example, have reduced or prevented interbreeding between the Catholics and Protestants. The net effect is the establishment of two breeding populations within what could have been a homogenous group. Similar examples can also be found in many other parts of the world where religious, economic, or political strife has resulted in a degree of isolation between groups (often referred to as ethnic groups).

Human differences are distributed in some rather interesting patterns around the world. If we take a single trait or several traits together, we see that many population groups vary widely from one another. The worldwide distribution of traits such as the ABO blood group, Rh blood group, abnormal hemoglobin, or the gene for taste sensitivity to phenylthiocarbamide show quite a wide difference between many populations. The fact remains, however, that these populations have been established because of conditions other than those determined by their genomes. The combinations of genes in these populations are found there because of social, geographical, and cultural conditions that have contributed to the growth and maintenance of the biological unit, which can be defined as a breeding population.

RACE AS A BIOLOGICAL UNIT

Explaining the arrangement of the varieties of organisms found in the natural world is as much a problem today as it always has been. With the newer techniques of taxonomy that use computer facilities, investigators can process thousands of items of information, many more than could the naturalists of previous generations. Rather than establishing and clarifying distinct boundaries between populations, this additional information will often raise new questions and cast doubts on the validity of many older, accepted taxonomic units. As noted earlier, anthropologists of the last century classified Melanesians with Africans because of similarities in skin color and hair. Such classification did not persist for long before anthropologists realized that there were numerous differences between the two groups. Over the decades many distinctive characteristics of cranial facial morphology were recorded that demonstrated the Melanesians were more closely related to other population groupings of the Pacific region. The similarities and degrees of relatedness are summarized by Howells (1973:40) in Figure 5-1.

The problem is not whether the earlier classifications were a true, accurate description of the natural world. The former methods merely had another way of viewing biological diversity, especially through those characteristics that were measured and considered at that time; groupings of all dark-skinned people together was logical to the early explorers and anthropologists. When other traits are considered, however, the boundaries of the first classifications break down. Since the development of genetic theory and description of DNA, life's diversity is now seen somewhat differently. Groups of organisms appear as dynamic units, many of whose characteristics change from generation to generation. Types or averages are no longer considered a sufficient means to describe groups of individuals participating in a breeding population. It is this dynamic condition that makes it extremely difficult to establish any all-inclusive taxonomic unit. The older definitions of such species as elementary units that are determined when collections of animals are sorted into groups are sufficient only as a first step.

The study of human diversity, especially the attempts to group people into subspecies or races, is hampered by the disagreement over several aspects of this diversity: its origin, its relation to the environment, and whether or not basic racial stocks are "real" and of great antiquity. The demographics of a population, that is, the growth and expansion or decline, is a more recent addition to the list of influences on distribution of biological diversity. Considering all of these factors it is best to return to a fundamental statement of biological classification. Species are considered natural biological units held together by gene flow, whereas subspecies are divisions made on an arbitrary basis. The subspecies (race) forms no

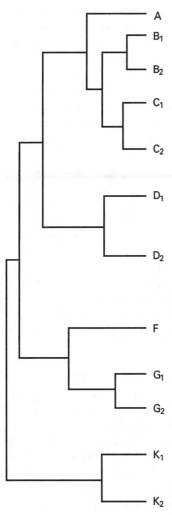

A   "Pygmies" of interior New Guinea

B_1 Baining of New Britain; central New Ireland; Timorini of west Irian

B_2 Nakanai of New Britain; south New Ireland; northeast Espiritu Santo

C_1 Many short people of north New Guinea, north New Ireland, Solomon Islands, Santa Cruz and New Hebrides

C_2 Slightly larger peoples of New Guinea, New Ireland, Bougainville (Solomons); western Micronesia (Palau, Yap, Marianas)

D_1 Moderately small and narrow-faced groups of north New Guinea, south Bougainville, Malaita, Carolines (Truk, Mortlocks, Kusaie), Ontong Java

D_2 Slightly larger, more narrow-faced groups of Carolines (7) and Marshalls; some possible Micro- or Polynesian-affected Melanesians in New Guinea, Bougainville, Malaita, Eromanga (New Hebrides)

F   Polynesia: Tonga, Samoa, north Cooks, Marquesas, Maori; Outliers Nukuoro and Kapingamarangi; Tanna of New Hebrides

G_1 Polynesia: (more broad-headed): Society Islands, Hawaii, south Cooks, Pukapuka

G_2 Fiji (broad head, face, nose): also one group each, Tonga and Kapingamarangi; southern New Caledonia

K_1 Australia (18 groups): continent-wide; also Tolai of New Britain, north New Caledonia Uvea of Loyalties

K_2 Australia (Arnhem Land, Cairns region, southeast coast, Murray River); also Loyalty Islands (Lifu and Mare); some Nakanai of New Britain

FIGURE 5-1 **Relationships of Pacific Peoples by Measurement** Comparisons of craniofacial and body measurements of 151 Pacific populations showed a clustering in three major branches: 1. Melanesian (A–D), with a subbranch of Micronesians (C_2 and D_2); 2. Polynesian (F–G); and 3. Australian (K). The degree of relationship or similarity is indicated by the length of the connecting branches in the diagram; for example, the K branches of the Australian samples are most distant from branch A of the Pygmies of interior New Guinea. Source: From Howells 1973. Reprinted by permission of George Weidenfeld and Nicolson Limited.

such "natural" unit, and the composition of each or the number described depends on the characteristics considered important. In other words, whether or not an individual or group of individuals are identified as a particular race is determined by their possession of certain traits, arbitrarily selected. More than fifty years ago, in studies of animal taxonomy, there was what was called the 75 percent rule. If 75 percent of the members of one population differed from another, then the two populations were considered to be distinct subspecies. This guideline worked more or less successfully depending on which criteria were used to assign the individuals. The second consideration is the geographical distribution of the populations and the history of contact, if any between them.

Most present-day concepts of race are founded in genetics and emphasize similarity throughout populations of a geographical region. This collection, or population complex, shares a close common ancestry and has been under the influence of similar selective forces. The existence of such conditions would result in a high degree of similarity between the genetic systems of these populations. According to many human biologists, the concept of race becomes much more useful if it is considered merely as an arbitrary grouping of populations identified for the purpose of a particular study. For example, the numerous studies today of ethnic group and disease emphasize sharing of a certain genome through common descent from recent ancestors. Certain components of this genome place the individuals at risk for some disease.

The various definitions listed in the first chapter, however, cover a broad range of understanding of the race concept.[1] The definitions do share a common factor; they consider the many racial differences that appear to relate to the geographical histories of each group. Dobzhansky (1944:252) stated: "It is recognized that most living species are more or less clearly differentiated into geographic races, each race occupying a portion of the species distribution." Many of the investigators today would likely subscribe to this definition with the additional qualifier of gene frequency differentiation. Few, however, view race as a natural unit.

The importance of geography to human diversity has often been recognized in the definition of races. Garn (1961) used spatial distribution of human varieties as a means of establishing racial groups. He provided us with geographical, local, and microraces, discussed earlier. Microgeographical races and local races are smaller, less inclusive groups, compa-

---

[1] I use the word "concept" as defined in Webster's dictionary, "an idea of a class of objects, a general notion." Most writers do also, I believe, even though they do not state a precise meaning. Used in this way, the implication is that race is a "real" object in nature awaiting to be discovered and labeled. There is much opposition against this view including my own objection as I will explain throughout the balance of the text. This implication of concept as defined raises many side issues, among them a failure of our language to adequately cope with a rapidly changing science of human biology and the understanding of our habitat.

rable with the breeding populations used by many workers who study human variation. These basic units are subject to localized natural selection, and population size is also effective in causing differentiation between groups. The largest, most inclusive group—the geographical race—includes many diverse local groups. In a way, this category is misleading, because often members of geographical races share only a few physical attributes. The geographical race conforms most closely to the older description of basic racial stocks or major races (usually the three: Mongoloid, Caucasoid, and Negroid).

Except for a superficial identification of the majority of the inhabitants of a continent, "basic stock" or "geographical race" tells us little about biological diversity or the interrelationships between breeding populations or the effects of the environment, which are the dimensions of the selective forces that act on the populations. "Basic stock" does not describe gene combinations but all too often contributes to stereotypes, the images generated when citizens of nations or regions are mentioned. That individuals seldom conform to an image is too large a disappointment to admit, a sin of which we are all guilty. Ripley's *Races of Europe*, mentioned in the first chapter, provided us with images of Europeans that tend to persist to this day, so it is important to recall an exhaustive study of human diversity within one of these "races." Hooton and Dupertius (1955) reported the results of their anthropometric study of ten thousand Irish males, residents of more than a dozen counties of Ireland. They found that few subjects fit the Irish stereotype so often used to depict one of the major "local races" of Europe. This and other surveys of local groups document that "geographical race" is merely a convenient label, an abstraction applied in a broad sense. To describe and study human variability, we must use a more restricted and precise grouping, because, otherwise, important interpopulation differences will be obscured.

Many characteristics show a disrespect for classical, time-honored boundaries. This was recognized many years ago when Hooton (1936:512), for example, observed: "There exists no single physical criterion for distinguishing race; races are delimited by the association in human groups of multiple variations of bodily form and structure." Another consideration is that race or any such label used to identify human groups is nothing more than an informational abstraction that provides us with a research tool to investigate biological variability (Baker, 1967:21). Such labels have no more reality than any of the others that we use to identify objects we encounter in our environment.

Each geographical grouping of *Homo sapiens* contains numerous local populations whose characteristics make it difficult to place. What causes this diversity of our species? Several sources have been described. First, independent or special creation had been widely advanced as an explanation. Though once popular, this belief that races were of great antiquity lacks any supporting archaeological evidence. On the contrary, people have been highly mobile since the earliest times overcoming natural and ethnographic boundaries to occupy every continent except Antarctica. Migrants have spread into new regions at times conquering the aboriginal inhabitants with a superior technology. The spread of the Neolithic with its agricultural technology out of the Middle East into Europe seven thousand to eight thousand years ago is an example from prehistory, whereas the Mongol invasion of eastern Europe in the fifteenth-century is an example from ancient history. On the other side of the world, in the central and south Pacific, the epic voyages of an ancient seafaring people led to the populating of unoccupied islands scattered over a vast expanse of ocean. Even throughout these millenia of population movements, there was extensive interbreeding that contributed to the maintenance of genetic continuity.

Another explanation of human diversity is that differing forces of natural selection caused the formation of relatively distinct groups. Before Darwin's theory of natural selection was published, several authors described the effects of climate and food on humans, and suggested that these factors may have contributed to human variation. Buffon, for example, observed in 1791:

> Three causes ... must be admitted, as concurring in the production of varieties which we have remarked among the different nations of this earth: (1) the influence of climate (2) food, which has a great dependence on climate; and, (3) manners, on which climate has, perhaps, a still greater influence. (Slotkin, 1965:185)

We must consider yet another factor: human differences—especially those often used to establish racial groups—are not as extreme or as great as generally supposed. This is most frequently seen in the case of morphological similarities that lead to the assumption that look-alikes denote common ancestry as discussed earlier. Intraracial variation is extensive in the major geographically determined races and is often overlooked. An example is the diversity found among native Americans. Rather than matching any stereotype, they vary greatly in size and form, from tall to very short (Table 5-1). Some populations are composed of people of heavy build who are prone to obesity, like the Papago of southern Arizona. In contrast are the short, slender-built people who dwell in the tropical rain forests of Central and South America. Face form also covers a wide range from broad, heavy faces to small, gracile faces with long, narrow noses; head shape varies over the range of cephalic indexes recorded for our species. Similar diversity is seen in several of the genetic markers of blood and taste sensitivity. Though Native Americans share a close common ancestry as descendants of populations who migrated from Siberia over the Bering Straits since approximately fifteen to twenty thousand years

TABLE 5-1   Mean Stature of a Sample of Native American
            Males

TRIBE	LOCATION	STATURE (CM)
Motilon	Brazil	146.2
Yanomama	Venezuela	153.2
Jivaro	Brazil	154.2
Maya	Yucatan	155.4
Otomi	Southern Mexico	158.0
Quechua	Peru	160.0
Hopi	Arizona	161.1
Zuni	New Mexico	161.4
Navaho	New Mexico	169.6
Aymara	Chile	161.8
Eskimo	St. Lawrence Island	165.0
Yaqui	Sonora	166.7
Papago	Arizona	168.8
Choctaw	Louisiana	171.4
Pima	Arizona	171.8
Blackfoot	North Dakota	177.4

Sources: Selected from Comas, 1960; Newman, 1953; and Eveleth and
Tanner, 1976.

ago, their present day variability should not be obscured by broad, all inclusive classification. This diversity among Native Americans is illustrated further by the "tree diagrams" in Figure 5-2. Diagram A is a dendrogram derived from genetic distance formula obtained from comparisons of gene frequencies at 14 genetic loci. This depicts the relative distance between Arctic peoples (North American and Siberian) and several sub-Arctic American Indians. Diagram B computes genetic relationships based on complex traits of dental morphology. Many of the same Arctic and sub-Arctic peoples are compared in addition to representatives of South American populations. Both genetic distance diagrams show a greater similarity between northern Siberian and sub-Arctic peoples of North America than with other Asian groups.

African peoples commonly grouped into a Negroid race are another example of millions of peoples being treated incorrectly as members of a homogenous geographical race. There are wide differences between many of the tribal groupings, and a careful study of breeding populations is necessary. Through several studies of East African peoples, Hiernaux, a French biologist, has shown significant differences in blood groups, stature, and face form among several populations living in East Africa. Other studies during the past fifty years have recorded broad ranges of diversity among Africans south of the Sahara, a factor that is overlooked too often in racial classification. Table 5-2 compares four physical characteristics of East-central African groups. They have been semi-isolated with little gene

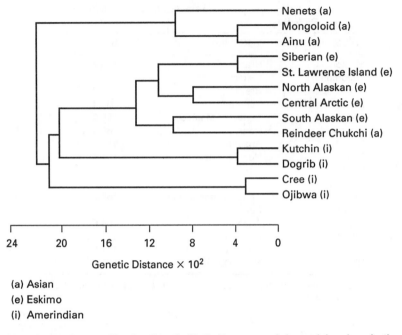

(a) Asian
(e) Eskimo
(i) Amerindian

FIGURE 5-2A   Dendrogram Showing Genetic Similarities among Asian and American Arctic and Sub-Arctic Populations. Szathmary, 1985. (Copyright 1985 by The Journal of Pacific History, Inc. Australian National University, Canberra, Australia.)

flow between them, so the selective forces of the individual environments have had a maximum opportunity to exert influence on each character (Hiernaux, 1966).

The diversity within each of the classical geographical race divisions is clearly established whether one examines the complex morphological traits or those inherited phenotypes of the blood. In fact, Lewontin (1974) emphasized that the intrapopulation diversity (the diversity among individuals) often exceeds that between populations. As he explained, 85 percent of genetic variability is among individuals within a nation or tribe. This is illustrated by his table of major genetic markers, their diversity within the species, and the proportion in populations or races (Table 5-3). Such variability has been recognized many times by human biologists and anthropologists, but it seldom prevented them from classifying subspecies of *Homo sapiens*. There was a growing discomfort with the race concept, however, and all of its related assumptions.

The problems that the race concept presented to field surveys of living human populations were described in detail by Hiernaux when he began to analyze the data collected during a biological anthropology field survey in central Africa in the 1950s. He noted that, though it was

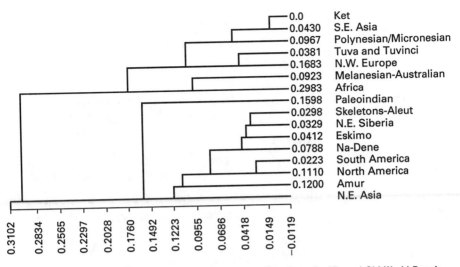

		0.0	Ket
		0.0430	S.E. Asia
		0.0967	Polynesian/Micronesian
		0.0381	Tuva and Tuvinci
		0.1683	N.W. Europe
		0.0923	Melanesian-Australian
		0.2983	Africa
		0.1598	Paleoindian
		0.0298	Skeletons-Aleut
		0.0329	N.E. Siberia
		0.0412	Eskimo
		0.0788	Na-Dene
		0.0223	South America
		0.1110	North America
		0.1200	Amur
			N.E. Asia

0.3102 0.2834 0.2565 0.2297 0.2028 0.1760 0.1492 0.1223 0.0955 0.0686 0.0418 0.0149 −0.0119

FIGURE 5-2B   Relationships within and between Native American, Pacific and Old World Populations. Based on twenty-eight dental trait mean measures of divergence clustered by unweighted pair group, arithmetic averages method. Turner, 1985. (Copyright 1985 by The Journal of Pacific History, Inc. Australian National University, Canberra, Australia.)

customary to start a description of survey results with a classification of the groups studied, the use of existing taxonomies rather than relying on the data collected is misleading. His observation led to the question, "what do we want to classify?" The answer seems unequivocal: the gene pools of the breeding population (Hiernaux, 1966:289). Most field studies of human diversity have followed this lead ever since.

TABLE 5-2   Means of Four Characters in the Mbuti Pygmies, Tutsi, and Bantu

	STATURE (CM)	NASAL INDEX	FACIAL INDEX	CEPHALIC INDEX
Mbuti Pygmies	144	103.8	78.3	77.0
Rwanda Tutsi	176	69.4	92.8	74.4
Bantu *Wet Forest*	164	94.0	81.9	76.1
Savannah	169	85.9	85.8	75.3
Arid Zone	171	85.0	89.7	74.8

Source: From Hiernaux J. 1966. "Human biological diversity in Central Africa," *Man* 1:287–306. Courtesy of Royal Anthropological Institute of Great Britain and Ireland.

TABLE 5-3   Major Genetic Markers in *Homo Sapiens*

LOCUS	ALLELE	POPULATIONS AND GENE FREQUENCIES
	SERUM PROTEINS	
Haptoglobin	Hp^1	0.09 (Tamils)—0.92 (Lacondon)
Lipoprotein	Lp^a	0.009 (Labrador)—0.267 (Germany)
	ENZYMES	
Red cell acid	p^a	0.09 (Tristan da Cunha—0.67 (Athabascan)
phosphatase	p^b	0.33 (Athabascan)—0.91—(Tristan da Cunha)
	p^c	0–.08 (Many)
Phosphoglucomutase	PGM$_1$	0.430 (Habbana Jews)—0.938 (Yanomama)
Adenylate kinase	AK^2	0 (Africans)—0.130 (Amerinds-Pakistanis)
	BLOOD GROUPS	
Kidd	JK^a	0.310 (Chinese-Dyaks)—1.000 (Eskimo)
Duffy	FY^a	0.061 (Bantu-Chenchu)—1.000 (Eskimo)
Lewis	Le^b	0.298 (Lapps)—0.667 (Kapinga)
Kell	K	0 (Many)—0.063 (Chenchu)
Lutheran	Lu^a	0 (Many)—0.86 (Brazilian Amerinds)
Rh	CDe	0 (Luo)—0.960 (Papuans)
	Cde	0 (Many)—0.166 (Chenchu)
	cDE	0 (Luo)—0.308 (Dyak-Japanese)
	cdE	0 (Many)—0.174 (Ainu)
	cDe	0 (Many)—0.865 (Luo)
	cde	0 (Many)—0.456 (Basques)
ABO	A	0.07 (Toba)—0.583 (Bloods)
	B	0 (Amerinds)—0.297 (Austr.-Toda)
	0	0.509 (Oraon)—0.993 (Toda)

Source: Selected from: Lewontin, 1972.

BREEDING POPULATIONS

The most suitable units for study are smaller local populations, groups of intermarrying persons whether tribes, castes, or inhabitants of a particular region. (Hiernaux, 1971:40)

Earlier we defined breeding population as a group of actually or potentially interbreeding individuals. This general definition fits most sexually reproducing organisms, but *Homo sapiens*, in many ways, is unique. Our elaborate social organization and culturally directed behavior make the human breeding population a unique result of the interaction of multiple biological and behavioral forces. Because of human behavior, the total genome of the species is distributed in space in clustered units. Society determines which individuals will mate to produce the next generation. A complex of social customs and taboos proscribe and prescribe sexual relations and establish the basis for family life, as well as family lineages, clans, caste systems, and religious affiliations; these present well-established culturally defined boundaries that in turn affect the gene combination of the next generation.

An example of how social systems may determine gene frequency is the case of the X-linked recessive gene that causes an individual to be deficient in G6PD. In patrilocal-patrilineal societies, where males remain in the community and bring their brides from outside, many of the X-linked genes are "lost" each generation because two-thirds of the X chromosomes are provided by the females in any population. Giles showed by a mathematical model that the X-linked G6PD-deficient gene may be less frequent in a patrilocal community, because the daughters of G6PD-deficient males leave, taking the gene with them, and the women moving into the community may come from a group that lacks the recessive trait or has a lower frequency. The opposite would be true in an example of a matrilocal community in which males leave to marry outside of their community. In this case, X-linked gene frequencies would be less disturbed. Such examples show how societies' decisions can indirectly influence gene exchange, which in turn causes change in gene frequencies. It is extremely important, then, to understand the functioning of a group as a social unit when one studies their genetic composition (Giles, 1962). Another example would be population admixture through the males of a dominant society frequently impregnating females of a subordinate group (European males mating with any number of females of the colonial areas). This process of gene exchange would likely influence sex-linked trait frequencies.

Geographical distance is another important consideration, for it obviously limits mating choices. In prehistoric times, and even among many peoples today, distance was a major restriction to gene flow. Brierley (1970), after studying census records, noted that in rural England during the nineteenth century, a man used to find his mate within six hundred yards of his residence. But, after the bicycle was invented, the average distance between prenuptial households jumped to sixteen hundred yards. If this increase in distance seems impressive, consider the mobility that has been brought about by the invention and wide use of the automobile. Even so, between 1940 and 1960, more than one-half of the marriages were between persons who had lived less than one mile apart. As modern transportation has increased mobility further still, a broader exchange of genes is to be expected. Whereas formerly, small breeding units were restricted by economics, politics, or geography to a village community, today, mating circles have expanded and the gene pool is much broader.

The effects that mating structures, distance, and population size have on gene frequencies is graphically illustrated by a study of modern Italian populations in the vicinity of the Parma Valley. Located in the north-

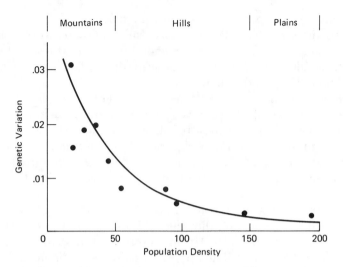

FIGURE 5-3A   Variations in the frequency of a blood type between one village and another was greatest, as predicted, in the isolated upland hamlets and declined as population density
increased farther down in the valley in the hill towns, on the plain, and in the city of
Parma. (From Cavalli-Sforza, Luigi Luca, "Genetic Drift in an Italian Population." Copyright © 1969 by Scientific American, Inc. All rights reserved.)

central part of Italy, this region contains a combination of rural villages
of various sizes and a few urban centers. In the foothills and surrounding
mountains, there are several smaller, relatively isolated villages that have
been occupied since prehistoric times. For several years, the geneticist
Cavalli-Sforza has carried on a thorough study of the genetic composition
of these populations. The sedentary nature of the populations, the varying
degree of their isolation, and the availability of marriage records from
church archives made these communities an excellent source of data for
the study of gene-frequency variation (Cavalli-Sforza, 1969).

The results of the study show a close correlation between village size
and gene-frequency differences. The villages in the mountains tend to be
smaller than those at lower elevations. This reduction in breeding population size contributes to genetic drift, which shows in the relationship
between population density and the genetic variation between communities
illustrated in Figure 5-3a. Those communities at the lower elevations show
less genetic difference. Genetic variation between villages is also influenced
by the relative lack of migration. Most marriages occur between persons
of the same church parish, and the next most frequent matings occur
between persons within eight kilometers (Figure 5-3b). Given these factors,
many consanguinial marriages occur in the mountain communities; more
special dispensations, granted by the Catholic church for cousin marriages,
are awarded to residents in these villages. As expected, the isolation, small

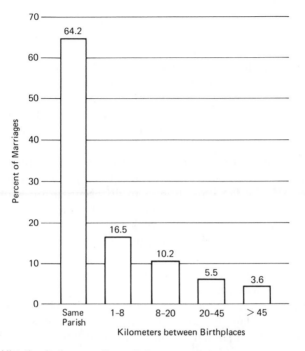

FIGURE 5-3B   Migration in the upper Parma Valley has been infrequent, a conclusion drawn from the fact that most marriages recorded from 1650 to 1950 in parish books united men and women who were from the same village. The number falls as the distance separating birthplaces increases. (From Cavalli-Sforza, Luigi Luca, "Genetic Drift in an Italian Population." Copyright © 1969 by Scientific American, Inc. All rights reserved.)

population size, and low rate of migration limit one's choice of a mate, which is reflected in the church records.

In less developed societies, environment together with poor transportation contribute even more to population isolation. People within remote villages may have scant opportunity to intermarry with others a short distance away, even if they are members of the same tribe. The rough, hilly terrain in the west Bengal region of eastern India causes the isolation of numerous groups. One of these groups, the Pahira, provides an example of the effects of this isolation. The fourteen hundred people of this primitive tribe of food collectors live in small hamlets scattered over three hundred square miles. They are clustered into three units or divisions. Each unit is an endogamous breeding population with little admixture of each generation. For example, considering three generations, the majority of individuals had both parents who were from the same unit. According to the Indian anthropologist Basu (1969), this endogamy has resulted in significant differences of the frequencies of the genes for the ABO blood group and taster phenotypes. Though members of the same tribe, these smaller units of hamlet clusters form distinct breeding populations. Thus, we must be extremely cautious in any statement about the gene frequencies of large groups, whether nations, states, tribes, or races. Reports describing the gene frequency of, say, several African Bantu tribes, the Lapps, the English, or the American Indians may be completely erroneous unless the sample is taken from representatives who are from the same breeding population within the social-political unit—a difficult task but a necessary one in an attempt to understand the genetics of human diversity.

The distribution of gene frequencies for certain alleles such as blood groups has been recorded for vast numbers of people. Boyd used these traits as sorting criteria in an attempt to differentiate races of humanity; the gene frequencies are summarized in Table 5-4. These groups cover large geographical regions and include numerous breeding populations; some of them tend to describe or imply homogeneity where little or none actually exists.

In more complex societies with caste and stratification, economic, religious, or political groupings, social distance plays a role similar to geographical distance. Peasant-aristocracy stratification in medieval Europe tended to isolate breeding populations and cluster genetic units within smaller areas. A similar situation exists even today in Latin America, and the persistence of rigid caste systems, as in India or in the peasant societies in Latin America, establishes an immense social distance between groups. The "untouchable" in India has no chance of mating with the higher-caste Brahman, for the Brahman would have to suffer religious sanctions.

The enforcement of religious beliefs has proved effective in isolating populations from the surrounding community even in modern U.S. society today. Strict sanctions are often imposed against marrying "outsiders," and there is very little gene flow between the religious isolate and neighboring populations. The Amish and Dunkers of Pennsylvania are examples of religious enclaves who have significantly different gene frequencies for traits such as the blood groups, as noted in chapter 2. The Hutterite colonies of South Dakota and Canada are further examples.

A majority of the Hutterites today, about 33,000 in three hundred colonies, can trace their ancestry back to 442 persons who migrated from Russia and settled in South Dakota between 1874 and 1877 (Oved, 1988). The high birth rate (an average of 8 children per marriage) has caused the colonies to grow to their present size even without gaining new immigrants. The Hutterite colonies are divided into three divisions called Leute, and there has been little interbreeding between them during the last century. This isolation of the divisions results in some unique gene frequencies when compared with North American and European populations because gene flow into the colonies from "outside" populations is

TABLE 5-4   Frequencies of ABO Blood Groups

POPULATION	PLACE	NUMBER TESTED	BLOOD-GROUP FREQUENCY O	A	B	AB
		Low A, virtually no B				
American Indians:						
Toba	Argentina	194	98.5	1.5	0.0	0.0
Sioux	South Dakota	100	91.0	7.0	2.0	.0
		Moderate A, virtually no B				
Navaho	New Mexico	359	77.7	22.5	0.0	.0
Pueblo	New Mexico:					
	Jemez, etc.	310	78.4	20.0	1.6	.0
		High A, little B				
Bloods	Montana	69	17.4	81.2	0.0	1.4
Eskimo	Baffin Land	146	55.5	43.8	.0	0.7
Australian						
Aborigines	Southern Australia	54	42.6	57.4	.0	.0
Basques	San Sebastian	91	57.2	41.7	1.1	.0
American Indians:						
Shoshone	Wyoming	60	51.6	45.0	1.6	1.6
Polynesians	Hawaii	413	36.5	60.8	2.2	0.5
		Fairly high A, some B				
English	London	422	47.9	42.4	8.3	1.4
French	Paris	1,265	39.8	42.3	11.8	6.1
Armenians	From Turkey	330	27.3	53.9	12.7	6.1
Lapps	Finland	94	33.0	52.1	12.8	2.1
Melanesians	New Guinea	500	37.6	44.4	13.2	4.8
Germans	Berlin	39,174	36.5	42.5	14.5	6.5
		High A and high B				
Welsh	North Towns	192	47.9	32.8	16.2	3.1
Italians	Sicily	540	45.9	33.4	17.3	3.4
Siamese	Bangkok	213	37.1	17.8	35.2	9.9
Finns	Hame	972	34.0	42.4	17.1	6.5
Germans	Danzig	1,888	33.1	41.6	18.0	7.3
Ukrainians	Kharkov	310	36.4	38.4	21.6	3.6
Asiastic Indians	Bengal	160	32.5	20.0	39.4	8.1

Source: From Boyd, W. C., "Genetics and the Human Race," *Science* 140:1057–1064, Table 2, 7 June 1963. Copyright © 1963 by American Association for the Advancement of Science. Reprinted by permission of the publisher.

near zero. For example, the frequency of type-A blood has increased whereas, type B has decreased to a low level and has even disappeared in some colonies. In addition to the RBC blood types, a recent study of the HLA system (WBC types) showed many of the HLA haplotypes common to Europeans, but the S Leut (Schmiedenleut) had high frequencies for seven HLA haplotypes that have been rarely detected among Europeans. The S Leut also differed significantly from the other two Leute in the combination of the forty-five haplotypes recorded (Kostyu et al., 1989).

This rapid growth from a few founders experienced by the Hutterites illustrate gene frequency change because of genetic drift.

Another example is the Amish of Pennsylvania, descendants of two hundred founders who entered Pennsylvania between 1720 and 1770; from these few, the population grew to forty-five thousand in 1960. This growth from a handful of ancestors, with few immigrants added to the colony, resulted in close inbreeding through past generations as demonstrated today by the few surnames that account for a majority of the population; 80 percent of the families in two Pennsylvania counties are accounted for by only eight surnames. Consequently, certain rare recessive genetic disorders occur in high frequency (McKusick, 1978). Further waves of migrants, about three thousand between 1815 to 1865, led to establishment of colonies in Ohio, Indiana, and Illinois. The Amish, because of high fertility, have a population growth of 3 percent per annum, a rate exceeded only by the Hutterites. By the 1980 census there were eighty thousand Amish living in twenty states and the province of Ontario, Canada.

In addition, founders or original colonists often are a select group, not a representative cross-section of a parent population from which they migrated. Hulse (1957) pointed out that a great many migrants to the British colonies in North America came from select regions of the British Isles. Also, he noted that certain physical characters often were possessed by these migrants, which set them apart from the general population. Additional data of the uniqueness of migrant groups is provided by his study of the Italian Swiss; Hulse observed that they were generally taller and heavier than the stay-at-home group. One may suppose that such groups as the Hutterites, Dunkers, and Amish may have descended from ancestors who were not representative of the general populations. This biased sample of a parent population can result in some unusual distributions of traits throughout future generations that sets the modern-day descendants apart. Though these factors are lumped under the term *founder's effect or principle*, they cover a multitude of events, some chance and some intentional. The founding group also may, by chance, have certain recessive genes that give rise to a high frequency of these alleles when the population expands. Livingstone (1969:58) noted:

> Since most of the world's populations have expanded rapidly in the last 1,000 years, much of the variability in the frequencies of lethal genes (or non-lethals for that matter) could be a consequence of the original expansion of the major populations.

Once a group is established as a breeding population, the size of the reproductive unit plays an important part in determining the composition of each succeeding generation. *Genetic Drift* or *Sewall Wright Effect* refers to chance events that alter gene frequencies in small breeding populations. The effect is accentuated because even fewer individuals contribute to the next generation. In large modern populations, one-fifth to one-sixth generally produce one-half of the next generation. In small, relatively isolated groups, the effective breeding population is even lower, and the fact that a few males father most of the children can have a profound effect on the gene fixation of each generation. The Dunker Isolate in western Pennsylvania presents a good example of genetic drift. Gene frequencies for blood groups have shown significant differences between this religious isolate and the parent population in western Germany as well as the surrounding Pennsylvania populations. Glass and coworkers (1952) explained these differences on the basis of the small size of the effective breeding population. This and several more recent studies show that genetic drift is an important factor, perhaps even the principal agent, in the formation of genetic variation among tribes, villages, clans, or any other socially defined breeding unit.

When an investigator studies groups such as the Hutterites, Amish, or Dunkers, written records are available to guide and aid that person in establishing genealogies. For nonliterate tribes such as the Amazonian Indians in South America or tribal groups in New Guinea, however, no records exist beyond a few notes provided by travelers, anthropologists, or missionaries, which are not adequate to establish the relationships between groups definitely. Therefore, identification of primitive populations is made, at least initially, on the basis of language similarities. The assumption is that tribes who speak the same language or similar dialects of a language are related genetically and share close common ancestry. Often the analogy is made between the spread of language and the spread of genes, as if the processes were the same—which they are not. As noted earlier, language is not inherited but learned. Several writers, though, have dealt with language groups, families, dialects, and so on, as if they were genetically determined phenotypes and as if dialect coincided with breeding population boundaries. For some broad surveys, genetic differentiation parallels major linguistic boundaries as in the case of a description of sub-Saharan Africa (Excoffier et al., 1987). Excoffier and coworkers noted that genetic differentiation clearly parallels the clustering of major linguistic units. Hence, significant distinctions were recorded between Afro-Asiatic, West Africans, and Khoisan (!Kung and Hottentots) on the basis of their Rh, GM, and HLA types. This study, however, dealt with large continental-wide populations; the data for linguistic-genetic boundary coincidence is not as convincing for smaller groupings.

An example is the comparison of blood-group gene frequencies in populations of several villages of the New Guinea highlands. Livingstone showed significant differences in the gene frequencies between villages, though all spoke the same language and shared common ancestry. He cautioned that blood-group frequency and language do not correlate. These genetic differences are probably due to a combination of genetic drift and founder's effect (Livingstone, 1963:512).

Even the comparison of gene-frequency differences or similarities between two or more populations is not a reliable means of determining relationships or closeness of common ancestry. Though the groups may have separated into two different units only within the recent past, they still may have quite different gene frequencies. Villages of the Xavente and Yanomama, both South American tribes in the upper Amazon basin, divide into groups to establish new villages when the old settlement reaches a certain critical size. They decide who belongs to which group on the basis of family membership, and the division is usually made along family lines. The effect is to produce villages whose populations' gene frequencies differ significantly even though they are closely related. The population divergence that results from this process of population subdivision is described as the "lineal effect" by James Neel (1970:816).

Other examples of gene-frequency divergence are also offered by the Yanomama, a fierce people who until recently were continually at war with their neighbors, and village raids were often for the purpose of obtaining captive women. In one example, young women from the Makiritare tribe were brought back from a raid on a nearby village. They proved to be fertile over the years and produced an average of 7.3 children compared with the 3.8 average for Yanomama women. Chagnon and associates (1970) described this event as responsible for the unusually high frequency of the Diego gene among this particular group of Yanomama.

Polygamy may have been the preferred form of marriage in former times, and it can be an important factor influencing the composition of the next generation. In some modern groups in which this form of marriage is practiced, several South American tribes—for example, 70 to 80 percent of the offspring—are from polygamous unions. Because some males are able to acquire more than one wife, it is obvious that many other males have limited opportunity to reproduce; hence, the genetic contribution to succeeding generations is limited to a very few males. Some males, because of their dominant position as clan leaders or relatives of high-status individuals contribute disproportionately to future generations. This reduces gene flow and acts much like the founder's principle in producing a certain gene combination. Polygamy may have been an important force in human evolution, especially during periods when the strongest, bravest, or best hunter was able to acquire more wives. The Eskimo, for example, have been very practical in caring for widows and orphans. The surviving family of a recently deceased hunter of the band is moved into the household of the most successful hunter, whose duty it is to care for them by taking the widow as his second or third wife and the children as his own.

TABLE 5-5   Regional Increases of Populations (in millions)

REGION	A.D. 1	1000	1500	1650	1750	1850
Africa	16	33	46	55	61	81
China	53	66	110	140	225	435
India	35	79	105	150	175	230
Eastern Europe	5	7	20	32	48	100
Southern Europe	18	12	20	28	35	58
Western Europe	10	15	33	50	60	110
North America	1.8	3.5	6	4.5	7	34.25

Chance or "fate," and natural events or intentional acts (such as of migration) play an important role in determining the growth, size, isolation, and, ultimately, gene frequency of the population. A typhoon may wipe out most of an island population, as on Puka Puka in the South Pacific, where an eighteenth-century typhoon left but seventeen survivors. These seventeen were all from the lower class in the Polynesian social structure, and persons of this class throughout Polynesia are, on the average, shorter. Shapiro (1942) explained the shorter stature of today's populations as a consequence of this chance event. Starvation and disease, too, have often decimated populations, leaving only a handful to start a new generation. Descendants often have traits or combinations of traits quite different from those expected. When studying a particular human group, the geneticist should be fully aware of its past history. Gadjusek (1964:134) notes: "The vicissitudes of history caused by social, psychological, and natural events operating on small bands have contributed greatly to the determination of the evolutionary course that has led to man." It has also added to the characteristics that set many modern human groups apart. Favorable location is another major factor in population diversity and growth; consider the eightfold increase of populations of western European—especially those of British origin during the past four centuries (Table 5-5).

In the case of chance events mediated by certain human actions, the founder's principle discussed earlier has been a major factor in the evolution of the human gene pool. When *Homo sapiens*, as a species, was very small in numbers during prehistoric times, the recurrence of the founder's principle would have produced much intergroup variability. The dangers of prehistoric existence probably destroyed many small groups, whereas in others a few hardy and lucky souls were able to survive and reestablish the population. As long as *Homo sapiens* remained at the nomadic hunting and gathering level, a chance fluctuation in population size because of random, natural events would cause the species to remain small. There was little possibility for the formation of large, homogenous breeding populations.

CLINAL DISTRIBUTION OF TRAITS

We now consider another concept of human trait distribution. *Clinal distribution* or *clinal variation* traces the geographical range of phenotypic or genetic characteristics of our species and assumes that they are distributed in a meaningful way. Clines locate a trait, gene, or characteristic on a map in much the same way as barometric pressure or temperature is plotted to depict weather. the location of the sampled data is marked on a map, and then the data points of the same size are connected. These clines express traits that vary continuously or by gradual progression of some feature from one geographical region to the next. The geographical plot of the variation of skin color among the world's population is an example (see Figure 1-11). This map shows that the density of melanin content of the skin is highly correlated with latitude; the more northerly peoples have a lighter skin pigmentation. Likewise, Figure 5-4 traces a clinal distribution of the type-B blood group frequency throughout Europe. The frequency of the allele decreases on a cline toward the west and probably is a genetic reminder of the invasions of Asian pastoral nomads into eastern and central Europe many times over the last two thousand years. These invaders, from an area that today has populations of high type-B frequency, contributed to the founding of many of the populations of the region.

Geographical variability of our species is self-evident, as discussed earlier, and it has often been considered in relationship to certain environmental features like temperature, humidity, or sunlight. To the observer there is an apparent covariation of certain inherited biological traits and climatic conditions. Peoples living in colder climates tend to have a certain body form. Nose form is closely related to vapor pressure and, of course, skin color is correlated with the quantities of solar radiation striking the earth's surface.

These distributions pass through many populations as if they were entirely independent of the boundaries constructed by human mating habits. The spatial location of the populations, however, causes the formation of a gradual series of genetic or phenotypic frequencies. The construction of a line through these forms the *cline*. The fact that the location of populations forms the cline makes it difficult to explain the distribution of a single gene, though several workers have advocated such an approach. Livingstone (1964:54) claims: "The variability in the frequency of any gene can be plotted in the same way that temperature is plotted on a weather map." This method is not without its problems, however.

Clines represent genetic distribution over broad areas, which frequently may obscure sharp differences in gene frequencies between adjacent populations. When there is an increase sampling of local popu-

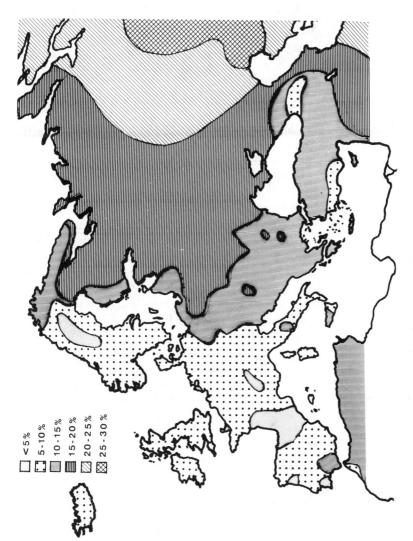

FIGURE 5-4 Frequencies of B allele in Europe. (From Mourant, A., *The Distribution of the Human Blood Groups*, 1954. Copyright © 1954 by Blackwell Scientific Publications, Ltd. Reprinted by permission of the publisher.)

Legend:
- □ < 5 %
- ⊡ 5 - 10 %
- ▤ 10 - 15 %
- ▥ 15 - 20 %
- ▧ 20 - 25 %
- ▨ 25 - 30 %

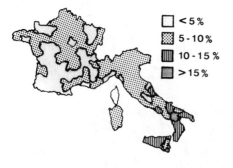

☐ < 5 %

▦ 5 - 10 %

▥ 10 - 15 %

▧ > 15 %

FIGURE 5-5
Distributions of B allele in France and Italy.
(From Morganti, G., "Distribution of blood groups in Italy." Copyright © 1959 by Churchill. Reprinted by permission.)

lations, these differences are identified, and the clinical boundaries of gene frequencies must be redrawn (Figure 5-5). This figure illustrates that as gene-frequency distribution becomes better known, the broader, more encompassing clinal expressions break down. Compare those regions of France and Italy that list the frequencies of the B allele with those noted in the clinal distribution plotted in Figure 5-4.

There are several possible explanations for clinal distributions. The most frequently offered is that clines indicate the effect of natural selection. This means that gene frequency follows the distribution of selective forces, but clines can also reflect the history of an exchange or flow of genes between populations. Livingstone has suggested that clines may be due to recent advances of advantageous genes or to gene flow between populations with different equilibrium frequencies for the gene. Figure 5-6 shows the geographical distribution of the hemoglobin S gene in the Old World superimposed on a map of the distribution of Falciparum malaria. The gene appears to provide a selective advantage in a malarial environment, as is explained in the next chapter. Note that hemoglobin S is not confined to Africa, but occurs in many other areas and in numerous diverse populations.

BREEDING POPULATIONS VERSUS CLINES

> It has often been assumed that subspecific groupings based on the distribution of one, or at most a few characters will necessarily be concordant with the distributions of other variable characters. This, it seems, may be so for populations isolated in mountains, islands, caves or other restricted and special habitats, but is not usually the case in wider, more continuous regions. (Barnicot, 1964:198)

Here is one of the major objections to the use of geographic races as units of study. Some think that the proper method for studying human variability is the single trait, as it is distributed across populations boundaries. In contrast, others focus on the combination of characters in breeding

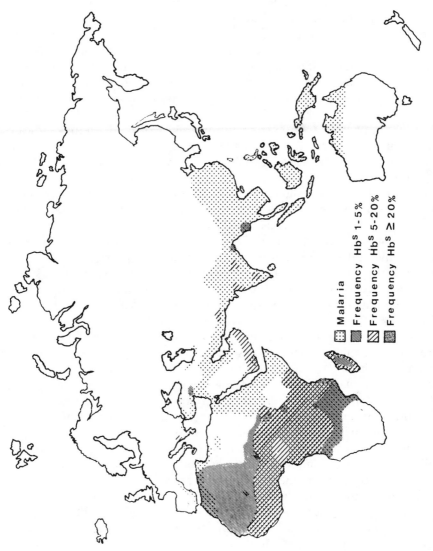

FIGURE 5-6 Distribution of malaria and sickle-cell anemia. (Redrawn from Buettner-Janusch, 1966.)

207

populations. What we should be concerned with is not taxonomic units but the distribution of traits among the world's peoples and the meaning of this variation.

A portion of this variation is illustrated by the maps in Figures 1-11, 5-4, and 5-6. These genes coincide with the distribution of certain selective forces and, in several striking examples, also with massive population movements. The presence of a cline of darkly pigmented skin in North America together with hemoglobin S (Hb^S and $Fy-$) is due to movements of many Africans to the New World during the seventeenth and eighteenth centuries. This illustrates why contemporary populations may not provide evidence of the correlation of a gene frequency and selected force. The distribution of $Rh-$ (cde) type in Europe and North Africa may indicate prior contact between groups living in these areas (the occupation of Spain and parts of southern Europe by North Africans during the seventh and eighth centuries). Numerous populations in eastern and central Europe today contain certain gene combinations because of their ancestors being overrun by nomadic invaders from Asia. The presence of a cline of high type-B frequency may be considered as one example.

The clines illustrated in the figures describe the distribution of both monogenic and polygenic traits, and there are, as previously discussed, major distinctions between them. Morphological phenotypes such as skin color or body size vary continuously, and each population or group grades imperceptibly into another, so that no sharp, clear-cut divisions are discernible. This forms a smooth clinal distribution. In the case of monogenetic traits, the differing gene frequencies between populations are used to establish a cline. These frequencies can and often do change rapidly within one or two generations as was illustrated by the examples of island populations or isolated colonies. In addition, there are often steep clines between adjacent tribal groups. This is illustrated by the significant differences in blood-group frequencies between four tribes in central Australia who share adjacent boundaries. Crossing from one to another shows a change in frequencies of as much as 60 percent (Birdsell, 1950). Therefore, simple comparisons between trait distribution and selective forces are not always possible. The population's size, its history, and mating patterns must be clearly defined.

If we consider all those factors that cause changes in gene frequency: (1) mutation; (2) natural selection; (3) genetic drift; (4) migration; and (5) breeding behavior, then we find that factors 1 and 2 act on certain alleles in unique ways. Factor 2, natural selection, is determined by environmental conditions and a population's adaptation to them, and is distributed geographically; of course, it often cuts across population boundaries. The other factors, also, have a strong influence on gene frequency, but they are behaviorally determined and they have an intense effect on the gene frequency from generation to generation. Genes are not passed on one at a time, nor is individual fitness usually determined by single genes. An individual's genes are transmitted as a group, and fitness is a compromise between the interaction of all the genes.

Gene flow is often described as a major cause of clinal variation, but it is not descriptive of actual events, because genes do not flow or "float around in space." They are transmitted as a group or an array by the chromosomes, and the way these groups are combined to produce the next generation is determined by society. These factors lend considerable support to the breeding population concept. Hiernaux (1964:32) remarks:

> To me, as to many others, it seems that the only useful way of grouping individuals for anthropological analysis is to group together the people participating within the same circle of matings.

The clinal approach has its strength, but only when used in conjunction with the actual basis for trait distribution through time and space—the population. The argument that one approach is more efficient as a means of studying human variation than the other is without foundation. We must consider the adaptive significance or survival value of each trait in the context of the population, and pay heed to those conditions of environment and human adaptation that contributed to an increase of our species from a few million to more than five billion today.

RECOMMENDED READINGS AND LITERATURE CITED

BAKER, P. T. 1967. "The biological race concept as a research tool," *Am. J. Phys. Anthrop.*, 27:21–25.

BARNICOT, N. A. 1964. "Taxonomy and variation in modern man," in *The Concept of Race*, ed. Ashley Montagu. New York: Free Press.

BASU, A. 1969. "The Pahira: A population genetical survey." *Am. J. Phys. Anthrop.*, 31:399–416.

BIRDSELL, J. B. 1950. "Some implications of the genetical concept of race in terms of spatial analysis," Cold Spring Harbor Symposium on Quantitative Biology, vol. 15, *Origin and Evolution of Man*. Cold Spring Harbor, N.Y.

BOYD, W. C. 1963. "Genetics and the human race," *Science*, 140:1057–1064.

BRIERLEY, J. K. 1970. *A Natural History of Man*. Madison, N.J.: Fairleigh Dickinson University Press.

BUETTNER-JANUSCH, J. 1966. *Origins of Man*. New York: John Wiley.

CAVALLI-SFORZA, L. 1969. "Genetic drift in an Italian population," in *Readings from Scientific American-Biological Anthropology*. New York: W. H. Freeman.

CHAGNON, N. A., J. V. NEEL, L. WEITKAMP, H. GERSHOWITZ, AND M. AYRES. 1970. "The influence of cultural factors on the demography and pattern of gene flow from the Makiritare to the Yanomama Indians," *Am. J. Phys. Anthrop.*, 32:339–350.

COMAS, J. 1960. *Manual of Physical Anthropology*. Springfield, Ill.: Charles C Thomas.

DOBZHANSKY, T. 1944. "On species and races of living and fossil man," *Am. J. Phys. Anthrop.*, 2:251–255.

EVELETH, P. B., AND J. M. TANNER. 1976. *Worldwide Variation in Human Growth*, International Biological Program 8. New York: Cambridge University Press.

EXCOFFIER, L., B. PELLEGRINI, A. SANCHEZ-MAZAS, C. SIMON, AND A. LANGANEY. 1987. "Genetics and History of Sub-Saharan Africa," *Yearbook of Physical Anthropology*, vol. 30. New York: Alan Liss.

GADJUSEK, D. C. 1964. "Factors governing the genetics of primitive human populations," *Cold Spring Harbor Symposia in Quantitative Biology*, 29:121–135.

GARN, S. M. 1961. *Human Races*. Springfield, Ill.: Charles C Thomas.

GILES, E. 1962. Favism, sex-linkage, and the Indo-European kinship system. *Southwest. J. Anthropol.*, 18:286–290.

GLASS, B., M. S. SACKS, E. F. JAHN, AND C. HESS. 1952. "Genetic drift in a religious isolate: An analysis of the causes of variation in blood group and other gene frequencies in a small population," *The American Naturalist*, 86:145–159.

HIERNAUX, J. 1964. "The concept of race and the taxonomy of mankind," in *The Concept of Race*, ed. Ashley Montagu. New York: Free Press.

HIERNAUX, J. 1966. "Human biological diversity in Central Africa," *Man*, 1:287–306.

HIERNAUX, J. 1971. "Ethnic differences in growth and development," in *The Biological and Social Meaning of Race*, ed. Richard H. Osborne. New York: W. H. Freeman.

HOOTON, E. A. 1936. "Plain statements about race," *Science*, 83:511–513.

HOOTON, E. A., AND C. W. DUPERTUIS. 1955. *The Physical Anthropology of Ireland*, Peabody Museum of Archaeology and Ethnology, vol. 30, nos. 1–2. Cambridge, Mass.: Harvard University.

HOWELLS, W. 1973. *The Pacific Islanders*. London: George Weidenfeld and Nicolson Limited.

HULSE, F. S. 1957. "Some factors influencing the relative proportions of human racial stocks," *Cold Spring Harbor Symposia in Quantitative Biology*, 22:33–45.

KOSTYU, D. D., C. L. OBER, D. V. DAWSON, M. GHANAYEM, S. ELIAS, AND A. O. MARTIN. 1989. "Genetic analysis of HLA in the U.S. Schmiedenleut Hutterites," *Am. J. Hum. Gen.*, 45:261–269.

LEWONTIN, R. C. 1972. "The apportionment of human diversity," in *Evolutionary Biology*, vol. 6, eds. T. Dobzhansky, M. K. Hecht, and W. C. Steers. New York: Appleton-Century-Crofts.

LEWONTIN, R. C. 1974. *Genetic Basis of Evolutionary Change*. New York: Columbia University Press.

LIVINGSTONE, F. B. 1963. "Blood groups and ancestry: A test case from the New Guinea highlands," *Current Anthrop.*, 4:541–542.

LIVINGSTONE, F. B. 1964. "On the nonexistence of human races," in *The Concept of Race*, ed. Ashley Montagu. New York: Free Press.

LIVINGSTONE, F. B. 1969. "The founder effect and deleterious genes," *Am. J. Phys. Anthrop.*, 30:55–60.

MCKUSICK, V. A. 1978. *Mendelian Inheritance in Man*, 5th ed. Baltimore: Johns Hopkins University Press.

MORGANTI, G. 1959. "Distributions of blood groups in Italy," in *Medical Biology and Etruscan Origins*, eds. G. E. W. Wolstenholme and C. M. O'Connor, Ciba Foundation Symposium, Churchill, London. Boston: Little, Brown.

MOURANT, A. E. 1954. *Distribution of the Human Blood Groups*. Oxford: Blackwell Scientific.

NEEL, J. V. 1970. "Lessons from a 'primitive' people," *Science*, 170:815–822.

NEWMAN, M. 1953. "The application of ecological rules to the racial anthropology of the aboriginal New World," *Am. Anthrop.*, 55:311–327.

OVED, Y. 1988. *Two Hundred Years of American Communes*. New Brunswick: Transaction Books.

POLEDNAK, A. P. 1989. *Racial and Ethnic Differences in Disease*. New York: Oxford University Press.

SHAPIRO, H. L. 1942. "The anthropometry of Puka Puka," *Anthrop. Papers Mus. Nat. His.*, 38:141–169.

SLOTKIN, J. S. 1965. *Readings in Early Anthropology*, no. 40. New York: Viking Fund Publications in Anthropology.

SZATHMARY, E. 1985. "Peopling of North America: Clues from genetic studies," in *Out of Asia: Peopling the Americas and the Pacific*, eds. R. Kirk and E. Szathmary. The Journal of Pacific History, Inc. Canberra, Australia: Australian National University.

TURNER II, C. G. 1985. "The dental search for Native American origins," in *Out of Asia:*

Peopling the Americas and the Pacific, eds. R. Kirk and E. Szathmary. The Journal of Pacific History, Inc. Canberra, Australia: Australian National University.

VALLOIS, H. V., AND P. MARQUER. 1964. "La répartition en France des groupes sanguins ABO," 9th series. Bulletins et Mémoires de la Sociéte d'Anthropologie, Paris, 6:1–200.

_6_

The Adaptive Significance of Human Variation

An all too often forgotten and yet most basic fact is that the genes do not determine traits or characters, but rather the ways in which the organism responds to the environment. (Dobzhansky, 1971:121)

Correlated Variation.—In man, as in the lower animals, many structures are so intimately related, that when one part varies so does another, without our being able, in most cases, to assign any reason. We cannot say whether the one part governs the other, or whether both are governed by some earlier developed part. (Darwin, 1871:427)

The preceding chapters described the diversity of characteristics of both simple and complex genetic origin, and their distribution was traced throughout the species. This distribution, that is, the clustering of traits into certain breeding populations or the broad-ranging clines of individual gene frequencies, may be explained in several ways. A most obvious explanation is a population's history. Migrations, warfare, and chance events have brought together many peoples of diverse genomes; the colonial expansion of the last few centuries is a prime example of major population movements influencing distribution of inherited traits. European settlers moved into the Western Hemisphere with a deadly effect on the aboriginal populations who could not compete with western technology nor could they resist the diseases carried by the colonists, like measles and smallpox, which went through the population with deadly force. Another and smaller-scale example is the peopling of unoccupied islands by small founding populations, two thousand to four thousand years ago throughout the Pacific. These events contributed to unique distributions of traits that we typically use as markers to distinguish between populations and groups. Because *Homo sapiens* has been particularly successful at increasing numbers of people in all environments, at least since the last ten thousand years, the species has continued to migrate. The result is that much of the dispersion of human traits may be explained through the history of growth and migration of founding populations.

Because these founding populations were small, chance played a major role in the genetic combination represented as we discussed in the last chapter. Further, natural events—either catastrophic or simply the arduous nature of the new environments—exerted particular stresses on the new colonists. Some colonies grew very slowly, and some did not survive beyond a generation or two with the only evidence of their ever having existed are the debris and skeletal remains found among the archaeological excavations. Whether by chance or through adaptation to the environmental stresses, the spread of *Homo sapiens* eventually led to our dominance of most of the earth's environments much to the amazement of early explorers and naturalists like Charles Darwin (1871:178) who commented, "Man can long resist conditions which appear extremely unfavorable for his existence."

The third important factor contributing to the distribution of human diversity is natural selection. We assume that gene combinations for several well-known characteristics are adaptively significant; that is, natural selection has acted over a period of time to form the gene pool of the populations so it is composed of a majority of individuals best suited physiologically to respond efficiently to environmental stresses. Our complex behavior and our often elaborate technology, however, interfere with and modify these stresses. The wearing of clothing, use of artificial shelter, cooking of food, use of domesticated plants and animals, medication, sanitation, and so on all have had their effects on the modification of environmental stresses. They have actually created what can truly be called a man-made environment. Human skill in manipulating the environment should not be looked on as a means of totally freeing us from the effects of natural selection, however. The environment still exerts stress on human populations and exacts a toll in the form of mortality rates, retarded growth, and disease incidence.

Human responses to the demands of the environment are generally lumped together under the term *adaptation*. This term is broadly used and refers to all adjustments made by the individual that promote its welfare or, in a more comprehensive sense, the welfare of the population. Another way of describing adaptation is: "the fit of the organism to its environment." The breadth of meaning and its frequent use make it difficult to define adaptation accurately. Actually, adaptation has several levels of meaning. The first is the physiological adjustments to cope with changing stresses, or rather acclimatization.[1] People can acclimate to cold or heat (within certain limits), altitude, vapor pressure, and an enormous diversity of nutrients. This ability to acclimatize is due to the broad-ranging human plasticity, an ability or capacity to acclimate that is inherited. The second describes adaptations of behavior, particularly relevant in studies of humans. Through small or large adjustments in their behavior, humans adapt to a wide variety of environments. These two meanings may be described as *functional adaptations*. The third is genetic adaptation, which notes the significance of products of certain genes to survival under particular conditions; the ability to produce antibodies against disease or a particular hemoglobin form found in malarial environments are examples.

The many types of environmental stresses acting on our species are too numerous to list individually, and some have effects on the metabolism that are not altogether understood. For our purpose we consider the following environmental stresses, which have had important effects on human diversity: (1) temperature and humidity; (2) solar radiation; (3) altitude; (4) nutrition; and (5) disease. Unfortunately, none of these has a simple causal relationship with the species' genetic system, and a single stress may affect several genotypes. For example, body form and size are related to diet and climate, and also to the polygenic makeup that influences growth and form. The effects of natural selection may be reflected in several ways throughout future generations. The first example is the functional adaptation, or acclimatization, made by individuals to stresses encountered at high altitude.

ENVIRONMENTAL STRESSES AT HIGH ALTITUDE

The spread of human populations throughout the world during prehistoric times and their successful adaptation demonstrate the plasticity of human phenotypes in their capacity to acclimatize to a wide range of environments. This ability to survive and reproduce under a variety of stresses has enabled *Homo sapiens* to use most of the world's landmass, but the costs have often been high in terms of mortality rates. In some cases, it has required several generations to adjust to the selective forces. Among the

---

[1] Frisancho (1979) makes a distinction between acclimatization, changes occurring during a lifetime, to adjust to a variety of environmental stresses, and acclimation, biological changes in response to a simple experimentally induced stress.

more difficult environments are those in mountain areas above three thousand meters.

Certain high-altitude environments have been occupied for at least ten thousand years. Though poor in resources, areas such as the high plains of Ethiopia and the Atlas Mountains in Africa, eastern Turkey and Iran in the Middle East, the Himalayas and Tibetan Plateau, and the Andes in South America have sustained millions of people since the Neolithic. The best known area, perhaps, is the high plateau (Altiplano) of the central Andes, which spreads across parts of five countries, from Ecuador in the north to Chile in the south. It was in this area that the Inca Empire had established control over millions of people. At the time of the conquest by Pizarro in 1532, there were approximately ten million people living in this region above three thousand meters in elevation. Following the arrival of the Spanish, there was a major decline in population as millions died off because of warfare, starvation, and the infectious diseases of European origin to which the native populations had little resistance.

After this initial decline the Andean populations gradually recovered growing slowly during the centuries until, by 1960, they reached their former size. During the last twenty years rapid population growth has occurred; today, there are approximately thirty million living in the area within the boundaries of the ancient Incan Empire. Most of these people are descendants of the founders of communities established in the Altiplano as long ago as three hundred generations. They have been relatively isolated from lowland communities and, until recently, there has been little population movement. Today's residents of the Altiplano, especially in Peru, are excellent subjects for the study of human adaptation to altitude. The question of adaptation, particularly genetic adaptation, has been investigated most thoroughly among the Quechua Indians of Peru who have shown a remarkable ability to sustain life at the greatest limits of human habitation (from three thousand to five thousand meters). In this section we consider some of the findings of these studies and how they may add to our understanding of human variation.

High-Altitude Environment

The earth is surrounded by an envelope of gases that consists mostly of nitrogen (78 percent) and oxygen (21 percent), and this atmosphere is the densest at sea level (barometric pressure, 760 mm). The air becomes thinner as distance from sea level increases, and there is less of life-sustaining oxygen. This thinner air has important consequences for plant and animal life, and well-defined environmental zones exist in the mountains. For example, trees do not grow above an elevation of approximately four thousand meters, whereas grass and certain herbaceous plants that

TABLE 6-1   Environmental Stresses Related to High Altitude

Hypoxia (abnormally low levels of oxygen)
Intense ultraviolet radiation
Cold (greater radiant heat loss)
Aridity (owing to high winds and low humidity)
Limited nutritional base (because of reduced plant and animal fertility)

are used as pasture can grow up to fifty-five hundred meters. At these higher elevations, more of the shorter wave lengths of solar radiation (ultraviolet and cosmic rays) penetrate the thinner air. Also, there is greater radiant energy heat loss so temperatures are colder than at lower elevations of the same latitude. The conditions in an alpine environment that create microclimatological stresses are listed in Table 6-1.

Though the net effect of all of these stresses makes life at high altitudes very unpleasant and harsh, *Homo sapiens* has certain physiological and cultural means to cope with them. Cultural adjustments can alleviate the effects of cold temperature and high winds. For example, the use of shelter and dark clothing, which absorbs 95 percent of the sun's radiant heat (versus the 30 percent that light-colored clothing absorbs) are ways of protecting against the intense cold and ultraviolet radiation. The location of dwellings at strategic points in the valleys can compensate to some degree for the rough terrain. Adaptation to low oxygen requires certain physiological adjustments to enable individuals to sustain near-normal activities at higher elevations, however. Certain individuals appear better able to adjust than others.

Oxygen Requirements and High-Altitude Adaptations

The human physiology requires a certain minimum amount of oxygen for normal tissue function, and, measured in terms of barometric pressures, approximately 40 mm of oxygen is needed.[2] The body's arterial pressures are maintained at 95 mm to deliver this quantity to the tissues. The entire respiratory system and circulatory system functions to provide the required oxygen. In the dense atmosphere, at sea level, with an oxygen pressure of 159 mm, the human circulatory system easily absorbs and distributes oxygen whether a person is at rest or engaged in heavy work. It is more difficult at high altitude, however, and a person will suffer from *hypoxia*, a decrease below normal levels of oxygen in the air, blood, or tissues. The degree of hypoxia and its effects vary with altitude and

---

[2] Atmospheric pressures are measured in terms of the height of a column of mercury—for example, in a laboratory barometer familiar to generations of students. Hence, the air pressure at sea level will force the mercury column to a height of about 760 mm, which will fluctuate up or down depending on the air pressures of a passing weather front.

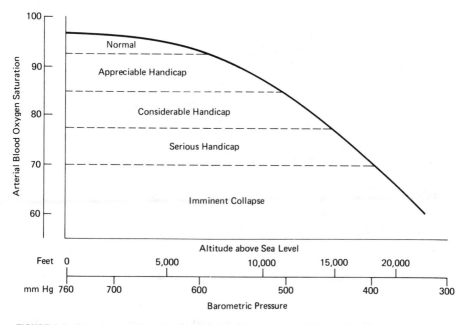

FIGURE 6-1   Percent saturation of arterial blood with oxygen and gross physiologic effect of acute exposure of sea level natives to high altitudes. (From Pace, N., *Man at Altitude*, 1961. Copyright © 1961. Courtesy of Charles C Thomas Publisher, Springfield, Ill.)

work level, and even simple movement is restricted. Figure 6-1 describes the degrees of handicap to human activities at several altitudes.

This major stress at high altitudes, low oxygen pressure, stimulates the metabolism to maintain a normal level of oxygen in circulation. There are several physiological adjustments to hypoxia that are possible; some are of long-range benefit and require a period of time for the person to acclimate to the stress. Certain adjustments are made immediately when a person, acclimatized to sea-level pressures, moves up to high altitude. These physiological responses are most acute at first, but they gradually decrease as other more long-term compensations become effective.

Increased respiration is the immediate reaction to lowered atmospheric oxygen, and there will be greater cardiac output to increase blood flow through the lungs and arteries. The resting pulse rate will rise from 70 to 105 beats per minute, for example, but will decline to normal levels after a few days. During the first year of residence at a high altitude, a person acclimatized to sea-level pressures will hyperventilate to increase the alveolar oxygen tension (pressure) that maintains the normal level of oxygen delivered to the tissues. A side effect of this hyperventilation is a decrease in the level of carbon dioxide (CO_2) in the blood. The decrease in CO_2 causes the blood to become more alkaline, and this rise in pH must be adjusted by the kidneys through excretion of greater quantities

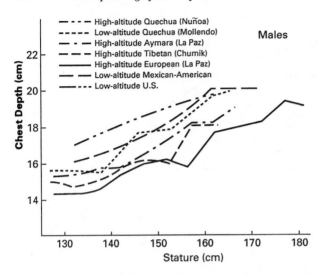

FIGURE 6-2   **Chest Depth Relative to Stature in Selected Populations.** (Adapted from Greksa, 1986.)

of sodium bicarbonate to maintain an acid-base balance of the blood at near-normal levels. Hyperventilation decreases with time and returns to near-normal levels after approximately a year as other mechanisms begin to compensate for lower atmospheric oxygen. The lungs function more efficiently, and the total volume (air inspired or expired) increases.

Given the respiratory requirements, pulmonary function appears to differ somewhat between highland natives and sea-level dwellers in many respects. The Quechua of Peru have proportionately much larger chests than Europeans and lungs with significantly greater volume (Figure 6-2) Interestingly, natives of the Himalayas do not have expanded chest dimensions (Greska and Beall, 1989). Expanded lung volume is able to bring greater amounts of air into contact with more capillaries that have increased in diameter (dilated). In addition, the lung tissues of high-altitude natives have a greater capacity to diffuse gases compared with those of natives at lower elevations, even after they have undergone a period of acclimatization to high altitude (Frisancho et al., 1989).

Another response to hypoxia is an increase in the number of red blood cells (RBC) in circulation. The body's capacity to produce new RBC is increased during the first three months of residence at a high altitude and then levels off; thus, a person may have up to 30 percent more RBC after a period of acclimatization. Persons participating in an expedition in the Himalayan mountains were examined periodically by the staff physician for their hemoglobin (Hb) concentration during a three-month period. The individuals' Hb concentration increased as the group moved from thirteen thousand feet to over nineteen thousand feet (Hock, 1970).

TABLE 6-2   Human Acclimatizations to Hypoxia

Red Blood Cells
  Increase in number
Hemoglobin-Oxygen Disassociation Curve
  An increase in an enzyme (DPG) in the RBC decreases the affinity of hemoglobin for oxygen, which in turn enhances the oxygen release to the tissues
Circulation
  Increase in cardiac output during the first days of exposure
Capillaries
  Increase in capillary network to aid diffusion to the tissues
Ventilation
  Hyperventilation occurs during the first year of exposure to hypoxia, which increases arterial oxygen saturation
Cellular Metabolism
  Several cellular changes have been reported in high-altitude arrivals which increase the resistance of the tissues to low oxygen

Several studies of long-term residents at altitudes above forty-five hundred meters have confirmed this change in red-cell density. The greater number of RBC increases the Hb concentration, which in turn increases the oxygen-carrying capacity per unit volume of blood. The upward adjustment in red blood cell density ensures that a greater cardiac output, such as occurs in heavy exercise, will expand the oxygen-carrying capacity per unit volume of blood. This will increase the oxygen transported to the tissues by about the same amount as it would be at sea level, where populations have a lower Hb concentration. This form of response is not without its costs because the greater number of blood cells increases blood viscosity making it more difficult for the heart to pump a given volume. This raises questions about the actual benefits of an increased number of blood cells (Ballew et al., 1989).

The affinity of the Hb molecule for oxygen is also changed; the disassociation curve (the measure of Hb's oxygen affinity) is altered through an increase in certain red-cell enzymes and by the carbon dioxide in the tissues. This enables the Hb to release more oxygen at the tissues than it would otherwise. The change in hemoglobin-oxygen affinity owing to conditions relating to hypoxia and any benefit derived from such a shift, however, is under close study because conflicting results are reported in both high and low altitude populations.

Table 6-2 summarizes the various mechanisms involved in human response to hypoxia. Considering all of these factors, acclimatization to high altitude occurs through increased respiration, cardiac output, increase in red-cell number with higher Hb concentration, and an improved diffusion of oxygen into a richer capillary net in the lungs. Though these adjustments to the hypoxia at high altitudes enable relatively normal physiological functions, the adaptation or acclimatization can be only partial because our species survives best in the denser atmosphere found below ten thousand feet. Certain populations, however, appear to be more efficient in these responses and, hence, appear to be adjusted to life at high altitudes. They seem to be better able to endure the stresses at a high altitude, perhaps because of their long history of residence at these higher elevations. The natives of the Altiplano area of the Andes, mainly the Quechua, have several characteristics that imply genetic adaptation to such environments.

CHARACTERISTICS OF A HIGH-ALTITUDE POPULATION

One of the frequently described characteristics of the Quechua is their *growth rate.* Children who have lived all their lives above four thousand meters grow considerably slower than do the Quechua children living below twenty-five hundred meters. Figure 6-3 shows that differences were found between populations resident at three different elevations. These high-altitude populations lagged far behind groups of American children except in one dimension, chest circumference. Though they were much shorter at all ages, the high-altitude Quechua had greater chest size, which provides a proportionately greater lung volume (Velasquez, 1976).

Another factor of growth that shows significant differences between populations is retarded development, illustrated by delayed eruption time of the teeth and slower motor development. Compared with North American standards, the growth of the skeleton is retarded and the epiphyses fuse later than they do in low-altitude populations. In addition, there is a retardation in the development of secondary sexual characteristics; little dimorphism is seen until about the fourteenth year because the onset of puberty is slowed. Growth is slow and prolonged in males with small increases of stature occurring into their early twenties, and they experience only a slight growth spurt, or none at all. Females fare somewhat better at high altitudes, though their sexual maturity is also delayed. Menarche (the onset of menses) occurs on the average a year later among high-altitude girls than among their counterparts at sea level (13.48 years versus 12.58). Females show a moderate adolescent growth spurt but less than at sea level (Frisancho, 1970).

It has long been known that temporary infertility is experienced when populations adapted to low elevations move to high-altitude regions. Low-altitude women experience menstrual disturbance, and there is greater risk of fetal loss (Hoff and Abelson, 1976). This decrease in fertility is reflected in higher infant mortality and lower birth weights, and it exists to some degree among long-term residents as well. Infants of low birth weight are at greater risk; their mortality is higher, and

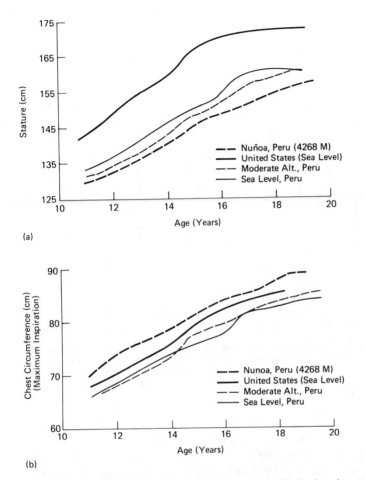

(a)

(b)

FIGURE 6-3   Development of (a) stature and (b) chest size of Nuñoa boys in comparison to U.S. norms and Peruvian samples from sea level and moderate altitudes. Despite their smaller stature, the Nuñoa boys have much greater chest circumference than the other Peruvian groups. (Reprinted from Frisancho, A. R., "Human Growth and Pulmonary Function of a High Altitude Peruvian Quechua Population," *Human Biology,* 41(3), 1969 by permission of the Wayne State University Press. Copyright © 1969 Wayne State University Press.)

congenital abnormality is more frequent.[3] A probable cause is the lowered oxygen levels reaching the fetus when the mother resides at a high altitude. Certain adjustments are made, however, to oxygen deprivation. The placenta is enlarged and has increased vascularization, and the fetus grows

[3] Low birth weight is a significant indication of problems of the neonatal period. Eighty to ninety percent of the infant deaths in the United States are associated directly or indirectly with birth weights of less than 2500 grams.

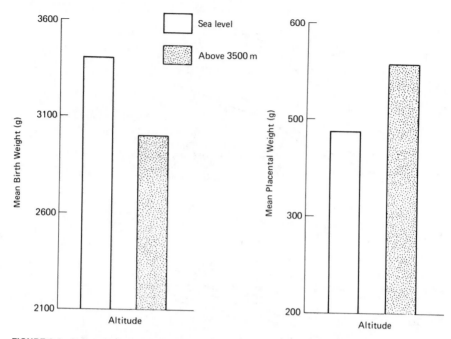

FIGURE 6-4   Comparison of Birth Weight and Placental Weight of Sea-Level and High-Altitude Natives. Residence at high altitude is associated with lower birth weight but increased weight of placenta. (From Frisancho, A. R., *Human Adaptation*, 1979. St. Louis: The C. V. Mosby Co.; modified from Miller, L. K., and L. Irving. 1962. *J. Appl. Physiol.* 17:449–465.)

more slowly. Females of different ethnic groups, however, have varying success in coping with low oxygen levels. Mestizo[4] women in Puno, Peru (elevation 3850 meters), have low-birth-weight infants about 23 percent of the time, whereas highland native women produce only 10 percent low-birth-weight infants (Mazess, 1975). This distinction between these groups may be genetically determined because the Mestizo are a group of mixed European and Indian ancestry (Figure 6-4).

Another stress encountered by the Quechua at high altitude is the low temperature throughout the year. Part of the response to the intense cold at a high altitude is cultural, as described earlier, but there are physiological adjustments that are made by the Andean natives to maintain a relatively stable body temperature, *homeostasis*, under cold stress conditions. Carefully conducted physiological tests of Quechua and European subjects point to two principal mechanisms of response when exposed to cold. The first is an elevated metabolism that generated greater body heat. This compensates for the heat lost through the extremities by an increase

[4] Individuals of Native American and European ancestry of a degree not specified.

of blood flow, which maintains a warm skin surface. Thus, body heat is expended to maintain the temperatures of the hands and feet to prevent frostbite. These mechanisms were more effective in the Quechua than in the European subjects tested; the Quechua maintained higher metabolic rates and greater peripheral blood flow (Frisancho, 1979).

In sum, the Quechua populations have sustained large population densities at high altitude for centuries and appear to be acclimatized to life in an oxygen-thin atmosphere. The human cost has been great, however, as measured in terms of higher infant mortality, more frequent congenital birth defects, slower growth, a smaller body size at all ages, and an increased frequency of respiratory diseases. In all comparative studies, Quechua residents at lower altitudes are healthier, larger, and have fewer problems common to their counterparts who live at elevations above three thousand meters.

SKIN COLOR, GEOGRAPHY, AND NATURAL SELECTION

As noted earlier, the darkest-skinned people inhabit a region roughly defined by the Tropics of Cancer and Capricorn. Within this zone there is the most intense solar radiation throughout the year, though total solar radiation varies little in relationship to latitude, the shorter wave lengths of the spectrum (in the ultraviolet 290-mμ to 320-mμ range) decreases rapidly with an increase in latitude, the greater the distance from the equator the greater the change. It is this part of the solar-radiation spectrum that causes sunburn and suntanning and stimulates the synthesis of vitamin D_3 from 7-dehydrocholesterol (Table 6-3). Seasonal changes cause wide variation in the amount of ultraviolet light reaching the earth's surface in the temperate zones. At, or near, the equator there is much less variation in solar intensity in the ultraviolet region of 290 to 320 mμ.

The distribution of dark-skinned peoples coincident with solar radiation intensity has caused writers for many years to argue that skin color has adaptive significance and that in some way these people are suited for the climatic conditions under which they live. Such an argument often was countered by observations that several of these populations lived in humid tropical rain forests where little sunlight reached the ground and that, in fact, these tropical peoples had the darkest skins. Further, such conditions would have prevented solar radiation in these regions from becoming an effective selective force. Other doubts have been raised by the presence of Arctic and sub-Arctic peoples, Eskimo and Siberia reindeer herders, for example, who have a considerable amount of melanin in contrast to the Lapplanders who are very pale. The objections to skin color as an adaptive trait have frequently been based on scant evidence of the degree of pigmentation and a considerable misunderstanding of

TABLE 6-3   Solar Radiation and the Ultraviolet Spectrum

WAVE LENGTH[1]	BIOLOGICAL EFFECTS[2]	PENETRATION[3]
Ultraviolet-C 190–290 mμ	germicidal; little skin penetration	scattered and absorbed by dust, water vapor and ozone; little or none reaches earth's surface
Ultraviolet-B 290–320 mμ	sunburn, cancer, tanning, and vit. D synthesis	more energy reaches earth's surface
Ultraviolet-A 320–400 mμ	same as above but less effective; the additional influence of photolysis on some vitamins	more energy reaches earth's surface than above

[1] The units of measure of solar spectrum are given in millimicrons (mμ) which are equal to 10 angstroms.

[2] The biological effects vary according to wave length and have greater or lesser effect on different cell structures or chemical compounds; e.g. the 290–320 range stimulates the production of melanin and also provides the energy for vitamin D synthesis from its provitamin. The higher range UVA also has some of these effects.

[3] The penetrating power of the UV energy spectrum is a function of its wave length; the shorter wave lengths are absorbed and scattered by more substances and little or no energy reaches the earth's surface. Likewise the longer wave lengths penetrate the skin deeper; e.g., at 360 mμ the penetration is twice as deep as it is at 240 mμ (see Faber, 1982).

several significant factors: the nature of solar radiation, its effect on the skin, physical geography, and the living conditions of many tropical peoples. Discussions of human pigmentation have often been purely speculative with little reference to the available data. We will examine these data and consider whether the melanin content of the human skin is, in fact, advantageous or disadvantageous under certain environmental conditions.

Solar Radiation

Figure 6-5 illustrates the spectrum of solar radiation and the intensity of various portions. The absorption bands provide a rough approximation of the effective interference that certain substances provide. Gases in the outer atmosphere, particularly ozone, dust, smoke, and water vapor block, absorb, or scatter solar radiation to varying degrees depending on the wave length of the radiation. The *visible portion*, 400 to 800 mμ (4000 to 8000 angstroms), is least affected by atmospheric conditions, but water vapor is especially influential in reducing the amounts of infrared striking the earth's surface daily. Infrared is the part of the spectrum that causes a rise in skin temperature and provides the warm feeling one gets while in sunlight. A large fraction of the *ultraviolet* portion, about 290 to 320 mμ (2900 to 3200 angstroms) is absorbed by ozone but is relatively unaffected by water vapor, a factor that explains why one may become sunburned even on an overcast summer day. The shorter wave lengths

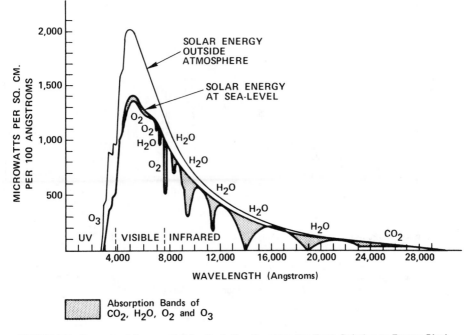

FIGURE 6-5   Measure of Energy of Solar Radiation Reaching the Earth Relative to Energy Dissipated in Atmosphere. (From M. Luckeish, *Applications of Germicidal, Erythemal, and Infrared Energy*, 1946. Copyright © 1946. Reprinted by permission of Wadsworth Publishing Company, Belmont, California 94002.)

are also influenced by the angle between the sun and the earth's surface; time of day as well as season of the year causes a reduction of radiation, especially in the temperate zone as shown by the diagram of the daily radiation count in Minneapolis (Figure 6-6).

Human Skin and Solar Radiation

The effects of solar energy on the skin vary considerably depending on wave length and there is deeper penetration of the skin by energy at the near infrared (1000 mμ), but little ultraviolet (290–400 mμ) reaches the lower layer of the epidermis (stratum germinativum). Corneum thickness and pigment have significant effects: darkly pigmented skin is penetrated much less deeply than fair skin. These differences may be important factors in adaptation to geographic regions of high solar radiation.

Because we judge skin color by the visible part of the spectrum, the differences in the reflective properties of human skin should be noted. Figure 6-7 shows skin-reflectance characteristics of American blacks and

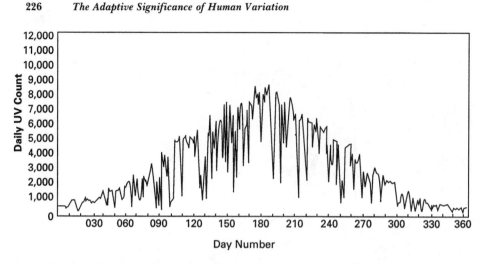

FIGURE 6-6   Daily total of Ultraviolet Radiation for 1974 in Minneapolis, USA

The record of UV measured in this North American city at 44.58° north latitude illustrates the broad range of difference between mid-summer (day 185) and mid-winter (day 350). (Source: From Faber, 1982. Reprinted with permission from: World Health Organization, Washington, D.C.)

whites. The curves indicate greater reflectance by the white skin over the entire spectral range tested. These curves, however, were constructed from average values of all subjects tested and may obscure range of variation of reflectance. Figure 6-8 illustrates the range of reflectance characteristics of several populations that have varying degrees of pigmentation. Reflectance was measured at the upper end of the visible range. The whites reflected roughly 50 percent of the light, and Aboriginals only reflected about 10 percent; other groups showed reflectance properties between these two extremes. The two groups that recorded male and female reflectance values showed males lower on the scale.

A word about geography and the living habits of tropical peoples is appropriate here. With the few exceptions of wandering, hunting, and gathering peoples who dwell in tropical rain forests as refuge areas, most populations who live in tropical areas sustain themselves by agriculture or herding. Agriculturists must remove forest and hence the protective shade covering is lost; pastoral herding peoples must live in open country. The argument that many darker-skinned peoples live in shaded areas of the tropical rain forests incorrectly assesses these environmental requirements. The fact is that a good many of these peoples live under conditions of a high incidence of solar radiation and spend most of their lives exposed to the harmful effects of ultraviolet rays. The few exceptions in the Old and New World tropics are explainable in terms of the population's history.

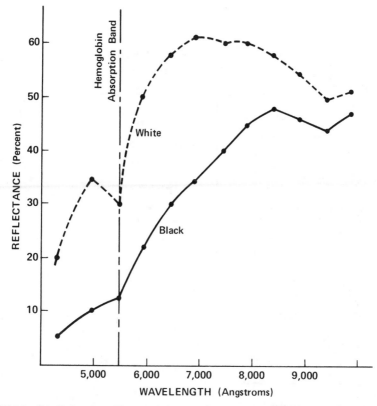

FIGURE 6-7 Skin-Reflectance Characteristics of a Sample of American Blacks and Whites. (Redrawn; based on Barnicot, 1957.)

Average reflectance characteristics of black and white skin on the flexor surface of the forearm. Measurements made from visible light to the near-infrared range with marked absorption indicated in the white sample at approximately 5500 angstroms (the absorption for hemoglobin).

NATURAL SELECTION AND SKIN COLOR

The further from the tropics, the fairer skinned are the people, and this fact has supported an argument for relationships between skin color and sunlight for centuries. We now consider some of the probable explanations that have been offered for this relationship. First, if we look on the epidermis as a filter that reduces the amount of ultraviolet radiation penetrating the skin, we can establish the relative advantages or disadvantages for high melanin content of the skin in various environments. Melanin blocks most of the ultraviolet radiation, so dark-skinned persons are less subject to the detrimental effects of overexposure to solar radiation, mainly sunburn and skin cancers.

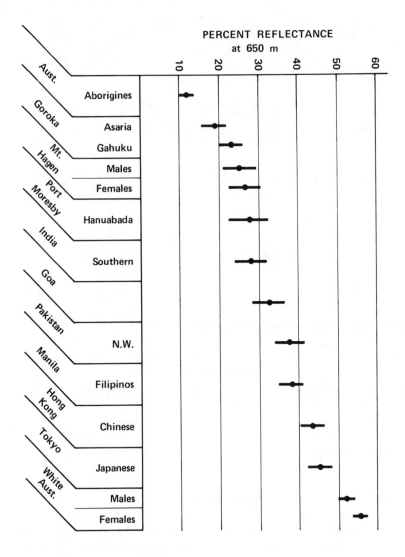

FIGURE 6-8   Skin-Reflectance Characteristics of Several Populations. (After Walsh, R. J., "Variations of melanin pigmentation of the skin in some Asian and Pacific peoples." Copyright © 1963 by the Journal of the Royal Anthropological Institute. Reprinted by permission of the publisher.)

The mean percentage of reflectance from the foreheads of samples of several populations is indicated by the dot, and the range of plus or minus one standard deviation is indicated by the line.

Sunburn, depending on the degree, causes congestion of the subcutaneous capillaries, destruction of cells, and edema (collection of fluids under the skin's surface). Besides being painful, sunburn can be very dangerous, opening the way for many secondary effects including infection and heat exhaustion. Prolonged exposure to the sun can also cause permanent damage. Premature wrinkling of the skin due to a disintegration of collagen and elastic fibers is another effect of long-term exposure. Darkly pigmented peoples are less prone to this solar radiation damage because of the filtering effects of the melanin, and hence such people appear to "age" more slowly.

Of course, our species can and often does use some kind of shelter or covering, but in certain climates the high temperature and humidity make clothing a disadvantage and reduces the body's capacity for heat dissipation. Skin pigmentation enables humans to be more mobile and functional in tropical sunlight, where ambient temperatures are close to normal body temperature, making heat dissipation difficult especially when clothing is worn. An exception is seen among desert peoples like the Saharan tribes. These people live in one of the hottest regions of the world and go about with their bodies completely clothed. The clothing is loose fitting, however, and traps air between the skin surface and the outer garment. Perspiration is collected by the cloth and is quickly evaporated by the dry air. The garment serves both as a shield from the sun's rays and as a cooling aid through evaporation.

Skin cancer, basal and squamous cell types, is another risk of overexposure to sunlight. The incidence of skin cancer is highest among fair-skinned persons who are exposed for prolonged periods. Persons whose occupations keep them out of doors have a greater chance of developing skin lesions, usually on the face or on the back of the hand. The highest frequencies of skin cancers in the world are among white Australians living in Queensland—about 265 cases reported per 100,000 males and 156 per 100,000 females. The incidence among whites living in South Africa is much lower—133 per 100,000 males and 72 per 100,000 females. In contrast, British populations have a low of only 28 per 100,000 males and 15 per 100,000 females. In the United States the rate of new skin cancer cases has radically increased; up to 600,000 are predicted for 1990, and some 27,000 of these are of the third type, malignant *melanoma*. The relation to sunlight is clear; Tucson, Arizona, has seven times the number of skin cancers as does Minneapolis (Faber, 1982). Among the darker-skinned populations, problems related to solar radiation are minimal, and skin cancers rarely, if ever, occur. Recently, skin cancers have received more attention because they have increased during the past decade and are expected to rise further because of a depletion of the ozone layer that surrounds the earth and functions as a major filter of solar energy at the shorter wavelengths.

Photochemical Effects of Ultraviolet Light

Several chemicals essential for metabolism are sensitive to ultraviolet and undergo decomposition (photolysis) when exposed to sunlight. Among these sensitive chemicals are several vitamins: folic acid (B_c), riboflavin (B_2), and vitamin E. The photosensitivity of these substances has led to the suggestions that dark skin may protect certain critical metabolites in the blood and dermis from the photo-decomposition caused by ultraviolet radiation. Several experiments have shown that levels of folic acid in the blood were depressed by ultraviolet light; such was the case with patients of Scandinavian descent undergoing treatment for skin ailments by exposure to ultraviolet light. Branda and Eaton (1978) reported that folic-acid levels in such patients dropped significantly during the course of their treatment. Though no comparable study has been reported for vitamin E or riboflavin in humans, these substances are known to be photosensitive as demonstrated by laboratory experiments.

As explained earlier, *vitamin D* is essential for proper calcium metabolism and the development of the calcified tissues of bones and teeth. Vitamin D is scarce in all foods except in fish oils, and it is usually difficult to get through dietary sources. The vitamin, however, is synthesized by the action of ultraviolet light on a *sterol* compound, 7-dehydrocholesterol, found in the lower layers of the epidermis. Because the amount required for proper maintenance of calcium is small (only about 300 to 400 units per day), the exposure of a small area of the body to the sun for a short period is sufficient. It has been estimated that 20 cm², or about the area of the skin covering a human infant's face, is sufficient. Any interference with this amount of exposure (reduction in time, in ultraviolet light, or in surface area) correspondingly diminishes the amount of vitamin D synthesized. The effects caused by a reduction in the vitamin vary between individuals, depending on their age. Rickets, once a frequent disease in northern Europe, will develop in children deprived of vitamin D. Their rapidly growing bones will fail to mineralize properly and the weight-bearing parts of the skeleton, the legs and pelvis in particular, will become distorted and misshapen as the infant begins to walk. In its severest form, rickets can even result in death. Children living in crowded slums of industrial cities of England suffered from a high frequency of rickets. The smoke-laden air and the crowded streets with no open space and little sunlight reduced the chance of satisfying the body's requirements for the vitamin. Given the environmental influences, rickets has been called the first air pollution disease (Loomis, 1970).

These vitamin-D deficiency diseases have occurred in a wide variety of environments, even in the tropics. Women of some cultures more frequently suffer because of a tradition that causes them to be confined to the household from early childhood and are allowed in public only if they are completely covered. The restriction on their daily activities and their required clothing reduces the amount of sunlight striking the skin to a low level. For example, Bedouin women in North Africa and the Middle East remain inside the family's tents most of the day, and if they venture outside they must clothe themselves completely with skirts and veils. Only the small area of skin around their eyes is exposed to sunlight. This seclusion of women indoors also affects the health of infants and children. Infants in Muslim cultures and among high-caste Hindus frequently develop rickets during infancy, but many recover as young children when they are allowed to play out of doors. Females, often married at twelve years of age and then forced into the seclusion of the home and veil, frequently develop the disease again.

Rickets can also occur in a modern urban population. For example, among the large numbers of east Indians and Pakistanis who have settled in the British Isles during the last thirty-five years, cases of rickets and osteomalacia frequently occur. The combination of low incidence of sunlight in these northern latitudes, deeply pigmented skin, and dietary customs significantly reduces the chance of the synthesis of an adequate amount of vitamin D. The pathological results—skeletal malformations—have been reported in several clinical studies. this is similar to the experience of American black populations living in North American cities a half century ago. Before the widespread use of vitamin D supplements, rickets was suffered by many children, but most frequently among blacks.

Rickets and osteomalacia are most effective as selective forces among females because these diseases may lead to distortion of the pelvis. Figure 6-9 diagrams a normal and distorted pelvis inlet comparing the influence of rickets. Even a slight deformation of the pelvis reduces the birth canal and interferes with normal childbirth, increasing the risk of death of the mother or the fetus during childbirth. The effects of the disease can be measured by the frequency of deformed pelvis among females; only 2 percent of white women had a deformed pelvis compared with 15 percent of black women. Since the addition of vitamin D_2 to milk in the United States and most European countries, however, rickets has nearly been eliminated as a childhood disease.

Despite the disadvantages of dark skin in the temperate zone, it can be advantageous to be deeply pigmented in the tropics when overexposure to ultraviolet rays could cause not only sunburn and skin cancer, but also hypervitaminosis (an overproduction of vitamin D). Too much vitamin D is harmful; as little as 2000 IU (international units) per day synthesized or ingested over a period of time causes calcification of many soft tissues throughout the body and impairs kidney function. The toxic level may be as low as 40,000 IU for infants to 100,000 IU for adults (normal individual needs vary between 400 and 1000 IU per day). Whole-body radiation has been estimated to produce upward of 120,000 units per hour, which is

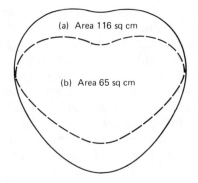

FIGURE 6-9 Outline of normal pelvic inlet (solid line) and contracted pelvic inlet due to severe child-hood rickets (broken line). (From Frisancho, A. R., *Human Adaptation*, 1979. St. Louis: The C. V. Mosby Co.; modified from Eastman, N. J., *Obstetrics*, 11 ed., 1956. New York: Appleton-Century-Crofts.

well above the toxic level (between 10,000 and 100,000 IU per day). Clothing, of course, reduces the amount of skin exposed, but the reader should remember the relatively little use of clothing by tropical peoples. Besides, during the first few years, children seldom wear any clothing at all and during the day are much more active than adults. This would add to the degree of their exposure and hence the potential for producing toxic levels of vitamin D.

SKIN COLOR AND EVOLUTION

The preceding discussions of the harmful and helpful effects of solar radiation provide some evidence of the direct effects on human survival. Considering all those factors that relate skeletal structure, calcium metabolism, skin pigmentation, and incidence of ultraviolet radiation, we now ask: How have they affected human evolution? Is the color of *Homo sapiens* "naturally dark" and, if so, what accounts for the relative depigmentation of the Europeans and the medium pigment of Asians?

The wealth of fossil evidence accumulating today supports earlier hypotheses that *Homo sapiens* evolved in the tropics. Our immediate ancestors spread into and "permanently" occupied the northern latitudes relatively recently in time, probably not before the third interglacial period (about 120,000 years ago). At this time these prehistoric populations were likely dark skinned and suffered the detrimental effects common to deeply pigmented peoples living in regions of low ultraviolet radiation. Many skeletal and dental lesions found among fossilized Neanderthal remains[5] suggest that they had suffered from an imbalance in their calcium metabolism probably brought on by low levels of vitamin D. Under such conditions of low incidence of ultraviolet energy and diets with little or no vitamin D, natural selection would favor those individuals with fairer skin.

The selection for peoples that could thrive under such conditions— that is, relatively depigmented fair-skinned peoples—has lasted until the present century. There is evidence that the adjustment to these selective forces must have taken thousands of years. Even during the Mesolithic period, between ten thousand and fifteen thousand years ago, northern European populations suffered from poor mineralization. Skeletal remains from Sweden and other areas of northern Europe dating to this period show many signs of poor calcium in their teeth and bones. Likewise, evidence is seen among skeletal materials dating from medieval times.

Two things made possible the continuous survival of *Homo sapiens* in the northern latitudes. The first is the steady decline in pigmentation throughout hundreds of generations or, rather, selection favoring the survival of individuals whose genetic systems caused them to have lighter skins. The second is the increased use of fish in the diet during the past six thousand years—particularly herring, which is rich in vitamin-D– bearing oil. Eventually, though no one knows where the custom began, a home remedy for rickets was introduced: the use of fish liver oils to cure this childhood disease. Also, there developed the practice of placing infants outside, even during the coldest months, to gain a little "fresh air and sunshine." Both of these measures have the same end results and have helped our species to sustain life and maintain large populations in northern Europe.

A discussion of the protective effects of melanin must also consider the changes of *photolysis* (light-caused chemical breakdown). Experiments with human and laboratory animals, noted previously, have shown that photolysis reduces folic-acid levels. If individuals live on diets marginal in folic-acid content, as many tropical populations do, then they will be particularly susceptible to a reduction in vitamin action owing to the destructive effects of the sun. The impaired growth in children and low reproductive capacity are a result of folic-acid deficiency, and would be a strong selective influence for dense pigmentation as protection against photo-decomposition of this essential vitamin. A similar argument could be made for protection of riboflavin and vitamin E. The probability that

[5] Francis Ivanhoe (1970) discussed the probability that Neanderthals during the final glaciation (Wurm) suffered from vitamin-D deficiency. He claims that there are numerous skeletal lesions similar to the type caused by vitamin-D deficiency. Though his claims are not generally accepted, he does raise an interesting point. Other studies since have pointed to a likelihood of calcium imbalance (Molnar and Molnar, 1985; Ogilvie et al., 1989).

melanin functions to reduce photo-decomposition of certain vitamins and prevents overproduction of vitamin D argues strongly for natural selection of dark-skinned peoples in areas of intense solar radiation.

If another feature of human skin is considered, its tanning ability, then evidence can be added to that already discussed. Selection appears to have been for skin that will vary in pigmentation according to the incidence of ultraviolet. The best adapted, then, would have skin that tanned well in the summer (reducing vitamin-D synthesis as exposure to sunlight increased with the long summer days) and lightened during the winter to take all possible advantage of the weak winter sun. Europeans native to southern Europe, North Africans, and western Asian populations have skins with a higher degree of melanin content than their northern neighbors, so they tan much better—a feature that is a significant advantage in their climates.[6]

Skin coloration happens to be much more complex and variable than is usually appreciated, and it requires far more discussion than can be given here; however, many of the interrelationships seem clearly established between sunlight and physiology. One final consideration we should note is the difference between the skin color of males and females in the same populations. Females have lighter skin, which, given their need for a more carefully regulated calcium metabolism, makes good adaptive sense. Children are also much fairer than their parents; often the infants of dark-skinned parents are pink, and their skin steadily darkens throughout childhood. This is another factor that shows the interrelationship between the human skin pigmentation system and solar radiation, demonstrating again the selective advantages that variable skin pigmentation can confer on the human population.

ABNORMAL HEMOGLOBINS AND RED-CELL VARIANTS

The population distributions of abnormal Hbs provide important clues to genetic adaptation of *Homo sapiens*. Populations with a long history of contact with the disease malaria usually exhibit the highest frequency of red-cell deficiencies or Hb abnormalities that were described earlier. The apparent relationships between these abnormalities and malaria are explained on the basis of a hypothesis that states: An individual who is a heterozygote (a carrier of the abnormal gene) enjoys a relative degree of

[6] The populations that prove to be exceptions to this general distribution scheme, northern Asians, American Indians, and Eskimos of the sub-Arctic, have a different history than northern Europeans. American and Siberian populations, for example, probably have not lived for very long in the regions where they are found now, and natural selection for light skin has not operated for the length of time that it has in Europeans.

immunity to infection by the malarial parasite in comparison with a person with the normal genotype. What mechanisms of cell metabolism actually convey this immunity has been under study for years, and several possibilities have been identified (Edelstein, 1986). The results show that red blood cells with some abnormal hemoglobin or cells that are deficient in the G6PD enzyme are less able to support the growth of the parasite; the red blood cells are more fragile with a shorter life-span or have a lower energy level. These factors prevent the multiplication of parasites and result in a reduced number in the circulation; hence, such a person would have a longer, healthier life-span and a higher rate of fertility. For example, in the case of the sickle-cell gene Hb^S, the heterozygote $Hb^A Hb^S$ would be at a selective advantage and reproduce at a higher rate than the normal $Hb^A Hb^A$. The greater fertility of the heterozygote would maintain the gene Hb^S at a high frequency in the population despite the loss of the gene through the near lethal combination in the homozygote $Hb^S Hb^S$ (a person homozygous for Hb^S seldom reaches adulthood).

Malaria and Natural Selection

The dreaded disease malaria occurs in endemic proportions in many areas of the world, mainly tropical and subtropical regions. It is a major cause of sickness and death, with about eight million new cases reported and approximately four million deaths annually. If deaths owing to complications arising from malarial infection are counted, then the death rate is much higher. In areas of the world where the death rate from all causes is extremely high, recent control of malaria has reduced this rate by one-third to one-half. This illustrates the rather stringent control that malaria has exerted on population size; it has probably been a major selective force acting on humanity for many generations. The negative effects of malaria, however, are seen in many other ways besides death rates. The endemic malarial conditions that exist among tropical populations mean that individuals carry a quantity of parasites in their bloodstream from time of birth, and in many areas are reinfected year around. This together with the burden of other parasites common to the tropics and limited nutrition causes a lowering of the general health, reduces energy levels, and increases susceptibility to other diseases, all of which affect life expectancy.

The disease we call malaria is caused by several species of the genus *Plasmodium*. This single-cell parasite has a complex life cycle, part of which is spent in the body of a mammalian host where it enters the red blood cell and, using the cells energy supply, divides eventually destroying the cell. The released parasites accumulate in the larger blood vessels, especially those in the liver and spleen. *Homo sapiens* is host[7] to four species of *Plasmodium*, which cause four different types of malaria: *vivax*, the most common form and with a wide geographical distribution; *ovale*, the rarest form native to West Africa; *malariae*, a broad but spotty-distributed parasite causing a mild form of the disease; and the fourth, and most deadly type of malaria, *falciparum*. This *Plasmodium* species requires a warm climate to flourish, and its distribution is limited to the tropics (Harrison, 1978).

The organism may be transmitted to humans by the bite of a female Anopheles mosquito infected with the parasites, or an uninfected mosquito may suck up the parasites when biting an infected human. The mosquito then becomes a carrier or vector that can deposit the malarial organism in many uninfected persons. Because mosquitoes are vectors for malarial transmission, the distribution and spread of the disease depends on the habits and life cycle of the *Anopheles* species. Of the one hundred species known to function as a vector of the *Plasmodium* parasites, there are only about twenty important ones because the parasites develop better in some species of *Anopheles* than in others. Each world region provides an environment that seems to favor certain species; for example, the species, *A. gambiae* is the major vector for distribution of falciparum malaria in Africa and Arabia, where *P. falciparum* accounts for 80 to 90 percent of the malaria infections found among the populations in these regions. Throughout India, Southeast Asia, and New Guinea, other species are important vectors of *vivax* and *falciparum* malarial parasites.

The part humans play in this host-vector disease organism scheme is important and complicated because several of the major species of mosquito depend on human disruption of the environment to provide breeding places. The *A. gambiae* mosquito is best adapted to the conditions that exist about human habitations, because it does not breed well in virgin tropical rain forests; also, sedentary human populations provide many more hosts than do wandering bands of nomads. In the past, the Anopheles, or their ancestral forms, may have preyed on nonhuman hosts, just as many species still do. Through the development of human sedentary life since the Neolithic, several mosquitoes have come to depend on humans as their major host. Primitive agricultural activities and adoption of sedentary village life brought about many changes in the environment that had been followed by a significant increase in the human population and a decline in the number of wild mammals in the vicinity of the settlements (Livingstone, 1958).

These changes are particularly evident in the example of slash-and-

---

[7] In addition to the human host, species of malarial parasites have been identified in several South American primates and in macaques of Southeast Asia. These cause forms of malaria similar to the vivax or malariae in humans. The hypothesis is that the primates act as a reservoir for the parasites, which can be transmitted to humans by certain mosquito vectors. Though of evolutionary importance, the hypothesis has not been fully tested.

burn techniques of the tropical rain forest horticulturist who radically alters the flora and drives away many mammals that might have been hosts to the mosquitoes. This style of agriculture involved the cutting and then burning of the trees, and this removal of the tropical rain forest cover exposes the thin soils to erosion in the high-rainfall areas. Stagnant pools of water collect and provide mosquito breeding places; further, humans locate their dwellings in groups where numerous families live in close contact. All of these events provide an ideal situation for the transmission of malarial parasites on a continuous basis, causing up to 100 percent of the population to be infected.

These relationships probably have existed for as long as humans have practiced agriculture in the tropics—about three thousand to four thousand years. The situation in the subtropics is more complex, and the insect vectors are different, as are the types of malarial disease that they transmit. The association between agriculture, settled village life, and malaria is probably the same, however. Skeletal remains from Greek Neolithic sites show extensive signs of bone modification associated with chronic anemia, and some investigators believe these conditions to be due to thalassemia, which, today, is found in many Mediterranean populations (Angel, 1966). Because these same populations are those suffering from a high incidence of malaria, it is assumed that the early agriculturists brought about environmental changes that contributed to a rise in the disease. The association has remained until this very day.

If the malarial hypothesis is accepted, then the genes for such abnormalities as Hb^S, Hb^E, thalassemia, and G6PD deficiency are an advantage for populations living in the area where malaria is endemic. The survival value of being a carrier living under malarious conditions outweighs the disadvantage. The selection for the heterozygote establishes a balanced polymorphism that maintains the abnormal gene at high frequencies.

The most clear-cut relationship between malaria and the red-cell variants appears in the case of Hb^S. Individuals who are carriers (heterozygotes) are less likely to die from *falciparum* malaria than persons with normal Hb; also, fertility is higher among sicklers living in areas where *falciparum* is endemic, and female sicklers have a higher live birth rate than nonsicklers. Overall, there is a significantly greater number of sicklers in the older than forty-five-year segments of the population, which indicates a longer life-span; in addition, fewer sicklers die in infancy. Though untested, male fertility is likely to be higher in sicklers because of fewer episodes of the high fever associated with malarial attacks. Because spermatogenesis is impaired by elevated body temperature, it is believed that sicklers are less subject to this impairment to fertility, because they have fewer malarial attacks.

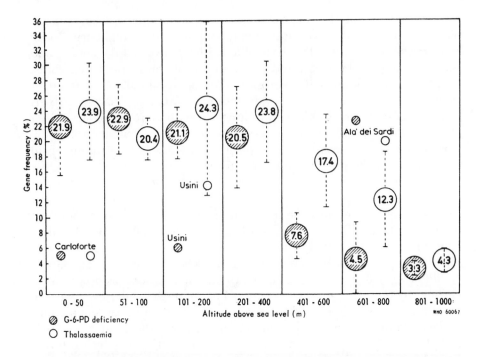

FIGURE 6-10   Incidence of G6PD Deficiency and of Thalassaemia Trait in Relation to Altitude above Sea-Level. (From Siniscalco, M. et al., "Population genetics of haemoglobin variants, thalassaemia and glucose-6-phosphate dehydrogenase deficiency, with particular reference to the malaria hypothesis." Copyright © 1966 by World Health Organization. Reprinted by permission of the publisher.)

The figures in each of the large circles are the averages of the gene frequencies found in the villages that fall within the ending altitude groupings (0–50 meters, 51–100 meters, etc.).

DISTRIBUTION OF RED-CELL VARIANTS

Evidence to support the relationships between thalassemia, G6PD deficiency (Gd^B −), and malaria is provided by a study carried out on the island of Sardinia, once an intensely malarious area. A clear inverse correlation was found between altitude and frequency of thalassemia and G6PD deficiency (Figure 6-10). At the higher elevations, as one moves away from the coastal plain, the rate of malarial infection decreases because the environment is less favorable to the mosquito vector. There are fewer carriers of the genes for Gd^B − and thalassemia among the populations of villages in the mountains and foothills. Some villages, however, do not fit the correlations. In other words, the selective force (malaria) is present, but there are few people who are carriers of the genetic traits (G6PD and thalassemia) that would provide them with a degree of immunity; an explanation must be sought elsewhere. The villages of Carloforte and Usini, both in a malarious area, were settled in the last two hundred years by immigrants from other regions, Spain (Usini) and Genoa (Carloforte). These founder's did not possess the Gd^B – or thalassemia genes. This reconstruction is further reinforced by the genealogical evidence; the few individuals with these traits can trace their ancestry to a Sardinian origin (Siniscalco et al., 1966).

This history and distribution of populations with high frequencies of Hb^S and suffering from endemic malaria is another correlation worthy of note. Populations with over 15 percent gene frequency for Hb^S are known from West Africa to northeast India and Bangladesh, and in each of these areas *falciparum* malaria is transmitted continuously throughout the year. The question of the origin of this Hb^S gene outside the African continent logically comes up, because it has been considered by many to have originated in Africa. In many areas of the Mediterranean there is historical evidence of contact with Arab populations, who have established colonies in many places along its northern shores in Spain, Italy, Sicily, and Greece. African slaves from sub-Saharan areas were often brought in, and it is likely that at least some of them were carriers of the Hb^S gene. In India, trade and some colonization from Africa are known to have occurred with some importation of the Hb^S gene.

It is difficult to explain the presence of such a high frequency of Hb^S in certain parts of India, however, solely on the basis of the importation of slaves or on the establishment of colonies (Figure 6-11). There is a possibility that such a gene as Hb^S, which is advantageous under certain conditions, appeared in several populations throughout human history by random mutations. The gene then would become fixed at high frequencies because of its advantage under conditions of endemic malaria. Such occurrence of spontaneous mutations would rule out the need to associate a gene with a particular race. Though the question is far from settled, there are supporters for both sides of the argument: for gene distribution by migration and for random mutation. One group explains that a few mutations in a central area initiated an advantageous gene such as Hb^S, and from that central area, supposedly in the southern Sudan of East Africa, the gene spread by population migration and interpopulation contact. This spread has been classically associated with the expansion of populations of Bantu speakers, early agriculturists who successfully exploited tropical rain forests. Such a scheme, however, would make it difficult to explain how the gene arrived in remoter areas noncontiguous with the main African homeland, such as Bangladesh.

Since the first edition of this book was written a great deal of work has been done on the Hb genes, especially the beta Hb. The structure of the DNA sequence has been defined as well as its chromosome location. In addition, the use of endonucleases (enzymes to cleave DNA at particular

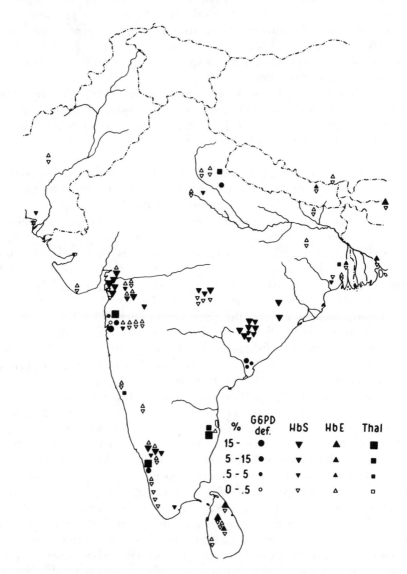

FIGURE 6-11   Hemoglobin S and Other Red-Cell Defects in India. (Reprinted from Livingstone, F.
B., *Abnormal Hemoglobins in Human Populations*, 1967. (Chicago: Aldine Publishing
Company, 1967); copyright © 1967 by Frank B. Livingstone. Reprinted by permission
of the author and Aldine Publishing Company.)

sites) have been applied to a wide range of samples from differing ethnic groups and geographical races (from India to African Americans). The results produced several RFLPs, and as discussed in chapters 2 and 3, the RFLPs on either side of the Hb^S gene differed between several populations sampled. Some of these haplotypes were identified in reference to the population where they were discovered: Senegal, Benin, and Bantu, and, a fourth, the Arab-Indian. The presence of different fragments with the Hb^S suggests to some observers that the gene underwent separate mutation; three different mutations in Africa, and another in the Middle East and India. Because of the diversity of haplotypes, the argument for independent mutation is convincing, but Livingstone (1989) views the present-day distribution as due to diffusion from an origin in the Middle East and the haplotypes the result of recombination as described earlier in chapter 3. Whatever explanation proves to be correct, the RFLP evidence provides more useful information about population diversity and offers additional documentation of the adaptation of the human hemoglobin complex.

NATURAL SELECTION AND GENETIC ADAPTATIONS AT OTHER LOCI

Human genetic adaptation to a particular selective force is difficult to establish. The generation time is too long, experimental procedures are restricted, and human behavior and physiological plasticity complicate the results. Because of the requirements of the malarial parasite and the dependence of some mosquito vectors on human use of the environments, however, selection at the beta-Hb locus has been well documented. More important is the fact that a single disease, malaria, with a high mortality rate, acts as the selective force differentiating between individual Hb genotypes as described earlier. Other examples of genetic adaptation are not so readily available. The red-cell antigens, especially the ABO, and certain serum proteins have all been implicated, in various ways, with the probability of survival within differing environments where there is contact with some of the major infectious diseases. No single disease has been established, however, as a selective force comparable with the malarial-Hb hypothesis. A complex of several disease organisms may be acting on different genotypes of blood components. It is this variety that makes it difficult to sort out the selective force and to establish a particular genotype's contribution to survival. Despite these problems, the environmental distribution of several inherited factors of the blood raise the question of natural selection, or rather, are these uneven distributions evidence of genetic adaptations? Because of the wealth of information gained from the long period of investigations and because of the uneven distributions of blood types throughout the world, the ABO blood groups provide an excellent source of data to examine the question of genetic adaptation further.

The discovery of inherited differences in ABO antigens and antibodies intrigued many investigators and led them on in a search for a function. Did the fact that type B was more frequent in parts of Asia, while type A was more prevalent among several northern Europeans have any relationship to the environmental variables in each region? Other investigators followed the route that treated the blood groups as nonadaptive (that is, selectively neutral) and reasoned that differing frequencies of the types among populations were due to other factors that influence gene frequencies (Boyd, 1950). Despite this latter position an enormous amount of work has gone into an effort to discover natural selection at the ABO locus. Since the initial discovery of the ABO system in 1900, many millions of persons around the world have been typed, and extensive research has been carried on in an attempt to discover correlations between blood type and the incidence of disease. The results have been inconclusive, but they have stimulated much speculation about the meaning of blood-group polymorphism in all of the red-cell antigens, plasma proteins, the HLA system, and the ABO blood groups in particular.

ABO Alleles

The average frequencies of the ABO alleles for the entire species may serve as a baseline against which individual populations or population complexes may be compared. Allele O (62.5 percent) is the most frequent and B (16 percent) the least, with allele A (21.5 percent) slightly higher. As discussed in chapter 3, populations in many parts of the world deviate widely from these averages, but, with a few exceptions (Australia and Native Americans in particular), alleles A and B are usually greater than zero and seldom rise above 50 percent. Figure 6-12 plots the A and B frequencies for 215 representative populations; most cluster within the ranges of 15 to 30 percent (type A) and 10 to 20 percent (type B) when gene frequency distribution is considered. Alice Brues (1954, 1963) argued that such a distribution could most adequately be explained by balanced polymorphism at the ABO locus, which was maintained by selection for the heterozygote, the AO genotype. Though the nature of the selection has yet to be fully understood, many workers now consider that the ABO alleles are adaptive and in some way influence survival, a factor that must be considered.

Though the search for the meaning of blood-group polymorphisms during more than a half century has been disappointing, several possible explanations have emerged. These explanations can be grouped into several categories of selection that act to regulate allele frequencies during

PERCENT OF GENE A

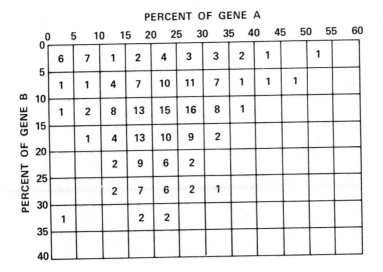

FIGURE 6-12   **Limits to the Range of Alleles A and B in the World's Populations.** (From Brues, A. M., "Selection and polymorphism in the ABO blood groups." Copyright © 1954 by The Wistar Institute Press. Reprinted by permission of the publisher.)

Quantitative distribution of 215 representative human populations in respect to frequencies of the ABO blood-group genes.

the period of human evolution and population diversification. Selection in *Homo sapiens* functions to cause differential fertility, differential mortality, and infant mortality in particular. There have been studies indicating that the ABO system is effective in each of these categories.

Differential Fertility

There was a difference in the rate of live births of type-O mothers, and these women produced fewer children than expected when the fathers were type A or B. Further, if the male parent was heterozygous AO or BO, then there was a significantly greater number of OO children produced by the type-O mother. The net result of matings incompatible for the ABO system is seen in Table 6-4.

The differential fertility acts in the following ways: First, there is a selection at the *prezygotic* stage. In a type-O female there appears to be a greater chance of fertilization by the sperm carrying the type-O gene, so the genotypes differ significantly from the expected frequency shown by the Hardy-Weinberg equilibrium, as in the following:

Parents   AO × OO

Children   AO   OO (> 50 percent)

TABLE 6-4   ABO Blood Type and Fertility

| | MATINGS WHERE THE ABO BLOOD TYPES OF MALE AND FEMALE ARE: | |
	Compatible	Incompatible
Total matings	812	617
Pregnancies	2639	1928
Abortions[a]	273 (0.10 per pregnancy)	295 (0.15 per pregnancy)
Living children[a]	2108	1341
Couples childless[a]	80 (0.10)	112 (0.18)
Couples as yet infertile[a]	66 (0.08)	72 (0.12)

[a] These differences between compatible and incompatible matings are statistically significant.
Sources: Based on Matsunaga and Itoh, 1958; and Matsunaga and Hiraizumi, 1962.

This selection for one male gamete over the other may be due to the antibodies in vaginal secretions, which react with sperm specific for type A. Sperm have been shown to possess specific antigen reactions, but the question still remains of whether such specificity is due to the alleles carried by the sperm.

The second reason for reduction of fertility of incompatible matings is fetal loss owing to antibodies A and B in the type-O mother. The naturally occurring A and B antibodies in the O mother do not readily cross the placenta, but some mothers make an anti-A and anti-B antibodies that can easily diffuse through the placenta membranes and enter the fetal bloodstream. Once there, they can disrupt development and cause fetal death. Overall, several studies show that women who carry fetuses with ABO blood types incompatible with their own have a greater risk of spontaneous abortion. The ease with which the antibodies from the maternal system can pass into the fetal bloodstream presents a clear danger similar to that known to exist for Rh hemolytic disease (Mourant, 1983).

In sum, fetal maternal incompatibility may contribute to a reduced fertility rate, increased abortion early in pregnancy, and hemolytic disease of the neonate. These are strong selective forces favoring the increase in the frequency of the O allele over A or B, and should lead to rapid fixation. In other words, all populations with such incompatible matings would eventually contain only type O (Figure 6-13). Such a condition exists in many Native American populations, but most of the world, as we have seen, have populations with a mixture of all three alleles. The question is what factors cause the A and B alleles to persist?

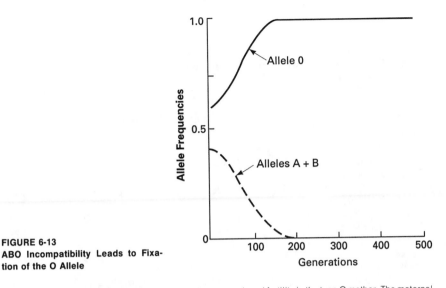

FIGURE 6-13
ABO Incompatibility Leads to Fixation of the O Allele

Fetal-maternal incompatibility of ABO type contributes to reduced fertility in the type O mother. The maternal antibodies select against a type A or type B fetus while favoring a type O. The result is that the allele O would become fixed in a population within about 200 generations if no counter selective forces are involved, that is, neither types A nor B persons have an advantage in certain environments. **(Source: Etkin and Eaton, 1983.)**

Disease Incidence and Blood Groups

The association between ABO blood types and certain diseases was considered early in the study of red-cell antigen systems. Analysis of thousand of hospital records compared the blood type of the patients with the disease for which they were treated. In this way a wide variety of diseases was listed, but the early results were disappointing and discouraged further investigation for nearly twenty-five years.

A study of the frequency of stomach cancer in England revealed a difference between regions; the mortality rate was higher in the north than in the south. Aird and associates (1953) at first thought the difference might be due to some environmental factor, and there did prove to be a difference in water hardness; a higher calcium concentration was found in those areas with the lowest stomach cancer rate. The correlation was slight but when the ABO blood types were compared, there was a significantly higher number of type-A persons with this type of cancer. These results encouraged a wide range of investigators to seek disease associations. Significant associations were found with several tumors as well as several other internal diseases (Table 6-5).

Though the distribution of secretors and nonsecretors throughout the world's populations is not as well known as that of the ABO red-cell types, their presence in tissues and fluids throughout the body may have

TABLE 6-5   Significant Associations between Blood Groups and Noninfectious Disease

DIAGNOSIS	NO. OF SERIES	NO. OF PATIENTS	CONTROLS	COMPARISON	
Neoplasias of the intestinal tract					
Cancer, stomach	101	55,434	1,852,288	A:O	1.22
Cancer of colon and rectum	17	7,435	183,286	A:O	1.11
Malignant tumors of salivary glands	2	285	12,968	A:O	1.64
Cancer, pancreas	13	817	108,408	A:O	1.24
Cancer, mouth and pharynx	2	757	41,098	A:O	1.25
Other neoplasias					
Cancer, cervix	19	11,927	197,577	A:O	1.13
Cancer, corpus uteri	14	2,598	160,602	A:O	1.15
Cancer, ovary	17	2,326	243,914	A:O	1.28
Cancer, breast	24	9,503	355,281	A:O	1.08
Multiple primary cancer	2	433	7,823	A:O	1.43
Nonmalignant tumors					
Nonmalignant salivary tumors	2	581	12,968	A:O	2.02
Other internal diseases					
Duodenal ulcers	44	26,039	407,518	O:A	1.35
				O:A+B+AB	1.33
Gastric ulcers	41	22,052	448,354	O:A	1.17
				O:A+B+AB	1.18
Duodenal and gastric ulcers	6	957	120,544	O:A	1.53
				O:A+B+AB	1.36
Bleeding ulcers (gastric and duodenal)	2	1,869	28,325	O:A	1.46
				O:A+B+AB	1.51
Rheumatic diseases	17	6,589	179,385	A:O	1.24
				A+B+AB:O	1.23
Pernicious anemia	13	2,077	119,989	A:O	1.25
Diabetes mellitus	20	15,778	612,819	A:O	1.07
				A+B+AB:O	1.07
Ischemic heart disease	12	2,763	218,727	A:O	1.18
				A+B+AB:O	1.17
Cholecystitis and cholelithiasis	10	5,950	112,928	A:O	1.17
Eosinophilia	3	730	1,096	A:O	2.38
				A+B+AB:O	2.13
Thromboembolic disease	5	1,026	287,246	A:O	1.61
				A+B+AB:O	1.60

Sources: Examples selected from Mourant and Kopec, 1978; Vogel and Motulsky, 1986.

a major significance in the response to foreign antigens. Some clues are provided by the relative gene frequencies at this locus. The record, to date, has established that most American Indians are secretors and that most nonsecretors are found in African populations south of the Sahara and in southern India. In the British Isles the alleles (Se, se) are approximately equal in frequency, and there are about 25 percent of nonsecretors (the se se genotype). The meaning of this distribution is not fully understood, but there is a possible relationship between the antigens and the digestive tract. There may be some interactions between the macromolecules of food and bacteria.

The presence of ABH in most people plus the fact that many food substances, once broken down into their molecular constituents, have specific reactions with the ABO substances make it highly probable that there is a complex series of reactions between antigens and macromolecules within the gastrointestinal tract. Many of these reactions may enhance digestion or retard it, depending on the substances involved, or there may be chronic irritation of the fine mucous linings of the intestines. At any rate, it is more than a coincidence that several diseases associated with the ABO system are localized within the digestive system. This area of research has not been fully explored, but immunological studies point out the likelihood of gut flora, similar to the blood group substances, stimulating the production of antibodies appropriate to the individual's RBC antigen. Hence, a type-A person will make anti-B antibodies in response to stimulus by substances in the gut flora and will tolerate antigens similar to type A (Roitt, 1988). Given the wide variety of foods that omnivorous *Homo sapiens* can and has subsisted on for thousands of years, the digestive system would be an area subject to natural selection.

In sum the chronic diseases listed in Table 6-5 have been used to demonstrate the correctness of the original hypotheses that selection has been acting to influence polymorphisms of the ABO system. Note, however, that these diseases are of the type that usually afflict an individual later in adult life, near the end of the reproductive period. It is unlikely, then, that ulceration, diabetes, or cancer is going to influence a person's reproductive fitness. Dietary-antigen relationships, however, should be looked at carefully as an area of strong environmental influence.

Infectious diseases offer several interesting possibilities for explanation of the adaptability of blood groups. Certain blood types may cause an individual to be more or less susceptible to disease-causing organisms, and several relationships between blood type and diseases are listed in Table 6-6.

Some of the organisms that cause these diseases have been demonstrated to be similar, antigenically, to either the A, B, or H antigens—that is, they have chemical structures on the coatings of their outer shells that are very similar in form to the antigens on the surface of the RBC. The

TABLE 6-6   ABO Blood Groups and Infectious Diseases

DISEASE	REPORTED GREATER SUSCEPTIBILITY (TYPE)
Parathypoid	O
Cholera	O
Plague	O
Scarlet fever	O and B
Escherichia coli (some strains)	B
Smallpox	A
Bronchial pneumonia	A
Rheumatic heart disease	A

Sources: Examples selected from Mourant and Kopec, 1978; Vogel and Motulsky, 1986.

explanation follows that the more similarity between the chemical structures of disease organisms and ABH antigens, the less likely is the individual's defense system to make antibodies against the disease organism. Thus the smallpox virus has a chemical specificity similar to type-A antigen. A person with type-A blood would be more susceptible to smallpox than would an O or B type. The findings of Vogel and associates (1975) described a mortality of 50 percent in type-A persons (approximately four times higher than in B or O persons) among populations in India. As a matter of fact, the frequency of A is much lower among populations of the Indian subcontinent than among Europeans.

Another organism, the plague bacteria with an H-antigen specificity, appears to be more lethal to type-O individuals, and if one considers the rate of mortality from this disease during the Middle Ages, when up to 90 percent of the populations of some European cities were wiped out, then the effectiveness of the disease as a selective agent can be appreciated. The areas of the world where plague has the longest history are the very areas where type O is found at the lowest frequency today. Areas that suffered from many outbreaks of the epidemic have a proportionately higher A and B frequency than regions where plague has never been reported or has been absent for several hundred years.

Vogel points to central Asia, India, and Mesopotamia as major plague centers, areas where populations have the lowest frequency of O. The selection against a type-O person in populations with a long history of plague would, over the generations, decrease the frequency of this allele. If in the same populations there was selection also against type-A allele because of smallpox, then both the A and O alleles would be present in low frequencies. Type-B allele would occur at high frequencies, as in India, where B frequencies are among the highest in the world (Figure 6-14).

Counter to this selection favoring B type in smallpox and plague

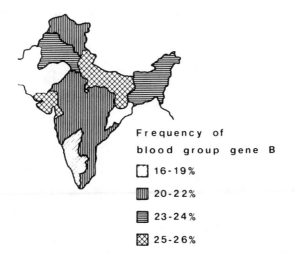

Frequency of
blood group gene B

☐ 16-19%

▥ 20-22%

▤ 23-24%

▨ 25-26%

Plague and smallpox have been major causes of death at all ages throughout India well into this century. These diseases were likely sources of natural selection at the ABO locus and are probable causes of the high frequency of type B.

FIGURE 6-14   Distribution of Blood Type B in India. (Based on Buchi, 1968.)

areas is the high rate of infant infectious diarrhea caused by various strains of *E. coli* bacteria. The shifting of A or B antigens specificity in *E. coli* strains during the epidemics in eastern Europe in the 1950s alternately caused more frequent episodes in type-B or type-A infants, and the disease was more acute in both than in type-O infants (Vogel and Motulsky, 1986).

Another possible source of natural selection is the peculiar behavior of insects. Some species of insect vectors appear to prefer one particular host over another. The temperature or color of the skin or the chemical compounds excreted may influence choice. Some studies have demonstrated that mosquitoes have preferences in the blood on which they chose to feed. How the insect choice was made or what chemical substance attracted them is not known, but type-O was the most frequent. Volunteers were used to record the frequency of bites, and those persons with type-O blood were bitten more often than those with type A or B. Should subsequent studies support these preliminary results, then malaria and other mosquito-borne diseases may be added to the list of disease selection at the ABO locus.

Population size is another factor that indirectly influences the course and intensity of natural selection. A glance at the chart of infectious diseases in Table 6-6 shows that many are of the type commonly found in larger populations that live in close contact within dense settlements and that are exposed to food and water pollution. One is tempted to

TABLE 6-7   Blood-Group Gene Frequencies in Isolates in and near Europe

ISOLATES	GENE PERCENTAGES					
	A	B	O	M	d	K
Icelanders	20	5	75	58	37	5
Irish (Republic)	17	7	76	57	43	4
Lapps	37	9	54	52	16	1
Basques	24	2	74	54	56	5
Béarnais	24	4	72	49	59	3
Corsicans	22	3	75	65	35	4
Sardinians	20	7	73	75	22	3
Walsers	21	5	73	51	41	8
Bergamasques	24	6	70	56	43	5
Valle Ladine	20	3	77	78	56	
Svani (Caucasia)	23	7	70	65	41	
Saudi Arabians	16	11	75	72	25	6
Towara Bedouin	16	9	74	52	31	13
Jebeliya Bedouin	12	26	62	66	54	18
Ait Haddidu Berbers	7	5	89	24	23	4

Source: Selected from Mourant, 1983.

speculate that only in recent times has selection operated to produce the ranges of gene-frequency variation from the ABO blood types—since the Neolithic, when *Homo sapiens* developed agriculture and adapted to settled village life. Supporting evidence is provided by the fact that the more isolated groups, especially those that have been involved with the development of dense sedentary life-styles only in the last few hundred generations, are the ones with the highest type-A and -O frequencies— groups such as the northwest Europeans. The Basques of northern Spain, Lapps, Australian Aboriginals, and Polynesians are some examples of isolation and high-A frequencies. Type B is consistently low except in a few Middle Eastern isolates (Table 6-7).

By contrast, the populations whose ancestors established the earliest large, densely populated, agriculturally based communities are those with the lowest A frequencies (American Indian groups excepted). Most of India's populations, Thailand, and many mideastern groups illustrate this relationship. This speculation is based on the diverse data of the reactions between the red-cell antigens of the ABO and several diseases. The problem is a highly complex one; some selective forces may be acting in opposition to each other, as in the case of smallpox and plague, but the net effect is to alter a breeding population's gene combinations.

With all the information that we possess on the blood groups, explanations for their adaptive significance still escape us, and several recent authoritative works on the human blood groups give little attention to natural selection. As Vogel (1968:366) states, however, the blood-group antigens probably played an important role in *Homo sapiens* evolution and adaptation:

> In earlier centuries, infections have killed a high percentage of mankind before reproductive age. Hence, selective pressure was very strong, and genetic adaptation to infections must have strongly influenced our present gene pool.

Infant mortality is the area where selection can be most influential in shaping the gene pool of future generations. High rates of infant deaths were once the norm among our ancestors, and even rates of more than 50 percent were typical among some nomadic populations, even during the last century. Often these deaths were due to various forms of gastrointestinal ailments, or infant diarrhea, which is especially severe in populations, even today, who make use of polluted water and account for a large percentage of infant and childhood mortality.

Differences in reactions of the blood type with several kinds of intestinal bacteria have been noted and, as a result, the severity of the diseases that the organisms cause varies with blood type. Involvement of the ABO antigens with bacteria in the intestinal tract has been described, and there is no more critical period than when an infant is adjusting to the microbial groups common to his or her environmental setting. This period, and the period of stress on the young child's system during weaning, are times of extreme selective pressures. Add to this all of the parasites and amoebas found in many tropical regions, plus marginal diets and the lack of suitable "weaning" foods, and one can easily see that any difference in susceptibility to infection, even though slight, will lead to extensive differences in mortality rates.

These are but a few possible demonstrations of the adaptive significance of the human ABO blood types. The other blood groups do not appear to be involved in an interaction with the environment; little is known about the possible action of natural selection on the several other blood groups. There has been an excess of MN genotypes reported in some populations, but the significance of this greater than expected MN frequency over MM, NN genotypes is not known. At least one disease affecting the MN locus has been described, however; type N has been found more frequently among persons with rheumatic diseases. The knowledge that *Homo sapiens* has no antibodies for this system does not aid our understanding. It should be recalled, also, that the M and N genes are evenly distributed throughout the world, except for American Indians, who have a much greater frequency of M, and Australian Aboriginals, who have a high type-N frequency.

The distribution of the Rh alleles shown in Figure 6-15 provides

FIGURE 6-15   Percentage Frequency of Blood-Type Allele r (RH negative). (After Hulse, 1971.)

evidence that strongly supports the argument that selection may have acted on this locus also, though the only disease association thus far reported has been a higher than expected *type-D allele* among patients suffering from rheumatic fever. The most frequent explanation offered for the Rh system is that hemolytic incompatibility (discussed in chapter 3) serves to regulate the frequency of d(r). This allele, responsible for approximately 95 percent of hemolytic disease in the newborn, approaches a frequency of zero in a population within a few generations when selection is most intense. Yet, despite the selection against offspring of Rh incompatibility matings, a high frequency of d(r) has been maintained in several populations throughout the generations. These high frequencies suggest that natural selection is operating to maintain a deleterious allele, probably through selection for the heterozygote as we have seen in other examples. We do not know what the advantage may be to a heterozygote carrier of d(r), but, whatever it is, a balance has been maintained and the allele persists at high frequencies in several European and African populations.

Of the other blood groups, two are worthy of note because of their peculiar distribution. The *Duffy group* shows a significant difference between Europeans and West Africans. According to Race and Sanger (1975:341) this group provides the greatest distinction between the two populations of all the blood groups; African populations have between 60 and 90 percent of Fy (a−b−), but this allele is seldom found in Europeans (less than 35 percent). The Fy-negative individual is immune to the vivax malarial parasite. The parasite attaches to the Fy^a or Fy^b site on the red-cell membrane and provides a point of entry. This resistance to vivax malaria, a common form in North America, would help explain why the African slaves imported to the New World did so well and grew rapidly in number, whereas the Native Americans in the tropics, who lacked any natural resistance to malaria, declined.

The second blood group is the *Diego*, which is due to a simple dominant and is confined to Mongoloid peoples. The frequency of this allele is highest among certain South American Indians (36 percent) and is virtually absent in Eskimos, though both have descended from Asian peoples. Some suggestion has been made that the gene, because it is most frequent in tropical populations, may in some way be adapted to that type of environment.

Finally, when all of the distributions of blood-group polymorphisms are considered and all explanations of selective forces are evaluated, definite adaptive value of each allele has not been established. The numerous interactions between environmental factors and blood types, and all variations of allele frequencies, offer evidence of some possibilities. The reader must remember, however, that allele frequencies are the end result of the sum total of several types of interactions, including natural selection acting at various growth stages. Additionally, though many blood types seem to be inherited as a single gene, it is likely that several, if not all, of the alleles for the different blood groups are pleiotropic; that is, they affect more than one phenotype. According to Harris (1980:174), "We are probably also naive in looking at selection exerted on a single gene locus; we should be thinking of selection acting on the whole genome." While the search continues for the survival value of the blood-group alleles, it is a reasonable assumption that diversity of these genes in our species is of adaptive value and has played a role at different stages in our evolution and selective influences vary at different points in our life cycles.

RECOMMENDED READINGS AND LITERATURE CITED

AIRD, I., H. H. BENTALL, AND J. A. F. ROBERTS. 1953. "A relationship between cancer of the stomach and the ABO groups," *Br. Med. J.*, 1:799–801.

ANGEL, J. L. 1966. "Porotic hyperostosis anemias, malarias and marshes in prehistoric eastern Mediterranean," *Science*, 153:760–763.

BALLEW, C., R. M. GARRUTO, AND J. D. HAAS. 1989. High altitude hematology: Paradigm or enigma? in *Human Population Biology: A Transdisciplinary Science*, ed. M. A. Little and J. D. Haas. New York: Oxford University Press.

BARNICOT, N. A. 1957. "Human pigmentation," *Man*, 57:114–120.

BLUM, H. F. 1962. "Does the melanin pigment of human skin have adaptive value? An essay in human ecology and the evolution of race," *Quart. Rev. Biol.*, 36:50–63.

BLUM, H. F. 1969. "Is sunlight a factor in the geographical distribution of human skin color?" *Geograph. Review*, 59:557–581.

BOYD, W. C. 1950. *Genetics and the Races of Man*. Boston: Little, Brown.

BRANDA, R. F., AND J. W. EATON. 1978. "Skin color and nutrient photolysis: An evolutionary hypothesis," *Science*, 201:625–626.

BRUES, A. M. 1954. "Selection and polymorphism in the ABO blood groups," *Am. J. Phys. Anthrop.*, 12:559–597.

BRUES, A. M. 1963. "Stochastic tests of selection in the ABO blood groups," *Am. J. Phys. Anthrop.*, 21:287–300.

BUCHI, E. C. 1968. "Somatic groups composing the modern population of India," in *Proceedings of the Eighth International Congress of Anthropological and Ethnological Sciences*. Tokyo, Japan: Science Council of Japan.

CLARKE, C. A. 1961. "Blood groups and disease," in *Progress in Medical Genetics*, vol. 1, ed. A. G. Steinberg. New York: Grune and Stratton.

COON, C. S. 1965. *The Living Races of Man*. New York: Alfred A. Knopf.

DARWIN, CHARLES. 1871 (reprinted, 1936). *The Descent of Man and Selection in Relation to Sex*. New York: Modern Library.

DOBZHANSKY, T. 1971. "Race equality," in *The Biological and Social Meaning of Race*, ed. Richard H. Osborne. New York: W. H. Freeman.

EDELSTEIN, S. J. 1986. *The Sickled Cell: From Myths to Molecules*. Cambridge, Mass.: Harvard University Press.

ETKIN, N. L., AND J. W. EATON. 1983. "Blood bankers, viruses and ABO blood groups" [abstract], *Am. J. Phys. Anthropol.*, 60:192.

FABER, M. 1982. "Ultraviolet radiation," in *Nonionizing Radiation Protection*, ed. M. J. Suess, European Series #10. Washington, D.C.: WHO Regional Publications.

FRISANCHO, A. R. 1969. "Human growth and pulmonary function of a high altitude Peruvian Quechua population," *Human Biol.*, 41:365–379.

FRISANCHO, A. R. 1970. "Developmental responses to high altitude hypoxia," *Am. J. Phys. Anthrop.*, 32:401–407.

FRISANCHO, A. R. 1979. *Human Adaptation: A Functional Interpretation*. St. Louis: C. V. Mosby.

FRISANCHO, A. R., AND L. P. GREKSA. 1989. "Developmental responses in the acquisition of functional adaptation to high altitude," in *Human Population Biology: A Transdisciplinary Science*, eds. M. A. Little and J. D. Haas. New York: Oxford University Press.

GANOG, W. F. 1977. *Review of Medical Physiology*, 8th ed. Los Altos, Calif.: Lange Medical Publications.

GREKSA, L. P., AND C. M. BEALL. 1989. "Development of chest size and lung function at high altitude," in *Human Population Biology: A Transdisciplinary Science*, eds. M. A. Little and J. D. Haas. New York: Oxford University Press.

HARDY, J. D., AND C. MUSCHENHEIM. 1934. "The radiation of heat from the human body: IV. The emission, reflection and transmission of infrared radiation by the human skin," *J. Clin. Invest.*, 13:817–831.

HARDY, J. D., AND C. MUSCHENHEIM. 1936. "Radiation of heat from the human body: V. The transmission of infrared radiation through the skin," *J. Clin. Invest.*, 15:1–9.

HARRIS, H. 1980. *The Principles of Human Biochemical Genetics*, 3rd ed. New York: Elsevier North-Holland.

HARRISON, G. 1978. *Mosquitoes, Malaria and Man: A History of the Hostilities Since 1880.* New York: E. P. Dutton.

HOCK, R. J. 1970. "The physiology of high altitude," in *Readings from Scientific American-Biological Anthropology.* New York: W. H. Freeman.

HOFF, C. J., AND E. ABELSON. 1976. "Fertility," in *Man in the Andes,* eds. P. Baker and M. Little. London: Hutchinson and Ross.

HULSE, F. S. 1971. *The Human Species.* New York: Random House.

IVANHOE, F. 1970. "Was Virchow right about Neanderthal?" *Nature,* 227:577–579.

KAN, Y. W., AND A. M. DOZY. 1980. "Evolution of the hemoglobin S and C genes in world populations," *Science,* 209:388–390.

KIRBY-SMITH, J. S., H. F. BLUM, AND H. G. GRADY. 1942. "Penetration of ultraviolet radiation into skin, as a factor in carcinogenesis," *J. Natl. Cancer Inst.,* 2:403–412.

LIVINGSTONE, F. B. 1958. Anthropological implications of sickle cell gene distribution in West Africa. *Am. Anthropol.,* 60:533–562.

LIVINGSTONE, F. B. 1967. *Abnormal Hemoglobins in Human Populations.* Chicago: Aldine.

LIVINGSTONE, F. B. 1989. "Who gave whom hemoglobin S: The use of restriction site haplotype variation for the interpretation of the evolution of the beta^S-globin gene." *Am. J. Human Biol.,* 1:289–302.

LOOMIS, F. W. 1967. "Skin-pigment regulation of vitamin D biosynthesis in man," *Science,* 157:501–506.

LOOMIS, F. W. 1970. "Rickets," *Sci. Am.,* 223:77–91.

LUCKEISH, M. 1946. *Applications of Germicidal, Erythemal, and Infrared Energy.* Belmont, Calif.: Wadsworth.

MATSUNAGA, E., AND Y. HIRAIZUMI. 1962. "Prezygotic selection in ABO blood groups," *Science,* 135:432–434.

MATSUNAGA, E., AND S. ITOH. 1958. "Blood groups and fertility in Japanese populations, with special reference to intra-uterine selection due to maternal-foetal incompatibility," *Ann. Hum. Genet.,* 22:111–131.

MAZESS, R. B. 1975. "Human adaptation to high altitude," in *Physiological Anthropology,* ed. A. Damon. New York: Oxford University Press.

MOLNAR, S., AND I. MOLNAR. 1985. "The incidence of enamel hypoplasia among Krapina Neanderthals," *Am. Anthrop.,* 87:536–549.

MOON, P. 1941. "Proposed standard solar-radiation curves for engineering use," *J. Franklin Inst.,* 230:583–617.

MOURANT, A. E. 1983. *Blood Relations: Blood Groups and Anthropology.* New York: Oxford University Press.

OGILVIE, M. D., B. K. CURRAN, AND E. TRINKAUS. 1989. "Incidence and patterning of dental enamel hypoplasia among the Neandertals." *Am. J. Phys. Anthrop.,* 79:25–41.

PACE, N. 1961. "Man at altitude," in *A Study of Man and His Environment,* eds. S. M. Farber and R. H. L. Wilson. Springfield, Ill.: Charles C Thomas.

RACE, R. R., AND R. SANGER. 1975. *Blood Groups in Man,* 6th ed. Philadelphia: F. A. Davis.

ROBERTS, D. F. 1978. *Climate and Human Variability,* 2nd ed. Menlo Park, Calif.: Cummings.

ROITT, I. 1988. *Essential Immunology,* 6th ed. Oxford: Blackwell Scientific.

SINISCALCO, M., L. L. BERNINI, G. FILIPPI, B. LATTE, P. MEERA KHAN, S. PIOMELLI, AND M. RATTAZZI. 1966. "Population genetics of haemoglobin variants, thalassemia and glucose-6-phosphate dehydrogenase deficiency with particular reference to the malaria hypothesis," *Bull. World Health Organ.,* 34:379–393.

THOMSON, M. L. 1955. "Relative efficiency of pigment and horny layer thickness in protecting the skin of Europeans and Africans against solar ultraviolet radiation," *J. Physiol.,* 127:236–246.

VELASQUEZ, T. 1976. "Pulmonary function and oxygen transport," in *Man in the Andes,* eds. P. Baker and M. Little. London: Hutchinson and Ross.

VOGEL, F. 1968. "Anthropological implications of the relationship between ABO blood groups and infections," *Proceedings of the Eighth International Congress of Anthropological and Ethnological Sciences,* 1:365–370.

VOGEL, F. 1975. "ABO blood groups, the HL-A system and diseases," in *The Role of Natural Selection in Human Evolution*, ed. F. M. Salzano. New York: American Elsevier.

VOGEL, F., AND A. G. MOTULSKY. 1986. *Human Genetics: Problems and Approaches*, 2nd ed. Berlin: Springer-Verlag.

WALSH, R. J. 1963. "Variations of melanin pigmentation of the skin in some Asian and Pacific peoples," *Journal of the Royal Anthropological Inst.*, 93:126–133.

_7_

Human Variability and Behavior

Individuals vary considerably in their behavior, as they do in many of their biological traits. One does not have to be an expert to recognize this. Just as we perceive differences in human size, shape, and color, we readily differentiate between persons on the basis of their personality traits. The behavioral differences we distinguish are difficult to measure and are influenced to an extraordinary degree by cultural factors, however. The family, religion, and nation have profound influences that establish lifetime patterns of behavior; even the era in which one lives shapes many of our responses, as any comparisons between generations in the twentieth century will show. An additional problem arises when we attempt to quantify such traits and try to draw conclusions about an individual's worth or quality, or ability. All too often we seek an easy answer and rely on group membership as the key to individual evaluation.

The study of human behavioral diversity is further complicated not only by prejudices and misconceptions but also by the confusion of social and biological definitions of race as described earlier. For example, by the end of the last century, beliefs in racial superiority reached a peak as entire nations and civilizations throughout human history were attributed to the "superior germ plasm of its citizens." Most frequently the Nordic was described as the bearer of this superior germ plasm. The French aristocrat, Count Gobineau, dedicated the contents of four volumes on *The Inequality of Races* to an attempt to prove that the Nordics, who he described as the "bearer's of the lamp of civilization," were above all other races. The rest of the species, including the bulk of Europeans, were grouped into races that were inferior. According to Gobineau, "It was the Nordic who created the high civilizations of the past and who were responsible for the formation of modern states" (Gobineau, in Barzun, 1965:54).

This conviction of racial superiority proved to be useful as a rationalization for the treatment of aboriginal peoples Europeans encountered during their world exploration and colonization. Confronted with the high mortality and declining populations that they were no doubt responsible for, the colonial government officials talked glibly of, "a passing of an inferior race." In New Zealand, where the Maori with their highly developed tribal government and efficient use of the land presented special problems of conquest, the reaction was the same after the defeat of the Maori armies. The general feeling of the English colonists is summed up by one official: "Taking all things into consideration, the disappearance of the race is scarcely subject for much regret. They are dying out in a quick, easy way, and are being supplanted by a superior race," (Belich, 1986:299). This kind of statement coming from the officials virtually anywhere in the far-flung European colonies was not surprising because it expressed the general feeling of the time. Even among the medical missionaries, who were charged with tending to the physical and spiritual needs of the people, there was the firm belief that the "race has run out" and, after two or three generations, only a remnant would remain to represent the people (Fenton, 1859:31). Many examples existed among peoples around the world; all non-Europeans, by definition, were incapable of higher development. Even among the Europeans, however, there was a scaling of biological inequality and southern Europeans were placed lower than northern populations, and eastern Europeans were at the bottom of the scale. Such beliefs were common in the nineteenth century and have persisted even into recent decades as shown by the dominant theme of a book that revived racism in the 1970s: "It must not be forgotten that certain races of man not only never attained independently to the status of civilization, but never independently reached the intermediate phase" (Baker, 1974:528).

Such brief statements note the direction of racist writings of the last century, which sought to understand human societies in terms of heredity. Of course, today we no longer speak of "superior germ plasm" as the source of civilization, nor do we define race and national character. There is, however, a continued interest in biological determinism, or genetic determinism of behavior, which has its modern roots in the application of various tests designed to measure aptitudes or intelligence. With the revival of Mendelian genetics in 1900, theories of social reform and human behavior were decidedly influenced by evidence of particulate inheritance. Many physical characteristics were determined at conception by combinations of parental genes, so it was considered probable that traits like mental ability, aggression, and social pathology were also inherited. Psychologists eagerly applied the new genetic theory to a host of social problems of the day, and the principal problem was believed to be the "flood" of immigrants entering America during the 1900s.

In the beginning of this century there was an attempt to discriminate between immigrant groups through the application of an intelligence test devised by the French psychologist, Binet. Goddard, one of the first psychologists to adapt the Binet test in America, was invited by government officials in 1912 to apply the test at the Ellis Island immigrant receiving station. Goddard administered a revised Binet test and its supplements to what he called representatives of the "great mass of average immigrants." Convinced of the accuracy of his results, Goddard reported that 83 percent of the Jews, 80 percent of the Hungarians, 79 percent of the Italians, and 87 percent of the Russians were "feebleminded" and unable to deal with abstractions. The effect of these results became all too clear when Goddard reported in 1917 that the number of aliens deported because of feeblemindedness increased approximately 350 percent in 1913 and 570 percent in 1914 because of the untiring efforts of the physicians, who were inspired by the belief that mental tests could be used for detection of "undesirables" (Kamin, 1974).

The interest of authorities in the mental quality of the immigrants at the turn of the century was grounded in a firm belief that racial and even certain national groups were biologically inferior. This interest was heightened by the change in countries of origin of immigrants, which had been a worrisome problem for some time to many Americans involved in the eugenics movement dedicated to the improvement of the species. Before 1890, most immigrants came from western Europe, but by the turn of the century this source declined, and a "new immigration" began. Eastern and southern Europe were the sources of this more recent migration, all with populations of "non-Nordics." The newly devised mental tests provided a ready means of sorting out the "undesirables." The results of comparisons of test scores achieved by the new immigrants with those of U.S. citizens of Nordic descent were interpreted as a decline in immigrant intelligence, which was believed to be a grave threat to Nordic survival. Psychologists like Goddard and Brigham, a participant in the testing program of army recruits during World War I, attributed this decline directly to the change in racial origin of the immigrants. Many writers warned that steps must be taken to preserve America's "precious heritage of germ plasma," and, in 1924, steps were taken in the form of restrictive immigration laws that limited the number of immigrants according to their national origin (Cravens, 1978:228).

These restrictive immigration quotas provide another example of the notion that the superficial differences, which set other peoples apart from us, are somehow indicative of inferior beings or lesser humans. Such an idea is of great antiquity, as discussed in chapter 1. Despite the thousands of pages written to present evidence to refute such misbeliefs, concepts of racial superiority and inferiority are, perhaps, as strong today as they ever were. Witness the increase of statements that attribute many aspects of human behavior to inheritance. The conviction that "biological determinism" or "genetic predestination" is a reality and offers a ready explanation for many of society's problems. How much simpler to attribute these problems to "instinctive behavior" than to deal with the complex underlying causes of famine, disease, crime, and aggression. It is but a short step to conclude then that some ethnic groups are inferior because of their genetic complement.

There is no need at this point to review those strongly held beliefs that associate a particular form of behavior with certain racial groups. We have all heard such arguments many times. Consider, though, that if there is a wide genetic diversity within each major geographic unit (race) of the several biological traits, which we have considered previously, then there should be an equally wide range of those genes related to people's behavior. Simply stated, there are "bright" and "dull" people in all groups of *Homo sapiens*. Just as the distribution of easily perceived traits was not understandable by clustering them into major geographical units, so it is difficult or downright impossible to talk of "racial" variation of behavior. The problem is further confused by the nature of whatever behavioral phenotypes we identify. Because of the complexity of human behavior, it is not possible to establish separate genetic and environmental components, though this was offered as a method by the leader of the more recent revival of sociobiology, E. O. Wilson, in his book, *On Human Nature*. The uniquely human capacity to learn and communicate is inherited, but our learning potential depends on the environment for the extent and kind of knowledge acquired. Each generation passes on its store of knowledge, or culture, to the next generation.

Description and comprehension of behavioral diversity is further complicated by the difficulties of measuring and identifying mental ability and behavior. The observer's own cultural background greatly influences his or her judgment or perception, particularly if he or she is studying a primitive society that lacks a written language, and whose people look and dress quite differently from those of the observer's group. It takes many months or years to gain insight and understanding under such conditions and, even then, most observers are only partly successful. This means that any comparisons between the "native" and "civilized" mind are speculative at best and will reveal little about the inheritance of behavioral diversity.

Another group, the American blacks, has been the object of many studies, and the results have frequently been used in attempts to show that there is something innately inferior about this group. Their lower average performance on certain standardized tests is often attributed to "inferior genes," and there is even a belief in certain circles that "the black has a gene for 'slow learning.'" Of course, the difficulty of attempting to unravel the inheritance of learning ability is compounded by the complexity of the learning processes, to say nothing of the difficulty of genetic identification. Even the detection of its presence in an individual is not possible, as is also the case with many other polygenic traits that have unknown gene combinations whose individual genes cannot be identified. About all that the many studies of the American black have shown is that, as a group, they have a lower average IQ, by a few points, than the white population. Much more has been made of this small difference than the data permit, especially when discussing genes, behavior, and race, because no control for gene admixture is ever made. That is, the individuals of the sample grouped as black in the United States are descendants of several generations of hybridization, and the European admixture varies widely.

The question of just how much of our behavior is determined biologically and how much by our experience is still open. Some claim that behavior is influenced minimally by one's inheritance in contrast to the vast changes that can be made by the environment. Others have revived the old "nature" argument used by the eugenists of last century, who claimed that a person's biological as well as behavioral makeup is determined by heredity. Few will deny, however, that there are inherited behavioral differences between individuals, and that there is probably a significant biological component underlying many of our behavior responses. An extreme form of biological influence can be easily illustrated by the mental retardation that often accompanies several kinds of chromosome abnormalities. The (XXY) and Down's (trisomy 21) syndromes possess mental impairment along with the physical defects that result from errors in chromosome number. Also, there are several possibilities for explaining certain clinically defined mental illnesses in terms of enzyme polymorphisms. The inherited diseases phenylketonuria, Tay-Sachs, and galactosemia, described in chapter 3, all have associated mental retardation. Beyond such pathological examples, no case can be made for inheritance of mental or behavioral traits. Environment looms large as a causal factor.

RACE AND BEHAVIOR

The categorizing of people according to their group membership (race or ethnic group) is a tempting exercise because it ultimately simplifies the scope of human diversity that exists. The behavioral variety that appears to exist, however, between races or ethnic groups is difficult, if not impossible, to attribute largely to a biological basis (the genes). Most, if not all, of the differences in life-style and world perception that have so puzzled observers have, at one time or another, been attributed to innate differences. That the "primitive" mind was not well developed in its reasoning powers was a frequent response of western European observers when confronted with strange, exotic societies. Many of the distinctions described, though were actually due to cultural influences, socioeconomic status, or the physical environment.

The cultural component is responsible for a great deal of variability, and often cultures are evaluated as being modern or primitive, simple or complex. The behavior of individuals participating in a culture other than our own differs from what we have come to know as "standard" behavior. The contrasts are striking, particularly when the technology is primitive or simple, such as in the cultures of New Guinea or Australia. Rather than make a value judgment, it would be more logical and would aid understanding if each culture were considered as an adaptation to the environment in which it is found. Whether it be the rigorous environment of the Australian "outback," which nurtured the culture of the Aboriginal, or that of the impoverished peoples in urban ghettos, the sociocultural framework of each enables the maintenance of human society.

When we consider language, we find a great deal of complexity even in so-called primitive cultures. Rather than measure mental capacity or evaluate a society on the basis of doubtful testing procedures, we might do better to look at the communication system and determine how each group copes with the demands of its environment. If one sees languages as a basis for human behavior and as a necessary foundation for society, then the investigator is forced to the conclusion that all groups are equal in their capacities and their intellectual ability to respond to the challenges of their environment.

Many times in the past, in the study of primitive societies, assumptions have been made by the investigator about the capacity of the people to deal with, in our terms, more complex or abstract subjects. Invariably, these assumptions proved to be wrong. The world view, individual experiences, society's behavioral roles, and the physical environment often proved to be the deciding factors. Misunderstanding of the society and its culture has often led to statements such as, "Inadequate neurological organization has been a major factor in the origin and persistence of a fundamental cultural inadequacy—lack of written communication" (Green, 1967:26). This comparative study of various Aboriginal populations attributed inadequate neurological development to the technique of child rearing, particularly when the infant is restrained, as on a cradle board, and not permitted to crawl. The investigator surveyed the ethnographic literature describing a limited number of Amazonian Indians and several African groups and reached his conclusions without considering the many variables and diversities within the cultures that affect child development.

In addition to ascribing race differences to inheritance, national character has often been described in this way: The antipathy, the hostile acts of aggression and at times even warfare, between ethnic groups, some even close biological relatives, is due to differences in genetic heritage. Darlington, a foremost human geneticist of his day, described the centuries of conflict between the English and Irish:

> This quarrel can be understood only in terms of the profound racial difference between the Gaelic-speaking natives and the English-speaking invaders, a difference which even today, after twenty generations of limited hybridization, is still not seriously blurred.
>
> The English were sober, industrious, mechanical, calculating and ruthless; characteristics invaluable in government. The native Irish by contrast were imaginative, unpredictable and even irresponsible. Their pre-Aryan and perhaps paleolithic speech had died out only in the ninth century and they had more left of their paleolithic instincts. (Darlington, 1969; 449–450)

Darlington appeared to explain away a long and very complex sociopolitical history on the basis of persistence of "paleolithic instincts," whatever they are.

The immigrants streaming through Ellis Island during the early part of this century provided a favorite target for snap judgments about inferior behavior; if their IQ did not give them away, their appearance would. As one psychologist noted:

> I have seen gatherings of the foreign-born in which narrow and sloping foreheads were the rule. . . . In every face there was something wrong—lips thick, mouth coarse . . . chin poorly formed . . . sugar-loaf heads . . . goose-bill noses . . . a set of skew molds discarded by the Creator. . . . Immigration officials . . . report vast troubles in extracting the truth from certain brunette nationalities. (Hirsch, 1926:74)

These physical and cultural differences were taken as evidence of inferiority and held up as a warning to the "superior" race (that is, Nordic) to beware of the dangers of being swamped by inferior beings. This set the theme of much literature on population studies over the first decades of the century, and after a seemingly quiescent period, is being revived again today. The modern-day feelings about inequality (now referred in more subtle terms such as *ethnic differences*) is dealt with from a perspective of "birth dearth" or the lower fertility rates of peoples of European origins in contrast to "others." This contributes to an imbalance of growth rates and, together with the high legal and illegal immigration, will result in a much lower proportion of west European stock. The implied or implicit concern is that such an ethnic imbalance will contribute to social turbulence (Wattenberg, 1985:114). Though this author is discussing the changes of ethnic balances in the U.S. population, the same may be said of the United Kingdom and several countries of western Europe. This illustrates, in a contemporary context, a concern with cultural, ethnic, and biological differences.

A frequent area of comment was the mental illness among American blacks, often cited in the nineteenth century. Mental illness was believed to be especially high among freed slaves who, according to the argument, were incapable of surviving and remaining healthy except under the care of the white slave owner. The results of the 1840 census added support to the generally held belief that racial mental inferiority was a fact. The census of 1840 recorded that blacks living in the North suffered a higher rate of mental illness (1 in 144) than in the South (1 in 1558), which supported the contention that blacks were healthier and happier under slavery than when given their freedom, as this high insanity rate among the free blacks of the North "proved." This census record was used by supporters of slavery despite the fact that Edward Jarvis showed that the census was completely inaccurate. Jarvis found, after a painstaking examination of the figures, that many towns were listed as having more insane blacks than the total number in residence. In some cases, a town had no blacks at all, but several were added, nevertheless, to the total for the insane recorded for the region. These errors, plus the fact that the "diagnoses" of mental illness were left up to the census taker, made the data highly suspect. Jarvis tried for many years to get Congress to amend these gross errors, but without success (Stanton, 1960:164). This image of a group in peril of destruction because of freedom persisted for a long time, as the following quote expresses:

> While laughter and music were common with the race before the war emancipation turned the race towards flashy clothes, intemperances, excesses of all kinds, and an accompanying "mental depression and anxiety." The Atlanta National conference of Charities and Corrections felt that the race was "in danger of being destroyed by insanity." (quoted in Haller, 1970:164)

Where do these beliefs come from and why are they frequently repeated by otherwise distinguished scientists? Well, these beliefs come from personal bias, to begin with, from the uncritical acceptance of broad generalizations reinforced by erroneous data, and through the use of new methods of measuring human abilities (mental tests, for example). Even examples from novels and travel books can be cited as sources of influence on racial opinions, as is well illustrated by Francis Galton's descriptions of his travel experiences (1869:395):

> The number among the negroes of those whom we should call half-witted

men is very large. Every book alluding to negro servants in America is full of instances. I was myself much impressed by this fact during my travels in Africa. The mistakes the negroes made in their own matters were so childish, stupid, and simpleton-like, as frequently to make me ashamed of my own species. I do not think it any exaggeration to say, that their C is as low as our E, which would be a difference of two grades, as before. I have no information as to actual idiocy among the negroes—I mean, of course, of that class of idiocy which is not due to disease.

Despite overwhelming evidence to the contrary, such beliefs have persisted, and a century later the following quotation illustrates this persistence:

> Nature has color-coded groups of individuals so that statistically reliable predictions and their adaptability to intellectually rewarding and effective lives can easily be made and profitably be used by the pragmatic man in the street. (Shockley, 1972:307)

What about this color coding? Are there really simple ways by which a "pragmatic man in the street" can evaluate the quality of another human being? Is it as easy as identifying a criminal type by the size of the nose or ears, as was proposed by Lombroso a century ago? Is "innate ability" as plain as the nose on your face or the shape of your head, or are many writers today again confusing and mixing traits that bear no relationship?

POPULATION, RACE, AND BEHAVIOR

The use of social stereotypes of ethnic groups may be a popular exercise, but in any attempt to study the genetic system, careful attention must be given to each population's composition. The frequent use of a social classification of a group based on a single known attribute, such as skin color, generally ignores all others, as in the case of American blacks. Their ancestry is quite mixed, comprising from 10 to 90 percent Caucasoid genes, with the average estimated as between 20 to 30 percent. Some interbreeding with Native Americans adds to American black heterogeneity; in addition, their African ancestry is anything but homogeneous. African populations are as diverse as any in the world, and the American blacks' African ancestry consists of contributions from a variety of these populations. Slaves imported into Charleston, South Carolina, between 1733 and 1807 came from a region extending from Senegambia to Angola, an area of 1000 by 600 miles that encompasses a variety of environments and cultures. Because of their diverse African ancestry and through centuries of admixture with persons of European descent, American blacks are distinct from all modern African populations.

If for no other reason, criticism of studies of racial differences in intelligence can be made on these grounds: The studies are often carried out on groups whose actual genetic composition is not known. Nor is the group distinguished or identified in any way as a breeding population, and its recent ancestry and history are ignored. The only concern with group identification is with the social definition of race—again pointing out the error and the handicap of the confusion of culture and biological variables. It is one thing to discuss genetic potential, gene frequency, or inherited ability within a breeding population whose members share a large number of genes in common; it is another matter to discuss these variables in reference to race (socially or biologically defined).

The claim has often been made that an admixture of Caucasoid genes actually causes an increased IQ in American blacks, as if Caucasoids were a homogeneous group all possessing the same gene combinations, regardless of whether northern or southern, eastern or western Europe in origin. Such statements on admixture and IQ are unfounded; data do not exist to support such a contention that intelligence varies with degree of ancestry. In fact, there is no connection between test performance of an individual and the number of that person's European ancestors as recently shown. Estimates of the degree of European ancestry of 350 African American residents of Philadelphia were made by careful analysis of blood groups and serum proteins, which is possible because, as we discussed in chapters 3 and 6, European and African populations differ in average frequencies of certain blood phenotypes. This method was used instead of the usual method of asking the subjects to identify their degree of European ancestry on the basis of known white ancestors. With their ancestry established through biochemical genetics methods, this group was given a variety of mental tests. Scarr and her associates reviewed the results and demonstrated that those persons with a high degree of African ancestry did no better and no worse than those individuals who had several European ancestors (Scarr, 1981; Scarr and Weinberg, 1978).

Correlations can be made between combinations of genes and behavior only when the ancestry and genetic admixture of each individual tested are known, and only when breeding-population boundaries are established can interpopulation comparisons be made. These are difficult criteria to fulfill, of course, but any study that purports to examine genotypes and the behavioral phenotype must carefully determine population composition. Anything less will produce misleading data. This is particularly true because confusion still surrounds the definition of race and especially the identification of an individual's racial heritage. Investigators who attempt to compare populations of differing racial composition often ignore this problem, as the following quotation illustrates:

> Although most of the studies of racial differences in intelligence are based on social definitions of race, it should be noted that there is usually a high

correlation between the social and the biological definitions, and it is most unlikely that results of the research would be very different if the investigators had used biological rather than social criteria of race in selecting groups for comparison. (Jensen, 1971:16–17)

Jensen, a leading proponent of the racial inequality argument, mixes a social classification with a genetic one. If he wishes to argue that American blacks score lower on IQ tests than American whites because of an inherited difference, then careful account must be taken of the genetic composition of the group. How else can genetic determination be identified unless population admixture is known? What about the tests themselves? What do they, in fact, measure?

RACIAL DIFFERENCES AND IQ: A MEASURE OF MENTAL ABILITY

The argument rages on endlessly over what standardized tests for mental ability actually measure. With all of the millions of tests administered during this century, no agreement has been reached as to what is actually tested. "Intelligence is what IQ tests measure," states one worker. "IQ tests measure learning experience," declares another. Whatever the test scores reveal about the individual, they are widely used in our society and often place individuals within a niche in our educational system. Such placement has far-reaching effects on a person's future development and achievement. The test scores of the individual vary four to five points on retesting over short intervals, but over intervals of several years, variations of twenty to thirty points are known, supporting the belief that tests are a measure of learning experience (Schiff and Lewontin, 1986:194).

Our testing procedures trace their origins to Alfred Binet, a French psychologist who developed the first usable intelligence test in 1905 (the Binet-Simon test). The purpose of the original test was to identify students with low academic aptitudes so they might be assisted by special programs. Binet was concerned with the development of therapeutic courses to aid students who had performed poorly on the tests. He did not attempt to describe the source of the problem nor did he determine whether their poor performance was due to environmental or congenital factors. In fact, he specifically rejected those who described intelligence as a fixed quantity. Nevertheless, subsequent adaptations of Binet's test have often concluded that the results revealed the quality of inherited intelligence.

Rather than attempt to define what intelligence was, Binet took the direct approach of establishing what was "normal mental development." Normal was simply the performance of a majority of children, of any age, on a series of tests. These tests were based on a collection of questions typically used in the classroom. The majority was set at between 65 to 75 percent and the lowest 25 percent were defined as backward. Because the questions selected were those taken from material commonly taught, it is not surprising that the test performance was highly predictive of academic achievement.

The Binet method was imported to this country and first used by Goddard to test immigrants at Ellis Island, as mentioned earlier. Also, the Binet-Simon test was tried on American school children with poor results until Lewis Terman of Stanford adapted the test to American standards. Terman used groups of California school children and adjusted the scores of each age group so the average was one hundred; that is, a person performing "normally" at his or her age level would be expected to score around one hundred because this was the score for the majority. The modified form was introduced in 1916 as the Stanford-Binet test, which purported to establish the subjects' IQ.

The IQ test was quickly accepted and applied by American psychologists, but the extent of these applications went far beyond the original purpose of identifying academic ability. Binet had carefully avoided consideration of test results in terms of inheritance of mental ability. In fact, he accused those who treated intelligence as a fixed quantity of having a brutal pessimism (Chase, 1977:236). Nevertheless, the pioneers of the mental testing in America—Terman, Goddard, and Yerkes—readily accepted test results as evidence of a person's inherited mental ability and discussions of feebleminded, bright, and dull were repeated frequently in the current psychological publications. This misuse of the IQ test to label individuals as mental defectives violates Binet's original intent and purpose, which was simply to identify those children, low in academic achievement, who were in need of special help.

A short time after its introduction, the modified Binet test was adapted for the testing of army recruits during World War I. Eventually nearly two million males were tested by the Alpha test (for literates) and the Beta test (for nonliterates). The results of this mass testing have been described in numerous reports and have generated considerable controversy, which still continues more than two generations later. Briefly, several of these reports concluded that the average mental age of American adult males was fourteen, a conclusion that led to statements about "the impossibility of democracy working with citizens of such low intellect." Also, the psychologists involved accepted the tests as a measure of "native" intelligence and concluded that efforts to improve the lot of many social groups would be fruitless.

Terman, accepting the test results as evidence of a high frequency of adults of such a low mental age, described the threat to the "welfare of the State." He warned that "the propagation of mental degenerates" must be curtailed. Such strong feelings expressed in 1917 by a respected scientist immediately gained wide public acceptance (Block and Dworkin, 1976:348–49). The reader today, before accepting this kind of rejection of charitable attempts of assistance for the more unfortunate, should ask who were the feebleminded to whom Terman was referring? They were, of course, those who scored lowest on the IQ tests and on the army tests that were so readily employed by psychologists as a diagnostic tool of mental capacity. Many of the groups who scored lowest were newly arrived immigrants from eastern and southern European countries, the grandparents and great-grandparents of so many Americans living today.

The ready acceptance of test scores by professionals and the general public alike revealed hidden dangers to any society that based government policy on these results. Some writers, realizing the problems imposed by overreliance on test scores, reacted with sharp comments laying bare some of the fallacies underlying the search for a single measure of innate ability. Foremost among the opponents was the editorialist Walter Lippman who observed: "The whole drift of the propaganda based on intelligence testing is to treat people with low intelligence quotients as congenitally and hopelessly inferior. The prominent testers believe that they are measuring the capacity of a human being for all time and that this capacity is fatally fixed by the child's heredity." He continued further in an exchange of letters with Terman and admitted that he was emotional in his response, "I hate the impudence of a claim that in fifty minutes you can judge and classify a human being's predestined fitness in life. I hate the abuse of a scientific method which it involved. I hate the sense of superiority which it creates and the sense of inferiority which it imposes".[1]

IQ Tests and American Blacks

Throughout World War II and the postwar decade, the mental testing issue was relatively ignored and the environmentalists seemed to dominate the heredity-environment problem that had been a battleground for a century. Then the issue was revived in the early 1960s. What was said about the IQ for immigrants at the turn of the century was repeated in reference to American blacks, but with considerably more emotion. "Their intelligence is significantly lower, they lack the ability to handle abstract reasoning (Jensen, 1969:81), and test performance of a group improves in proportion to the admixture of Caucasoid genes" are examples

[1] The original essay by Walter Lippman and the following exchange of letters with Lewis Terman were published in the *New Republic* in 1922 and outline a debate about the early applications of mental testing results. Block and Dworkin (1976) reprint these letters in a volume of essays, *The IQ Controversy*. Reading through the essays provides a background on the time and players in the psychological testing game early in this century.

of some frequent statements (Shockley, 1972:298). Such repetition of the early misapplication of IQ test scores forty years later to another socially disadvantaged group is disheartening, especially in light of the mass of work that has gone into development of intelligence-testing programs during recent decades. We still find claims that, "intelligence is inherited and relatively unchangéd by the environment (education) and IQ tests are a measure of this innate ability." These claims must still be examined and refuted (Weinberg, 1989:98). Though there are many more testing procedures today, there is still no basis for the argument that IQ is a measure of intelligence. It is, rather, a means of classifying people by a measure of their learning experiences, as we discuss later.

Arthur Jensen was one of those who introduced this modern version of the inappropriate use of heritability, race, and IQ. Before the American Educational Research Association meeting in 1967, Jensen launched an attack on compensatory education, which made him a famous but controversial figure. First, like many psychologists from the past, he accepted that IQ was inherited and then suggested that, "since intelligence is largely determined genetically, we need to know the proportion of difference between blacks and whites that is genetically determined" (Hirsch, 1967:437). He treated intelligence as a trait that was possessed in unequal proportions by different "pure races." Jensen continued his criticism of the new environmentalists in a series of books and papers. In 1969 he published a paper, "How Much Can We Boost IQ and Scholastic Achievement?," which examined compensatory-education programs for minority children (the Head Start program, for example). In his paper Jensen argued that IQ tests measure general ability, and individual differences in IQ were due to a high degree of genetic determination, which was the reason compensatory programs proved ineffective iñ overcoming the inherited differences between racial groups. Jensen's emphasis on genetic determination is surprising because, less than a decade earlier, he had presented convincing data that showed the opposite to be true. He had cited socioeconomic factors as the cause of differences in learning achievements of poor and nonpoor groups (Chase, 1977:46).

Jensen compiled vast amounts of data from studies of American blacks in support of his argument. A variety of tests, including the Stanford-Binet, all placed black achievement lower than white. Comparison of the two groups showed the average IQ for blacks about fifteen points below the average for whites. This difference between groups is an indisputable fact, but note that the range of variation is broad. Some studies report as little as ten points of difference or as much as twenty (Figure 7-1). Also, the distribution of the IQs of blacks overlaps that of whites, and the means will vary depending on the study sample. Recall that these differences between the two groups are similar to many of the differences between

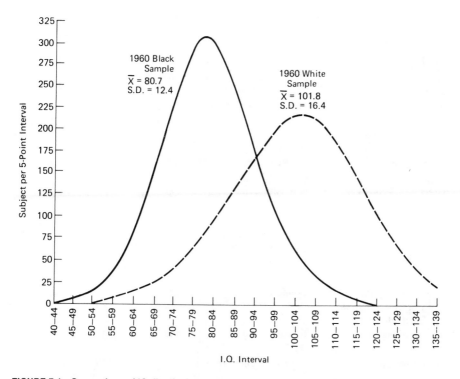

FIGURE 7-1 **Comparison of IQ distributions of American Black and White Elementary School Children.** The distribution of American black I.Q. is taken from a sample of 1800 children enrolled in elementary schools in five southern states. The mean of 80.7 contrasts with the 101.8 mean of a normative white sample and is the greatest difference reported. (From Kennedy, W. A., V. Van de Riet, and J. C. White, 1963. Copyright © 1963 The Society for Research in Child Development, Inc. Reprinted by permission of the publisher.)

native-born Americans and eastern European immigrants that were reported in the 1920s.

Comparisons of ethnic groups across international boundaries give similar results to those obtained in the United States. Most groups not native to or descendant from northwestern Europe scored between ten and twenty points lower. The exceptions were the subjects in Italy, and European descendants in New Zealand and Australia who performed at the mean. The rest of the sample populations were assigned IQs of about one standard deviation below the mean (100) on the basis of performance on a variety of mental tests that included the Stanford-Binet, Raven, and Cotell-Culture Fair tests (Table 7-1). These results are summarized by Lynn (1978) who attempted to interpret ethnic group performance on the basis of race, the implication being that the differences were of genetic origin. He had trouble, however, explaining the high IQ of Italian subjects

TABLE 7-1   Table of Comparisons of IQ in Several Populations

POPULATION	TEST	IQ SCORE
Northern Europe		
Scotland	Stanford-Binet and Terman-Merrill	100
Belgium	Cattell's Culture-Fair	104
France	Raven's Progressive Matrices	104
Southern Europe		
Italy	Raven's Progressive Matrices	100
Spain (army)	Raven's Progressive Matrices	87
Yugoslavia	Raven's Progressive Matrices	89
Greece	Wechsler Scale	89
Mideast		
Iraq	Goodenough DAM	80
Iran	Goodenough DAM	80
India		
Univ. of Calcutta	Stanford-Binet	95
Univ. of Calcutta (post- grad. students)	Raven's Progressive Matrices	75
Variety of Indian states	Raven's Progressive Matrices	81–94
Afro-Americans	Shuey (81 different ones)	85
Africa		
Uganda	Raven's Progressive Matrices	88
Uganda	Terman Vocabulary and Kohs Blocks	80
Jamaica	British Intelligence	75
Jamaica	Terman Vocabulary and Kohs Blocks	low 80s
Tanzania	Raven's Progressive Matrices	88
Ghana, Jahoda	Raven's Progressive Matrices	75
South Africa	British National Foundation for Edu- cations Research	87
South Africa—Zulu	Raven's Progressive Matrices	75
American Chinese	Stanford-Binet	97
Asians		
Japan	Wechsler Scale	106.6
Bandung, Java	Goodenough Draw-a-Man	96
Native Americans		
Eskimo	Raven's Progressive Matrices	70–80
Eskimo	Vernon—several	85
Amerinds (Canada)	Coleman—several	91–96
	Vernon—several	79

TABLE 7-1   Table of Comparisons of IQ in Several Populations *(Continued)*

POPULATION	TEST	IQ SCORE
Australia		
Europeans	American Otis	95
Aboriginals (Victoria)	Peabody Picture Vocabulary and Illinois Psycholinguistic Ability	80
Aboriginals (Queensland)	Queensland	78 in isolation 85 in close contact
Pacific		
Europeans (N. Zealand)	Otis	98.5
Maori (N. Zealand)	Otis	84
Maori (N. Zealand)	Queensland	94
Micronesia	Cattell's Cuture-Fair	88
Polynesia	Pacific Infants Performance Scale	88
Southern Africa		
!Kung (Kalahari)	Maze	55

Source: Data selected and adapted from Lynn, 1978.

(x = 100) while Spain, Greece, and Yugoslavia had the lowest for Europeans (x = 87). The European IQ scores had a north-south gradient except for the Italian. He offered that the gradient was due to the racial composition of the population:

> If these results from Caucasoid, Iranian, and Indo-Dravidian nations are considered in the light of the racial composition of the populations, it is apparent that where the people are predominantly of northern European stock, as in Britain, northwestern Europe, the United States, Australia, and New Zealand, their mean IQs are approximately 100. (Lynn, 1978:278)

This should not be hard to explain considering the tests were designed by and for northwestern Europeans. The differences all fall within that range reported for minorities in the United States, and scores from different tests vary as in the case of the two New Zealand Maori samples; a mean of 84 on the Otis and 94 on the Queensland tests. Also it should be noted in the table that Australian Aboriginal children varied in the test performance depending on closeness of their contact with European settlements. The children far removed and with little contact with Europeans scored the lowest.

WHAT INFLUENCES IQ

How can this consistently lower performance be explained? Some explain away the differences in terms of genetic variation as outlined by Lynn earlier. Many educators and psychologists, Jensen included, point out the strong role environment plays in academic achievement and IQ scores, however. Jensen (1969:60) notes that moving children from a deprived environment to an improved one can boost IQ twenty to thirty points. In addition, the socioeconomic status of the parents greatly affects the IQ performance of the children; also, there is a high correlation between performance and the quality of education, as demonstrated by a comparison of the army Alpha tests with the state expenditure on elementary education. Adults who had resided as children in states with the lower school expenditures scored lowest on the tests (Table 7-2).

TABLE 7-2   Median and Mean Negro and White Army Alpha Intelligence-Test Scores and School Expenditures Per Child Aged 5 to 18 Years By State

State (1)	WHITE N (2)	Median (3)	Mean (4)	NEGRO N (5)	Median (6)	Mean (7)	School expenditures (8)
Alabama	779	41.3	49.4	271	19.9	27.0	1.51
Arkansas	710	35.6	43.3	193	16.1	22.6	3.09
Florida	55	53.8	59.8	499	9.2	15.3	4.68
Georgia	762	39.3	48.3	416	10.0	17.2	2.68
Illinois	2,145	61.6	66.7	804	42.2	47.9	13.46
Indiana	1,171	56.0	62.2	269	41.5	47.6	11.75
Kansas	861	62.7	67.0	87	34.7	40.6	10.58
Kentucky	837	41.5	48.6	191	23.9	32.4	4.57
Louisiana	702	41.1	49.0	538	13.4	20.8	2.52
Maryland	616	55.3	60.2	148	22.7	30.7	8.44
Mississippi	759	37.6	43.7	773	10.2	16.8	2.63
Missouri	1,329	56.5	61.9	196	28.3	34.2	8.54
New Jersey	937	45.3	52.9	748	33.0	38.9	14.04
New York	3,300	58.4	63.7	1,188	38.6	45.3	19.22
North Carolina	702	38.2	45.9	211	16.3	22.1	1.51
Ohio	2,318	67.2	73.0	163	45.4	53.4	12.13
Oklahoma	865	43.0	50.6	98	31.4	35.9	5.50
Pennsylvania	3,280	62.0	67.1	790	34.8	40.5	12.85
South Carolina	581	45.1	51.1	334	14.2	19.2	1.93
Tennessee	710	44.0	52.0	504	29.7	35.9	2.71
Texas	1,426	43.5	50.2	854	12.2	18.2	4.38
Virginia	506	56.3	60.5	57	45.6	52.0	3.39
West Virginia	423	54.9	60.8	67	26.8	28.5	6.79
Subtotal (23 states)	25,774	49.53	56.00	9,399	26.09	32.30	6.91
District of Columbia	77	78.8	85.6	30	31.2	34.3	17.78
Total	25,851	50.75	57.23	9,429	26.43	32.39	7.36

Sources: From Spuhler andd Lindzey, 1967 (copyright © 1967 by McGraw-Hill Book Co.; reprinted by permission of the publisher); data from Yerkes, 1921; and *Statistical Abstract of the United States*, 1902.

Contrary to Jensen's claim that compensatory education has failed to boost IQ, there are several studies that show the opposite. One of the most successful educational enrichment programs boosted IQs of a group of black preschoolers by thirty-three points. This project, carried out in Milwaukee by Rick Heber, an expert on mental retardation, provided a major enrichment in the lives of children born to black mothers living in the most impoverished area of the city. The program included extensive training of the mothers in simple skills and offered personal one-on-one teaching for the children from a few weeks old until six years of age. The results were astounding. This group of volunteers, chosen at random, achieved skills far beyond those achieved by the control group who were not given the special training (Loehlin, Lindzey, and Spuhler, 1975:159–160).

There have been many demonstrations of the effects that environment has on test performance. The famous Coleman report, *Equality of Educational Opportunity*, described the results of an extensive study carried out on 650,000 school children in four thousand public schools. The part of the report that has been frequently seized on as "proof" of racial inequality is the achievement test scores showing that white students scored significantly higher than the nonwhites. The application of these results as evidence to support a particular brand of racist dogma ignores the bulk of the report, which dealt with the wide range of sociological factors related to the educational process and student performance. For example, the higher the socioeconomic level of the entire student body of a school, the higher the test scores of all ethnic groups (see Chase, 1977:498).

In the 1970s, a group of educational psychologists, headed by Mayeske, carefully reexamined the data published in the Coleman report. Their thorough analysis of each section isolated five significant sets of variables influencing test scores. Of these five, racial-group membership was the fourth lowest in its influence on test performance. When the scores are statistically weighted for socioenvironmental differences, the average scores of the several ethnic groups show very little difference. Figure 7-2 plots the percentage of difference between these groups when each of the environmental factors is considered. When adjusted for social background the differences dropped to insignificant levels.

Health factors can also exert a major influence on test performance. Early deafness can lower IQ by 20 points. Premature and underweight babies have significantly lower scores at several developmental stages; at ages three to five years, for example, their IQ mean was 94.4. Multiple births are also a significant factor: Twins score 5 points lower on the average than single births, and triplets were 9 points less (see Loehlin et al., 1975:196–229). Nutrition also affects test performance; in many studies increases of up to 10 points are reported for children placed on enriched diets provided through school programs. The maternal environment, as

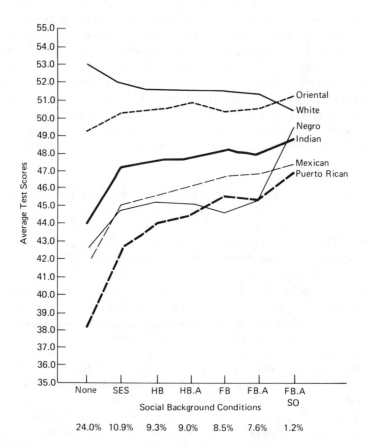

FIGURE 7-2   Racial-Ethnic Group Achievement Means Adjusted for Social Background Conditions. Percent of total difference among students in their achievement that is associated with their racial-ethnic group membership

SES = Socioeconomic status

HB = Home background; this set of variables includes both socioeconomic status and family structure

HB.A = Family attitudes about their ability to influence the course of their lives and the extent to which education benefits them

FB = Family background; educational, social, etc.

FB.A = Family background and area (of residence; regional; urban; rural; etc.)

$\frac{FB.A}{SO}$ = Quality and achievement-motivational mix of school attended

"... the differences among the various racial-ethnic groups in their achievement levels approach zero as more and more considerations related to differences in their respective social conditions are taken into account" (Mayeske, 1971, p. 112).

(From Mayeske, 1971, U.S. Department of Health, Education and Welfare.)

measured by prenatal nutrition, also shows a high correlation with the IQ of the offspring later.

WHAT DOES IQ MEASURE?

Since the introduction of intelligence testing, modifications have been made to allow testing groups of diverse backgrounds, languages, and experiences. The search has been for a "culture-free" test—that is, a series of questions that will reveal natural ability uninfluenced by a person's past experiences. Dozen of tests have been designed since the early days of the Stanford-Binet, but, to date, no culture-free test has been devised. This is not unexpected because ability to distinguish between objects, identify words, and so forth at any age is determined by a complex of interactions between inherited qualities, development, and experiences. It should be obvious that children, regardless of their ethnic backgrounds, raised in isolated rural communities will have experiences distinct from middle-class suburban children. This was reflected by the lower scores of certain social groups tested in the 1900s. Children living in a densely populated city ghetto have a vocabulary and language style unique to their experiences, in contrast to children raised in rural areas. Their sociocultural differences, some argue, affect IQ test performance just as it did in the case of the eastern European immigrants three generations ago.

Simply put, children from different social environments perform at different levels if given the same test. A case in point is the frequently used Stanford-Binet test, which was standardized on a sampling of U.S. middle-class white children and adolescents. Most Hispanic American, black, and Indian children perform below average on such a test, as should be expected given their different backgrounds. To overcome the difficulty imposed on the black children by the Stanford-Binet, Williams, a black psychologist, designed the Black Intelligence Test of Cultural Homogeneity, the BITCH test (Loehlin et al., 1975:69). Blacks, on the average, score higher on this multiple-choice vocabulary test based on words and phrases distinctive to the black culture.

Considering these factors that influence variability in test performance, the tragedy is that test results are too often accepted as a measure of innate potential. The similarity between the lower scores of the immigrants fifty years ago and the lower scores of the blacks today should warn against such an acceptance. The history of the eastern European immigrants has shown that they and their offspring increased their IQ with residence in the United States, and there is every expectation that as more opportunities open to them and the sociocultural differential decreases, the black IQ averages will increase as well. The many ethnic groups are not, as some writers continue to assert, handicapped by their genes. The question remains, though, of the degree to which heredity influences intelligence, however measured.

INHERITANCE OF IQ

> While it certainly is true that I started out to study the genetics of a behavior, in the course of much thinking and experimenting over more than a decade I have come to realize that it is impossible to study the genetics of a behavior. We can study the behavior of *an* organism, the genetics of *a* population, and individual differences in the expression of some behavior by members of *that* population. (Hirsch, 1969:43)

Among the many polygenic traits of our species, behavioral responses or intellectual capacity are the most difficult with which to deal. Not only is little known about the genetics influencing behavior, but extreme difficulty is encountered when attempts are made to identify or label the phenotypes. Witness the disagreement concerning what IQ is and the wide variation in diagnosis of mental illness or behavioral pathologies in our society. Given these factors, it is much more difficult to establish genetic relationships for behavior than for polygenic phenotypes such as skin color, face form, or stature. Because we are not concerned here with phenotypic labeling of "types" or behavior, we look only at the methods employed to determine the degree of genetic influence on the performance of standard IQ tests.

Heritability of IQ

Many of the assumptions of inherited inequality, as measured by intelligence tests, are based on studies of close relatives and on twins. The correlations of test scores of these relatives and especially twins raised together and apart range from less than 0.2 to a high of 0.87 for identical twins. The correlation coefficient of 0.8 has been derived from these studies and has found a prominent place in the literature discussing inherited inequality. This high correlation is interpreted as "evidence" that the genetic component influences intelligence more than environment (80 versus 20 percent) because correlation between subject groups is considered equivalent to heritability. The reliability of this evidence is questionable from many perspectives, but it is weak evidence of genetic influence mainly because the concept of heritability is often misunderstood and misused. We do not know how large is the component of heredity in mental ability, though many still continue to argue about this very issue of what is the precise proportion of the genetic determination of behavior.

Heritability, in the broadest sense, is that proportion of variation of a trait in a population that is due to a variation of genotypes. Earlier, in chapter 3, we described the phenotype as the result of the interaction between genotype and environment, and it is useful to point out again that genes only determine the potential for response to environments. They do not determine the phenotype directly but influence its expression. When a polygenic trait such as stature, for example, is measured in a population, there will be a mean and a range of sizes. The total variation or *variance* about the mean is due to the variance in genotypes among the individuals of the population and the variance of their environments during growth and development. In other words, the total population variation is due to both variation of genotypes and environment. This relationship can be expressed mathematically: variance in phenotype (V_p) = variance in genotypes (V_g) + variance in environment (V_e). Heritability (H^2), then, is that proportion of variance owing to genotypic variance and can be written as follows:

$$H^2 = \frac{V_g}{V_g + V_e}$$

Phenotypes that have a high degree of variance owing to high genetic variance will therefore have a high H^2. Likewise, phenotypes with low genotype variance will have low heritability. Those populations with less genotypic difference between the individuals will, thus, have a lower heritability. If the hypothetical case was considered in which all individuals were the offspring of a single fertilized egg, their genotypes would be identical copies of the original. Because there would be no genetic variance in our hypothetical population, the V_g would be zero and H^2 would then be zero.

Heritability then is not a measure of the genetic influence on a phenotype; it is merely a measure of the total effect of the genotype variance on phenotypic variability. As described by Gregg and Sanday (1971:59): "Heritability only tells what proportion of the variance is due to genetic differences, not the extent to which a trait is determined by genetic factors." Additionally, heritability is not a constant value that tells us the degree of genetic influence on the phenotype of any single individual. As stated by Jensen (1971:13–14):

> There is no single true value of the heritability of a trait. Heritability is not a constant, but a population statistic, and it can vary according to the test used and the particular population tested.

If the example is used of a group of individuals placed on a diet that contains a carefully controlled constant amount of the amino acid, phenylalanine (the $V_e = 0$), then any variance of phenylalanine blood levels (the V_p in the population) will be due to V_g or a variance in the genetic system. If later the diet is varied between members of the same group, then phenotypic variance will increase. This does not mean that the genetic contribution or the effect of the genes is any less, merely that the relative contributions of V_g and V_e will change. In neither case is the degree of genetic contribution or gene effect known.

H^2 of a phenotypic variance within a population tells us nothing about the genetic component in the individual; what it does describe is the degree of variance in a population that is due to the genes under a certain set of environmental circumstances. This simple formula actually describes a method employed by animal and plant breeders long before genetic inheritance was known or understood. Farmers could selectively breed their stock by the simple logic that any variation in animals living under a stable environment (the same food, pasturage, and so on) was due to some factors of inheritance ("blood lines") that could be passed on to the next generation. In this way, undesirable traits could be selected out and useful traits bred for. The egg producers in a flock of chickens, cows who produced the most milk, or cattle that showed the greatest weight gain could be used as breeders. The genetics were not known (and in many cases still are a mystery), but desirable effects of selective breeding could easily be seen, evaluated, and used to advantage.

Finally, heritability describes a property of populations, not of individuals, and does not distinguish the traits that they possess. H^2 is a limited piece of information that measures the degree of variance owing to genetic variance within a given population at a particular time under specific environmental conditions. It is a population statistic just as is mortality or fertility rates, and H^2 estimates derived from the variance of one population cannot be applied to another. Given the difficulty in studying human populations, however, how is this statistic derived?

Twin Studies

In an attempt to overcome the difficulties of determining genetic-environment influences in *Homo sapiens*, hundreds of studies of monozygous, or identical twins, offer a source of data for estimates of heritability. The importance of these studies cannot be overstated. These individuals, conceived from a single fertilized ova, have identical genomes. It follows then, any phenotypic differences are the result of environmental influences. Measurements of traits in large samples of both monozygotic (MZ) and dizygotic twins (DZ) have been made, and comparisons of the correlations have given considerable information about the heritability. The data most revealing of the genetic effects comes from studies of MZ twins reared in separate households that are, presumably, different environments. Unfortunately, not many such subjects have been located and carefully studied; there have been only four such studies to date with the recent addition of the Minnesota Twin Project (Bouchard et al., 1986). Before 1974 there was another, and by far the largest study, with fifty-three twin pairs described by an English psychologist, Cyril Burt. The results of a battery of mental and achievement tests in this investigation set the standard for twin studies and provided the basis for a correlation of IQ of twin pairs of 0.771, which was cited in many papers and texts that discussed inheritance of mental ability.

Questions about Burt's results began to be raised in the early 1970s. His results were just too consistent from the data described in one study to the next as additional separated twins were identified and enrolled in the project. As the number of twin pairs increased, the correlation coefficient remained the same to the third decimal place. The possibility of data manipulation and even scientific fraud, by the outright invention of subjects, was raised. Kamin went through the laborious work of checking the data step by step and noted the statistical impossibility of the correlations remaining the same from 1951 when twenty-one pairs were described and 1958 when the number was increased to thirty and finally to fifty-three pairs in 1964 (Kamin, 1974). Following Kamin's work, others began to examine Burt's many publications and uncovered numerous flaws, fictitious coauthors, nonexistent master's theses, and manufactured data. At this point the conclusion was inescapable; for several decades, a major fraud had been perpetrated on the scientific community (Hawkes, 1979; Hearnshaw, 1979).

The effect on educational psychology in general and on twin studies in particular would have been minimal if it had not been for the status of Burt among educational psychologists. His conclusions were quoted in many standard texts and even used as a guide to educational policies implicitly influencing the treatment of minority students. The exposure of the fraudulent data was a major blow to many who maintained that IQ had a high heritability, and hence was largely influenced by genetics. This group soon recovered, and argued that the other twin studies supported their position that environment only minimally affected mental ability as measured by the IQ tests. These arguments, however, neglected the lack of control for similarities or differences in the environments of twins raised apart. Though the Minnesota study has helped bolster a hereditarian position, the range of heritability quotients for traits other than IQ has been ignored (Table 7-3).

Despite the difficulties and doubts encountered in the separated twin studies, correlations or similarities of phenotypes of twins offer a means of estimating heritability. Figure 7-3 shows that MZ twins raised together are most similar (correlation of 0.73 to 0.95), which compares to correlations of siblings of around 0.42. Presumably, the similarities are due to genotypes shared by related individuals. In the case of the 0.20 to 0.30

TABLE 7-3   Correlations of Identical Twins Reared Together and Apart

	MINNESOTA MZA		MZT	
	R	PAIRS (NO.)	R	PAIRS (NO.)
Anthropometric variables				
Fingerprint ridge count	0.97	54	0.96	274
Height	0.86	56	0.93	274
Weight	0.73	56	0.83	274
Mental ability—general factor				
WAIS IQ—full scale	0.69	48	0.88	40
WAIS IQ—verbal	0.64	48	0.88	40
WAIS IQ—performance	0.71	48	0.79	40
Raven, Mill-Hill composite	0.78	42	0.76	37
First principal component of special mental abilities	0.78	43	NA	NA
Personality variables				
Mean of 11 Multidimensional Personality Questionnaire scales	0.50	44	0.49	217
Mean of 18 California Psychological Inventory scales	0.48	38	0.49	99

MZA = monozygotic twins raised apart; and MZT = monozygotic twins raised together.
Source: Data selected from Bouchard, T.J., Jr., 1990

correlation between foster parent and child, similarities of IQ are due to a sharing of the home environment.

The higher correlations between the identical-twin groups is a reflection of their genetic likeness. Because of their genetic identity, any differences between MZ twins are assumed to be due to environmental variables. Therefore, the proportion of gene influence on the phenotypes is equal to the correlations between twins, or $H^2 = r_{obs}$ derived from the following formula:

$$r \text{ observed } = r \text{ genetic } \times \frac{V_g}{V_g + V_e}$$

since r genetic $= 1$, then

$$r \text{ observed } = \frac{V_g}{V_g + V_e} \text{ or } H^2$$

Again, the reader is reminded that this refers to a variance observed in a "population" of twin pairs (the number of twin pairs tested) and *does not*

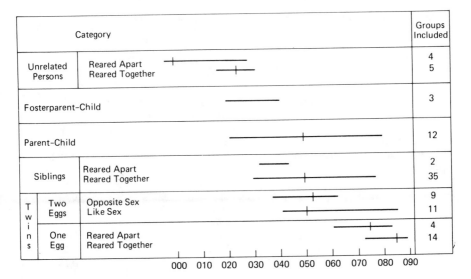
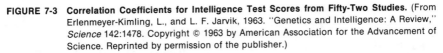

FIGURE 7-3   Correlation Coefficients for Intelligence Test Scores from Fifty-Two Studies. (From Erlenmeyer-Kimling, L., and L. F. Jarvik, 1963. "Genetics and Intelligence: A Review," *Science* 142:1478. Copyright © 1963 by American Association for the Advancement of Science. Reprinted by permission of the publisher.)

express degree of genetic influence in an individual. In other words, individuals may, and often do, perform quite differently from their twin, while others earn scores close to their twins (Table 7-4). The twins are treated as separate populations, with mean and variance; the two groups are then compared for covariance (correlation).

The H^2 covers a considerable range, and this single measure depends a great deal on the selection of twins and their environments, both for twins raised apart and for those raised together. The correlations that are used are based on a number of twin studies during the last fifty years, and each study has several inherent problems. First, in the case of twins (MZ) reared apart, the age at time of separation varies over a wide range from a few days to six years, which causes a wide variety of environmental influences on the development of the twins and in turn influence the correlations. Second, many of these studies encompass a time span of a half-century when techniques and methods differed considerably from those of today. Also, the twin studies were not standardized for sex and age, both of which are influential on IQ and improper correction for these factors will produce higher correlation values. The effects of environmental differences are indicated in Table 7-4, which also shows the relative degree of genetic influences. There are numerous other problems encountered when twin studies are attempted; even those MZ twins reared in separate households are often reared by relatives, uncles,

TABLE 7-4　Heritability Estimates in Twins Reared Apart and Together

REFERENCE	PSYCHOLOGICAL TEST VARIABLE (P)	NO. OF PAIRS (n)	INTRAPAIR CORRELA-TION (r_p)	ESTIMATES (H^2)
Husén (1959) year groups 1949–1952	IQ by I test	MZT 215	0.894	—
		DZT 416	0.703	—
Newman, Freeman, and Holzinger (1937)	Binet Mental Age	MZS 19	0.637	0.637
		MZT 50	0.922	±0.136
		DZT 50	0.831	
	Binet IQ	MZS 19	0.670	0.670
		MZT 50	0.910	±0.126
		DZT 50	0.640	
	Otis score	MTZ 50	0.947	—
		DZT 50	0.800	—
	Otis IQ	MZS 19	0.727	0.727
		MZT 50	0.922	±0.108
		DZT 50	0.621	
	Stanford Educat. Age	MZS 19	0.502	0.502
		MZT 50	0.955	±0.172
		DZT 50	0.883	
Shields (1962)	Dominoes Intell. Test	MZS 37	0.758	0.758
		MZT 34	0.735	±0.070
	Mill Hill Vocabul. scale	MZS 38	0.741	0.741
		MZT 36	0.742	±0.073

MZS = monozygotic twins separated; MZT = monozygotic twins (brought up together); and DZT = dizygotic twins (brought up together).
Source: Adapted from Vogel and Motulsky, 1986.

aunts, and so forth. There are also recorded cases in which twins had maintained close contact during various stages of their childhood, even attending the same schools, which raises the probability of many shared childhood experiences before they were ever tested as participants in a twin study program (Lewontin et al., 1984).

Many of the differences or variations are even more interesting than the similarities. Twins raised apart have up to 20 points of difference, which again shows the effect of environment. In the case of adopted children there is an average gain of some 20 points over their biological mothers, and the correlation between parents and children is approximately 0.5, but bright parents usually have children with lower IQs, which is described as "regression towards the mean." These comparisons were taken a significant step farther by studies of transracially adopted children (Scarr and Weinberg, 1983). The study tested parents in 101 adoptive families that had 176 adoptive children (130 were "socially" classified as black), and the families also included 143 biological children of the parents.

Most adoptees (111) were younger than one year old when adopted and 65 after their twelfth month. The homes were economically well off, and the parents scored in the bright-average range. Tests of all children were recorded; the black adopted children averaged 110 points IQ or 20 points above comparable children in the black community. The adopted black child averaged 6 points lower than the biological children in the families. Scarr and Weinberg (1983:261) interpreted these high IQ scores as an indication that genetic differences do not account for a major portion of the IQ differences between racial groups. Also, they concluded that black and interracial children reared in the "culture" of the tests perform as well as other adopted children in similar families. If all of these factors are considered, there is a basic error in the argument that lower IQs among certain ethnic or racial groups are due to "inferior" genes.

In an earlier study of genetic and environmental influences, Scarr (1971) described the results of 992 pairs of MZ twins in Philadelphia. First, and perhaps most important, was that 75 percent of the total variance on test scores of whites was due to genetic variance, whereas the proportion of genetic variance in disadvantaged black populations was less. This provided evidence for the correctness of the statement that studies of twins as a method of obtaining H^2 is not fully dependable for the general population, because twins are not a representative group.

Scarr-Salapatek (1971:1286) also tested the hypothesis that "Social class differences in phenotypic IQ are assumed to reflect primarily the mean differences in genotype distribution by social class; that is, environmental differences between social classes (and races) are seen as insignificant in determining total phenotypic variance in I.Q." Scarr and Weinberg (1983) found, through extensive black and white twin comparisons, that the hypothesis was false; the environment played a more significant role in population variance. These results, together with those obtained from later studies of transracial adoptions, provide a solid base from which to reexamine the degree of genetic influence on behavior. The conclusions they reached are clear: The class or rather the cultural environment is of equal or greater importance to a child's development than is the genetic component.

> The implications of the differences between race and social class for intellectual achievement is that there are more likely to be genetic differences in I.Q. scores between social class than racial groups. (Scarr, 1981:79)

It is of interest that these two researchers reach a point where social class is given such emphasis.

Class and Caste

An interesting book that deals thoroughly with the question of the effects of class and caste on IQ differences describes the relative environmental influences within and between populations; environmental influences are greater between populations than within a population (Ogbu, 1978). This is due to the fact that the two levels of comparisons are not the same. Within a population, the individual differences are comparisons of biological organisms, whereas the intergroup comparisons are treating groups (castes) sociologically defined. Even the perceived differences between black and white Americans are less biological than sociological, as noted earlier in the transracial adoptee studies. There are, to be sure, genetic differences, but the degree covers an enormous range because of more than three hundred years of interbreeding and, as shown by Scarr and Weinberg (1978), bear no relationship to the individual's test performance.

Ogbu considers the social classification of black Americans as a caste like status and suggests that their minority position and achievements are comparable with other minorities: Native Americans, Mexican-Americans, and Puerto Ricans. Society's expectations, the limited educational opportunities, and lower expectations of economic rewards, together with social barriers, have caused responses of "mental withdrawal," leading to a failure in educational achievement. Whether or not the reader accepts this observation, and, to be sure, the situation has changed somewhat in the last decade, the evidence of lower achievement of these minority groups is there to see. Each of these minorities score lower on the standard tests by, interestingly enough, fifteen points or one standard deviation. They also have the highest school dropout rate, the highest unemployment, and so on. The introduction of caste boundaries and expectations points out a further weakness of the inherited inequality arguments so often used as a simplistic explanation of group differences. It is interesting to compare the IQ scores of several races at this point as listed in Table 7-1. Northwestern Europeans are at the top with the standardized score of one hundred, whereas all others have lower scores—many about fifteen points lower. This says more about social boundaries limiting learning experiences than about innate mental ability. The San (Bushmen) of the Kalahari score at the "moron level" (on the European scale of standards, of course), yet they have survived for thousands of years, in fact they have thrived, in a demanding environment, as experts in animal and plant resources; they also have a finely developed social system and complex language. Of the groups listed in Table 7-1 they have had least contact with Western culture. Just as revealing are the differences in scores of Australian Aboriginals of remote regions and those in close contact with Euro-Australian communities.

Every nation has its minorities, relegated to some caste that is, by definition, biologically inferior, and socially undesirable as well. India is famous for its elaborate caste system codified by law and sanctioned by religious beliefs. The castes are arranged in social stratification from Brahmin at the top, with the greatest social prestige, wealth, and political status, to a middle group "nonpolluting caste" who performed services for the Brahmin, to the lowest-level untouchable castes who carried out the least desirable occupations of scavengers, sweepers, washermen and other laborers. Other nations also have established social castes, perhaps not as rigid in boundaries but still an identification of a minority group, be it the "guest worker"—usually from North Africa, southern Europe, or Turkey, in France or Germany, or the historically famous Gypsies, especially in central and eastern Europe. In the United States, of course, Blacks, Hispanics, and Native Americans have occupied these caste positions.

Most Asian minorities in the United States have, by and large, fared better, but in their homelands there are numerous and complex caste structures. Even in Japan, there are castelike minorities, the statement by Nakasone, the former Japanese prime minister, not withstanding. Nakasone, in a public speech, explained Japan's achievements by referring to the high levels of intelligence of its citizens. "Our average score is much higher than the United States. There are many Blacks, Puerto Ricans, and Mexicans in America. In consequence the average score over there is exceedingly low." Forced later to apologize, for what was perceived as a racial slur, Nakasone tried to explain with the observation that Japan was a monoracial society. He added that, "there are things that the Americans cannot do because of multiracial nationalities there," a statement that made matters worse.[2] On the contrary, Japan does have minorities. The best recognized are the Koreans, small in number to be sure (only 680,000) but forced by discrimination to remain on the fringe of society. A still smaller ethnic group, the Ainu descendants of the original inhabitants have suffered considerable economic and social deprivation during the centuries. Though numbering only about twenty-four thousand today, they too took offense at Nakasone's remarks. Another group that disturbs the notion of a homogeneous society is the Burakumin, a social minority caste who are limited, by centuries old tradition, to undesirable occupations (the sweepers, slaughter house workers, and so on). This social caste occupies a position in Japanese society comparable with that of the *untouchables* of India. Though there has been intermarriage with Koreans during past generations, there has been little with the Burakumin who rank lowest on the social scales of Japanese society; in fact, during the prewar era intermarriage was forbidden by law. The purpose of pointing out the existence of this low caste is to note that the school performance of the Burakumin children is well below the national norm; they score,

---

[2] Though these remarks by the then prime minister of Japan were later qualified and a form of apology was published, the initial comment stated his firmly held belief in the inequality of ethnic groups (*New York Times*, 3 January 1986). Several news magazines published essays discussing the issues raised and were severely critical of Nakasone (*Time*, 6 October 1986; *Newsweek*, 6 October 1986).

on average, fifteen points lower (one standard deviation) below the Japanese average.

Ogbu suggests that this is evidence of children's reaction to society's expectations and to a teacher's attitude toward low caste children. He emphasizes that when persons of this caste had migrated to Hawaii or the West Coast their school performance was equal to that of the other Japanese children since the American school teachers were not aware of the caste differences. The teachers simply dealt with all children of Japanese ancestry, or, for that matter, all Asians in the same way—they had high expectations of school performance. The story could be continued by relating the experiences of Orientals, Yemennites, Ethiopians, and other Jews in contact with the dominant group, the Ashkenazin, in Israel, but the contrasts are the same as related earlier. The same expectations, stereotypes, and treatment are found in Israeli society (Schiff and Lewontin, 1986).

Finally, the point is that no one, single measure may represent innate ability, and the norms are standardized by tests administered to the majority groups and used as a standard against which all others are compared. We are dealing with a complex combination of genes when we consider mental ability, and the polygenic nature of this phenotype means that a considerable number of interactions occur between genes, their products, and the environment. It is misleading to attempt to partition the relative influence of environment and genetics in such a complex organism as *Homo sapiens.* The nature of much of the genetic system is its potential to interact with environmental stimuli. A gene-enzyme response syndrome is an example, and the level of the enzymatic response is probably a result of the storage of information. The central nervous system stores and retrieves information as an adaptation to the environment, and a feedback loop is formed. The cultural environment, the genes, and stored experience all provide a mental template that will vary from population to population and from generation to generation.

> It is a truism that behavior cannot be biologically inherited but must be developed and elicited under the combined influence of genetic and environmental factors. The effects of genes must be expressed through physiological action, and it has long been known that genes modify each other's effects so that only when a gene has a major and usually disruptive effect is there a one-to-one relationship between gene and character. (Scott, 1969:64)

In addition to this definition, a statement by Weinberg should be added that stresses influences of environment. It is especially important if one considers that caste status creates a particularly unique environment in contrast to all others.

> Environments can affect whether the full range of gene activity is expressed.

Thus, how people behave or what their measured I.Q.s turn out to be or how quickly they learn depend on the nature of their environments and on their genetic endowments bestowed at conception (Weinberg, 1989:101).

GENETICS, INTELLIGENCE, AND THE FUTURE

The final, definitive research must await a racially integrated America in which opportunities are the same for both races. . . . The important conclusion for the present, however, is that if there are any inherent distinctions, they are inconsequential. Even now, differences in I.Q. within any one race greatly exceed the differences between the races. Race as such is simply not an accurate way to judge an individual's intelligence. (Pettigrew, 1971:116)

For many decades we have been warned of the possibility of a decline in human intelligence because of disproportionate fertility rates of certain segments in our society. The prediction that collective intelligence would decrease one to four points per generation has proved to be false, however. For a time it looked like an accurate prediction, since the "least intelligent" (that is, those with the lowest IQs or least number of years in schooling) appeared to be producing more children, but longitudinal data have shown that there has been no decline in general intelligence. In fact, the often-expressed concern about birth rates among low-IQ groups is based on earlier studies that showed that women with low IQs had more children, but these studies did not count those women who never had children. This, of course, resulted in an incorrect estimate of fertility among low-IQ groups. Actually, because many women of this group never have children (about 30 percent versus only 10 percent in the over-130 IQ group), the results of comparisons between the two groups show that the reproductive rate of the high-IQ group is greater.

The measure of mental ability or IQ differences between social groups (or racial groups) has been questioned many times and is often attributed to differences in a central theme involving survival and lifestyles of complex industrial societies. The basis for variance in IQ may lie in discriminatory practices, economics, and language. Groups consistently scoring lower on standardized tests do not necessarily come from an "inferior" environment but from one that is distinct from the environment of the group on which the test was originally standardized. The various tests were designed as predictive devices, and as such they work very well to a limited extent in that they are predictive of academic success—but, unfortunately, people have tried to use them for other purposes. Lewontin and many others have raised the question of what these tests actually measure and what is more important how the results are applied (Lewontin et al., 1984). In addition, IQ tests as predictors of competence or success in a vocation after formal training has been seriously challenged (Fallows

1989). Fallows argues that though the test scores are good predictors of academic achievement they are poor or useless as indication of career success. He suggests that opportunity and motivation to achieve are more important. For examples, he listed a variety of occupations and professions where the person's class standing or grades in college or training programs had little bearing on professional competence. He cited, among other examples, the success of the G.I. bill that supported millions of veterans in college—persons who otherwise would not have had the opportunity to gain an advanced education. Finally, to be comparable, two persons taking the same test should have been exposed to the same material and experiences and be in the same state of physical development. Or, as Scarr-Salapatek (1971:1287) stated:

> Only if black children could be reared as though they were white, and vice versa, could the effects of different rearing environments on the genotype distribution of the two races be estimated.

Careful use of biological or social definitions of race and controlled or modified tests matter little if we simplistically assume that humans are "color coded." It is dangerous and inaccurate to assume that, if the variation of trait X in one population differs from the variation of that trait in another population, then all inherited traits differ at the same rate between the two groups. "Races" are not inferior or superior; there is no "gene for slow learning," and the genetics of whatever IQ measures has yet to be determined; if it ever will be possible is another matter. The future may look bleak to some who claim a decline in IQ, but there are no data to demonstrate such a decline. On the contrary, there is every indication that environmental improvement will increase with an expansion of the opportunities for persons to realize their full potential. As Dobzhansky states:

> Correctly understood, heredity is not the "dice of destiny." It is rather a bundle of potentialities. Which part of the multitude of potentialities will be realized is for the environments, for the biography of the person, to decide. Only fanatic believers in the myth of genetic predestination can doubt that the life of every person offers numerous options, of which only a part, probably a miniscule part, is realized. (1976:160)

A personal observation as a conclusion for this chapter is in order: I would like to warn any reader to approach studies of genetics and behavior or behavioral genetics with great caution. Often, and I fear more frequently than not, the authors who describe in many ways the relationship of genetics to behavior approach the task with some bias. It is to be expected. We are, after all, the product of our experiences and training within a society and, however we try to be objective, our conclusions are biased to some degree. The revival of the nature-nurture controversy and the development of behavioral genetics in the last decade are good examples. Too frequently, authors will accuse one another of covert or even overt racism or will refer to a political bias (that is, Marxism) and then discount the data reported or the criticisms because of these alleged biases. Without citing specific works beyond those mentioned earlier, I would argue that we are all guilty to some degree. The major sin of writers on all sides of the question is clear but generally ignored, that is, the sin of omission. Those who write about human variability, as a group, avoid a close examination of the concept of race and its validity for the study of human variability. Nowhere are personal biases more apparent than in the taxonomy of our species. The use of racial stock, race, hybrid, or ethnic group is too frequently mixed with the sociological classification, a classification based on a group's self-identification or by the labels imposed by the majority population. This casual use of stereotyping in the name of classification must stop if objectivity is to be introduced to the study of human diversity at any level, but especially in the investigation of behavioral differences and measured abilities.

RECOMMENDED READINGS AND LITERATURE CITED

BAKER, J. R. 1974. *Science, Racism and Social Darwinism: A Review of Race.* London: Oxford University Press.

BARZUN, J. 1965. *Race: A Study in Superstition.* New York: Harper and Row.

BELICH, J. 1986. *The New Zealand Wars.* Auckland: Auckland University Press.

BLOCK, N. J., AND G. DWORKIN, eds. 1976. *The IQ Controversy.* New York: Pantheon Books.

BODMER, W. F., AND L. CAVALLI-SFORZA. 1970. "Intelligence and race," *Sci. Am.*, 223:19–29.

BOUCHARD, T. J., JR., D. T. LYKKEN, M. MCGUE, N. L. SEGAL, AND A. TELLEGEN. 1990. Sources of human psychological differences: The Minnesota study of twins reared apart. *Science*, 250:223–250.

BOUCHARD, T. J., JR., D. T. LYKKEN, N. L. SEGAL, AND K. J. WILCOX. 1986. "Development in twins reared apart: A test of the chronogenetic hypothesis," in *Human Growth: A Multidisciplinary Review*, eds. A. Demirjian and M. Brault. Philadelphia: Taylor & Francis.

CHASE, A. 1977. *The Legacy of Malthus: The Social Costs of the New Scientific Racism.* New York: Alfred A. Knopf.

CRAVENS, H. 1978. *The Triumph of Evolution: American Scientists and the Heredity-Environment Controversy, 1900, 1941.* Philadelphia: University of Pennsylvania Press.

DARLINGTON, C. D. 1969. *The Evolution of Man and Society.* New York: Simon & Schuster.

DOBZHANSKY, T. 1976. "The myths of genetic predestination and of tabula rasa," *Perspectives in Biology and Medicine*, 19:156–170.

ERLENMEYER-KIMLING, L., AND L. F. JARVIK. 1963. "Genetics and intelligence: A review," *Science*, 142:1477–1479.

FALLOWS, J. 1989. *More Like Us.* Boston: Houghton Mifflin.

FENTON, F. D. 1859. *Aboriginal Inhabitants of New Zealand.* Auckland: W. C. Wilson.

GALTON, F. 1869 (reprinted, 1962). *Hereditary Genius.* New York: MacMillan.

GREEN, L. J. 1967. "Functional neurological performance in primitive cultures," *Hum. Poten.*, 1:19–26.

GREGG, T. G., AND P. R. SANDAY. 1971. "Genetic and environmental components of differential intelligence," in *Race and Intelligence*, eds. C. L. Brace, G. R. Gamble, and J. T. Bond. Washington, D.C.: American Anthropological Association.

HALLER, J. S., JR. 1970. "The physician versus the Negro: Medical and anthropological concepts of race in the late nineteenth century," *Bulletin of the History of Medicine*, 44:154–167.

HALLER, J. S., JR. 1971. *Outcasts from Evolution, Scientific Attitudes of Racial Inferiority, 1859–1900*. Urbana: University of Illinois Press.

HAWKES, N. 1979. "Tracing Burt's Descent to Scientific Fraud," *Science*, 205:673–675.

HEARNSHAW, L. S. 1979. *Cyril Burt: Psychologist*. London: Hodder and Stoughton.

HIRSCH, J., ed. 1967. *Behavior-Genetic Analysis*. New York: McGraw-Hill.

HIRSCH, J. 1969. "Behavior genetics, or 'Experimental,' analysis: The challenge of science versus the lure of technology," in *Behavioral Genetics: Methods and Research*, eds. M. Manosevitz, G. Lindzey, and D. D. Thiessen. New York: Appleton-Century-Crofts.

HIRSCH, N. D. M. 1926. "A study of natro-racial mental differences," *Genetic Psychology Monographs*, 1 (numbers 3 and 4).

JENSEN, A. R. 1969. "How much can we boost IQ and scholastic achievement?" in *Environment, Heredity, and Intelligence*. Cambridge, Mass.: Harvard Educational Review.

JENSEN, A. R. 1971. "Can we and should we study race differences?" in *Race and Intelligence*, eds. C. L. Brace, G. R. Gamble, and J. T. Bond. Washington, D.C.: American Anthropological Association.

KAMIN, L. J. 1974. *The Science and Politics of IQ*. Hillsdale, N.J.: Lawrence Erlbaum Associates.

KENNEDY, W. A., V. VAN DE RIET, AND J. C. WHITE. 1963. *A Normative Sample of Intelligence and Achievement of Negro Elementary School Children in Southeastern United States*, Monograph 28, no. 6. Chicago: Society for Research on Child Development.

LADIMEJI, O. A. 1974. Book Review: *Race*, by John R. Baker (New York: Oxford University Press.) *Race* 16:101–110.

LEWONTIN, R. C., S. ROSE, AND L. KAMIN. 1984. *Not in Our Genes*. New York: Pantheon Books.

LOEHLIN, J. C., G. LINDZEY, AND J. N. SPUHLER. 1975. *Race Differences in Intelligence*. New York: W. H. Freeman.

LYNN, R. 1978. "Ethnic and racial differences in intelligence: International comparisons," in *Human Variation: The Biopsychology of Age, Race, and Sex*, eds. R. T. Osborne, C. E. Noble, and N. Weyl. New York: Academic Press.

MAYESKE, G. W. 1971. *On the Explanation of Racial-Ethnic Group Differences in Achievement Test Scores*. Washington, D.C.: Office of Education, U.S. Department of Health, Education and Welfare.

OGBU, J. U. 1978. *Minority Education and Caste: The American System in Cross-Cultural Perspective*. New York: Academic Press.

PENROSE, L. S. 1951. "Measurement of pleiotropic effects in phenylketonuria," *Annals of Eugenics*, 16:134–141.

PETTIGREW, T. F. 1971. "Race, mental illness and intelligence: A social psychological view," in *The Biological and Social Meaning of Race*, ed. R. H. Osborne. New York: W. H. Freeman.

SCARR-SALAPATEK, S. 1971. "Race, social class and IQ," *Science*, 174:1285–1295.

SCARR, S. 1981. "Toward a more biological psychology," in *Science and the Question of Human Equality*, eds. M. S. Collins, I. W. D. Wainer, and T. A. Bremner. Boulder, Colo.: Westview Press.

SCARR, S., AND R. A. WEINBERG. 1978. "Attitudes, interests, and IQ," *Hum. Nature*, 1:29–36.

SCARR, S., AND R. A. WEINBERG. 1983. "The Minnesota adoption studies: Genetic differences and malleability," *Child Develop.*, 54:260–267.

SCHIFF, M., AND R. LEWONTIN. 1986. *Education and Class: The Irrelevance of IQ Genetic Studies*. New York: Clarendon Press.

SCOTT, J. P. 1969. "Discussion," in *Science and the Concept of Race*, eds. M. Mead, T. Dobzhansky, E. Tobach, and R. E. Light. New York: Columbia University Press.

SHOCKLEY, W. 1972. "Dysgenics, geneticity, raceology: A challenge to the intellectual responsibility of educators," *Phi Delta Kappan*, 53:297–307.

SPUHLER, J. N., AND G. LINDZEY. 1967. "Racial differences in behavior," in *Behavior Genetic Analysis*, ed. Jerry Hirsch. New York: McGraw-Hill.

STANTON, W. R. 1960. *The Leopard's Spots: Scientific Attitudes Toward Race in America, 1815–59.* Chicago: University of Chicago Press.

VOGEL, F., AND A. G. MOTULSKY. 1986. *Human Genetics: Problems and Approaches.* Berlin: Springer-Verlag.

WADE, N. 1976. "IQ and heredity: Suspicion of fraud beclouds classic experiment," *Science*, 194:916–919.

WATTENBERG, B. J. 1985. *The Birth Dearth.* New York: Pharos Books.

WEINBERG, R. A. 1989. "Intelligence and IQ: Landmark issues and great debates. *Am. Psychol.*, 44:98–104.

WILSON, E. O. 1978. *On Human Nature.* Cambridge, Mass.: Harvard University Press.

YERKES, R. M., ed. 1921. "Psychological examining in the U.S. Army," *Mem. Natl. Acad. Sci.*, 15.

_8

_The Future
of the
Human Species___

Viewed from an evolutionary perspective our species has been extraor-
dinarily successful in adapting and increasing in numbers. If natural
selection is for reproductive success of a species, we rank among the more
successful. Not only have we increased and improved our adaptation, but
we have gained in the ability to alter environments to suit our needs.
These environmental alterations and population increases have created a
feedback system that has a profound influence on biological variability
and, in turn, places limits on our adaptive responses. Human population
growth, however, is determined primarily by the social system and depends
on effective behavior within an environmental context (Washburn, 1964).
The effectiveness of our behavior has contributed to an expansion and
dispersal of *Homo sapiens* about the globe, breaking down older population
boundaries, establishing new ones while, at the same time, creating new
dimensions of biological diversity.

Throughout the preceding chapters I have described the many ways
in which *Homo sapiens* vary and have considered the probable causes.
Among these many causes relating to diversity is the increase in the variety
of ways our species exploits natural resources. Development of technology
and improved organization, for example, have aided human response to
the forces of natural selection. The results have been dramatic during the

past ten thousand years, the last three hundred years in particular. Environments have been changed to fit human needs, but there are still many problems confronting us today. Natural selection is still operating though, but in different forms, and it is continuing to shape the composition and diversity of human populations. The dimensions and scope of these ongoing processes require careful consideration, especially the increase in numbers of people and the burden these expanded populations place on the environment. Demographic factors of this expansion exert a major influence on gene frequencies. Epidemiology, the types and distributions of disease, is also altered each generation as new diseases gain in population influence while older ones decline as threats to human health.

POPULATION GROWTH

Two million years ago our ancestors numbered only a few hundred thousand and, from this small number, our species evolved and increased until, by the time of the Neolithic (the invention of agriculture), we had reached a total of five million. This growth was painfully slow during hundreds of thousands of years and, throughout this period, we could not be judged to be very successful as a species; in fact, many other primates far outnumbered us. With the development of agriculture, however, *Homo sapiens* began a more rapid increase (Figure 8-1). Even with this increased rate of growth, it still took an average of fifteen hundred years for our species to double in size, but from A.D. 1650, when the world contained approximately five hundred million people, it took only two hundred years to increase to one billion (Table 8-1). From then on the annual rate of population growth increased; today, we grow at a rate of 1.8 percent and about ninety-five million new people are added each year, up from seventy-seven million in 1982.

The accelerated population growth since the advent of agriculture has had many causes, and some are difficult to identify. A major influence, though, was a more dependable food supply, because food had been a primary factor limiting population size. During much of their annual cycle, prehistoric hunters and gatherers probably had an ample food supply that, judging from studies of modern hunters, could have supported a much larger population. The lean periods—those times of scarcity that occurred periodically—kept population numbers below the "carrying capacity" of the environment, however. The major achievement of the agriculturists at the time of the Neolithic was their ability to produce and to store a surplus of food, which enabled them to survive times of scarcity

WORLD POPULATION GROWTH

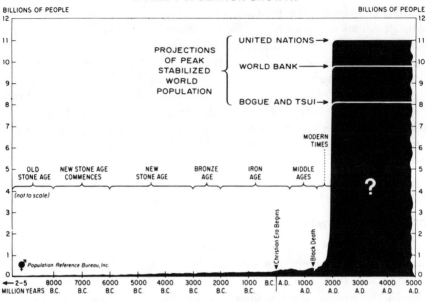

FIGURE 8-1   **Growth in Numbers of *Homo sapiens* and their Ancestors.** (From Inter-change, 1980, Population Reference Bureau, Inc.)

TABLE 8-1   **World Population Doubling Times**

YEAR	POPULATION	DOUBLING TIME (YEARS)
8000 B.C.	5,000,000[a]	1500
A.D. 1	250,000,000[a]	1500
1650	545,000,000[a]	200
1750	728,000,000[a]	200
1850	1,171,000,000[a]	100
1950	2,486,000,000	50
1970	3,632,000,000	35
1975	4,000,000,000	36
1990	5,321,000,000	39
2000[a]	6,292,000,000	43
2020[a]	8,228,000,000	53

[a] These are estimated population sizes and doubling times in years.

Sources: Based on data from the Population Council, 1990; and Deevey, 1960.

between harvests.[1] This capability helped sustain a larger average number of people than had existed before the Neolithic.

Another possible factor contributing to population growth was the radical change in life-styles brought about by agricultural subsistence. Formerly, during the hunting and gathering phase of existence, females could only nurse one child at a time; in addition, infants had to be breast-fed for up to three years because of the lack of an adequate weaning food. This prolonged nursing period, plus the heavy work load, and the frequent movement of camp sites reduced female fertility and caused infanticide to be a common practice (Birdsell, 1981). By contrast, a major feature of life since the earliest advent of agriculture was the establishment of semipermanent settlements, and this more sedentary life had an important effect on female fertility. The less arduous existence encountered in a sedentary village, in contrast to a nomadic hunting life, reduced the strain on females and extended their reproductive period. The number of children they could bear increased from an average of four to six or even more as estimated from studies of recent primitive agriculturists. No longer were females forced to transport an infant while going about their daily round of food collecting over many miles of territory, as in former times. Also, improved infant care and nutrition reduced mortality and increased the number of children reaching adolescence.

Though settled village life had certain advantages, many new problems affecting human survival were created. Greater numbers of people living in close contact during long periods provided the type of environment necessary to sustain a variety of disease organisms that took a heavy toll on the population and shortened life expectancy. In early agricultural periods, judging from skeletal remains, there was a high mortality among young adults and adolescents. Though comparatively improved since the days of the Paleolithic hunter, human existence was still precarious for several millennia after the introduction of agriculture.

In recent centuries there was an acceleration of population growth but the contributing factors are numerous and complex and are subjects of much recent debate: did a more dependable food supply contribute to an increase in numbers or did the greater number of people provide the impetus to develop improved food-producing technology (Boserup, 1981)? During the nineteenth century we can point to the control of infectious disease as a major reason for declining death rates, but, in the seventeenth, eighteenth, and early decades of the nineteenth century, control of disease

---

[1] Agriculturists were more or less successful in producing surpluses to carry them through the years of crop failures, but not always. Many times during the Middle Ages and even into recent centuries, two or more successive years of crop failures resulted in famine and, together with epidemics, caused high mortality rates. A recent and interesting historical account of these episodes in Europe details the impact of crop failures on populations in Europe (Ladurie, 1988)

was probably not the single most important reason for growth. It is likely that increased efficiency in food production was more important. New food crops were introduced into Europe from the Americas. Plants like potato and corn, in particular, enabled agricultural production to increase radically because of their shorter growing season and a yield of a greater amount of calories per unit measure than the grains traditionally grown. The same amount of land planted in such crops could sustain many more people than previously possible; also these New World crops could grow well on soils unsuited for wheat and barley, the staple European crops.

By this period, toward the end of the eighteenth century, European populations had increased as much as 133 percent, and population pressures had reached the point at which many millions from western Europe migrated to new lands. With this rapid expansion, the modern era began, and the conditions under which we live today were initiated. These modern living conditions, though varied and complex, have the capacity to change rapidly; as they change, selective forces are altered readily. Natural selection, which in a previous period favored one group over another, changed and resulted in a shift in population size and reproduction rate. All populations of *Homo sapiens* were not affected equally, however, nor were the same selective forces present everywhere at the same time. While the technologically advanced societies were seeking new space, many, perhaps most, of the world's populations were living at preseventeenth-century levels. African and New World peoples were less numerous in proportion to the carrying capacity of their lands than were Asians and Europeans. Figure 8-2 shows a gain of Europeans and persons of European origins in North American of 8 percent of the world total between A.D. 1750 and 1900 compared with only 4 percent for all of Asia, whereas Africa and the Mideast showed a net decline in proportion of the total world population. If more reliable estimates were available for the Neolithic populations in Europe and the Mideast, disproportionate population gains would likely be seen. The point is, because growth is greater in some world regions than in others, some population boundaries expand, whereas others remain stable or may even contract, thus changing relative sizes of ethnic group representation throughout prehistoric and even modern times.

Bands of hunting nomads were much more numerous in places like Australia and the Western Hemisphere before European colonial expansion. Probably, during the Neolithic they were even more numerous than many of the sedentary agriculturists. Even the !Kung, who today occupy Africa's Kalahari Desert, were probably as numerous as Europeans ten thousand years ago. Europeans have expanded and successfully occupied new areas of the world, and the few thousand !Kung have been pushed into a harsh refuge area by expanding agriculturalist and pastoral peoples, such as the tribes of Bantu speakers and more recently the Europeans

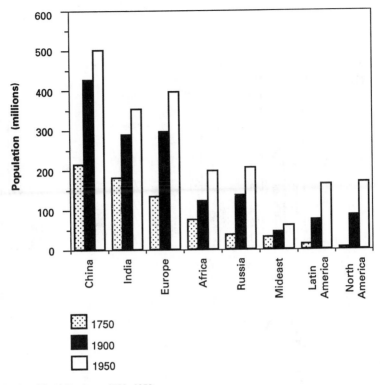

FIGURE 8-2a   World Regions, 1750–1950

The populations in major world regions have grown disproportionately over the last two centuries with Europe exceeding all others between 1750 and 1950. Even allowing for the wide range of error in these estimates, the changes in regional increases have been impressive.

(Hulse, 1955). The Aboriginal peoples of Australia and North and South America had much the same experiences. The end result of disproportionate increases of the world's peoples we see today is a population distribution that differs radically from that of prehistoric times. The hunters have all but disappeared except in a very few refuge areas and even primitive agriculturalists are but a fraction of their former number and are rapidly diminishing as their environments and resources are destroyed. By contrast, many populations have sustained phenomenal growth over the last few generations.

The future, if growth projections are reasonably accurate, will see an even greater change in the distribution of the world's peoples (Figure 8-3). The growth trends of two centuries ago have been reversed. Those countries with more natural and technological resources have a slower projected growth rate than the less developed areas of the world. The majority of the more than six billion people in the year 2000 will live in

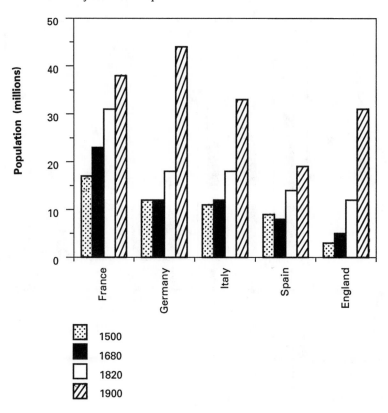

FIGURE 8-2b   Western Europe, 1500–1900

The rate of growth in Europe was greatest in England where the population more than doubled, 1680–1820 and then doubled again, 1820–1900. This rate was approached only by Germany which increased by greater than twice its size during the years, 1820–1900. Sources: Population estimates taken from historical demography studies by: Durand, 1977; Langer, 1963; McEvedy, 1978.

the *less developed countries* (LDC).[2] There will be an estimated 79 percent of the world living in the LDC, *a significant increase from the 66 percent living in these regions of the world in 1950.* The more developed countries (MDC) will continue to grow but very slowly, only about 0.5 percent per year. The LDC, though slowing from their 1975 rate of 2.1 percent, will increase their population by 1.8 percent per annum. At this rate the doubling time will be 33 years in contrast to the 93 to 266 years doubling time for North America and Europe. If China, with a rate of natural increase of 1.4

---

[2] Classification of the "more developed" and "less developed" regions follows that of the United Nations—that is, the "more developed" regions comprise all of Europe, North America (United States and Canada), Australia and New Zealand, Japan, the Soviet Union, and temperate South America (Argentina, Chile, and Uruguay). The rest of the world is regarded as "less developed."

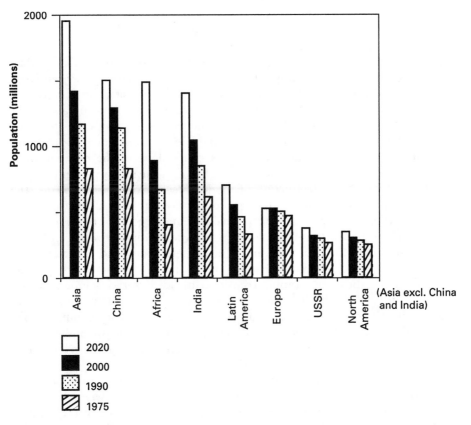

FIGURE 8-3   Regional Populations, 1975–2020

Given the current growth rates of major world regions the projections for the year 2020 will place Asia and Africa far ahead of the other regions. Latin America will nearly double in size in contrast to those areas that experience only slow growth (Europe, North America, and the USSR). **(Data selected from Population Reference Bureau, 1990.)**

percent and doubling time of 49 years, is excluded from the calculations than the LDC doubling time is 29 years.

The major differences in growth during the past three decades are due to a dramatic lowering of the death rate. When both birth and death rates were high, a reduction in only the death rates would, of course, result in rapid population growth, as experienced by Africa, Asia, and Latin America in the past few decades. The effects that these growth phenomena have on evolution depend a great deal on the population structure, its mating circles, social systems, and age structure. Some investigators believe that since death rates have been lowered, natural selection operates through a variation in birth rates. This variation is effected mostly through a voluntary decision of the parents, made according to the dictates of their culture or society, often with consideration of the advantage to the family.

Countries with rapidly growing populations such as Mexico, India, and Nigeria are undergoing what is described as a *demographic transition*. This term is used by demographers to describe a transition in the growth potential of a population. In the past, a relatively stable population was maintained with little or no net increase between the generations because a high birth was counterbalanced by high death rates. Such populations begin to change when they enter the second phase of the demographic transition by reducing death rates through various health measures (usually associated with the introduction of modern technology), while births still remain high. Populations then begin to increase rapidly. A third phase is entered when birth rates decline until replacement equals or barely exceeds loss, and the population approaches a zero population-growth condition. Western European countries and the United States and Canada have reached this stage. A critical factor in the future will be the length of time required for the demographic transition in the lesser developed world. The continuous high birth rates in the LDC will cause many populations to double their size in less than a generation. Mexico, for example, has a natural increase of 2.4 percent, which adds more than two million new people each year to its population. If continued at this rate of growth, the population will double within twenty-nine years.

Populations undergoing rapid growth have age structures as illustrated by the example of Mexico where persons born between 1960 and 1974 make up the largest population segment, in contrast to the United States (a slow-growth nation). Sweden is an example of a "no-growth" nation; each age segment between birth and sixty years is nearly equal in size (Figure 8-4). The distinction between developed and developing countries in age distribution is shown even more graphically by the diagram in Figure 8-5. The more developed countries have maintained the proportion of children under age fifteen at about 22 percent since 1950, while this age groups has nearly doubled in the developing countries and may even rise in some.

An important consideration of the age structure of a population in determination of society's needs is the dependency ratio. This is the ratio between the productive portion of the population, set typically at fifteen to sixty-four years, and the dependent age groups, the individuals younger than fifteen years and older than sixty-four years. The larger the dependent group, the larger will be the *dependency* ratio (DR). Populations in the LDC have a very high dependency ratio. Comparisons between slow-growth and rapid-growth countries show a wide difference in the DR (Figure 8-6). These figures are based on estimates provided by the Population Reference Bureau but do not consider the probable use of

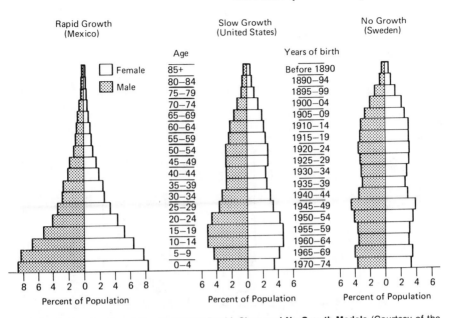

FIGURE 8-4   Age-Sex Population Pyramids: Rapid, Slow, and No Growth Models (Courtesy of the Population Reference Bureau, Inc., Washington, D.C.)

child labor, which, of course, would reduce the number of dependents. Even allowing for this, the dependency ratios are high in the LDC whose poorer economics are less able to support such a burden of dependents. This large proportion of children will, as they enter adulthood, provide a high reproduction potential and a source for rapid population growth in the future.

The dramatic effects that these population shifts have on the economy, the environment, and the social institutions of the LDC are almost beyond comprehension. One way of gauging the impact of rapid growth on a nation's resources, is to consider the age structure created by high birth rates. When, within less than a generation of rapid growth, many persons of the same *age cohort* (persons born within a given period) must fit within the socioeconomic structure. For example, in the United States, the group born during the "baby-boom" period, considered as that period between 1946 to 1964 when fertility rate peaked at 3.6 percent, followed the age cohort born during the depression years, 1929 to 1941, when fertility rates were 2.5 to 2.1. The baby boom was a seventy-five-million-person bulge in the population, which placed a heavy burden on our hospital and educational facilities as they moved through childhood. As they entered adulthood, however, they were followed by a smaller group because of the decreased birth rates during the past ten years (fertility below 2.1). The result is that many more persons entered the labor market

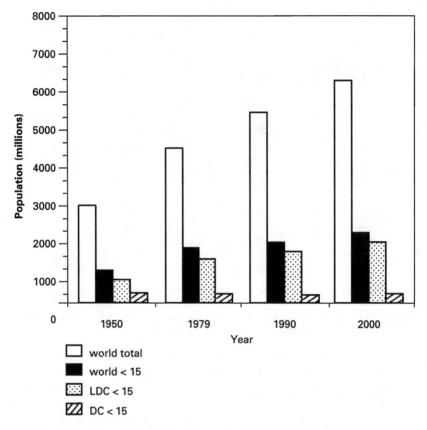

FIGURE 8-5   Children Younger Than Fifteen Years of Age, 1950–2000. (Data selected from Population Reference Bureau, 1990.)

in the 1970s than in previous decades, whereas there were fewer children to enroll in elementary school, a factor that has forced the closing of schools in many cities.[3] We witnessed, in the United States, some major stresses on our social system—particularly reduced numbers of job opportunities and an increased demand for certain types of housing. Magnify the problem many times and consider the effects on lesser developed countries in which approximately 40 percent of the total population is younger than fifteen years of age. This disproportionate number of young will be a prime source of social and political upheaval in the near future.

[3] Now, in the 1990s, we are experiencing what is called the "baby boom echo" with larger numbers of school-aged children requiring the expansion of school programs in certain areas.

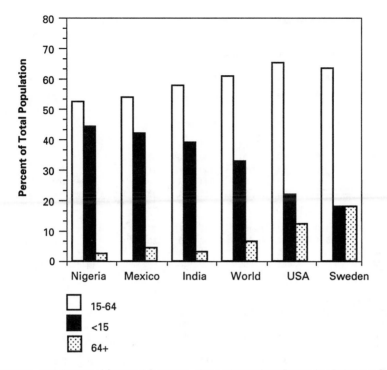

FIGURE 8-6   **Age Groups of Selected Countries.** (Data selected from Population Reference Bureau, 1990.)

DEMOGRAPHIC FACTORS OF POPULATION CHANGES

A significant aspect of the phenomenal population growth in this century has been the reduction in mortality rates (Table 8-2). The lowering of infant mortality, especially, has been a major contributing factor which, together with improvement in maternal care, has radically driven up fertility rates (average number of live births per female in their reproductive years). Life expectancy has been extended, and major causes of death have altered. The net effect, in addition to an increase in population size, has been an alteration in the forces of natural selection acting on each generation. Individuals who, in prior times, would have died before adolescence are now surviving through their reproductive years. This shift in population fitness in all parts of the world has far-reaching effects for the gene pool of future populations and will contribute to ongoing evolution. The demographic factor with the greatest influence on population size is the infant mortality rate, an influence well understood by every society and Aboriginal nomads. Infant mortality rates have varied

TABLE 8-2   Population Growth Rates of Selected World Regions

	POPULATION ESTIMATES[1]				BIRTH[2] RATES		DEATH[3] RATES		NATURAL[4] INCREASE		DOUBLING[5] TIME	
	1930	1950	1972	1990	1972	1990	1972	1990	1972	1990	1972	1990
World	2178	2674	3782	5321	33	27	13	10	2.0	1.8	35	39
Major Areas												
Africa	164	222	364	661	47	44	21	15	2.6	2.9	27	24
West Africa	48	67	107	206	49	47	24	17	2.5	3.0	28	23
East Africa	46	63	103	199	47	47	22	17	2.5	3.0	28	23
North Africa	39	53	92	144	47	38	17	10	3.0	2.8	23	25
Middle Africa	21	25	38	68	44	45	24	16	2.1	3.0	33	23
South Africa	10	14	24	45	41	36	18	9	2.4	2.7	29	26
Asia	1120	1381	2154	3116	37	27	14	9	2.3	1.9	30	37
East Asia	591	684	962	1336	29	20	12	6	1.7	1.3	41	52
Western Asia	31	44	82	132	44	36	16	8	2.8	2.8	25	24
Southern Asia	371	481	806	1192	44	35	17	12	2.6	2.3	27	30
Southeast Asia	127	173	304	455	49	29	15	8	2.9	2.1	24	34
Western Hemisphere												
North America	134	166	233	278	17	16	9	9	1.1	0.7	63	93
Latin America	108	163	300	447	38	28	10	7	2.8	2.1	25	33
Tropical South America	55	84	160	247	40	29	10	8	3.0	2.1	23	33
Central America	22	35	72	118	43	32	11	6	3.2	2.5	22	27
Temperate South America	19	27	41	49	25	21	9	8	1.7	1.4	41	51
Caribbean	12	17	27	34	33	25	11	8	2.2	1.7	32	40
Europe	355	392	469	501	16	13	10	10	0.7	0.3	99	266
W. Europe	108	123	151	159	15	12	11	10	0.5	0.2	139	326
S. Europe	93	108	151	145	18	12	9	9	0.9	0.3	77	250
E. Europe	89	88	106	113	17	14	10	11	0.7	0.3	99	215
N. Europe	65	73	82	84	16	14	11	11	0.5	0.2	139	286
USSR	179	180	248	291	17.4	19	8.2	10	0.9	0.9	77	80
Oceania	10.0	12.7	20.2	27	25	20	10	8	2.0	1.2	35	57

[1] Estimates given in millions. [2] Births/1000. [3] Deaths/1000. [4] Birth rate minus the death rate. [5] The time population to double if rate of increase continues.
Sources: Population Reference Bureau, Inc. 1990, and Demographic Yearbook, 1969, 1974, and 1979.

widely from ancient to recent times, and slight changes had major effects on the future generations.

Infant Mortality

In the United States today, 98 percent of all children born alive reach their thirteenth birthday compared with only 50 percent who did so one hundred years ago. This major demographic change is due,

TABLE 8-3   Infant Mortality Since 1898 of Selected Countries

COUNTRY	1898–1902	1918–1922	1956–1960	1972	1990
Group I[a]					
Sweden	98	65	17	11.7	5.8
Japan	155	172	36	13	4.8
Norway	88	—	20	13.8	8.4
Denmark	131	84	24	14.8	7.8
France	154	112	32	15.1	7.5
United Kingdom	152	85	23	18.4	9.5
United States	162	85	26	19.2	9.7
Group II					
Soviet Union	—	—	81	24.4	29
Hungary	204	—	—	34	15.8
Spain	190	158	49	27.9	9.0
Italy	167	141	47	29.2	9.5
Argentina	—	—	61	58	32
Group III					
Nigeria	—	—	—	180	121
Kenya	—	—	—	135	62
India	200	212	198	139	95
Mexico	—	—	76	69	50
Guatemala	—	—	95	92	59

[a] Groups of countries arranged according to relative infant mortality rates.

Sources: Selected from Population Reference Bureau, 1990; and Demographic Yearbook, 1979, 1990.

primarily, to a dramatic lowering of infant mortality rates since the turn of the century followed by eradication of many of the childhood diseases affecting preadolescents. Other developed countries, particularly those of western Europe, have had the same experience. Table 8-3 shows comparative data on infant mortality for selected countries. Group I countries have death rates of less than 10 per 1000 live births, whereas group III countries have rates as high as 121 per 1000. All countries listed in this table have experienced a dramatic reduction of death rates during the past eighty years. The greatest decreases have been among the developed countries, groups I and II, but developing countries also show an improvement in infant health.

The United States, at the turn of the century, had a frighteningly high infant mortality rate that would be comparable to that of many of the underdeveloped countries today, but this rate has now been reduced to 9.7 per 1000. Still, there are twenty countries with lower infant mortality rates. All of these countries have shown a 70 to 80 percent reduction in infant deaths since the turn of the century (a graphical comparison of sixteen selected countries is shown in Figure 8-7). The reduced infant

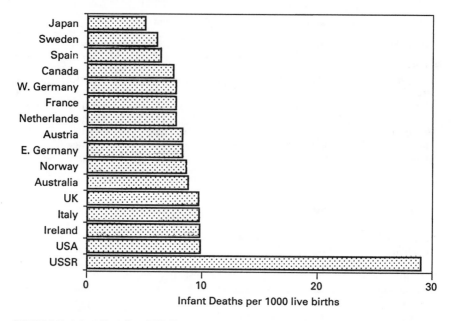

FIGURE 8-7   Infant Mortality, 1990. (Data selected from Population Reference Bureau, 1990.)

mortality has been achieved through a variety of changes; improved diets, better maternal care, and control of infectious diseases have all contributed. As of 1987, Sweden led the world in improvements of infant health, a fact that is reflected by Sweden's having one of the lowest infant mortality rates in the world. Because of the completeness of health records extending back nearly two centuries, Sweden may be used as an example of what can be achieved in the field of infant health. From 250 per 1000 infant deaths a century and a half ago, the rate was reduced to 9 per 1000 by 1980, which was thought to be the minimum that can be achieved given the knowledge of fetal development. The rate has undergone a significant reduction since, and even the lower rate of 5.8 has been surpassed in Japan in 1990 with 4.6 (See Table 8-3).

Sweden achieved this low level of infant death through major innovations in prenatal care and obstetrical services; a countrywide network ensures that every woman is within an hour of a maternity health center, which offers free services. The Swedish experience indicates the importance of socioeconomic factors. The high rates of mortality among those ethnic groups that occupy a lower socioeconomic position in many countries provide additional statistics that emphasize the influences of social factors. Where adequate data are available, mortality rates vary by national region; urban centers with available medical services are usually lower than in the rural areas. In the United States, for example, significant differences

TABLE 8-4   Causes of Death by Color and Sex in United States, 1955–1987[a]

	TOTAL		WHITE (1955)		NONWHITE (1955)		WHITE (1987)		NONWHITE (1987)	
	1955	1987	MALES	FE-MALES	MALES	FE-MALES	MALES	FE-MALES	MALES	FE-MALES
All Causes		872.4					668.2	384.1	1023.2	586.2
Diseases of heart	355.8	312.4	437.9	292.4	317.6	255.8	225.9	116.3	287.1	180.8
Malignant neo-plasms	146.5	195.9	160.1	141.0	119.8	108.5	158.4	109.7	227.9	132.0
Cerebrovascular diseases	106.0	61.6	102.3	106.2	117.8	112.9	30.3	26.3	57.1	46.7
Influenza and pneumonia	27.1	28.4	27.8	21.3	57.5	40.1	16.8	9.7	26.4	12.2
Arteriosclerosis	19.8	9.2	20.5	20.7	14.2	11.7	7.6	12.4	4.8	6.0
Diabetes mellitus	15.5	15.8	12.8	18.5	9.7	18.6	9.5	8.1	18.3	21.3
Tuberculosis	9.1	0.7	11.2	4.1	28.4	15.0	0.7	0.3	2.8	1.2
Infant mortality per 1000 live births	26.4	10.5	23.6		42.8		8.6		17.9	

[a] Rates per 100,000 population.
Sources: Adapted from Smith, 1960; and U.S. Bureau of Census, 1990.

between races have been recorded ever since health statistics have been compiled. Blacks have the highest infant mortality of any racial group; a black infant is twice as likely to die as a white infant. In addition, though great gains have been made in this century, life expectancy is still lowest among blacks (Table 8-4). A variety of explanations are offered from lack of access to medical facilities to younger age at first pregnancy, but whatever the causes significant differences have been recorded throughout this century.

Maternal Health, Infant Mortality, and Natural Selection

Throughout the last few generations, as infant mortality has declined and maternal health has improved, childbirth-related deaths have been reduced drastically. Maternal death rates of 320 per 100,000 a century ago in the developed world have decreased to 30 per 100,000 today. The combined effects of lower infant and maternal mortality rates have been an increase in fertility and a growth of population. Maternal mortality rates vary widely among the LDC and though still high are probably much lower than a few generations ago. Further improvement in prenatal care and maternity services should reduce the risks of pregnancy and raise fertility rates. As shown in Table 8-5 there is a wide disparity between countries, and most have rates as high or higher than recorded in the developed world at the turn of the century.

TABLE 8-5   Estimates of Maternal Mortality by Region

REGION	NUMBER OF MATERNAL DEATHS (THOUSANDS)	MATERNAL-MORTALITY RATE (PER 100,000 LIVE BIRTHS)
Africa	150	640
North	24	500
West	54	700
East	46	660
Central	18	690
Southern	8	570
Asia	308	420
West	14	340
South	230	650
Southeast	52	420
East	12	55
Latin America	34	270
Central	9	240
Caribbean	2	220
Tropical South	22	310
Temperate South	1	110
Oceania	2	100
Developing Countries	494	450
Developed Countries	6	30
World	500	390

Source: Adapted from *Population Today*, Population Reference Bureau, 1990.

These factors of maternal and infant health are radically altering the selective forces acting on the human population. A reduction of the selection against those genetic defects that contribute to early death or which affect infant susceptibility to disease will undoubtedly increase the genetic load in future populations. Likewise, improved maternity services enable many women to give birth to healthy infants when they might otherwise not have been able to because of hormonal deficiencies, poor general health, or defective pelvic structure (discussed earlier as an example of rickets influencing female growth). In vitro fertilization and embryo implants have opened up a whole new area of possibilities for reproduction by women who otherwise could not have conceived and carried a fetus to term. These reproductive services are expensive and require sophisticated medical procedures available to only a few.

In addition to the variation in mortality rate, reduction between world areas, and changes in fertility rates, there are significant differences between social classes. These differences have caused shifts in population percentages of various classes during the past three generations and are likely to continue, but alteration in fertility and growth rates among socioeconomic classes and ethnic groups within any country are much more difficult to define or predict. Social statuses often shift, and fashions change as preferences for large or small families alter. The immediate result is a continuation of the wide fluctuation in group size and proportion, just as observed earlier by Osborn (1971:370):

> The first result of the reduction in births was greatly to increase differential fertility between social, economic and educational groups. . . . The great post-war baby boom was largely a phenomenon of the white-collar classes. Their birth rate almost doubled between 1940 and 1960 and accounted for most of the rise in births in that period. The proportion of families of five or more children continued its long decline. Group differentials lost much of their significance.

Socioeconomic influences on decisions to have children is even more clearly illustrated by the rapidly changing events in Europe in the last twenty years; the lack of housing, low family income, and high inflation rates have caused many young couples to decide against having children, resulting in significant drops in fertility rates in many countries. Several Eastern European countries have reduced total fertility rates (TFR)[4] below replacement level (TFR of 2.1) but Romania and Poland have maintained a replacement level TFR despite the hardships confronting young families. The TFR for the Soviet Union is 2.5, which is an average for the total population of 291 million people, while the religious beliefs of the central Asian Republics of the Soviet Union have influenced a tradition of large families and have contributed to fertility rates two to three times the national average. On the other hand, improved economic circumstances can also have the same results, a reduction in family size. Spain and Italy have significantly improved their economic positions over the last decade while the TFR reduced from 2.6 to 1.5 (Spain) and 2.0 to 1.3 (Italy). These examples serve to illustrate that fluctuations of population sizes between generations or between ethnic groups are the result of complex forces which may quickly alter demographic processes because of social or natural factors.

EPIDEMIOLOGICAL TRANSITION

The developed countries of the Western world have passed through several stages of what may be termed an "epidemiological transition" (Omran, 1982). The first stage was periodic episodes of high mortality

---

[4] The average number of live births for all women living through their reproductive years.

from outbreaks of infectious diseases like smallpox, cholera, typhoid, the black plague, and a variety of respiratory diseases. One or another of these diseases would spread throughout the poorly housed, poorly fed populations crowded into the growing cities of western Europe of the eighteenth century. These diseases caused the highest mortality among the young child and infant; life expectancy at birth was between 20 to 40 years. The improvements in sanitation, housing, and living conditions in general quickly reduced the impact of many of these infectious diseases and shifted the higher mortality rates to older age groups; children were now more likely to survive to adulthood. This was the second stage when life expectancy increased to fifty years.

The third stage of the transition was beginning at about 1900 when there were major shifts in causes of death. Because of preventive measures several infectious diseases no longer plagued populations of the developed countries, though they remained a problem in many of the developing countries. The incidence of gastrointestinal diseases, several childhood diseases, tuberculosis, and pneumonia, all once the leading causes of death have been reduced to insignificant levels in the U.S. The major causes of death are now the chronic, degenerate types of disease, such as cardio-vascular disease, cancer, and respiratory disease (Table 8-6), which begin to appear at middle age and are major causes of mortality in older and older age groups each decade. Several kinds of cancers and cardiovascular disease have steadily increased to replace tuberculosis and pneumonia as number-one causes of death. By midcentury, life expectancy had increased to sixty-five years, and there is a greater risk of dying from one of several of the chronic degenerate diseases. New threats occur in the form of chronic respiratory diseases, like emphysema and bronchitis, and have become significant factors in the death rates. In the 1980s acquired immune deficiency syndrome (AIDS), which became the fifteenth leading cause of death (5.5 per 100,000 population) in 1987,[5] is a new cause of mortality.

Improved nutrition, cleaner water, and more effective waste disposal had brought on the decline of the infectious diseases. Our changing life-style accompanying urbanization and the rise of industrialization and its pollution, together with tobacco smoking and overeating however, have contributed to the increase of heart, lung, and cancer diseases. Overeating, especially of animal fats, and limited exercise are believed to be contributing factors to cardiovascular diseases. The American Heart Association, for example, has recommended for years that Americans reduce total caloric intake and limit fat consumption, and has bolstered its recommendation

---

[5] AIDS is caused by a virus, human immune deficiency virus (HIV), which has a latent period of several years before symptoms begin to appear and, given the number of known carriers today, future mortality rates are expected to rise significantly.

TABLE 8-6 Average Annual Death Rates per 100,000 from Fifteen Leading Causes, United States, 1900 and 1987

1900		1987	
ALL CAUSES	1,755.0	ALL CAUSES	872.4
1. Tuberculosis	201.9	1. Diseases of heart	312.4
2. Influenza and pneumonia	181.5	2. Malignant neoplasms	195.9
3. Diarrhea and enteritis	133.2	3. Cerebrovascular diseases	61.6
4. Diseases of heart	132.1	4. All Accidents	39.0
5. Congenital malformations[1]	91.8	5. Chronic obstructive pulmonary disease	32.2
6. Acute & chronic nephritis	89.0	6. Pneumonia and influenza	28.4
7. Cerebral hemorrhage, embolism	75.0	7. Diabetes mellitus	15.8
8. Bronchitis and broncho-pneumonia	67.6	8. Suicide	12.7
9. Cancer & other malignant tumors	63.0	9. Chronic liver disease & cirrhosis	10.8
10. Diphtheria	43.3	10. Atherosclerosis	9.2
11. Typhoid & paratyphoid	35.9	11. Nephritis, nephrotic syndrome & nephrosis	9.1
12. Cirrhosis of the liver	12.9	12. Homicide	8.7
13. Measles	12.5	13. Septicemia	8.2
14. Whooping Cough	12.1	14. Certain conditions originating in the perinatal period	7.5
15. Diabetes mellitus	9.7	15. Human immunodeficiency virus infection	5.5

[1] Classification includes all diseases and malformations of early infancy contributing to deaths after the first year of life.

Sources: U.S. Government Printing Office, 1930; U.S. Dept. of Health and Human Services, 1989, and U.S. Department of Commerce, 1976.

with convincing statistics that show that high cholesterol and overweight contribute to heart disease.

Just as in the case of infant-mortality rates discussed previously, the leading causes of death also differ between the two groups of countries, the MDC and LDC. Whereas heart disease, cancer, and vascular disease head the list in the developed countries, gastroenteritis, pneumonia, and malaria aggravated by malnutrition are the major causes of death in the developing nations. World Health Organization surveys show that whenever people adopt the dietary habits of the more affluent nations, however, certain chronic diseases increase.

Cardiovascular Diseases

Arteriosclerosis, particularly of the coronary arteries of the heart, is the leading cause of death in the affluent societies. This disease is literally a "hardening" of the arteries through an accumulation of lipids (mainly cholesterol) and calcium salts, which gradually blocks blood flow. The smaller coronary arteries that feed the heart muscles are often the first to suffer restricted blood circulation, and coronary heart disease results. Once a rare affliction mainly of the elderly, coronary and other vascular diseases occur more and more frequently in younger adults. The presence of arteriosclerosis was seen in 77 percent of the autopsies of American soldiers killed during the Korean War. These were young (the average age was twenty-two) and apparently healthy individuals (Newman, 1961).

In the United States this disease accounts for one in three deaths, and in western Europe this cause of fatalities is nearly as high. Certain developing countries are suffering an increase in coronary disease among the wealthier classes who are adopting western lifestyles. As their incomes rise, so does their consumption of animal protein and fats together with an overabundance of total calories. The dietary influence is underscored by the experiences of several European populations during World War II. The incidence of coronary heart disease dropped to one-third of the prewar incidence in Finland and the Netherlands, but after the war, as nutrition rose back up to prewar levels, so did coronary heart disease, which reached a peak in most MDC in the early 1970s and then began to decline. A realization of the importance of proper diet and exercise began to influence a change in lifestyle, and several countries showed a dramatic decrease. The United States reduced the rate from 470 in 1975 to 312.4 per 100,000 in 1987.

A ranking of 52 nations for mortality rates from all types of cardiovascular diseases showed a broad difference, from a low of 119.4 per 100,000 deaths in Guatemala to a high of 449.7 in Romania (54 percent of deaths from all causes). Other high rates are found throughout Eastern Europe. By contrast, Finland, New Zealand, northern Ireland, and Denmark, are in the midrange of cardiovascular rates (36, 33, 39, and 18) but rank at the top for death rates from coronary heart disease (47, 46, 52, and 42). Considering only highly developed countries, Japan has the third lowest mortality rate, whereas France is the fourth lowest for all cardiovascular diseases (World Health Organization, 1987; see also Polednak, 1989: 67–72). These differences are a source of numerous questions regarding lifestyles that relate to health, as well as genetic influences. In all nations reporting health statistics of individuals by ethnic group significant variation is seen between the groups.

In Finland, for example, a country with one of the higher coronary heart disease rates, the Lapps have a significantly lower rate than the national average. Finns living in a region of northern Norway have higher coronary heart disease rates than Norwegians and Lapps living in the same area. Careful studies of populations in another high-rate country, New Zealand, also reveal considerable ethnic group differences. Maori, the Aboriginal inhabitants, had a higher rate than those of European descent; there was even a significant difference between Maori who followed the Mormon religion and those who did not. The Mormon Maori had the lower incidence, but an interesting aspect of the study was the finding that Maori women were at higher risk from coronary heart disease, the reverse of results from so many other studies that showed males at a higher risk (Prior, et al., 1986).

Coronary heart diseases, their debilitating sequel of reduced physical activity and risk of early death are problems confronting all people. The chance of heart disease is increased with aging, by certain life-styles, and with some diets. In the many epidemiological studies, high-risk groups have been identified: Sex is the first distinction made (males are at greater risk than females), and the list goes on to include smoking, the use of alcohol, and overeating. A familial factor, the history of heart disease in the family, is noted as well but whether there are gene products affecting heart disease risk is not clear though several possibilities have been proposed. Ethnic group risk is even more difficult to define because so often minorities (frequently identified as one or another ethnic group) lead significantly different life-styles; Maori of New Zealand, Samoans, or recent Asian immigrants in the United States are some examples (see Baker et al., 1986). During most of this century, however, attention has been directed to studies of the higher mortality and morbidity rates among American blacks because of the varying frequencies of several diseases and because of the frequent reports of hypertension among this group.

Hypertension

On average, blood pressure rises with age, at least among populations of the developed world. Though there is no clear-cut division between normal and high blood pressure, significant differences have been reported among national groups, and between social and ethnic groups within a country. In the United States, American blacks—both males and females—have consistently higher pressures than whites. These differences have been attributed to dietary habits, the frequent and heavy use of common table salt (sodium chloride), for example, and probably genetic factors as well. It has been hypothesized that American blacks may be highly sensitive to sodium intake because of their ancestors' genetic adaptation to diets that were assumed to be low in salt because their original homeland, West Central Africa, is a region low in available salt supplies (Wilson, 1986). A more likely explanation is the frustration and tensions encountered in the daily lives of persons of lower socioeconomic status. African-Americans as well as other minority groups around the world encounter many stressful situations in their daily lives, and there is ample physiological evidence that anxiety and tension brought about by many causes can quickly elevate blood pressure. Even the measurement procedure itself is often a sufficient cause of anxiety.

The stresses of modern living certainly influence us all to some degree. Populations living in isolated rural communities frequently show lower average blood pressures than their relatives living in urban areas. When Aboriginal peoples move to cities and adopt Western life-styles, one of the earliest detectable physiological responses is increased blood pressures. This relocation effect has been measured in peoples as diverse as Eskimo, New Guinea highlanders, Solomon Islanders, and Australian Aboriginals. In their native environments, not only is there no hypertension, but there is no increase in blood pressure with age, as is typically recorded for Europeans and persons of European ancestry. In addition, nomadic tribes of East Africa, normally with low pressure patterns, increase blood pressure when they adopt a sedentary life-style. The same experience is shared by numerous other tribal groups throughout Africa (Hutt and Burkitt, 1986). A feature common among these low blood pressure communities is a low salt intake, while diverse ethnic groups on high-salt diets show a similar history of rising blood pressure with age. The salt intake level and blood pressure relationship is not as simple as once thought, however. Other factors such as the intake of potassium are influential; an increase in this element in proportion to sodium lowers the "salt risk" factor.

Regardless of the causes, hypertension is a serious risk factor in cardiovascular diseases, and together with diet (the rich high-fat, high-protein diet of developed countries) affect an increase in the mortality from these diseases. The rate has been declining during the past decade in the United States, partly because of the realization of the dietary influences and an appreciation of the need for exercise. Cardiovascular mortality, however, remains at the top of the list of leading causes of death and is often referred to as a disease of "affluence." The consumption of an excess of calories, through a refined carbohydrate high-fat diet leads to a state of overnutrition and its disease sequel, as can be clearly demonstrated by the increases observed among developing countries when a segment of the population adopts a Western diet and sedentary life-style.

Cancer

A variety of malignant neoplasms are grouped under the term *cancer* because they have certain characteristics in common. A malignant neoplasm is formed when a collection of cells radically change their normal functions and begin to multiply rapidly in uncontrolled growth, which eventually leads to a spreading and an overcoming of healthy tissues in other parts of the body. There are one hundred varieties of this disease classified according to the site or organ in which its originates (lung, skin, breast, prostate, and so on). Certain cancers are more lethal than others, and approximately 50 percent of the malignancies may prove to be fatal. The fatality rate depends a great deal on the type of neoplasm, the length of time it had grown before detection, and, of course, the treatment. The cure rate of skin cancers (basal and squamous types) is close to 100 percent, whereas it is less than 50 percent for lung cancer and the third type of skin cancer, melanoma. About 22 percent of the deaths in the United States are due to malignant neoplasms compared with the 35 percent caused by cardiovascular disease. Though heart disease-related deaths leveled off about 1970, deaths from cancers continued to climb during this period. The cancer death rate increased 5.2 percent in 1975 over the previous year, which contrasts to the steady 1 percent annual increase since 1933. The rate decreased slightly in 1988 and 1989 in the United States, however, while increasing among many of the LDC.

Causes of many cancers are still obscure—that is, the mechanisms that cause cells to become malignant are not known for certain, though there are several studies that suggest a mutation in the somatic cells' DNA as a probable cause (Ames, 1979, 1983). Ionizing radiation from x-rays, nuclear power, or cosmic rays have long been known to have mutagenic effects. In addition, persons who have been exposed to fallout from atomic testing have two to three times the national average for leukemia. Another source, ultraviolet rays from the sun, causes skin cancer, which occurs most frequently in fairer skinned persons and usually on the backs of the hands and parts of the face. Skin cancer is more likely in those fair-skinned persons whose occupations keep them outdoors a good part of the day (see chapter 6).

In addition, relationships have been suggested between malignancy and a number of factors. Close correlations are seen between certain diets and cancers of the stomach and colon; between alcohol and esophagus, throat, and mouth cancer; and between tobacco smoke and lung cancer. A long list of organic chemicals and substances like asbestos fibers are also implicated as causes of cancers of the lung, liver, and bladder, especially because workers exposed to them through their occupations have an extremely high incidence of certain types of cancer (lung cancer among asbestos plant workers, for example). Cancers of the lung, large intestine, and breast cause about half of all cancer deaths. Lung cancer, described by Cairns (1975:69) as "a disease of the twentieth century" is closely related to cigarette smoking; the risk of lung cancer is fifty times greater in smokers (Figure 8-8) than in nonsmokers. Many health officials have pointed out that if tobacco smoking were abolished, this form of cancer would be nearly eliminated, though air pollution is considered a contributing cause. Further evidence is provided by the rising incidence of lung cancer among females who, as a group, began to adopt the smoking habit some twenty to thirty years after the males. The rate among women was more than three times as great in 1985 as in 1950, whereas the male rate

Packs per Person   **Deaths per 100,000**

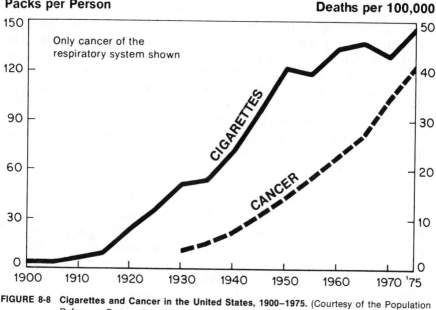

FIGURE 8-8   **Cigarettes and Cancer in the United States, 1900–1975.** (Courtesy of the Population Reference Bureau, Inc., Washington, D.C.)

increased 2.7 times during this period. Though tobacco use in much of the developed world has declined this past decade, especially in the United States, it is on the increase in many Third World countries, especially throughout Asia, and lung diseases of all types are expected to increase while a decline is already evident in the developed countries (Lopez, 1990).

Food habits are another likely cause of certain types of cancers. A diet high in meat and fat but low in cereals (especially unrefined) appears to be closely linked to cancer of the large intestine; a significant factor appears to be the low amount of dietary fibers in the high meat, fat, and refined carbohydrate diet. The distribution of colon cancer corresponds closely with dietary quality, and this form of cancer varies considerably between countries; the MDC have the highest incidence (Burkitt, 1971). Because of this relationship to polysaturated fats of the diet, a great deal of attention has been directed to the fat and fiber content consumed by wealthy nations. The results have reinforced the earlier observations of dietary influences (Cohen, 1987).

The most frequent cancer of women, breast cancer, has a world distribution similar to that of colon cancer in males. Because this distribution closely follows dietary quality, it is possible that some factor(s) are lost in the refined diet. Women on refined diets lacking in whole grain have higher rates of breast cancer (American women, for example). Though the evidence is not all in yet, it seems that the element selenium and vitamin E may be the factors involved because these substances are found in abundance in many whole grains but are mostly lost during refining processes. Test results have shown the antioxidant properties of selenium and vitamin E which work to protect cell membranes from oxidation by products of cell metabolism (Combs and Scott, 1977). The general functions of selenium in human nutrition are becoming better understood as well as its influence on certain cancer sites (Levander, 1987). The environmental influence (dietary), rather than genetic, is supported by the examples of Japanese women who migrated to Hawaii. Here, within two generations, their breast cancer rates were nearer those of Hawaiian women (80 per 100,000) than in Japan (11 per 100,000).

The preceding examples plus others suggest that many cancers, perhaps 70 to 90 percent of the cases, are environmentally determined (Cairns, 1975; Mayer, 1983). The data on diet, the incidence of environmental pollutants, the use of alcohol, and smoking all point to this possibility. Additional evidence is provided by a comparison of ethnic groups that have migrated and adopted the new diets in their new homeland. Japan has a very high rate of stomach cancer, but Japanese immigrants in California have significantly lower incidences. Sons of the immigrants have an even lower incidence, one which is much closer to that experienced by Americans of European ancestry (Figure 8-9). The high frequency of stomach cancer in Japan may be due to the diet that contains large quantities of salt fish and pickled vegetables. Other groups with similar diets also have high rates of this disease: Iceland, Finland, and Norway, for example, where large quantities of dried, salted fish are eaten.

Further evidence of the environmental effects on the course of the disease is offered by the increase of cancer incidence with age. Cairns described the older than 60 years of age population as the group at greatest risk. He reasoned that the longer one is exposed to carcinogenic factors, the greater the chance of the disease; the effects of many carcinogenic substances may not show up until twenty to forty years after exposure. With an increased number of persons living into their eighties, a higher cancer rate is to be expected. Finally, for many, the work environment has proved to contain many substances that are carcinogenic, but the tumors will not show up until years later. Asbestos fibers, silicates in quartz dust, and polyvinyl chloride (cause of liver cancer) lead the list of dangerous substances, which includes insecticides and organic solvents, many of which have been too recently introduced into the environment to understand their long-term biological effects fully.

Diabetes

This disease, diabetes mellitus, is a complex syndrome principally characterized by the inability to maintain blood sugar levels within a normal range. This condition of "glucose intolerance" has a variety of

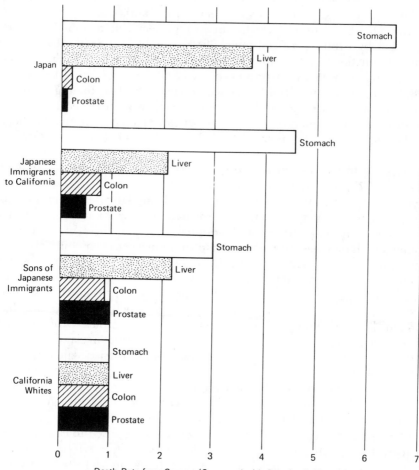

Death Rate from Cancers (Compared with Rate for California Whites)

Change in incidence of various cancers with migration from Japan to the United States provides evidence that the cancers are caused by components of the environment that differ in the two countries. The incidence of each kind of cancer is expressed as the ratio of the death rate in the population being considered to that in a hypothetical population of California whites with the same age distribution; the death rates for whites are thus defined as 1. The death rates among immigrants and immigrants' sons tend consistently toward California norms, but the change required more than a generation, suggesting that causative agents are factors influenced by culture rather than hazards to which all are exposed equally.

FIGURE 8-9   Death Rate from Cancers. (From Cairns, J., "The Cancer Problem." Copyright © 1975 by Scientific American, Inc. All Rights Reserved.)

causes; the insufficiency of insulin (a pancreatic hormone regulating glucose levels), cellular insensitivity to the action of insulin, an excess of glucagon (another hormone of the pancreas), and a host of other causes—some caused by rare genetic defects of carbohydrate metabolism. The most frequent expressions of the disease are classified into two categories: type I, juvenile or insulin dependent (IDDM), and type II, an adult-onset form or noninsulin dependent (NIDDM). The juvenile or IDDM type is least frequent, has a significant genetic influence for susceptibility to certain pancreatic virus, and the symptoms appear by adolescence or young adult age. It is controlled, principally by insulin injection. Type II, NIDDM, is the most common form, and the symptoms of high blood glucose levels usually appear after 40 years of age. There is a genetic component influencing susceptibility suggested by family and twin studies, but there are significant environmental influences, principally dietary, which have been identified. With major dietary and life-style changes in many populations, type II diabetes has increased dramatically over the past decades and continues to rise (Harris, 1990). Because it has become a significant health threat and is now one of the leading causes of death, the balance of the discussion will consider only this type of diabetes.

Once only the twenty-seventh commonest cause of death, diabetes has now reached near-epidemic proportions and is the seventh most frequent cause of death in the United States. Though medical treatment has kept the death rate from rising further, the number of diabetics has increased by 60 percent among whites and 120 percent among blacks between 1966 and 1981. Today, there are approximately ten million cases reported in the United States with five hundred thousand new cases added each year. Because a diabetic, over the years, gradually develops impaired circulation and is more prone to kidney failure, heart disease, and blindness by late middle age, the number of people involved and the cost to a population in diabetic-related illness and death is even higher (Diabetes in America, USDHHS, 1985).

Though there is a hereditary influence, this disease is closely linked to overeating; it follows the spread of an affluent diet and one high in refined carbohydrates. In developing countries diabetes is found mainly in urban areas that contain the wealthier populations. For example, among the rich urban residents of India, diabetes is twice as likely to develop as among the rural poor. Further, though rare among Japanese women before the end of World War II, diabetes is now the eighth most frequent cause of death among this group. In Puerto Rico, though the general health of the population improved during the economic boom of the 1960s, diabetes rose from twelfth place to become the eighth most frequent cause of death (Eckholm, 1977).

Further evidence of the influence of Western-type[6] diets is provided by the experiences of populations like Australian Aboriginals and several groups of Native Americans. The Pima and Papago of Southern Arizona are especially predisposed to diabetes in middle age; more than 60 percent of the adults, aged forty-five to sixty-five, were diagnosed as diabetic, which was a 50 percent increase since the epidemiological survey of 1965. Other Native American groups also have significantly higher rates than the U.S. average (up to nineteen times as high); in addition, Mexican Americans also show a high incidence of diabetes (Knowler et al., 1990). Other ethnic differences are seen among American blacks who had twice the diabetic rate as that found among whites, with females of both groups higher than the males (Harris, 1990). Among Australian Aboriginals who have adopted Western diets (high in sugar and flour), the incidence of diabetes has been found to be 10 percent compared with only 2.3 percent among a European population living near the Aboriginal reserve where the study was carried out (Kirk et al., 1985).

Throughout the Pacific, similar high diabetes rates are reported for those Polynesians or Melanesians who have "urbanized" and adopted the Western diet, ceased to work as hard as formerly, and have substantially increased average body weight. People on the island of Nauru are a classic example of detrimental health effects of a changing life-style. This small Pacific island is populated by people with one of the world's highest diabetic rates, about 42.2 percent. The disease was unknown before 1945 but, following the mining of the island's rich phosphate deposits, the population's income rose to thirty-four thousand dollars per capita, another world record. With this newfound wealth they radically changed their living habits, purchasing all of the available goods of the developed world from airplanes to motorcycles, and especially imported foods. The result is near universal obesity and a record incidence of diabetes (Zimmet, 1982).

There is no single explanation for this dramatic difference between ethnic groups. There is a probability, however, that certain groups are genetically better adapted to the type of diet humans had consumed for 99 percent of the species' existence, a diet highly variable in quantity with a large mixture of complex carbohydrates. Neel (1962, 1982) offered a hypothesis he called the "thrifty genotype," which could explain the food-storage capacity of certain peoples. He noted that hunters' and gatherers' diets range between "feast to famine," times of scarcity alternated by plenty, when the people gorge themselves. During these times, persons with the physiological ability to convert and store the excess food as fat are at an advantage. The surplus food energy enables them to endure the

---

[6] Western-type diets refer to the typical diet consumed in developed countries, emphasizing highly refined carbohydrates in particular.

periodic episodes of starvation. Neel proposed that their insulin-producing beta cells in the pancreas are more sensitive to stimulus, and the insulin increased rapidly and aided in this energy storage. If such persons, however, continuously consumed large quantities of refined carbohydrates during a long period, as in the case of so many peoples today, they would exhaust their insulin-secreting potential by middle age. They would then become unable to regulate their blood-glucose levels within physiologically acceptable limits. Another advantage of efficient energy storage is offered by Prior (1971) who suggested that Polynesians, famous for their long sea voyages, were another example of a population who rapidly became obese on a food surplus, a characteristic that served them well in ancient times on the open ocean. Even in the tropical climate of the South Pacific, cold temperatures can be a problem when the sun goes down; the temperature drops rapidly and people in small outrigger canoes are exposed to cold winds causing a rapid loss of body heat. Persons with thicker fatty layers were better insulated and thus protected from metabolic heat loss; such individuals would also have an excess of stored energy. In modern times this tendency for rapid weight gain, once an advantage, now contributes to a high incidence of type II diabetes.

These examples of epidemiological transition illustrate some aspects of environmental influence on human survival and, hence, on the composition of the human genome. These environmental changes, however, occur very rapidly through human intervention, and the pace of change is ever accelerating as technology increases in its complexity. We use space differently from before, and we readily shift from one dietary complex to another, gaining more food energy per unit mass but taxing our metabolism with the unwanted results described earlier.

DISEASE EPIDEMICS AND SELECTION

The scourge of epidemics throughout human history that have caused wide fluctuation in population growth gives evidence of the probability that many of our genetic polymorphisms today are the result of past natural selection. We have given examples of probable resistance of certain genotypes of the ABO blood groups to disease in our previous discussions in chapter 6. Though these examples are based on statistical correlations, as we noted earlier, infectious diseases, which have periodically killed thousands during the past millennia, should be seriously considered as probable agents of natural selection. Plague, cholera, typhus, smallpox, and typhoid, to mention a few, have had dramatic effects on civilization throughout recorded history. Wars were won or lost, cities were abandoned, and civilizations have fallen because of epidemics. In past warfare, often more casualties were caused by disease than by bullets. An example is typhus, which, along with freezing weather and malnutrition, accounted for most of the deaths among Napoleon's troops in 1812 during their war with Russia. Typhoid fever killed more Union soldiers during the American Civil War than died in all of the battles fought. In fact, of the 364,000 deaths, only 140,400 were from battle wounds; the remaining 224,000 fatalities were due to disease.

Smallpox

The invasion of the Americans by Europeans more than four hundred years ago demonstrated the effect of infectious diseases on peoples without a history of prior contact and who, therefore, had low resistance. Millions of American Indians died—an estimated 1.5 million in Mexico alone—and smallpox is believed to have been the main cause. This deadly disease, which killed even Europeans at a rate of four out of ten, passed from village to village, from the time of its introduction in Vera Cruz in 1507. Eventually the "pox" extended northward into what is now Arizona and New Mexico. Entire populations in the Southwest died from epidemics even before they were visited by Europeans (McNeill, 1976).

In modern times smallpox has been responsible for many deaths even in those populations with a long history of contact with the disease. There were an estimated 2.5 million cases in 1967, mainly in South America, Africa, and parts of South Asia, but stringent vaccination regulations brought this number down to slightly more than 100,000 by 1972. No cases were reported for 1978, and the disease is believed to have been eradicated entirely, but a constant watch is maintained by the World Health Organization.[7] This control of smallpox and other infectious diseases, a remarkable achievement of modern health science, should not be allowed to make us complacent, however. There is a continuous struggle between humans and microbes, and to maintain the low death rates enjoyed by the last two generations, perpetual vigilance is necessary (DuBos, 1968).

Cholera

Cholera, a major cause of epidemics spread by transmission of the bacteria through contaminated food and water, has reappeared periodically, killing millions. When crowded conditions exist, accompanied by poor sanitation, the population is at grave risk for infection from these bacteria. For example, 50,000 cases were reported in New York in 1866,

---

[7] The last endemic case of smallpox in Africa and worldwide was located in Somalia on 26 October 1977. The patient, a twenty-three-year-old hospital cook, made a complete recovery. In 1980 at the thirty-third World Health Assembly meeting in Geneva, smallpox was declared officially eradicated from the planet.

but there were only a few reported in 1900. The provision of clear water and improved sanitation reduced the danger of a reoccurrence in many areas. In the same year (1900) that New York suffered only a few cases of cholera, nearly a million persons died of the disease in India. Since a major world epidemic reported in 1919, the disease has appeared sporadically throughout Africa and Asia. Spreading from a base in Indonesia, cholera broke out in a new epidemic in 1970, but major efforts by the World Health Organization brought it under control. Cholera has continued to decline since 1972, but it still remains a danger to world health, as witnessed by experiences in the South Pacific where cholera had never been identified before. The disease was introduced onto the island of Tarawa through bacteria carried by an unsuspecting traveler and spread quickly throughout many of the islands in the Gilbert chain (Maung, 1979). Between September and December 1977, the first cholera epidemic in South Pacific history claimed 21 victims. A total of 1102 cases was reported, but the death toll was kept to a minimum by early diagnosis and the ready availability of modern treatment.

The experiences of Peru in the first half of 1991 further illustrates the ever present threat of cholera when modern societies are disrupted. The breakdown in sanitation services, water distribution, and the grossly overcrowded capital city of Lima have contributed to a modern epidemic. As of February, 23,000 cases have been reported; fortunately there have been only a few hundred deaths, but at this time the epidemic is still spreading.

CHANGING ENVIRONMENT AND NATURAL SELECTION

During those recent times just a few generations ago, when bacterial and protozoan diseases were at their peak, any gene or gene combination that reduced susceptibility would have had a marked effect on survival. The selective advantage of certain genotypes in an era of massive epidemics would have been an important factor in the biological evolution of *Homo sapiens*, particularly with rapid growth rates and major population shifts during the past few thousand years. The most recent outbreaks, summarized in Table 8-7, can be used to trace a significant change in our disease environment. The total effect has been the alteration of combinations of disease organisms with which humans are in most frequent contact (McKeown, 1985).

These changing patterns of disease and mortality undoubtedly cause alteration in gene frequencies, and certain polymorphisms will be selected for or against in the future. Examination of disease influences can provide a way of interpreting population variation and selection through time. Anthropologists attempting to understand human diversity several gen-

TABLE 8-7   Historical Outline of Three Selected Diseases

DISEASE	DATE	EPIDEMIC HISTORY	DEATHS REPORTED
Plague	540	Beginning of first Pandemic, which lasted 50 to 60 years in Europe	100,000,000 (estimated)
	1338	Start of second Pandemic, which lasted nearly three centuries	25–43,000,000
	1664	Last outbreak of plague of the second Pandemic in London	
	1855	Start of third Pandemic, which covered a greater land area, including the U.S., India, China, and Mongolia, which suffered the worst	13,000,000 (mostly 1896–1917)
	1907	Year of maximum death rate of third Pandemic	1,315,892
	1923	Third Pandemic	250,000
	1942	Last outbreak of third Pandemic	10,577
Smallpox	15–17th centuries	American Indian populations	Millions of deaths estimated
	17th century	Outbreak in Europe	60,000,000
	1707	Iceland	18,000 of total population of 50,000
	1721	Boston's sixth epidemic—5985 with disease	895
	1770	India	3,000,000 .
	1776	Almost half of Revolutionary army of 10,000 suffered from the disease	
	1870	France, time of Franco-Prussian War, 100,000 cases	25,000
	1873	India	500,000
	1885	Montreal, Canada, 20,000 cases	3000
	1921	United States, 89,357 cases	481
	1945	United States, 346 cases	12
	1950	United States, 42 cases	None
	1977	Somalia, 1 case	
Cholera	1817	With India as a focal point, disease spread to Ceylon, Java, Borneo, and Indonesia	100,000 (reported in Java)
	1831	Mecca	18,000 (in 3 weeks)
	1832	England	5432
	1832	Belgium	8000
	1832	Canada—disease spread through United States to Mexico, Peru, and Chile	1000 (in 2 weeks)

TABLE 8-7 Historical Outline of Three Selected Diseases (*Continued*)

DISEASE	DATE	EPIDEMIC HISTORY	DEATHS REPORTED
Cholera	1866	The fourth Pandemic dates from this year with a major outbreak in Russia	90,000
	1866	United States	50,000
	1867	Sardinia	130,000
	1875	Hungary	190,000
	1877	China	89,000 (estimated)
	1899	Start of sixth Pandemic, which lasted until 1923	
	1900	Worst year of cholera on record, a major outbreak in India	800,000
	1906	India	682,649
	1919	India	565,166
	1960–1970	A total world caseload of 70,000 per year	21,000 (estimated)
	1991	Peru	1200

Sources: Based on Gallagher, 1969; Stamp, 1964; and World Population Data Sheet, 1980.

erations in the future will likely be puzzled by the persistence of many seemingly deleterious genes, unless, of course, they understand human history and consider the alteration of environmental factors and natural selection.

Genetic Load

The usual measure of genetic load is the frequency of lethal or deleterious genes within a population. Every gene pool contains a quantity of alleles, either dominant or recessive, which may reduce the fitness of the carrier. As environments are altered, the selective forces also change and the intensity of selection at a particular locus may be reduced. An allele that had been detrimental in the former environment may no longer reduce fitness, and in theory the frequency of the allele would rise through the generations, increasing the "genetic load" of the populations. Today, for example, individuals with some genetic diseases can be maintained by medical treatment and will in many cases live through their reproductive years. They may even pass on the defective allele. Should their environment ever change again—for example, revert back to its original state— then selection would increase to its formerly high intensity and the homozygous recessives would have reduced fitness. The magnitude of a population's genetic load, however, is generally underestimated though some gloomy appraisals of the species point out that everyone is heterozygous for many deleterious genes, and new mutations are continuously added to this load.

Modern medicine, after its success with infectious diseases, is now developing treatments for genetic disease. Medical intervention enables the survival of individuals who suffer from any one of a number of types of inherited metabolic defects and congenital abnormalities. Although such treatment may not eliminate natural selection altogether, it does reduce its effects.

Congenital Defects[8]

There are a number of disorders which, in former times, would have reduced the chances of survival beyond childhood or even beyond infancy. Many defects are now correctable by medical or surgical intervention, and the individuals can survive and lead normal lives. A common disorder like *cleft palate* (which occurs in one out of twenty-five hundred births) often resulted in an early death for the severest cases before this century, but it has been correctable by surgery for many years. A relatively minor muscular defect, *pyloric stenosis*, an enlargement of the muscle ring controlling the opening between the stomach and small intestine, killed most infants who had it before 1912, because food was prevented from entering the digestive tract from the stomach. Since 1912, this fairly common defect (two out of one thousand births) has been corrected by a minor surgical procedure. Numerous other developmental defects of the digestive tract can now be corrected by surgery. Likewise many defects of the musculo-skeletal system may be repaired; dislocation of the hip or clubfoot are examples of conditions that were once significant impairments to an active, healthy life that are now treatable.

Among the greatest achievements in the corrections of congenital malformations is in the treatment of heart defects. Since the development of advanced heart surgery techniques, numerous commonly occurring defects of the heart and major blood vessels that were formerly the chief cardiovascular causes of infant death can be repaired. Table 8-8 list some of the more frequent conditions whose early diagnosis and treatment has saved the lives of thousands of infants. Patent ductus arteriosus is one of the important examples. This blood vessel shutting some of the blood flow from the aorta (the large artery carrying blood from the heart) to the pulmonary artery during the fetal stage may remain open and functioning, depriving the infant of a portion of the oxygenated blood leaving the heart. Wastefully, this oxygenated blood is shifted back to the lungs without passing through the rest of the circulatory system. Such a condition places the infant at high risk, and even if the person survives, growth and physical activity is seriously impaired. This and other more

---

[8] A defect present at birth that may be determined genetically or may be due to external influences on the intrauterine environment (for example, maternal drug addiction or disease).

TABLE 8-8   Examples of Congential Cardiovascular Abnormalities Amenable to Surgery in Infants*

Ventricular septal defect	Coarction of aorta
Atrial septal defect	Truncus arteriosis
Patent ductus arteriosus	Transposition of great arteries
Pulmonary stenosis	Tricuspid atresia
Aortic stenosis	

* With the rapid advances in the diagnosis and treatment of the neonate and even the fetus, many congenital deformities which formerly caused death can now be corrected. This partial listing adapted from *The Merck Manual of Diagnosis and Therapy* provides some examples.

critical defects are amenable to surgical correction and has been of great advantage to those populations where modern medicine is available. In much of the Third World, however, infant deaths from these and other congenital defects are high because of the lack of medical care.

Genetic Disease

In all, there are more than two thousand simply inherited disorders known, and several can now be successfully treated to enable the afflicted person to lead a relatively normal life. A classic example is *hemophilia A*, which is inherited as an X-linked recessive that causes a deficiency in the action of a globulin factor (factor VII) and prevents the normal clotting of blood. This affliction occurs in approximately one in twenty-five thousand males. Before treatment was available, it usually caused death at an early age. Through treatment with blood coagulant factors, many of the hemophiliac's problems have been reduced, and life expectancy has been extended well beyond the previously expected eighteen years.[9] A more common genetic disease, inherited as an autosomal recessive gene, is *cystic fibrosis*—one of the most commonly known errors of metabolism in Caucasian populations (one out of every two thousand or three thousand live births). Persons with this condition have a malfunctioning of the exocrine glands in many of their tissues (the pancreas in particular). They suffer from clogged bronchial tubes that become obstructed with an accumulation of thick mucous deposits and are prone to respiratory infections and malfunctioning of the pancreas. Before treatment was available, most people with this disease died in early childhood; now, careful management of cystic fibrosis patients has extended their life expectancy into adulthood, about the midthirties.

Another affliction, *retinoblastoma*, an inherited malignancy of the retina of the eye that appears early in childhood, will cause death if

---

[9] Because the treatment requires the use of blood products (clotting factors), a tragic side effect has been the infection of many hemophiliacs with the human immune deficiency virus.

untreated. Surgical and medical treatment can now increase the chances of survival. In addition to such genetic defects, several hormone deficiencies influencing metabolic processes have also been identified, and treatments have been developed. Growth hormones and other pituitary deficiencies can also be alleviated, and persons with such defects can lead normal lives and reproduce with the chance of passing on that genetic component that influenced the appearance of the defect.

The survival of individuals with these genetic diseases increases the frequency of the defective genes in future populations. The increase in gene defects, however, will not result in a "plague" overwhelming our gene pool. Most of the defects occur at low frequencies, and any increase would be a slow process over a long period of many generations.

Ethnic Groups and Diseases

There are several of these congenital abnormalities and genetic diseases that occur more frequently in some populations than in others. Certain afflictions are associated with one or more of the ethnic groups, and several of the major diseases are listed in Table 8-9. The explanation for the relative frequencies of these ailments that are at least partially influenced by genetic factors is not easy to come by. We might consider that in some ways we are more a product of our environment than of our genes and that in any example of inherited disease, expression of the disease depends on environmental influences. Differences in diet, living habits, and the population's history all contribute to interpopulation variability. In the case of several conditions, though, breeding behavior and population size have played a major role. Thus we find that among Hawaiians, for instance, clubfoot (caused by a partially penetrant dominant allele) occurs at a frequency of sixty-eight per 10,000 births in contrast to the eleven per 10,000 in Caucasians and six per 10,000 in Asians. The high frequency among Hawaiians probably relates to the small size of the original founder population, in addition to a high degree of inbreeding during the earlier generations. The high rate of diabetes among several groups of American Indians may have other causes, as discussed earlier; one of the most likely is their adoption of a modern diet rich in refined carbohydrates. Their insulin-secreting cells, adapted through evolution to another type of diet, are ill equipped to cope with diets that require a steady maintenance of high insulin levels.

Examples of race and genetic disease are illustrated by three autosomal recessive diseases, Tay-Sachs, cystic fibrosis, and PKU, which are most commonly found among Europeans or persons of European ancestry, and seldom among Asians or Africans. Even within this rather narrow distribution, there are striking differences among the several European ethnic groups. Tay-Sachs, for example, has a gene frequency of approx-

TABLE 8-9   Disease Incidence in Selected Ethnic Groups

ETHNIC GROUPS	RELATIVELY HIGH PREVALENCE OF THESE DISORDERS
African Black	Abnormal hemoglobin HB^s, Hb^c, thalassemia G6PD deficiency (African type) Hypertension Polydactyly Cervical cancer Sarcoidosis

American Indians
    Papago
    Apache
	
	Diabetes mellitus
	Congential hip dislocation

Ashkenazic Jews	Tay-Sachs disease Pentosuria Stub fingers Bloom's disease Leukemia Diabetes mellitus
Chinese	Thalassemia G6PD deficiency (Chinese type) Nasopharyngeal cancer

Europeans
    Northern
 	
    Southern
	
	Phenylketonuria
	Pernicious anemia
	Cleft palate
	G6PD deficiency (Mediterranean type)
	Thalassemia

Japanese	Acatalasia Oguchi's disease Cleft lip-palate Gastric cancer

Sources: Damon, 1962, 1971; and McKusick, 1967.

imately 0.015 in eastern European Jews. By contrast, other Jewish populations and non-Jewish Europeans have a frequency of less than 0.001.
This high frequency may be explained by the founder's effect. Also, it
has been suggested that the heterozygote may be more resistant to
tuberculosis, which was endemic among these populations at one time;
those families with a history of Tay-Sachs had a lower than average death
rate from tuberculosis (Rotter and Diamond, 1987). Similar explanations
have been offered for the high frequencies of PKU among western
Europeans, including the possible advantage of the heterozygote (who has
paler skin) in a region with an incidence of low ultraviolet radiation
(McCullough, 1978). The question of the frequency of cystic fibrosis is

more difficult, though the factor of the high excretion of sodium chloride by the skin through the sweat glands may hold some clues. The final explanation of the distributions of these genes will have to await further study of their biochemical influences on the general metabolism of the heterozygote.

GENETIC COUNSELING AND SELECTIVE BREEDING

With the rise of the genetic load of *Homo sapiens*, a logical course might seem to be regulation and control of mating to attempt to counteract the increase of detrimental mutants. It is fairly obvious that persons who carry a dominant gene that results in some defective development like achondrodystrophy, retinoblastoma, or Huntington's disease should carefully consider before producing children, but the case of carriers of recessive genes of low frequency is somewhat different. The chance that two persons who carry the same recessive alleles will mate is fairly remote, except in the case of cousins or individuals from the same small endogamous population. In such cases, professional genetic counseling would alert the potential mates to the possibilities of producing defective offspring, particularly if defects are known to have occurred in previous generations.

Now with recombinant DNA techniques, the actual locus of each gene can be identified as has been done for many (Carter and Willey, 1986). This method of testing can be applied to determine if a person is a carrier for a deleterious gene. The absolute control of human breeding or the use of sperm banks as advocated in the past is another matter. The full or even partial application of eugenics methods leaves much to be desired because of many unanswered questions. One of these is the possible higher fitness of the heterozygote; another is simply a question of what trait is to be selected for or against, which is a serious consideration because our species has survived and evolved through millennia because of our genetic variability. Some or perhaps most of our genetic load may even be desirable to maintain our variety. We owe our success as a species to cultural or exogenetic factors in addition to genetic adaptations. It is not the single gene in relation to the environment that determines fitness. The total fitness of an individual or a population is not measured by single or even groups of genotypes; it is the end result of the sum total of all genotypic interactions or, rather, the total genome.

We are a species whose genetic adaptations are to life-styles of an evolutionary past, mostly to a preagricultural, paleolithic form of life when population density was low and people were constantly on the move. This was the life-style of our species until approximately twelve thousand years ago, when many *Homo sapiens* became sedentary and adopted an agricultural technology. At that time, selection began to favor new forms, aided by increases in certain diseases, alteration in mating circles, and an increase in population sizes. Gradually, through the millennia, we have altered our gene frequencies. Because our environments are still changing, the frequencies of several genes will continue to alter. With an elaboration of our technologies, however, we are capable of quickly changing environments within a time span much shorter than a human generation. This factor introduces a new element into human evolution: the rapid change in selective forces, which places a heavy burden on our social systems and culture. Evolution is still very much a factor affecting our species, and "ongoing evolution" is still a reality though we have a larger hand in directing it, wittingly or unwittingly.

ONGOING EVOLUTION: EVIDENCE FROM PREHISTORY

Evidence for the evolution of recent *Homo sapiens* is difficult to identify and obtain. Evidence of an indirect sort exists, however, if we compare modern humans living in highly industrialized societies with peoples living under conditions comparable with those that have existed several thousands of years ago. Life expectancy was lower in primitive societies, and fewer individuals lived to reach adulthood. By contrast the longer life expectancy and greater population sizes among modern societies suggest a relaxation of natural selection. This *relaxed selection* has the apparent effect of increasing the frequency of defective phenotypes in a population, as explained in the preceding examples. Impressive evidence along these lines has turned up in studies of the relative frequencies of color blindness among primitive and industrialized societies. Australian Aboriginal males have a rate of only 2 percent, whereas Chinese and Japanese populations have between 4 and 7 percent, which contrasts with the 5 to 10 percent of the European and western Asian populations studied. The argument is that our preagricultural ancestors probably had a low frequency of this visual defect, which presumably would have been a handicap in their hunting activities. Those populations furthest removed in time from their hunting past would have accumulated a larger number of color-vision defectives, just as these studies have demonstrated. Visual acuity, in general, is better among "primitives" tested than among "civilized" populations, particularly in the case of myopia. There are fewer nearsighted individuals among hunters and gatherers today; also, many more people are found with exceptionally good vision. We can appreciate the obvious advantage when we consider the rigors of hunters' life-styles and their reliance on foraging activities. An example of the effect that poor eyesight may have on a person in a hunting society is offered by the story of a male in a !Kung population (Bushmen) who was not allowed to marry because he had never been able to demonstrate his skills as a hunter. His poor eyesight prevented him from hunting and caused him to be dependent on his sister for support (Post, 1965).

Several other characteristics are worth investigating, particularly those that relate to pregnancy, birth, and infant mortality. An example is the evidence that insufficiency of breast milk in newly delivered mothers is, at least in part, genetically based. There is a higher frequency of this deficiency in populations that have had the longest history of possessing dairy animals. Also, infant mortality rates are generally higher and birth rates lower in wandering, primitive, hunting groups; hence a stronger, more intense selection exists than in sedentary agricultural groups. Many other factors related to diet and disease may cause genetic differentiation among populations of various cultural forms, however.

Because we have spent approximately 99 percent of our time as a species sustained by hunting and foraging activities, we should take note of these contrasts. The greater number of skeletal defects and the higher frequency of color blindness and visual deficiency among peoples whose ancestors had been sedentary agriculturalists the longest are explained by the argument that this "new" mode of life for *Homo sapiens* reduced many of the stringent selective forces that acted during the hunting and gathering phase of our evolution. This relaxation of selection adds to the numbers of defects present in each generation.

These studies in themselves are quite interesting but are obviously limited by time; only three generations, at most, can be examined. A record of developmental defects of the skeletal and dental systems, however, is preserved for thousands of years. The skeletons of contemporary and recent populations have a greater number of defects than skeletons of groups who lived earlier. For example, there are a significantly higher number with developmental defects in the nasal septal region. These deviations in the size and shape of the nasal passages are of the kind that would have impaired breathing and would have been a focal point for infection (Wolpoff, 1969). There are several other abnormalities, such as the persistence of the metopic suture, a suture that divides the frontal bone at birth and normally fuses by one year of age. The occurrence of "peg-shaped" teeth (usually upper lateral incisors and third molars) and congenitally missing teeth are other developmental defects frequently seen; of course, there is the greater frequency of malocclusion (82 percent of American children today versus about 5 percent or fewer among Europeans several centuries ago). If a scale were set up listing the frequency of disturbance in skeletal development, *Homo sapiens* of today would be at the top of the scale with the greater number of defects, and preagriculture groups would be at the bottom; the early agriculturists would range somewhat in between.

These dental-skeletal type defects are polygenic and show a wide variation in their expression; thus, it is difficult to demonstrate precisely what selective forces may be operating. Comparisons of collections of prehistoric skeletons from different regions, however, show that a distinction exists between time periods and cultural levels. This evidence suggests a relaxation of selection over time; persons with skeletal deformation would be more likely to survive since the Neolithic than before. The reduced face, smaller tooth size, and missing teeth are a few of these features seen often in humans today; there is every chance that anomalies in development will increase in the future.

ONGOING EVOLUTION AND *HOMO SAPIENS* OF THE FUTURE

Science-fiction writers over the decades have been fond of depicting the human of the future as having evolved into a creature with an enormous head (to house the expanded brain) just barely supported by a frail and grotesque body. This body, with reduced digits on thin appendages, would be just capable of operating the buttons and switches that turn on machines that would perform all types of marvelous tasks: to feed, to comfort, and to entertain. The enlarged brain would be necessary, but such "vestiges" as the little toe would have long since "vanished," a victim of evolutionary processes. Well, I do not foresee such a creature in the future as a model of what our descendants will look like in the millennia to come. There will be changes in our biological makeup, to be sure, as we discussed, mainly an increase in variability and in the frequency of certain developmental abnormalities—but none of these changes will be as drastic as those predicted by the science-fiction writers. There has been no selection for increased brain size during the last one hundred thousand years, and the little toe is not in any danger of being lost, no matter how we cramp it into tight-fitting footwear. What changes will occur then?

There will be a continuing evolution of several aspects of human physiology, probably those that relate to life in the modern, cramped, and polluted environments of a highly industrialized society. Populations of the future will be crowded into increasingly larger urban centers and especially in the Third World countries. This will increase the potential for disease transmission, not only of those organisms long familiar as causes of epidemics but also of newer and more virulent strains that are likely to appear. We have been witnessing the appearance of insects resistant to DDT, for example, which has contributed to a rise in malaria. The *falciparum* parasite, the cause of the most deadly type of malaria, is resistant to several of the antimalarial drugs and treatment must shift to new drugs.

The change in dwelling space will intensify psychological stresses of twentieth-century society. Natural selection will apparently operate more

TABLE 8-10   Registered Deaths in London Administrative County by Age: Comparison of 7-Day Period before the 1952 Episode with the 7-Day Period that Included the Episode of Air Pollution

AGE	7-DAY PERIOD PRECEDING THE EPISODE	7-DAY PERIOD INCLUDING THE EPISODE
Under 4 weeks	16	28
4 weeks to 1 year	12	26
1–14 years	10	13
15–44 years	61	99
45–64 years	237	652
65–74 years	254	717
75 years and over	355	949

Source: From Dubos, 1968.

stringently on the urban dweller, subjected to noise, crowding, and foul air. These conditions place a burden on our neuroendocrine system, often stretching our psychological balance to the breaking point. The high mental-illness rate (one-fourth of all hospital admissions), the increased use of mood-altering drugs, and the rise of stress-related diseases are all part of the cost of urban living. The effect of air pollution is illustrated by the current incidence of respiratory diseases, notably bronchitis and emphysema, which have shown a steady increase in the last twenty-five years.

These stresses of living in an urban setting will likely reduce the frequency of certain genotypes and increase others. We have at least one genotype to which we can point as an example. The reports of air pollution in the cities list the increase of deaths during the worst episodes. Table 8-10 shows the significant increase in deaths from respiratory diseases during one of London's worst periods of air pollution. The elderly and persons with respiratory problems are usually the victims, and a major respiratory condition, emphysema, though rare before 1950, increases in frequency each year. A major symptom of emphysema is the loss of elasticity of the alveoli (air sacs of the lungs) and progressive reduction in pulmonary capacity. Many persons with this condition are deficient for an enzyme, alpha-1-anti-trypsin, proteinase inhibitor, which has the function of neutralizing the activity of enzymes that break down proteins. Certain alleles, inherited as recessives, are less effective in their inhibitory effect. These enzymes, mainly elastase are then free to degrade (by partial digestion) certain of the mucous membranes of the body. The tissues of the lungs are among those most sensitive and, hence, the progressive loss of elasticity appears to be greater among antitrypsin deficients. Major environmental conditions contribute to emphysema (cigarette smoking and air pollution), but the probability of the greater susceptibility of certain genotypes is an interesting phenomenon to examine (Khoury et al., 1986).

One could propose that, given clear air to breathe and without the smoking habit, the alpha-1-anti-trypsin–deficient person would stand less risk of developing emphysema. This presents a strong argument for natural selection acting against this genotype in a modern urban setting.

Another example of selection in the future would be the narrowing of the nutritional base. As food quantity becomes more of a problem, less attention will be paid to quality and nutritional balance will be more difficult to obtain. Also, for years, refinement and processing have been taking out many substances (trace elements and vitamins) and adding various adulterates to color and preserve our food. The cumulative effects of such processes are difficult to appreciate at this point in time, but already many coloring agents and preservatives have been implicated as suspected carcinogens. The removal of trace elements and vitamins may prove to be harmful as well; many of these substances are becoming recognized as essential for human nutrition; note our previous discussion of selenium and vitamin E. Food processing in the future will probably make greater use of such substitutes as algae and cellulose as sources of nutrients, but the effects on the human gene pool cannot be measured at this time.

Modern population mobility is probably another major factor contributing to gene-frequency changes today. Increasingly, we are becoming more urban, and mating circles are ever-widening. A few generations ago, matings almost always occurred between persons within a limited geographic area—usually the mates' childhood residences had been within a few thousand or even hundreds of yards of each other. In much of the world this remains the case; village, class, or caste endogamy still is maintained. As industrialization and urbanization continues to increase and spread throughout the world, our habits and customs are breaking down, and important alterations are occurring in matings circles. Gene exchange occur over ever-widening areas. In the nineteenth-century and in this century, transportation and especially the automobile have had an even more significant influence on extending population boundaries. This mobility and expansion of mating circles increases heterozygosity of the human species and decreases the chance of producing homozygous recessives. It increases the influence of assortative mating, however, particularly the preference for mating within one's own socioeconomic group or at the same educational level.

The reduced maternal mortality rate and the overall extension of the female reproductive years are also influential in changing gene frequencies. Last century the average age at menarche was eighteen; however, today, in many countries, it is between twelve and thirteen or as low as eleven years. A later onset of menopause is usual today and has increased from age forty-four, the average a century ago, to age fifty. Thus, in many societies, female reproductive span has been extended from a total of twenty-seven to thirty-six years. Though contraceptives reduce fecundity, the increased reproductive span and lower mortality rates are major contributions to the rise in fertility, particularly in underdeveloped countries.

All of these factors—the shift in selective forces, population mobility, increased reproductive span, and entirely new disease stresses—contribute to ongoing evolution of modern *Homo sapiens*. What the future holds is difficult to say, but evidence is accumulating and more is being learned about the genetic basis for human physiological response to the environment. Human variation exists now as it has in the past, though the boundaries, as defined, keep shifting, and new ethnic groups arise while others disappear. Whether we will remain as diverse in the future, a few hundred generations hence, is not possible to predict. We do know, however, that our species is capable of numerous responses to environmental stresses, both by individual homeostatic adjustments in the short term and genetic combination changes in the population over the long term.

Finally, we should note the prospects held out to us by developments such as recombinant DNA. Will "gene splicing" or genetic engineering enable us to direct our own evolution? We have the capability to breed those animals whose varieties are deemed most desirable and economically beneficial but will we be capable of applying this ability to develop a species of humans that possesses all of the "ideal" attributes? Will we be able to clone or engineer human life at will and in turn confront all the moral, ethical dilemmas of "playing God," as one author put it (Goodfield, 1977)? I doubt it, not just because of the technical problems presented by such a project, though they are monumental. Rather, it is the complexity of social organization required for such controlled mating or biological engineering that is overwhelming. There are many positive aspects of genetic engineering to look forward to, however. Great strides have been made in DNA research and treatment of cells, deficient in enzyme production, which can be achieved by injection of a manufactured gene with the right code.

The news that approval has been given to use genetically altered cells for the trial treatment of two diseases was just released as I was finishing this chapter (Fackelmann, 1990). In the first trial, WBC, genetically altered to infiltrate and destroy tumors, will be injected into volunteers suffering from *melanoma* (the deadly form of skin cancer). The second disease (adenosine deaminase deficiency) is an inherited immune disorder in which the child lacks a crucial enzyme that normally protects the T-lymphocyte cells from toxic chemicals. The accumulation of these toxins destroys the body's immune system. Lymphocyte cells withdrawn from the person with this defect will be altered to carry the DNA code for the missing enzyme, and the cells will be injected back into the child's bloodstream. Should these trials prove as successful as predicted given the results from the laboratory experiments, then two lethal diseases will be amenable to treatment by genetically "engineered" cells.

A more immediate application has been the synthesis of human insulin by specially programmed bacterial cell cultures. Such a process carried out in the laboratory is much less expensive than the older method of extraction of insulin from animal glands. At this time there are a dozen or more human proteins produced by bacteria with DNA altered to synthesize the desired product. Also plant genetics will likely continue to make great achievements with new hybrids and even with bacterial control.

Even with accomplishment of the necessary technical means, the logistics and priorities are overwhelming in their complexity. First, each of these achievements costs, and these costs are enormous in terms of money, resources, and trained personnel.[10] The "pay-off" or return for investment will be relatively small, in contrast to the yields, for investments of the resources in other areas: plant pathology, high-bred seeds, new energy sources, and so on. As the future unfolds, demands on all resources will increase radically, and priorities will likely be more and more rigidly enforced. There will probably be little support for the kind of technology that put us on the moon or its equivalent in genetic engineering unless the scientists can promise an immediate return in increased food production or energy sources. In the final analysis, however, what will keep evolutionary control out of human hands will be humans themselves.

The chief problem in dealing with growing population requirements at this point in our history lies not in our technology, but in the social institutions that have failed to keep pace with technological advances. Over population, pollution, and the energy crisis are all problems that were described and predicted by several writers decades ago (in a sense, some were like a latter-day Malthus). Many of their predictions proved to be all too accurate but few, if any, societies have been able or willing to prepare for these events that engulf us at the end of this century. We cannot blame such inadequacy only on indifferences or lack of foresight, but rather on an inertia. Our social institutions are just slow to respond, and it is this long reaction time to the appearance of new challenges or new technologies that hampers us as we seek to direct events or to control our fate. For example, much as been accomplished in the fields of genetics and medicine but children still die from "old fashioned diseases". There remains broad differences in mortality rates and life expectancies experienced by populations of all countries.

Throughout the book I have described several aspects of human diversity, but our knowledge is still limited at this point in time approaching

---

[10] The successful race to find the cystic fibrosis gene is an example of the intense competition that goes on today in the field of molecular genetics (Marx, 1989).

the start of a new century and the dawn of a new technological era. Many facets of human biology have yet to be explored. We need to expand our research on human variation and the collection of cellular material from populations around the world to record the restriction DNA fragments is a major advance, but, more important, we need to change our attitude and perspective. We need to appreciate human diversity for what it is—the result of a species gene pool responding to the stresses of natural selection as modified by behavior or culture. It is not a simple matter of explaining all diversity by the action of natural selection. Other factors are involved and should be considered, such as the breeding population size, the social system, and the population's history. Extensive comparative studies must be made; contrasts should be drawn between members of breeding populations; and the reliance on large, all-encompassing taxons must be avoided. The challenges are there, the frontiers broad: Students must rise to meet these challenges with their questions.

RECOMMENDED READINGS AND LITERATURE CITED

AMES, B. 1979. "Identifiying environmental chemicals causing mutations and cancer," *Science*, 204:587–593.

AMES, B. 1983 "Dietary carcinogens and anticarcinogens," *Science* 221:1256–1263.

BAKER, P. T., J. M. HANNA, AND T. S. BAKER, eds. 1986. *The Changing Samoans*. New York: Oxford University Press.

BERKOW, R., ed. 1977. *The Merck Manual of Diagnosis and Therapy*. Rahway, N.J.: Merck Sharp and Dohme Research Laboratories.

BIRDSELL, J. B. 1978. "Spacing mechanisms and adaptive behavior of Australian Aborigines," in *Population Control by Social Behavior*. F. J. Ebling and D. M. Stoddart, eds. New York: Praeger Publishers.

BIRDSELL, J. B. 1981. *Human Evolution: An Introduction to the New Physical Anthropology*. Boston: Houghton Mifflin.

BOSERUP, E. 1981. *Population and Technological Change: A Study of Long Term Trends*. Chicago: University of Chicago Press.

BOUVIER, L. F., AND J. VAN DER TAK. 1976. *Infant Mortality—Progress and Problems*. Washington, D.C.: Population Reference Bureau.

BURKITT, D. F. 1971. "Epidemiology of cancer of the colon and rectum," *Cancer*, 28:3–13.

CAIRNS, J. 1975. "The cancer problem," *Scientific American*, 233:64–78.

CARTER, T. P., AND A. M. WILLEY, eds. 1986. *Genetic Disease: Screening and Management*. New York: Alan R. Liss.

CLEGG, E. J., AND J. P. GARLICK, eds. 1980. *Disease and Urbanization*. Symposia of the Society for the Study of Human Biology, vol. 20. London: Taylor and Francis.

COHEN, L. A. 1987 "Diet and cancer," *Sci. Am.*, 257:42–48.

COMBS, G, F., JR., AND M. L. SCOTT. 1977. "Nutritional interrelationships of vitamin E and selenium," *Biol. Sci.*, 27:467–473.

DAMON, A. 1962. "Some host factors in disease: Sex, race, ethnic group, and body form," *Nat. Med. Assoc. J.*, 54:424–431.

DEEVEY, E. S., JR. 1970. "Mineral cycles," *Sci. Am.*, 223:148–158.

Demographic Yearbook. 1977. New York: United Nations 28th issue.

Demographic Yearbook. 1979. New York: United Nations 31st issue.

Demographic Yearbook. 1990. New York: United Nations 42nd issue.

DUBOS, R. 1968. *Man Adapting*. New Haven, Conn.: Yale University Press.

Durand, J. D. 1977. Historical estimates of world population: An evaluation. *Population and Development Review* 3:253.

Eckholm, E. P. 1977. *The Picture of Health*. New York: W. W. Norton.

Fackelman, K. A. 1990. "Human Gene Therapy Wins Crucial Victory," *Science News*, 38:68

Gallagher, R. 1969. *Diseases That Plague Modern Man, A History of Ten Communicable Diseases*. Dobbs Ferry, New York: Oceana Publications.

Goodfield, J. 1977. *Playing God: Genetic Engineering and the Manipulation of Life*. New York: Random House.

Harris, M. I. 1990. "Noninsulin-dependent diabetes mellitus in black and white Americans," *Diabetes/Metabol. Rev.* 6:71–90.

Historical Statistics of the United States, Colonial Times to 1957. 1960. Washington, D.C.: U. S. Department of Commerce, Bureau of Census.

Hoekstra, W. G. 1975. "Biochemical function of selenium and its relation to Vitamin E," *Federation Proceedings*, 34:2083–2089.

Hulse, F. S. 1955. "Technological advance and major racial stocks," *Hum. Biol.*, 27:184–192.

Hutt, M. S. R., and D. P. Burkitt. 1986. *The Geography of Non-Infectious Disease*. Oxford: Oxford University Press.

Inter-Change. Washington, D.C.: Population Reference Bureau.

Khoury, M. J., T. H. Beaty, C. A. Newill, 1986. "Genetic-environmental interactions in chronic airways obstruction". *International Journal Epidemiology*. 15:64–71.

Kirk, R. L., S. W. Serjeantson, H. King, and P. Zimmet. 1985. "The genetic epidemiology of diabetes mellitus," in *Diseases of Complex Etiology in Small Populations: Ethnic Differences and Research Approaches*, eds. R. Chakraborty and E. J. E. Szathmary. New York: Alan R. Liss.

Knowler, W. C., D. J. Pettitt, M. F. Saad, and P. H. Bennett. 1990. "Diabetes mellitus in the Pima Indians: Incidence, risk factors and pathogenesis," *Diabetes/Metab. Rev.*, 6:1–27.

Ladurie, E. L. 1988. *Times of Feast, Times of Famine: A History of Climate Since the Year 1000*. New York: Farrar, Straus and Giroux.

Langer, W. L. 1963. Europe's initial population explosion. *Am. Historical Review*. Volume LXIX, pp 1–17.

Levander, O. A. 1987. "A global view of human selenium nutrition," *Ann. Rev. Nutr.* 7:227–250.

Lopez, A. D. 1990. "Causes of death: An assessment of global patterns of mortality around 1985," *World Health Stat. Quart.*, 43:91–104.

Lopez, A. D. 1990. "Who dies of what? A comparative analysis of mortality conditions in developed countries around 1987," *World Health Stat. Quart.* 43:105–114.

McCullough, J. M. 1978. "Phenylketonuria-balanced polymorphism in Europe," *J. Hum. Evol.*, 7:231–237.

McEvedy, C. and R. Jones. 1978. *Atlas of World Population History*. New York: Penguin Books.

McKeown, T. 1985. "Looking at disease in the light of human development," *World Health Forum*, 6:70–75.

McKusick, V. A.1967. "The ethnic distribution of disease in the United States," *J. Chronic Dis.*, 20:115–118.

McNeill, W. H. 1976. *Plagues and Peoples*. New York: Anchor Press/Doubleday.

Marx, J. L. 1989. "The cystic fibrosis gene is found," *Science*, 245:923–925.

Maung, T. 1979. "Cholera in the Gilberts," *World Health*, January: 6–9.

Mayer, J. D. 1983. "The role of spatial analysis and geographic data in the detection of disease causation," *Soc. Sci. Med.*, 17:1213.

Neel, J. V. 1962. "Diabetes mellitus: A 'thrifty' genotype rendered detrimental by progress?" *Am. J. Hum. Genet.*, 14:353–362.

Neel, J. V. 1982. "The thrifty genotype revisited," in *The Genetics of Diabetes Mellitus*, ed. J. Kobberling and R. Tattersall. London: Academic Press.

Newman, M. T. 1961. "Biological adaptation of man to his environment: Heat, cold, altitude and nutrition," *Ann. N.Y. Acad. Sci.*, 91:617–633.

Omran, A. R. 1982. "Epidemiologic transition," in *International Encyclopedia of Population*. J. A. Ross, ed. New York: Free Press.

Osborn, F. 1971. "A return to the principles of natural selection," in *Natural Selection in Human Populations*, ed. Carl J. Bajema. New York: John Wiley.

POLEDNAK, A. P. 1989. *Racial and Ethnic Differences in Disease.* New York: Oxford University Press.

POST, R. H. 1965. "Population differences in red and green color deficiency: A review and a query on selection relaxation," *Eugen. Quart.*, 12:28–29.

PRIOR, I. A. M. 1971. "The price of civilization," *Nutr. Today*, 6:2–11.

PRIOR, I. A. M., et al. 1986. "Cardiovascular epidemiological studies in New Zealand and the Pacific and the Tokelau Island migrant study," *Research Review.* Medical Research Council of New Zealand.

ROTTER, J. I., AND J. M. DIAMOND. 1987. "What maintains the frequencies of human genetic diseases?" *Nature*, 329:289–290.

SMITH, T. L. 1960. *Fundamentals of Population Study.* J. B. Lippincott.

STAMP, L. D. 1964. *The Geography of Life and Death.* Ithaca, N.Y.: Cornell University Press.

U. S. Department of Health and Human Services. 1985. *Diabetes in America*, NIH Publication No. 85-1468. Washington, D.C.: U.S. Department of Health and Human Services.

U. S. Department of Health and Human Services. 1989. *Monthly Vital Statistics Report*, vol. 38, no. 5. Washington, D.C.: U.S. Department of Health and Human Services.

U. S. Government Printing Office. 1930. *Statistical Abstract of the United States.* Washington, D. C.: U.S. Government Printing Office.

VOGEL, F., AND A. G. MOTULSKY. 1986. *Human Genetics: Problems and Approaches*, 2nd ed. Berlin: Springer-Verlag.

WADE, N. 1979. "Recombinant DNA: Warming up for big payoff," *Science*, 206:663–665.

WASHBURN, S. L. 1964. "The study of race," in *The Concept of Race*, A. Montagu, ed. New York: Free Press.

WILSON, T. W. 1986. "History of salt supplies in West Africa and blood pressures today," *Lancet* 1:784–786.

WOLPOFF, M. H. 1969. "Climate influence on the skeletal nasal aperture," *Am. J. Phys. Anthrop.*, 3:405–424.

World Health Statistics Annual. 1978. Geneva: World Health Organization.

World Health Statistics Annual. 1979. Geneva: World Health Organization.

World Health Statistics Annual. 1987. Geneva: World Health Organization.

"World Population Data Sheet," 1980. Washington, D. C.: Population Reference Bureau.

"World Population Data Sheet," 1990. Washington, D. C.: Population Reference Bureau.

YINGER, N. 1990. "Focus on maternal mortality," in *Population Today.* Washington, D.C.: Population Reference Bureau.

ZIMMET, P. 1982. "Review articles: Type 2 (non-insulin-dependent) diabetes: An epidemiological overview," *Diabetologia*, 22:399–411.

Glossary

adaptation   response to environmental conditions by adjustments of physiological processes or behavior to improve an organism's chance of survival; may be short-term (functional), sometimes referred to as acclimatization, or a long-term response of a population's genetic variability, that is affected by natural selection over several generations.

age cohorts   individuals who share a common demographic attribute; most frequently, members of the same age group.

agglutination   the clinging together of cells caused by the attraction of antibodies and antigens, as in the case of blood cells with specific antibodies.

albumin   a type of simple, soluble protein distributed throughout the tissue fluids.

allele   alternate genetic forms of the same locus.

amino acids   small organic compounds, containing the amino group, that are combined to form protein compounds.

anthropometry   the measurements of human body form.

antibodies   protein molecules in the blood serum that will react with foreign proteins and protect against invading organisms.

antigen   a substance capable of stimulating the production of an antibody; or inherited antigen forms, such as those of the red blood cell—the blood groups.

assortative mating   the preferential selection of a mate with a particular trait or attribute; most frequently seen in positive assortative mating.

autosome   all chromosomes except the sex chromosomes, X and Y.

brachycephalic   describes a short, broad-shaped head whose breadth is approximately 80 percent or more of its length.

breeding population   a group of individuals who are potentially interbreeding, who occupy a local area, and who make up a basic unit of our species.

brow ridge   the ridge of bone over the eyes.

carpals   wrist bones.

cartilage   a dense, firm, but flexible connective tissue, that is the major part of most of the skeleton and that calcifies at various stages of growth.

centromere   the part of the chromosome where the chromatids are joined.

cephalic index   the ratio of the breadth to the length of the head or skull.

cerumen   the waxy substance secreted by glands in the external ear.

chiasma   crossing over of chromatids of homologous chromosomes during an early stage of meiosis.

chromatid   one of the two strands that make up the chromosome.

chromosome   the darkly staining rod-shaped structure, located in the nucleus of a cell, that is composed of DNA molecules.

clinal distribution   traces the geographical range of phenotypic or genetic characteristics of our species.

coefficient of inbreeding   the probability of like alleles from a common ancestor. The coefficient is higher, for example, in matings of first cousins ($\frac{1}{16}$) than in second cousins ($\frac{1}{64}$).

collagen   a fibrous protein that is the chief constituent part of connective tissue and bone.

congenital defect   a defective organ, system, or anatomical structure that is present at birth.

consanguineous   genetic relative; related because of a common ancestor.

cormic index   the ratio of sitting height to standing height, that shows the proportion of body height due to the head and trunk.

corneum   outer layer of the epidermis.

correlation   the degree of correspondence between two measurements.

cranial capacity   the volume of the skull; used to estimate brain volume.

craniology   a science dealing with variations in size, shape, and proportions of skulls among *Homo sapiens*.

crossover   the exchange of genetic material between homologous chromosomes when in synapse during meiosis.

culture   the learned behavioral pattern that *Homo sapiens* uses to manipulate the environment.

Darwinian fitness   states characteristic of those who produce the most offspring.

deme   see *breeding population*.

demographic transition   a transition in the growth potential of a population.

demography   the study of a population's growth, size, and composition.

deoxyribonucleic acid (DNA)   a large organic molecule composed of two intertwined strands of similar units, nucleotides; each nucleotide contains an organic base, deoxyribose sugar, and a phosphate molecule.

dependency ratio   the ratio between the economically productive portion of the population and the dependent age groups, usually taken as those under fifteen and over sixty-five years.

dermis   inner layer of skin where the blood vessels, nerves, glands, and hair follicles are located.

diaphysis   the shaft of long bones.

diploid number   the number of chromosomes in all cells except a germinal cell.

distal   referring to the direction away from the point of attachment of a limb.

DNA   see *deoxyribonucleic acid*.

dolichocephalic   describes a long, narrow head whose breadth is 75 percent or less of its length.

dominant inheritance one allele is dominant to another and, in the heterozygote, will cause the expression of the trait.

dysgenic those factors that reduce hereditary qualities; frequently applied to the preservation in the gene of defective traits through modern medical treatment of the affected individual; the opposite of eugenics.

effective breeding population that proportion of the population who are in their reproductive years.

electrophoresis a method of separating proteins by applying an electric charge to a solution of proteins.

embryo organism that results from the first eight weeks of in-utero development of *Homo sapiens*.

endemic the continuous presence of a disease in a community; often used in reference to a disease like malaria that continually infects a tropical population on a year-round basis.

endogamy inbreeding within a certain social unit, population, or deme.

endonucleases enzymes that break bonds at specific nucleotide sites along strands of DNA or RNA.

enzyme a protein catalyst that causes a chemical reaction to occur in a living organism.

epidemiology the study of the distribution and causes of a disease.

epidermis outer layer of skin; a tissue of four layers.

epiphysis the portion of bone that develops from secondary centers of ossification and remains separate throughout the period of bone growth; the ends of the long bones connected to the main shaft, the diaphysis.

erythroblastosis fetalis the hemolytic blood disease of the newborn; the blood cells of a Rh+ infant are destroyed by maternal antibodies from an Rh− mother.

erythrocytes red blood cells.

ethnic group a group of persons who share the same language and customs and who identify with certain recent origins.

eugenics efforts to improve the human species by controlled breeding.

evolution change in gene frequency of a population through time; descent with modification.

exogamy matings between members of different social groups, populations, or demes; outbreeding.

exon the segments of DNA that are transcribed into mRNA that are then translated into a polypeptide chain.

fetus human organism from eight weeks of development until birth.

fitness see *Darwinian Fitness*.

Founder's Effect establishment of a new population by a few original migrants or "founders" whose genetic composition may be an aberrant sample of the gene pool of the large population from that it migrated.

gametes germ cells, either ova or sperm.

gamma globulin a serum protein consisting of antibodies that act as a defense against infection.

gene that region of the DNA molecule that contains the nucleotide sequence code for the production of a polypeptide chain relayed by a messenger RNA.

gene flow exchange of genetical material between populations due to dispersion of gametes through interbreeding.

genetic disease an inherited disorder, usually caused by recessive alleles but sometimes by dominants.

genetic drift refers to chance events that alter gene frequencies in small breeding populations; the reduction in gene frequency is due to a sampling error because of a small number of matings.

genetic load   the total frequency of a population's lethal or sublethal genes that may affect an individual's growth, development, health, or chance of survival.

genotype   actual genetic composition of an organism; the pair of alleles at a locus of homologous chromosomes determined at conception.

globulins   a major group of proteins in blood plasma that include: alpha, beta, and gamma globulins.

haploid   refers to the number of chromosomes in sperm or ova (twenty-three), that is one-half the number of a somatic cell (forty-six).

haplotypes   a series or combination of closely linked loci.

haptoglobins   a protein in the serum portion of blood whose function is to bind with free hemoglobin to prevent its excretion.

Hardy-Weinberg Equilibrium   a mathematical formula stating the proportions between alleles within a stable population.

hemoglobin   red respiratory protein comprising more than 90 percent of the protein of a red cell and functioning to transport oxygen to the tissues of the body.

heritability   that proportion of variation of a trait in a population that is due to the variation of genotypes.

heterozygote   a pair of different alleles.

homeostasis   a maintenance of an equilibrium of various metabolic functions in the body.

hominid   the primate family taxon that includes *Homo sapiens* and extinct ancestral forms such as the Australopithecines.

homologous   having a likeness in structure.

Homo sapiens   the human species; genus *Homo*, species *sapiens*.

homozygote   a pair of identical alleles.

hypoxia   less than normal levels of oxygen in air, blood, or tissues; also refers to a general physiological state in response to low levels of atmospheric oxygen, particularly among persons at higher elevations.

incest taboo   matings forbidden between certain classes of relatives.

intron   a noncoding region of DNA that is transcribed but excised from mature mRNA.

isolate   a population or a group of populations who maintain a high degree of breeding isolation from other groups because marriages with outsiders are forbidden or restricted.

keratin   a protein; the major constituent of the outer skin layers.

Law of Independent Assortment   two traits, simultaneously considered, will sort and recombine independently of each other; Mendel's second law.

Law of Independent Segregation   traits are transmitted as discrete units that do not blend with or contaminate each other: Mendel's first law.

linkage   two or more genes located at loci close to one another on a chromosome.

locus   a chromosome position or space for the coded unit of the gene.

mandible   the lower jaw; the bone containing the lower teeth.

matrilocal   the settlement pattern in that adult males leave to marry outside of their natal community while the females remain.

maxilla   bone of the major portion of the face; contains the teeth and upper jaw.

meiosis   process of cell division and chromosome replication in germinal cells followed by cell fission and reduction in chromosome number.

melanin   dark pigment granules of the skin and hair of animals and of structures of plants.

melanocytes pigment cells of the skin.

menarche the onset of menstruation; the first menstrual period.

Mendelian ratio the ratio of genotypes of homozygote and heterozygote combinations.

mesocephalic describes an intermediate head shape between brachycephalic (broad headed) and dolichocephalic (long headed).

metacarpals the bones of the hands connecting the phalanges with the carpals (bones of the wrist).

microevolution alteration in the frequency of occurrence of certain genes from generation to generation.

mitosis cell division that occurs in somatic cells producing two identical daughter cells.

mutation a change in the genetic code; a change in the sequence of base pairs of the DNA molecule.

nasal index a ratio of the width to the length of the nose.

natal associated with one's birth; applied to location, native or community, where one's birth took place.

natural selection due to certain natural conditions in the environment, some individuals, because of their genetic endowment, produce more offspring who, in turn, reproduce at a higher rate than do other individuals. Through this process the less well-adapted are gradually reduced in number over the generations.

Neolithic the "new Stone Age," a period beginning approximately 10,000 to 12,000 years ago when *Homo sapiens* began to domesticate plants and, later, animals. A major feature of the Neolithic is the sedentary life style that it encouraged.

orthognathic straight faced; the teeth and supporting bone in the anterior part of the face lie close to the line drawn between the chin and the brow.

osteomalacia failure of the collagen of the newly formed bone to mineralize. A similar condition in children and juveniles is referred to as rickets.

patrilocal the settlement pattern in that females leave to marry outside of their natal community while the males remain.

penetrance the frequency of expression of the phenotype; some genes are expressed less than 100 percent of the time, so they have a low penetrance.

phalanges the long bones of the fingers and toes.

phenotype the trait expressed as a result of the interaction of the environment and genotype.

photolysis the destruction of chemical compounds by light; usually in reference to the ultraviolet range.

plasma the yellowish fluid part of the blood containing nutrients, many proteins, and the red and white blood cells.

pleiotropic the genes that influence the expression of more than one trait.

polygenic multiple genes that influence a single trait.

polymorphic describes variability between individuals within a population.

polytypic describes variability between populations.

porphyrins complex pigment molecules widely dispersed in plants and animals. Examples in humans are: heme (of hemoglobin), bile, and cytochrome.

prognathic the forward protrusion of the midfacial region due primarily to large teeth and robust dental arches.

race a geographically and culturally determined collection of individuals who share in a common gene pool and are similar in many characteristics (also referred to as a subspecies).

random mating   matings that occur without regard to genotype.

recessive inheritance   a trait determined by a pair of recessive alleles.

recombination   the formation of new combinations of linked genes by crossover between parts of homologous chromosomes during meiosis.

RFLP   restriction fragment length polymorphisms of DNA molecules produced by nucleotide specific enzymes (endonucleases).

ribonucleic acid (RNA)   a single-strand molecule of organic bases, sugars (ribose), and phosphates; used to translate the coded sequence of the DNA (RNA), or carry amino acids to the sites of protein synthesis (+ RNA).

ribosomes   these small spherical structures in the cell cytoplasm are made up of proteins and RNA, and are the site for protein synthesis.

rickets   a bone disease of young children and juveniles in that their rapidly growing bones fail to mineralize properly; the bones-especially the weight-bearing ones-easily bend or may become distorted.

RNA   see *ribonucleic acid*.

sampling error   a change in gene frequencies within a population that is due to an error caused by the small size of the effective breeding population.

secular trend   continuing for a long term or over a generation.

sex-linked   a trait determined by a gene carried on the sex chromosomes, usually the X chromosome.

sexual dimorphism   refers to the difference in form or size in males and females.

shovel-shaped incisors   incisor tooth that has thickened margins on the lingual surface (tongue side of the tooth)

somatology   the science that deals with the body, its form, and function; usually applied to comparative studies of body forms of different ethnic groups.

species   groups of interbreeding organisms reproductively isolated from other such groups.

steatopygia   an excessive accumulation of fat and probably fibrous tissue in the buttocks; particularly in evidence among females of certain ethnic groups such as the Bushmen and Hottentots of southern Africa.

subspecies   a grouping of individuals or populations who share a number of characteristics in common; frequently geographically limited.

synapsis   the pairing of homologous chromosomes during the anaphase stage of meiosis.

syndrome   the group or aggregate of symptoms associated with any disease or abnormal condition; for example, *Down's Syndrome*, a group of physical and neurological deformities appearing in a person with an extra chromosome of the twenty-first pair.

transferrins   a group of iron-binding proteins found in the serum portion of blood.

twins (dizygotic)   twins who are developed from a pair of fertilized ova and who are no more identical in their genotypes than sibs; also called fraternal twins.

twins (monozygotic)   twins developed from a cleavage of a single fertilized ovum; hence, they have identical genotypes; identical twins.

variance   the measure of the dispersion of values about a population mean.

zygomatic arches   cheek bones.

zygote   the fertilized egg.

Index